Scripture of the Lotus Blossom of the Fine Dharma

Prepared for the Columbia College Program
of Translations from the Asian Classics

Buddhist Studies and Translations
sponsored by
The Columbia University Seminar in Oriental Thought and Religion
with the cooperation of
The Institute for Advanced Studies of World Religions

Scripture of the Lotus Blossom of the Fine Dharma

Translated from the Chinese of Kumārajīva
by Leon Hurvitz

Columbia University Press · New York

Records of Civilization: Sources and Studies, No. XCIV

Portions of this work were prepared under a contract with the U.S. Office of Education for the production of texts to be used in undergraduate education. The texts so produced have been used in the Columbia College Oriental Humanities program and have subsequently been revised and expanded for publication in the present form. Copyright is claimed only in those portions of the work not submitted in fulfillment of the contract with the U.S. Office of Education. The U.S. Office of Education is not the author, owner, publisher, or proprietor of this publication, and is not to be understood as approving by virtue of its support any of the statements made or views expressed therein.

Library of Congress Cataloging in Publication Data

Tripiṭaka. Sūtrapiṭaka. Saddharmapuṇḍarīka.
English.
Scripture of the lotus blossom of the fine dharma.

(IASWR series)
Reprint. Originally published: New York: Columbia University Press, 1976. (Buddhist studies and translations) (Translations from Asian classics) (Records of civilization, sources and studies; no. 94)
Includes bibliographical references and index.
I. Kumārajīva, d. 412? II. Hurwitz, Leon, 1923- . III. Title. IV. Series.
V. Series: Buddhist studies and translations.
VI. Series: Translations from Asian classics.
VII. Series: Records of civilization, sources and studies; no. 94.
BQ2052.E5 1982 294.3'823 82-4329
ISBN 0-231-03920-4 AACR2

Columbia University Press
New York, Chichester, West Sussex

Printed in the United States of America
20 19 18 17 16 15 14 13 12 11

Translations from the Asian Classics

Editorial Board

Wm. Theodore de Bary, Chairman

Paul Anderer
Irene Bloom
Donald Keene
George A. Saliba
Haruo Shirane
David D. W. Wang
Burton Watson
Philip B. Yampolsky

Committee on Buddhist Studies and Translations

Wm. Theodore de Bary, Horace Walpole Carpentier
Professor of Oriental Studies
Yoshito S. Hakeda, Associate Professor of Japanese
Frederic Underwood, Assistant Professor of Religion
Alex Wayman, Professor of Sanskrit
Philip B. Yampolsky, Adjunct Associate Professor of Japanese

IASWR Series

Buddhist Monastic Discipline: The Sanskrit Prātimokṣa Sūtras of the Mahāsāṃghikas and Mūlasarvāstivādins, by Charles S. Prebish (The Pennsylvania State University Press).

Sūtra of the Past Vows of Earth Store Bodhisattva, tr. Heng Ching.

Avatāra: The Humanization of Philosophy Through the Bhagavad Gītā, by Antonio T. deNicolás (Nicolas Hays Ltd.).

The Holy Teaching of Vimalakīrti: A Mahāyāna Scripture, tr. Robert A. F. Thurman (The Pennsylvania State University Press).

Scripture of the Lotus Blossom of the Fine Dharma (The Lotus Sūtra), tr. Leon Hurvitz (Columbia University Press).

Hua-yen Buddhism: The Jewel Net of Indra, by Francis H. Cook (The Pennsylvania State University Press).

A Buddhist Leader in Ming China: The Life and Thought of Han-shan Te-ch'ing, by Sung-peng Hsu (The Pennsylvania State University Press).

The Syncretic Religion of Lin Chao-en, by Judith A. Berling (Columbia University Press).

The Renewal of Buddhism in China: Chu-hung and the Late Ming Synthesis, by Chun-fang Yü (Columbia University Press).

Foreword

The *Lotus Sutra* is one of the Translations from the Asian Classics by which the Committee on Asian Studies has sought to transmit to Western readers representative works of the major Asian traditions in thought and literature. Our intention is to provide translations based on scholarly study but written for the general reader rather than primarily for other specialists.

Of all the writings in the Buddhist canon none qualifies like the *Lotus Sutra* as a major religious scripture of enduring importance. It is a comprehensive and effective statement of the teachings of Mahāyāna Buddhism, most inspiring for its religious imagery and for its dramatic presentation of those teachings in a form readily appreciated by millions of Buddhists in China, Japan, and Korea. Moreover the Chinese version translated here, that of Kumārajīva about A.D. 400, has been widely accepted, and indeed, enjoyed, over the last fifteen centuries in East Asia. No collection of oriental classics could be complete without it.

Fortunately, in Leon Hurvitz the Lotus and Kumārajīva have a translator into English whose competence and devotion to the study of the text match its importance. Professor Hurvitz has spent almost a lifetime in the study of the Lotus, its commentaries, and the philosophies derived from it. Here he brings that great store of learning to the translation of the Lotus into an English version that is illuminated, not overlaid and burdened, by it.

WM. THEODORE DE BARY

Preface

The *Lotus Sūtra*, or *Saddharmapuṇḍarīkasūtra*, is by any standard one of the most influential of the scriptures of Mahāyāna Buddhism, one of the few whose original text, written in Buddhist Sanskrit, survives. Under the circumstances, perhaps the best course would have been to translate directly from the Sanskrit. However, in view of the purposes which this translation was meant to serve, it was made instead from the Chinese.

Chinese translations of the *Lotus* are known to have been made in the years 255, 286, 290, 335, 406, and 601. Of these, only the third, fifth, and sixth survive, but the sixth is scarcely more than a revision of the fifth. The third was made by Dharmarakṣa (circa 223–300), the Chinese-born descendant of Iranians who had settled in West China generations before. The fifth, on which the present translation is based, is that of Kumārajīva (circa 350–410), an Indo-Iranian missionary who numbers among the most outstanding of all the translators. Dharmarakṣa presumably did his translation without help, being perfectly at home in both Buddhist Sanskrit and Chinese. Kumārajīva, on the other hand, was the head of the most elaborate state-sponsored translation bureau yet to exist on the soil of China. However, not only did he have his collaborators, but in all likelihood they were indispensable to him, for it is extremely improbable that he could read or write Chinese at all. Whether or not he could, the fact remains that in the course of the years his bureau worked out a method of translation that, to judge from the clarity of the style, must have been very efficient indeed. Kumārajīva's version is much easier reading than Dharmarakṣa's, which goes a long way toward explaining why and how it eclipsed the latter totally.

In a way, Johnannes Nobel has set the tone for this sort of thing, by editing the Sanskrit, Tibetan, and Chinese versions of another Mahāyāna scripture, the *Suvarṇaprabhāsa*, as well as German translations based on each of them. In the light of that, possibly the best thing speakers of

English could have done with the *Lotus* would have been to produce separate translations of the Sanskrit, the Tibetan, and the two Chinese versions just mentioned. That, however, is a task for the future. What has been attempted here is to satisfy two demands simultaneously, that of the series to which the present translation belongs and that of the translator's philological conscience. That is to say, the *Lotus* occupied a position of enormous importance in the Buddhist church throughout the Far East, where, for want of a knowledge of Sanskrit, it was read only in Kumārajīva's version, the original for which must have differed in many particulars from the Sanskrit that exists today. At the same time, the *Lotus* is a work of Indian origin, and it is no use treating the Sanskrit as if it did not exist. Accordingly, a compromise was reached: (*a*) The translation throughout is based on Kumārajīva. (*b*) Where the Sanskrit and the Chinese are, in the translator's judgment, close enough, the English represents them both. (*c*) Where they mean the same thing, but the particular Sanskrit word or phrase is felt to be of interest in its own right to Sanskrit-oriented readers, the Sanskrit is given either in parentheses or in the notes in the back of the book. (*d*) Where the difference between the two versions is sufficient to merit comment, the Sanskrit is given in English translation in the notes. The same applies to passages in the Sanskrit that do not appear in the Chinese at all. (*e*) The Tibetan version and that of Dharmarakṣa were not consulted.

There follows now a summary of the contents chapter by chapter.

1. As the scene opens, the Buddha has just entered a state of concentration (*samādhi*). While in this state he emits from between his brows a ray of light that illuminates the entire universe. Mañjuśrī, asked by Maitreya what is the cause of this, replies that the Buddha is indicating by this ray of light that he is about to preach the *Lotus*.

2. Emerging from his concentration, the Buddha tells his listeners that there is only one Path to salvation, not three, and that every Buddha who makes his appearance in the world does so for the sole purpose of teaching this truth to the beings.

3. The Buddha now prophesies to his disciple Śāriputra the latter's future attainment of Buddhahood. Śāriputra, though encouraged

by this prophecy, still wishes to know why, if there are not three paths to salvation, the Buddha has so often preached their existence in the past. The Buddha replies with a parable:

> A rich man had a very large house. The house had only one entrance, and the timber of which it was made had dried out thoroughly over the years. One day the house caught fire, and the rich man's many children, heedless of the fire, continued to play in the house. Their father called to them from outside that the house was afire and that they would perish in the flames if they did not come out. The children, not knowing the meaning of "fire" or "perish," continued to play as before. The man called out once more, "Come out, children, and I will give you ox-drawn carriages, goat-drawn carriages, and deer-drawn carriages!" Tempted by the desire for new playthings, the children left the burning house, only to find a single great ox-drawn carriage awaiting them.

Asked whether the father can be rightly accused of having deceived his children, Śāriputra says that he cannot, since he was merely employing a device to save their lives. Just so, says the Buddha. The world is a great house afire with the flame of passion. When taught the way to Buddhahood, the beings, not understanding what is meant, remain in the passion-trap. Then the Buddha, in order to rescue them, devises a scheme. This scheme is the doctrine of the three paths to salvation. Just as the father cannot be accused of having deceived his children, so the Buddha cannot be accused of deceiving the beings with this doctrine, although in the ultimate sense the doctrine is not true.

4. Upon hearing the Buddha's announcement to Śāriputra that he, too, shall one day become a Buddha, several other disciples express amazement. One of them, Mahākāśyapa, gives voice to their feelings in the following parable:

> A father and son parted company while the son was still a very young man. In the course of time the father became very rich, while the son sank into the depths of poverty and beggary. Once, during the course of his wanderings, he happened to come to the palatial home of his father. The father, at once recognizing him, had him brought into his presence. This only frightened the poor man, and the father let him go. Then he sent two men to ask the beggar whether he wished to

> do menial labor on the rich man's estate. The beggar consented, and worked in this way for many years. One day the rich man told the beggar that in view of his many years of honest and conscientious service he would reward him with the charge of all his possessions. After several years more had passed, the rich man gathered his entire household and clan and told them that the beggar was his son, from whom he had been parted many years before, and that he was now reclaiming him and declaring him heir to all his possessions. When the beggar heard this, he was amazed, thinking that he had received something quite unexpected.

Just so, says Mahākāśyapa, is the śrāvaka, who in his own mind is headed for the goal of arhattva, when he is told by the Buddha that Buddhahood is his goal, too.

5. The Buddha explains further that Buddhahood is the only goal of Buddhism, and that nirvāṇa, if properly understood, is only another name for Buddhahood itself. (The Skt. adds the following, missing from Kumārajīva: The Buddha tells his listeners that the ordinary fellow is like a man born blind, the Hīnayāna practitioner like a formerly blind man whose blindness has been cured, the Mahāyāna practitioner like a worldling who has acquired powers out of the ordinary.)

6. The Buddha prophesies future Buddhahood to four other śrāvakas.

7. The Buddha tells the story of his career as a Buddha in a previous era and concludes with the following parable, also illustrating the main point of this scripture:

> A guide was leading a group of travelers to a spot where a treasure lay buried. On the way the travelers wearied, and some spoke of turning back. The guide accordingly conjured up an apparent city on the way, and successfully urged his companions to rest and refresh themselves there. When they had done so, they went on and reached the spot where the treasure was concealed. Then the guide told them that the city they had seen a while back had been an illusory city, and not a real one, which he had conjured up for the purpose of conquering their discouragement.

Just so, says the Buddha, are the beings. They tire quickly of the quest for salvation, and the Buddha conjures up imaginary forms of salvation for them midway, e.g., the vehicles of the śrāvaka and pratyekabuddha.

8. The Buddha preaches future Buddhahood to more śrāvakas, who relate the following parable:

> A person sewed a jewel into one corner of his friend's garment. The friend, not aware of this, made no attempt to use the jewel even when in serious straits. Then the man who had sewed it into his garment pointed it out to him and thus enabled him to get out of his difficulties.

Just so, say the disciples, is the Buddha. He proffers ultimate salvation to the beings, but they, unaware of it, do not avail themselves of it. The arhant, thinking himself to have attained nirvāṇa, receives an unexpected favor from the Buddha when the latter points out to him the existence of a higher form of salvation which is available to him.

9. More prophecies of future Buddhahood.

10. The Buddha now tells his listeners of the merit that lies in store for whoever shows the proper veneration to the *Lotus*.

11. An immense stūpa arises out of the earth, and the Buddha tells his listeners that it contains the body of a Buddha named Prabhūtaratna, who in a previous age preached the *Lotus*, vowing to produce his reliquary, after his nirvāṇa, wherever and whenever the *Lotus* should happen to be preached. Then the stūpa opens up, and Prabhūtaratna, seated within it, offers half his seat to the Buddha. A number of beings salute both Buddhas.

12. (In the Sanskrit, the following is still part of chapter 11. The numbers of the next chapters have a corresponding gap between the Sanskrit and Kumārajīva's version.) The Buddha says, "In a former age, I was a king. A seer preached the *Lotus* to me, thus enabling me to gain salvation. That seer now is my cousin Devadatta. In time to come he himself shall be a Buddha, Devarāja by name. Anyone who hears what I have said about Devadatta and believes it shall himself gain salvation." As the bodhisattva Prajñākūṭa was about to leave, the Buddha detained him, saying Mañjuśrī wished to speak with him. Prajñākūṭa asked Mañjuśrī how many beings he had converted, and Mañjuśrī told him, adding that the most distinguished was the daughter of the nāga king

Sāgara. Prajñākūṭa protested, saying that, as woman's body is filthy, no woman could become a Buddha. The nāga king's daughter instantly turned into a man, performed the necessary practices, and attained Buddhahood.

13. More prophecies of future Buddhahood, and promises on the part of sundry beings to propagate the *Lotus* diligently.

14. The four *sukhavihāras*, the dharmas of the bodhisattva.

15. Countless bodhisattvas from all over the universe come to pay homage to the Buddha and to receive his commission to propagate the *Lotus*. The Buddha explains to his listeners that the number of bodhisattvas whom he has so commissioned is literally incalculable. Maitreya then asks the Buddha how that could have been possible in the short space of the Buddha's preaching career.

16. The Buddha replies that the commonly accepted notions about the Buddha's life-span and teaching career have no ultimate truth, that the Buddha is in fact limitless in both time and space, assuming various forms in different ages and under different circumstances but all for one and the same purpose, namely, the salvation of the beings. He illustrates this with the following parable:

> A physician who had been away from home a long time returned to find his sons suffering from an ailment. He prescribed for them an appropriate medicine, which certain of them took but which others, mad from the poison, refused. Those who took it were immediately cured, while the others continued to languish in their malady. The physician accordingly went away and circulated the rumor that he had died. This shocked the ailing sons back to their senses, after which they too took their father's medicine and were cured. When he heard of this, the father made his appearance again.

Just so, says the Buddha, are the beings. When offered salvation some of them refuse it; so the Buddha stages a docetic nirvāṇa. This instills in them a sense of urgency, born of the fear that the Buddha will not always be among them. But for this, certain of the beings would continue forever to forego their own salvation.

17. The Buddha narrates the merit which shall accrue to those

who venerate the foregoing chapter of the *Lotus* telling of the unlimited nature of the Buddha's life-span.

18. More on the merit accruing to one who extols the *Lotus*.

19. More on the same.

20. More on the same, followed by the Buddha's narration of his own behavior in a previous era, in which, as the bodhisattva Sadāparibhūta, he was the object of much contempt and violence, but requited all actions with love and patience.

21. The bodhisattvas who have assembled from all over the universe promise to propagate the *Lotus*, whereupon both Buddhas stretch out their tongues, which extend very far, and emit a ray of light that illuminates the entire universe.

22. (This corresponds to chapter 27 in the Sanskrit.) The Buddha leaves the *Lotus* in the care of his listeners, all of whom then go their several ways.

23. (This corresponds to chapter 22 of the Sanskrit; the relationship which began with chapter 12 of Kumārajīva's version is hereby resumed.) The Buddha narrates an incident from a former incarnation of the bodhisattva Bhaiṣajyarāja.

24. The bodhisattva Gadgadasvara comes out of his own world to salute both Buddhas, and the Buddha tells his listeners about the deeds of this bodhisattva in a previous incarnation.

25. The Buddha tells his listeners about the efficacy of invoking Avalokiteśvara.

26. (This corresponds to chapter 21 of the Sanskrit.) More on the merit accruing to the person who extols the *Lotus*, followed by spells pronounced by several persons for the protection of such persons from all ills.

27. (This corresponds to chapter 25 of the Sanskrit.) More about deeds of certain bodhisattvas in previous incarnations.

28. (This corresponds to chapter 26 of the original.) Samantabhadra vows to be the protector of all who extol the *Lotus* and of all who appeal to him for help. The Buddha then entrusts the *Lotus* to him, once more dwelling on the merit which shall accrue to those who extol this scripture, as well as the afflictions that shall attend all who harm such persons.

A comparative catalogue of chapter titles shall appear separately below.

Before anything can be said about the *Lotus's* doctrinal content, a word or two must be devoted to the makeup of the text itself. This, in turn, involves one in a certain amount of Indian Buddhist history—a hazardous venture, since virtually none of it is written, at least not in historical form. Everything that is about to be said, therefore, is at best conjecture, at worst guesswork.

The *Lotus of the True* ("Fine") *Dharma* represents a Buddhist tendency that calls itself *mahāyāna*, apparently signifying the "great course," but later traditionally interpreted to mean the "great vehicle." To oversimplify, this movement distinguished itself from the older schools (to which it referred derisively as *hīnayāna*, "the defective course" or "vehicle") in two respects. First, it boasted that its practitioners were aiming at the salvation not merely of themselves but of all animate beings as well. Second, it concerned itself with the Universal and the Absolute, though these meant different things to different schools within that movement.

This is not to say, by any means, that these two features were totally absent from the earlier schools. Virtually all features of the Mahāyāna can be found in germ in the earlier forms of Buddhism. What this does seem to mean is that by the time the Mahāyāna made its appearance *as such*, the older and established forms of Buddhism were divided into discrete schools, each having its own written canon. (It must be stressed that the *written* canon in Buddhism is sectarian from the outset, and that presectarian Buddhism must be deduced from the writings as they now exist). In other words, the fledgling Mahayanists are trying to have their doctrines and their uncanonized texts accepted as the good coin of Buddhism by a Buddhist community accustomed to very different fare.

To proceed with the conjecture, each one of the Mahāyāna scriptures, at least of the early ones, appears to have been presenting itself as a self-contained rival to the *entire* Tripiṭaka (the alleged sermons of the Buddha concerning doctrine and monastic conduct, and the earliest systematizations of doctrine by his disciples), then as now a corpus of considerable scope. Now, once a certain Mahāyāna sūtra gained standing in the Indian Buddhist community, authors of minor works, even adherents of lateral schools, would wish to endow the respective minor works with greater dignity by simply tacking them on to works of established repute. There is, it certainly seems, unmistakable evidence of this in the *Lotus*.

There is a further complication. The *Lotus*, like all the Buddhist scriptures, presumably was not written down until long after it had gained general currency. By the time it was written down—ruling out the accretions just mentioned—it consisted of two self-evident layers, the older in verse, the younger in prose. The word "self-evident" here means two things:

(*a*) The verse is in what the late Mr. Franklin Edgerton called "Buddhist hybrid Sanskrit." That is to say, the meter of the verses is based on their original prakritic form, prakritic because the verses were popular homilies meant to reach a large general audience. Later, when the Mahayanists felt obliged to sanskritize in order to endow their form of Buddhism with greater dignity (as they, at least, understood it), they tried their hand at both prose and verse. Frequently, however, the Sanskrit form of a word would be so different from the Prakrit that it could alter the meter significantly in the verse. In those cases, sanskritization had to be abandoned. The hybrid quality of the language is evident to anyone who knows even a modicum of Sanskrit.

(*b*) The prose is much more explicit than the verse, which leads one to suspect that it originated as a commentary, in spite of the fact that the prose always comes first, followed by the remark that the Buddha, wishing to express himself "at greater length," resorted to verse. This is an old device, going back to the early canon (where, unless I am mistaken, the process was also historically set on its head). The prose is also much more sanskritized. While it might not pass muster with Pāṇini, nonetheless there are far fewer glaring prakritisms in it than in the verse.

Thus the oldest layer in the *Lotus* is presumably one of verse. Even there, however, there may be two separate scriptures, one saying that there is only one Path to salvation, not three, the other saying that the Buddha is not to be delimited in time or space, or indeed in any finite terms. To this oldest layer (in other words, to both scriptures, which by this time seem to have been united in one text), now a sacred text in mixed prose and verse, are added several smaller scriptures, the older ones, if I am not mistaken, in mixed prose and verse, the younger ones in prose alone. These "accretions" end with the remark that the assembled listeners, overjoyed, saluted the Buddha and took their leave.

Apart from the above-mentioned accretions, to which no space will be devoted in the present treatment, the *Lotus*, as has just been seen, makes two essential points, the former being that the Buddha is not to be delimited in time or space, the latter being that the attainment of Buddhahood is the only form of salvation, the only thing worthy to be called by the name nirvāṇa. Let us now have a somewhat closer look at these two ideas.

The earlier schools imagined Gautama Buddha to be but one in a series of Buddhas, each of whom would pursue a career similar in certain key respects: he would be born a prince, have experiences that would turn him away from the world and the flesh, try extreme asceticism and find it wanting, have an intuitive experience that would explain everything to him, reveal the content of that experience to others, then experience "extinction," i.e., a death followed by no reincarnation. When the Mahāyāna became full-blown, it declared this to be but one of three "Buddha-bodies," The first was the "body of transformation" (Skt. *nirmāṇakāya*, Ch. *hua shen* or, more commonly *ying shen*, "body of response"). The second, in ascending order, was the "body of bliss" (*saṃbhogakāya*, Ch. *pao shen*, "body of retribution"), a guise in which the Buddha was visible to *bodhisattvas*, i.e., to advanced candidates for Buddhahood. The highest was the "Dharma-body" (*dharmakāya*, Ch. *fa shen*), to which no predications can possibly apply. In the *Lotus* the Buddha tells his listeners, by resort to the most exaggerated hyperbole, that his person is, in effect, superior to both time and space. This is, in short, a statement that the only real Buddha-body is the Dharma-body.

On the oldest layers, the world *buddha* ("awakened") appears to have denoted one who had himself experienced the beatific truth, and to have connoted one that turned about to reveal that truth to others. As the monastic community proceeded to produce a series of clerics concerned with their own enlightenment to the exclusion of the spiritual welfare of anyone else, the Mahāyāna, motivated by other considerations as well, made its appearance. It characterized the course of religious practice just mentioned with the pejorative designation *hīnayāna*, "the deficient course"—"deficient" in the sense that it conduced to the salvation of no one other than the practitioner himself. To it was counterposed the *mahāyāna*, the "great course," "great" because it sought nothing less than the salvation of all animate beings. Thus there were two sets of practitioners, both acknowledged by the Mahāyāna to be legitimate: the *bodhisattva* (a word of obscure etymology, which appears on the surface, however, to mean "one whose essence is enlightened intuition"), whose aim is to be a buddha, and who in the very process of becoming one converts and saves untold living beings; and the *śrāvaka* ("auditor"), whose aim is to be an *arhant* ("worthy one, able one" on the face of it, but this word, too, is a bit mysterious), i.e., one who achieves his own salvation alone. It might be mentioned in passing that *buddha* is usually not translated by the Chinese but transcribed *fo* (ancient pronunciation was approximately *but*), as is *bodhisattva*, usually given as *p'u-sa* (abbreviated from *p'u-t'i-sa-to*, ancient pronunciation approximately *bo-dei-sat-twa*), while *śrāvaka* is always translated. The Ch. translation is apparently based on a folk-etymology, one that derives the word from the verb *śru* ("to hear") and the noun *vāc* ("voice"). Thus *śrāvaka* is rendered *sheng wen*, the "voice-hearer."

To these two is added a third, the Sanskrit form of which is *pratyekabuddha*. On the face of it, this would mean "individually awakened," i.e., having attained to enlightenment by his own efforts, not by listening to the preachings of a Buddha. While this is true of him, the important fact is that his enlightenment comes from observing the pattern of interdependent development or, to oversimplify, of cause (*hetu*) and condition (*pratyaya*). Kumārajīva either transcribes *pi-chi-fo* (ancient pronunciation approximately *pyek-či-but*) or translates *yüan chüeh*, "condition perceiver." The Pāli form of the word is *paccekabuddha*, which could as easily go back to *prātyayikabuddha*, "Buddha related to [causes and] conditions," as to *pratyekabuddha*. The latter is obviously a sanskritization postdating Kumārajīva or rejected by him.

By the time the *Lotus* makes its appearance, the saints are a trio, bodhisattva (aiming at the salvation of self and others), pratyekabuddha (aiming at the salvation of self by his own efforts), and śrāvaka (aiming at arhattva, i.e., the salvation of self by listening to a Buddha and taking his sermons to heart), all legitimate from the Mahāyāna point of view. The *Lotus* says, "No! The second and third do not exist. The only form of salvation is Buddhahood. The ostensible pratyekabuddha and śrāvaka are either bodhisattvas putting on a show or bodhisattvas deceiving themselves. Why, even the arhant is not real!"

I digress now to summarize what is, to my knowledge, the best statement to date of the issue of One vehicle versus three, namely, that of Mr. Fujita Kōtatsu on pp. 388–401 of *Hokke shisō*, a book published by Heirakuji Shoten in Kyōto in 1969.

By the time of the appearance of the *Lotus*, says Mr. Fujita, the schools, the northern ones in particular, are firmly convinced that there are three paths to salvation, each characterized by its own unique doctrine. Once embarked on any of the three, so this theory went, the practitioner is committed to it alone, and is unable to leave it for either of the other two. The *ekayāna* (One Vehicle) doctrine of the *Lotus*, Mr. Fujita goes on to surmise, was a reaction to this view of the threefold Path, and to the Sarvāstivāda version in particular. An interesting twist then takes place. The śrāvaka, who imagines himself destined for arhattva, says to himself, "I *can*not become a Buddha." "What he really means, Śāriputra," says the Buddha in the *Lotus*, "is, 'I *need* not become one!' This is noting but arrogance. They may think of themselves as pratyekabuddhas, śrāvakas, even arhants, for that matter, but, if *this* is their attitude, then they are no disciples of mine, to say nothing of their being enlightened!" Thus *buddhayāna*, a word the *Lotus* has in common with the schools, means something quite different, for it is a course open (or a vehicle available) to śrāvaka and pratyekabuddha as well. It is not only available to them, it is *incumbent* upon them, for there is no other road to salvation. Because the word means different things, one actually finds different words being used to represent it, words such as "the unique Vehicle," "the One Vehicle," "the unique Buddha Vehicle," "the Great Vehicle," "the unique Great Vehicle," "the bodhisattva-vehicle," etc.

Since the imagined enlightenment of the pratyekabuddha and of the arhant is in fact no enlightenment at all, the quest for it, in ignorance of this fact, is designated a "lesser" vehicle. The "greater" one is only the other, the one that aims at the deliverance of all living beings. The Buddha, still speaking to Śāriputra, says:

> Again, there are others who, in their desire for all-knowing gnosis, for the Buddhas' gnosis, for the gnosis which is so of itself, for the gnosis owed to no teacher, for the weal of many men, for the happiness of many men, out of compassion for the world, for the sake of the great body of men, for the weal and happiness of gods and humans, for the complete extinction (*parinirvāṇa*) of all living beings and in order to enable them to understand the gnosis, the strengths, and the confidences of the Thus Gone One, attach themselves to the Thus Gone One's teaching. Of them it is said that they "run away from the triple sphere in their keen desire for the Great Vehicle." For that reason they are called "enlightenment-beings, great beings" (*bodhisattvā mahāsattvāḥ*).*

> If there are beings who, having heard the Dharma from the World-Honored One, believe and accept it; who, vigorously practicing and striving, seek all-knowledge, Buddha knowledge, the knowledge which is so of itself, knowledge without a teacher, the knowledge and insight of the Thus Come One, his strengths, and his various sorts of fearlessness; who, mercifully recalling and comforting incalculable living beings and benefiting gods and men, convey all to deliverance, these are named the Great Vehicle. It is because the bodhisattvas seek this Vehicle that they are named Mahāsattvas.†

The word *bodhisattva* antedates the Mahāyāna, to be sure. In early Buddhism, however, its use was confined to Gautama, his well-known predecessors, and Maitreya, while in the *Lotus* its use is extended to include all who seek enlightenment, which for that scripture is synonymous with Buddhahood. The number of bodhisattvas is, for the *Lotus*, potentially infinite. The very life of the *Lotus* hinges on one point, namely, the statement that the One Vehicle, it and nothing else, is the Buddha Vehicle, the Great Vehicle, the bodhisattva-vehicle, the unique Vehicle.

* Translated from H. Kern and Bunyiu Nanjio, eds., *Saddharmapuṇḍarīka*, Bibliotheca Buddhica, vol. 10 (St. Petersburg: Académie Impériale des Sciences, 1912) p. 80 f.

† Translated from *Miao fa lien hua ching*, Kumārajīva's Chinese version, vol. 9 of the *Taishō shinshū dai-zōkyō* (Tokyo: Taishō issai-kyō kankō-kai, 1924–32), p. 13b.

Mr. Fujita points to the traditional division among the Chinese who believe that the One Vehicle and the buddhayāna of the three vehicles are the same and those who hold that they are different. The resort is to the famous parable of the burning house, which occupies most of the third chapter of the *Lotus*. There the father (Buddha) lures his children (all living beings) out of the burning house (the round of births and deaths) by offering them a goat-drawn carriage (*śrāvakayāna*), a deer-drawn carriage (*pratyekabuddhayāna*), and an ox-drawn carriage (*bodhisattvayāna*). Once they are out of the house, he gives them a carriage drawn by a great white ox (*buddhayāna*). Some of the Chinese said that the two ox-carts are the same, that, in other words, there are only three carriages, while others maintained that they are all different, meaning to say that there are in all four carriages.

Mr. Fujita holds that the text of the *Lotus* will support either interpretation. Three passages are cited in which the Buddha says that the buddhayāna/bodhisattvayāna is the only real one, and that the Buddha's own mention of the other two elsewhere than in the *Lotus* was no more than a device (*upāya*). Yet it must be noted that the *Lotus*, when it speaks of this *upāya*, says that all three, never the lower two alone, are a "device." The solution to the problem of the apparent inconsistency, says Mr. Fujita, is in the doctrine of "emptiness," which, he says, is eloquently expressed in the *Lotus* in the following passage:

> Like as a blind man who gains eyesight, just so is he to be viewed who is embarked on the course of the auditor or of the individually enlightened. He severs the defilements that bind him to continued existence. Freed of the bonds of the defilements, he is then released from the triple sphere with its six destinies. Thanks to this, the one embarked on the auditor's course has the following knowledge and utters the following speech: "There are no more Dharmas to be intuited! I have attained extinction!" It is then that the Thus Gone One teaches him the Dharma, for he endows him with enlightened intuition with these words: "If all dharmas are unattained, whence comes the extinction of them?" Once the thought of enlightened intuition has arisen within him, he neither continues to exist nor attains extinction. With this understanding he sees the world with its three spheres as being in all ten directions empty, like a conjuror's trick, like an illusion, like a dream, a will-o'-the-wisp, an echo. He

> views all dharmas as being unarisen, unsuppressed, unbound, unreleased, not dark, not light. Whoever sees the profound dharmas in this way, he sees, by not seeing, the whole triple sphere, filled with beings each of whom feels an inclination for the abodes of all the others.*

All the same, the *Lotus*'s references to "emptiness," if laid end to end, would not amount to much. The *Lotus*'s concern, after all, is much less with theory than with practice. The central issue is the One Vehicle, the availability of Buddhahood to all living beings; the *Lotus*'s message, so it alleges, was the Buddha's sole purpose in coming into the world. Thus the resolution of the apparent contradiction between the "three chariots" and the "four," i.e., the definition of the One Vehicle, is to be sought in the doctrine of "emptiness," but that, in turn, refers to the One Vehicle.

The question naturally arises: If the Buddha's career is not a matter of fact, why does he speak of it as if it were? If the three courses to salvation are not real, why does the Buddha dwell on them in such detail? The answer has already been suggested: it is a device, employed for the purpose of rendering more acquiescent those beings who would be frightened away by the ultimate message baldly stated. In the former case, the Buddha thinks, "If these fellows have the notion that I am always going to be around anyway, they may dawdle over their religious practice. If, on the other hand, they imagine, albeit falsely, that I am soon to be extinguished in nirvāṇa, the likelihood is that they will have a sense of urgency." In the latter case, the śrāvaka goes the full course to arhattva, only to say to himself, "Why, this is not real!" He then proceeds to Buddhahood, which *is* real.

The above is a bit oversimplified, but with it as a backdrop the accompanying English translation may be less puzzling.

The Buddha himself is frequently referred to by the epithet *tathāgata*, "Thus Come One" in my translation of Kumārajīva's text. Without much doubt, *tathāgata* is a non-Indic word refurbished to have an Indic appearance long after it had come into current use among India's Buddhists. When Kumārajīva transcribes it, for instance—which

* Translated from Kern-Nanjio, p. 234.

he does only seldom—he writes *tathagada*, which, on the face of it, means nothing. It was accordingly changed to *tathāgata*, then etymologized into *tathā gata*, "thus gone," and *tathā āgata*, "thus come." The Chinese appear to be rendering the latter, for they write *ju lai*, but even that word is not free of problems. In any case, the word signifies one who has actually attained what the others are seeking and thus can speak with authority about it.

There follows a comparative catalogue of the chapter titles in the two versions.

Kumārajīva	*Extant Sanskrit*
1. Introduction (*hsü p'in*)	1. Introduction (*nidānaparivarta*)
2. Expedient devices (*fang pien p.*)	2. Skill in means (*upāyakauśalya°*)
3. Parable (*p'i yü p.*)	3. Parable (*aupamya°*)
4. Belief and understanding (*hsin chieh p.*)	4. Strong inclination, attachment (*adhimukti°*)
5. Parable of medicinal herbs (*yao ts'ao yü p.*)	5. Medicinal herbs (*auṣadhī°*)
6. Bestowal of prophecy (*shou chi p.*)	6. Prophecy (*vyākaraṇa°*)
7. Parable of the conjured city (*hua ch'eng yü p.*)	7. Former connection (*pūrvayoga°*)
8. Receipt of prophecy by five hundred disciples (*wu pai ti tzu shou chi p.*)	8. Prophecy to five hundred mendicant monks (*pañcabhiksuśatavyākaraṇa°*)
9. Prophecies conferred on learners and adepts (*shou hsüeh wu hsüeh jen chi p.*)	9. Prophecy to Ānanda and others (*Ānandādivyākaraṇa°*)
10. Preachers of Dharma (*fa shih p.*)	10. Preachers of Dharma (*dharmabhāṇaka°*)
11. Apparition of the jeweled *stūpa* (*hsien pao t'a p.*)	11. Apparition of the *stūpa* (*stūpasaṃdarśana°*)
12. Devadatta (*T'i-p'o-ta-to p.*)	
13. Fortitude (*ch'üan ch'ih p.*)	12. Fortitude (*utsāha°*)
14. Comfortable conduct (*an lo hsing p.*)	13. Pleasant conduct (*sukhavihāra°*)
15. Welling up out of the earth (*ts'ung ti yung ch'u p.*)	14. Rise of *bodhisattvas* out of an aperture in the earth (*bodhisattvapṛthivīvivarasamudgama°*)
16. The life span of the Thus Come One (*ju lai shou liang p.*)	15. The life span of the Thus Gone One (*tathāgatāyuṣpramāṇa°*)

17. Discrimination of merits (*fen pieh kung te p.*)	16. Circuit of merits (*puṇyaparyāya*°)
18. The merits of appropriate joy (*sui hsi kung te p.*)	17. Exposition of the merits of appropriate joy (*anumodanāpuṇyanirdeśa*°)
19. The merits of the Dharma-preachers (*fa shih kung te p.*)	18. Praise of the Dharma-preachers (*dharmabhāṇakānuśaṃsā*°)
20. The bodhisattva Never Disparaging (*ch'ang pu ch'ing p'u-sa p.*)	19. Sadāparibhūta°
21. The supernatural powers of the Thus Come One (*ju lai shen li p.*)	20. The constituents of magic power of the Thus Gone One (*tathāgatarddhyabhisaṃskāra*°)
22. Entrustment (*chu lei p.*)	21. Entrustment (*anuparīndanā*°)
23. The former affairs of the bodhisattva Medicine King (*yao wang p'u-sa pen shih p.*)	22. The former connection of Bhaiṣajyarāja (*Bhaiṣajyarājapūrvayoga*°)
24. The bodhisattva Fine Sound (*miao yin p'u-sa p.*)	23. Gadgadasvara°
25. The gateway to everywhere of the bodhisattva He Who Observes the Sounds of the World (*Kuan shih yin p'u-sa p'u men p.*)	24. The exposition of the miracles of Avalokiteśvara, entitled the Chapter of Samantamukha (*samantamukhaparivarto nāmāvalokiteśvaravikurvaṇanirdeśaḥ*)
26. Dhāraṇī (*t'o-lo-ni p.*)	21. Magic formulas (*dhāraṇī*°)
27. The former affairs of the King Fine Adornment (*miao chuang yen wang pen shih p.*)	25. The former connection of Śubhavyūharāja (*Śubhavyūharājapūrvayoga*°)
28. The encouragements of the bodhisattva Universally Worthy (*p'u hsien p'u-sa ch'üan fa p.*)	26. The encouragements of Samantabhadra (*Samantabhadrotsāhanaparivarta*)

When dealing with Chinese Buddhist texts, it is most customary to use the recension of the *Taishō shinshū dai-zōkyō*. While I did consult it, nevertheless, since this is not a close textual study, and since the *Taishō* is so notoriously full of misprints, my basic text was the *Kunten kōsei Myōhō renge kyō*, edited by Akamatsu Kōyō (Kyoto: Yamada Hoendō, 1891). While, by comparison with the *Taishō*, it has the disadvantage of no variant readings, it is a work of scholarship and editorship of the highest order. There are no textual irregularities, the punctuation is meticulously correct, and the obscure passages are eked out with Japanese diacritics (the *kunten* of the title)—in all, a superb piece of work.

Where transcription and English translation are concerned, I follow Kumārajīva. That is, where he translates into Chinese, I translate into English. Where he transcribes phonetically, so do I. The one exception is the word *dharma*, which he translates (*fa*) and which I nevertheless transcribe. Sanskrit words in the text are translated in brief at their first appearance, and it is to be hoped that the Sanskrit-English glossary at the end will make them all clear.

VANCOUVER, BRITISH COLUMBIA — LEON HURVITZ

Contents

Roll Seven

Roll Eight

Scripture of the Lotus Blossom of the Fine Dharma

Roll 1

Chapter One: Introduction

Thus have I heard. At one time, the Buddha was dwelling in the city of King's House (Rājagṛha), on Gṛdhrakūṭa mountain, together with twelve thousand [Skt., twelve hundred] great *bhikṣus* [mendicant monks]. All were *arhants* [men enlightened but not Buddhas], their outflows already exhausted, never again subject to anguish (*kleśa*); they had achieved their own advantage and annihilated the bonds of existence, and their minds had achieved self-mastery. Their names were Ājñātakauṇḍinya, Mahākāśyapa, Uruvilvākāśyapa, Gayākāśyapa, Nadīkāśyapa, Śāriputra, Great Maudgalyāyana, Mahākātyāyana, Aniruddha, Kapphina, Gavāṃpati, Revata, Piliṅgavatsa (Pilindavatsa), Bakkula, Mahākauṣṭhila, Nanda, Sundarananda, Pūrṇo Maitrāyaṇīputraḥ, Subhūti, Ānanda, and Rāhula—such great arhants as these, known to the multitude. There were also another two thousand persons, including those who had more to learn and those who had not. There was Mahāprajāpatī, the *bhikṣuṇī* [mendicant nun], together with six thousand followers. Rāhula's mother Yaśodharā, the bhikṣuṇī, was also there together with her followers. There were eighty thousand *bodhisattva-mahāsattvas*, all nonbacksliders in *anuttarasamyaksaṃbodhi* [perfect enlightenment, that of a Buddha], all having mastered the *dhāraṇīs* [magic charms], preaching with joy and eloquence, turning the irreversible *Dharma*-wheel; having made offerings to incalculable hundreds of thousands of Buddhas, having planted many seeds of merit; constantly being praised by the Buddhas; cultivating themselves with compassion; having entered well into the Buddha's wisdom, having penetrated great wisdom, having reached the yonder shore; their fame bruited widely in countless worlds; able to save numberless hundreds of thousands of living beings. Their names were Mañjuśrī bodhisattva, the bodhisattva He Who Observes the Sounds of the World (Avalokiteśvara), the bodhisattva Gainer of Great Strength (Mahāsthāmaprāpta), the bodhisattva Constantly Exerting Himself

(Nityodyukta), the bodhisattva He Who Does Not Rest (Anikṣiptadhura), the bodhisattva of the Jeweled Palm (Ratnapāṇi), the bodhisattva Medicine King (Bhaiṣajyarāja), the bodhisattva Brave Donor (Pradānaśūra), the bodhisattva of the Jeweled Moon (Ratnacandra), the bodhisattva of Moonglow (Ratnaprabha), the bodhisattva of the Full Moon (Pūrṇacandra), the bodhisattva of Great Strength (Mahāvikrāmin), the bodhisattva of Immeasurable Strength (Anantavikrāmin), the bodhisattva He Who Transcends the Three Worlds (Trailokyavikrāmin), the bodhisattva Bhadrapāla, the bodhisattva Maitreya, the bodhisattva of the Heap of Jewels (Ratnākara), the bodhisattva He Who Leads the Multitude (Susārthavāha). He was with such bodhisattvas as these, to the number of eighty thousand.

At that time, Śakro Devānām Indraḥ was [there] with his following, consisting of twenty thousand sons of gods, among whom, further, were those named the God's Son of the Moon (Candra), the God's Son of All-Pervading Fragrance (Samantagandha), and the God's Son of the Glow of Jewels (Ratnaprabha). There were the four great god kings* together with their retinue of ten thousand sons of gods. There were the God's Son of Self-Mastery (Īśvara) and the God's Son of Great Self-Mastery (Maheśvara), together with their retinue of thirty thousand sons of gods. There were the Lord of the Sabhā (*Sahā*) world, Brahmā, the king of the gods; the great Brahmā Śikhin; and the great Brahmā, Bright Luster (Jyotiṣprabha), together with their retinue of twelve thousand sons of gods. There were eight dragon kings (*nāgarāja*), namely the dragon king Nanda, the dragon king Upananda, the dragon king Sāgara, the dragon king Vāsuki, the dragon king Takṣaka, the dragon king Anavatapta, the dragon king Manasvin, and the dragon king Utpalaka, each with several hundreds of thousands of followers. There were four *kinnara* [mythical being, half horse, half man], kings, namely, the kinnara king Law [Skt. has Druma], the kinnara king Fine Law (Sudharma), the kinnara king Great Law (Mahādharma),

* Jambudvīpa, the continent that we are supposed to occupy in the Buddhist cosmology, is dominated by a mountain range named Sumeru. One of the mountains in that range, Yugandhara, has four peaks. On the eastern peak dwells the god king Dhṛtarāṣṭra, on the southern Virūḍhaka, on the western Virūpākṣa, on the northern Vaiśravaṇa, acting as guardians of all Jambudvīpa.

and the kinnara king Law-Holder (Dharmadhara), each with several hundreds of thousands of followers. There were four *gandharva* [musician-demigod] kings, namely, the gandharva king Pleasant (Manojña), the gandharva king Pleasant Sound (Manojñasvara), the gandharva king Beautiful (Madhura), and the gandharva king Beautiful Sound (Madhurasvara), each with several hundreds of thousands of followers. There were four *asura* [titan] kings, namely, the asura king Balin, the asura king Kharaskandha, the asura king Vemacitrin, and the asura king Rāhu, each with several hundreds of thousands of followers. There were four *garuḍa* [mythical bird] kings, namely, the garuḍa king Great Majesty (Mahātejas), the garuḍa king Great Body (Mahākāya), the garuḍa king Very Full (Mahāpūrṇa), and the garuḍa king He Who Has His Wish (Maharddhiprāpta), each with several hundreds of thousands of followers. There was Vaidehī's son, King Ajātaśatru, with several hundreds of thousands of his followers. Each, having made obeisance to the Buddha's feet, withdrew and sat to one side.

At that time, the World-Honored One, surrounded by the fourfold multitude, showered with offerings, deferentially treated and revered, for the bodhisattvas' sake preached a scripture of the Great Vehicle named the Immeasurable Doctrine (Anantanirdeśa), a dharma to be taught to bodhisattvas, a dharma which the Buddha keeps ever in mind. When he had preached this scripture, cross-legged he entered into the *samādhi* [state of concentration] of the Abode of the Immeasurable Doctrine (Anantanirdeśapratiṣṭhānasamādhi), where his body and mind were motionless. At this time Heaven rained down *māndārava* [coral tree] flowers, *mahāmāndārava* [*mahā*, "great"] flowers, *mañjūṣaka* flowers [kind of celestial flower], and *mahāmañjūṣaka* flowers, scattering them over the Buddha and his bands of followers. The whole Buddha-world trembled in six different ways. At that time, in the company, the bhikṣus, bhikṣuṇīs, *upāsakas*, *upāsikās* [lay brothers and sisters], gods, dragons (*nāga*), *yakṣas* [spirits], gandharvas, asuras, garuḍas, kinnaras, *mahoragas* [great snakes], humans and nonhumans (*manuṣyāmanuṣya*), as well as petty kings and wheel-turning kings—these great assemblies felt that this had never happened before, and, joyously joining palms, single-mindedly they beheld the Buddha.

At that time the Buddha emitted a glow from the tuft of white hair between his brows that illuminated eighteen thousand worlds to the east, omitting none of them, reaching downward as far as the Avīci [the lowest] hell and upward as far as the Akaniṣṭha [highest] gods. In these worlds there could be fully seen the six kinds of living beings in those lands. There could also be seen the Buddhas present in those lands, and the *sūtradharmas* preached by those Buddhas could be heard. At the same time there could be seen those among the bhikṣus, bhikṣuṇīs, upāsakas, and upāsikās who through practice had attained the Path. Further there could be seen the various background causes and conditions of the bodhisattva-mahāsattvas, their various degrees of belief and understanding (*adhimukti*), and the various appearances with which they trod the bodhisattva-path. There could also be seen those Buddhas who achieved *parinirvāṇa* [perfect extinction]. Further, there could be seen how, after the Buddhas' parinirvāṇa, a *stūpa* [reliquary mound] of the seven jewels would be erected with the Buddhaśarīra [the Buddha's relics].

At that time, the bodhisattva Maitreya had this thought: "Now that the World-Honored One has shown these extraordinary signs, [we must ask] for what reason we have had these portents. Now that the Buddha, the World-Honored One, has entered into samādhi, whom shall I question about these rare apparitions, beyond reckoning and discussion? Who can answer?"

Further, he thought: "This Mañjuśrī the Dharma-prince, having already approached and served incalculable Buddhas in the past, must surely see these rare signs. I will now ask him."

At that time the bhikṣus, bhikṣuṇīs, upāsakas, and upāsikās, as well as the gods, dragons, ghosts, and the like, thought: "Whom shall we question about these lustrous and supernatural signs of the Buddha?"

At that time, the bodhisattva Maitreya wished to resolve his own doubts. He was also considering the thoughts of the four groups, the bhikṣus, bhikṣuṇīs, upāsakas, and upāsikās, as well as those of the assembled multitude of gods, dragons, ghosts, and the like. Then he questioned the bodhisattva Mañjuśrī, saying: "For what reason do we have these wondrous and supernatural signs, a great ray emitted which illuminates eighteen thousand lands to the east, making visible all the adornments of those Buddha-lands?"

Thereupon the bodhisattva Maitreya, wishing to restate this meaning, questioned in *gāthās* [a form of verse]:

Mañjuśrī,
  Why from the Leader's
Tuft of white hair does a great
  Ray shine in all directions,
Raining down māndārava and
  Mañjūṣaka flowers,
And with a breeze of sandalwood scent
  Gladden many hearts?
For this reason
  The earth is wholly purified,
And this world
  Trembles in six different ways.
Now the four bands in the assembly
  Are all delighted,
Their bodies and minds pleased,
  As if gaining something unprecedented.
When the ray from between his brows
  Illuminates the east,
Eighteen thousand lands
  Are all the color of gold.
From the Avīci hell
  To the Pinnacle of Existence (*bhavāgra*),
In the various worlds
  The living beings on the six courses,*

* The "six courses" are the forms of rebirth. Beginning at the bottom, they are (1) *naraka* (hell-dweller), (2) *preta* (the living dead, beings imagined to have necks the size of needles and stomachs the size of mountains, so that they are condemned to perpetual hunger), (3) *tiryagyonigata* (all members of the animal kingdom except man), (4) *asura* (titan), (5) *manuṣya* (human), and (6) *deva* (god). For category (3) the Skt. frequently has *tiryañcaḥ*, "horizontal beasts," which the Chinese, being principally an agricultural people, translated as *hsü sheng*, "domestic animals." Here, however, the term is rendered simply "beasts" throughout.

What they face in birth and death,
  The conditions arising from their good and evil deeds,
The pleasant and unpleasant they receive in retribution (*vipāka*)—
  All are seen herein.
I also see Buddhas,
  The lions among saintly lords,
Preaching the scriptures,
  The supremely subtle.
Their voices are pure,
  Emitting delicate sounds,
With which they teach bodhisattvas
  In numberless millions of myriads.
Their brahmā sound is subtle and profound,
  Making men to desire to hear it.
Each in his own world
  Preaches the true Dharma,
For various causes and conditions
  And by resort to numberless parables
Clarifying the Buddhadharma
  And enlightening the living beings.
If a man, encountering woe,
  Sickens of old age, illness, and death,
For his sake they preach *nirvāṇa*,
  Bringing to an end the uttermost vestige of woe.
If a man has merit,
  Formerly having made offerings to Buddhas,
And if he resolves to seek a superior dharma,
  For his sake they preach the rank of a perceiver of conditions
    (*pratyekabuddha*).
If there is a son of Buddha who,
  Cultivating many kinds of conduct,
Seeks unexceeded wisdom,
  For him they preach the Pure Path.
Mañjuśrī,
  I, dwelling here,
Have seen and heard things of this sort

Reaching to the thousands of millions.
As many as they are,
I will now tell them briefly.
I see in that land
Bodhisattvas like Ganges' sands,
Through various causes and conditions
Seeking the Buddha's Path.
Some perform the act of giving, presenting
Gold, silver, coral,
Pearls, *maṇi* [jewels]
Precious seashells, agate,
Diamonds and other treasures,
Bondmen and bondwomen, wagons and chariots,
Hand-drawn carriages and palanquins ornamented with jewels:
These in joy they give,
Applying them to the Path of the Buddha
And praying to attain this Vehicle,
The first in the three worlds,
Which the Buddhas praise.
Now there are bodhisattvas by whom
Jeweled four-horse carriages,
With spears and shields, and with flowered canopies
Arrayed on their seats, are presented.
Then I see bodhisattvas by whom
Bodily flesh, hands and feet,
Even wives and children are presented
In quest of the Unexcelled Path.
Again, I see bodhisattvas by whom
Heads and eyes, torso and limbs,
Are joyously presented
In quest of the Buddha's wisdom.
Mañjuśrī,
I see princes
Going before the Buddha
To ask of the Unexcelled Path,
Then abandoning pleasant lands,

Palaces and halls, courtiers and concubines,
Shaving their beards and hair,
And donning the Dharma-garb.
Now I see bodhisattvas
Who became bhikṣus,
Dwelling alone in serenity,
Taking pleasure in reciting the scriptures.
Then I see bodhisattvas
Striving with courage and determination,
Entering deep into the mountains,
And aspiring to the Path of the Buddha.
Again, I see them separating themselves from desire,
Constantly dwelling in desolation and serenity,
Profoundly cultivating *dhyāna*-concentration [meditation, mystic trance]
And attaining the five supernatural penetrations (*abhijñā*).
Then again I see bodhisattvas
Secure in dhyāna, their palms joined,
With thousands of myriads of gāthās
Praising the Dharma Kings.
Yet again, I see bodhisattvas
Of profound knowledge, and firm resolve,
Able to question the Buddhas,
To hear, to understand thoroughly, to receive, to keep.
I also see sons of the Buddhas,
Fully endowed with concentration and wisdom,
By resort to incalculable parables
For the multitude's sake preaching the Dharma,
Taking pleasure in preaching the Dharma,
Converting the bodhisattvas,
Smashing Māra's host
And beating the Dharma-drum.
Further, I see bodhisattvas,
Calm and silent in their quietude,
Revered by gods and dragons,
Yet taking no pleasure therein.

Again, I see bodhisattvas
  Dwelling in forests and emitting rays,
With which they rescue sufferers from the pains of hell
  And cause them to enter the Path of the Buddhas.
Again, I see Buddha-sons
  Who have never slept,
Going through forests
  In earnest quest of the Buddhas' Path.
I see further those perfect in disciplined conduct,
  Faultless in bearing,
Pure as precious gems,
  With these attributes seeking the Buddhas' Path.
Again, I see sons of the Buddhas
  Dwelling in the strength of forbearance, who,
Though men of overweening pride
  Hatefully revile and beat them,
Can bear all, without exception,
  Thus seeking the Buddhas' Path.
Again, I see bodhisattvas
  Who have separated themselves from all manner of frivolity
And from deluded followers,
  Who personally approach those of wisdom,
Single-mindedly removing distractions,
  On mountain and in forest composing their thoughts
For millions of thousands of myriads of years,
  Thereby seeking the Buddhas' Path.
Now I see bodhisattvas by whom
  Delicacies of food and drink
And a hundred varieties of broths and herbs
  Are offered to the Buddha and his *saṃgha* [brotherhood of monks];
By whom famous robes and superior garments,
  Their value in the thousands of myriads,
Or utterly priceless robes
  Are presented to the Buddha and his saṃgha;
By whom thousands of myriads of millions of kinds

Of houses of jeweled sandalwood,
As well as much fine bedding,
Are presented to the Buddha and his saṃgha;
By whom immaculate gardens and groves,
Their blossoms and fruits in full bloom,
With running springs and bathing ponds,
Are presented to the Buddha and his saṃgha:
By whom, with offerings such as these,
Supremely fine in many ways,
And with joy untiring,
The Unexcelled Path is sought.
Now there are bodhisattvas
Who preach the dharma of quiet extinction (*nirvāṇa*),
In various ways instructing
Numberless living beings.
Now I see bodhisattvas
Who view the nature of the *dharmas* ["things," phenomena]
As unmarked by duality,
Just like space.
Then I see sons of the Buddhas,
Their minds attached to no objects,
With this subtle knowledge
Seeking the Unexcelled Path.
Mañjuśrī,
There are also bodhisattvas
Who, after the Buddha's passage into extinction,
Shall make offerings to his *śarīra* [relics].
Further, I see sons of the Buddhas
Making stūpa-shrines
As numberless as Ganges' sands,
With which to adorn the realms and their territories,
Jeweled stūpas to the lovely height
Of five thousand *yojanas* [a *yojana* is several miles],
Both in length and breadth
Two thousand yojanas,
Every individual stūpa-shrine

Having on it a thousand banners,
Banners with jewels like intermingled dewdrops,
Their jeweled bells chiming in harmony;
To which gods, dragons, and spirits [*shen*; Skt. original unclear],
Humans and nonhumans
Of sweet flowers and skillfully played music*
Constantly present offerings.
Mañjuśrī,
The sons of the Buddhas,
In order to make offerings to the śarīra,
Adorn the stūpa-shrines,
So that the realms and their territories, in and of themselves,
Are of a most particularly refined beauty,
Like the king of divine trees
When his blossoms open out.
The Buddha has emitted a ray whereby
I and the assembled multitude
See these realms and territories,
Variously and peculiarly fine.
The Buddhas' supernatural power,
Their wisdom, is so rare
That, by the emission of a single pure beam,
They illuminate incalculable realms.
Seeing this, we
Gain something we have never had.
Son of the Buddha, O Mañju,
Pray resolve the multitude's doubts.
The fourfold multitude, in joyous supplication,
Looks up to you and me.
Why has the World-Honored One
Emitted this beam?
O Buddha's son, make timely answer
And, resolving doubts, cause joy.
What profit is there

* *Chi yüeh*, music played by professional performers.

In sending forth this ray?
When the Buddha sat on the Platform of the Path (*bodhimaṇḍa*),
What subtle dharmas he gained,
Because he wished to set them forth,
And in order to confer prophecy (*vyākaraṇa*),
He showed us the Buddha-lands,
Adorned and purified with many jewels,
And he saw the Buddhas.
The reason for all this is not a trifling one.
Mañju, you must know.
The fourfold multitude, the dragons, and the spirits
Look up to you,
Wondering what you will say to them.

At that time, the bodhisattva-mahāsattva Mañjuśrī said to the bodhisattva-mahāsattva Maitreya and the sundry great worthies (bodhisattva): "Good men, I surmise that the Buddha, the World-Honored One, now wishes to preach the great Dharma, to precipitate the great Dharma-rain, to blow the great Dharma-conch, to beat the great Dharma-drum, to set forth the great Dharma-doctrine. You good men, once before, in the presence of past Buddhas, I saw this portent: when the Buddhas had emitted this light, straightway they preached the great Dharma. Thus it should be understood that the present Buddha's display of light is also of this sort. It is because he wishes all the living beings to be able to hear and know the Dharma, difficult of belief for all the worlds, that he displays this portent.

"You good men, it is just as it was incalculable, infinite, inconceivable *asaṃkhyeyakalpas* [incalculable cosmic ages] ago. At that time there was a Buddha named Sun-and-Moon-Glow, a Thus Come One, worthy of offerings, of right and universal knowledge, his clarity and conduct perfect, well gone, understanding the world, an unexcelled Worthy, a Regulator of men of stature, a Teacher of gods and men, a Buddha, a World-Honored One,[1] who expounded the true Dharma which is good at its beginning, good in its middle, and good at its end, its meaning profound and recondite, its words subtle and refined, pure and without alloy, fully endowed with the marks of pure, white brahman-conduct (*brahmacaryā*). For the sake of those who sought to be voice-hearers (*śrāvaka*), his preachings corresponded to the dharma of the four truths, with which to cross over birth, old age, sickness, and death into ultimate nirvāṇa. For the sake of those who sought to be *pratyekabuddhas* [self-enlightened ones], his preachings corresponded to the dharma of the twelve causes and conditions. For the sake of the bodhisattvas, his preachings corresponded to the six *pāramitās* [perfections], with which he caused them to gain anuttarasamyaksaṃbodhi and to perfect the knowledge of all modes.

"Then, there was again a Buddha, also named Sun-and-Moon-Glow. Then, there was again another Buddha, also named Sun-and-Moon-Glow. In this way there were twenty thousand Buddhas, all having the same name, to wit, Sun-and-Moon-Glow, all belonging as well to the same clan, namely, that of Bharadvāja. Maitreya, it should be known that the first Buddha and the last were both of the same name, to wit, Sun-and-Moon-Glow, both fully endowed with the ten subsidiary designations and both preaching that which it is well to preach, the Dharma good at beginning, middle, and end.

"Before that last Buddha left his household, he had eight princely sons. The first was named Having a Mind (Mati), the second was named Good Mind (Sumati), the third was named Immeasurable Mind (Anantamati), the fourth was named Jewel-like Mind (Ratnamati), the fifth was named Superior Mind (Viśeṣamati), the sixth was named Mind Free of Doubt (Vimatisamudghāṭin), the seventh was named Echo Mind (Ghoṣamati), the eighth was named Dharma Mind (Dharmamati). These eight princes, each holding sway over four Heaven-spanning realms, were men to whom regal bearing came quite naturally. When they heard that their father had left his household and gained anuttarasamyaksaṃbodhi, these princes all cast aside their princely status and followed him out of the household life. Opening up their minds to the Great Vehicle and constantly cultivating brahman-conduct, they all became Dharma-masters, and planted roots of goodness in the presence of a thousand myriads of Buddhas.

"At that time, the Buddha Sun-and-Moon-Glow preached a scripture of the Great Vehicle named the Immeasurable Doctrine

(Anantanirdeśa), a dharma to be taught to bodhisattvas, one which Buddhas keep in mind. When he had preached this scripture, straightway, in the midst of the great multitude, seated with legs crossed, he entered into a samādhi called the Palace of the Immeasurable Doctrine (Anantanirdeśapratiṣṭhāna), body and mind motionless. At that time the gods rained down māndārava flowers, mahāmāndārava flowers, mañjūṣaka flowers, and mahāmañjūṣaka flowers and scattered them over the Buddha and his great multitude, and the whole Buddha-world trembled in six different ways. At that time, in the midst of the assembly, bhikṣus, bhikṣuṇīs, upāsakas, upāsikās, gods (*deva*), dragons, yakṣas, gandharvas, asuras, garuḍas, kinnaras, and mahoragas, humans and nonhumans, as well as petty kings and wheel-turning sage-kings (*balacakravartinaś caturdvīpakacakravartinaś ca*)—these multitudes, having gained something they had never had before, clasped their hands in joy and single-mindedly beheld the Buddha.

"At that time the Thus Come One emitted a glow from the tuft of white hair between his brows that illuminated eighteen thousand Buddha-lands to the east, omitting none of them, just like the Buddha-lands now visible.

"Maitreya, be it known that at that time in the assembly there were two thousand million bodhisattvas who wished to listen to the Dharma. These bodhisattvas, seeing this glow illuminate the whole Buddha-land and gaining something they had never had before, wished to know the reason for this glow.

"At that time, there was a bodhisattva whose name was Fine Luster (Varaprabha) and who had eight hundred disciples. The Buddha Sun-and-Moon-Glow, rising from samādhi, through the bodhisattva Fine Luster preached a scripture of the Great Vehicle named the Lotus Blossom of the Fine Dharma (*Saddharmapuṇḍarīka*), a Dharma to be taught to bodhisattvas, one which Buddhas keep in mind, [Sun-and-Moon-Glow] for sixty minor kalpas not rising from his seat. At that time, those assembled to listen also sat in one place, for sixty minor kalpas motionless in body and mind, listening to the Buddha's preachings as if for the space of a meal. At this time, there was not one person within the multitude who felt weariness, whether in body or in mind.

"The Buddha Sun-and-Moon-Glow, having preached this scripture for sixty minor kalpas, straightway, in the midst of the multitude of Brahmā, Māra, *śramaṇas* [ascetics], and Brahmans, as well as gods, men, and asuras, proclaimed these words: 'This day at midnight the Thus Come One shall enter nirvāṇa without residue.'

"At that time, there was a bodhisattva named Womb of Excellence [Śrīgarbha, "Embryo of Good Fortune"]. The Buddha Sun-and-Moon-Glow straightway conferred upon him a prophecy, announcing to the bhikṣus: 'This bodhisattva, Womb of Excellence, shall next become a Buddha named Pure Body [Vimalanetra, "Pure Eyes" (for *vimaladeha*?)] *tathāgato 'rhan samyaksaṃbuddhaḥ* [a Thus Come One, a Worthy One, a Properly and Fully Enlightened One].'

"When the Buddha had conferred this prophecy, he then, at midnight, entered nirvāṇa without residue. After the Buddha's passage into extinction, the bodhisattva Fine Luster kept the Scripture of the Lotus Blossom of the Fine Dharma, which for full eighty minor kalpas he expounded to others. The eight sons of the Buddha Sun-and-Moon-Glow all placed themselves under the tutelage of Fine Luster. Fine Luster's instruction enabled them to solidify their anuttarasamyaksaṃbodhi. These princes, having made offerings to hundreds of thousands of myriads of millions of Buddhas, all achieved the Buddha Path. The last to achieve Buddhahood was named Torch-Burner (Dīpaṃkara).

"Among the eight hundred disciples was one named Seeker of Fame (Yaśaskāma), who craved advantage and profit, who though he read and committed to memory a multitude of scriptures derived no profit from them, completely forgetting most—for which reason he was called Seeker of Fame. This man also, since he had planted roots of goodness, was able to meet incalculable hundreds of thousands of myriads of millions of Buddhas, to make offerings, to revere and honor them, and to praise them. Maitreya, be it known: at that time can the bodhisattva Fine Luster have been anyone else? I myself was he. You yourself were the bodhisattva Seeker of Fame. We see these portents, now just as before. For this reason I surmise that the Buddha will this day preach a scripture of the Great Vehicle named the Lotus Blossom of the Fine Dharma, a Dharma to be taught to bodhisattvas, one which the Buddha keeps in mind."

At that time Mañjuśrī, wishing to restate this message, in the midst of the great multitude proclaimed gāthās, saying:

I recall that in a past age,
  Incalculable, numberless kalpas ago,
There was a Buddha, supreme among men,
  Whose name was Sun-and-Moon-Glow.
He, the World-Honored One, expounded the Dharma,
  Saving incalculable living beings;
And innumerable millions of bodhisattvas
  Did he cause to enter into Buddha-knowledge.
Before this Buddha left his household,
  The eight princely sons whom he had begotten,
Seeing the Great Saint leave his household,
  Also followed him in the cultivation of brahman-conduct.
At that time, this Buddha preached of the Great Vehicle
  A scripture named Incalculable Doctrine,
In the midst of great multitudes
  And for their sakes making broad distinctions.
Having preached this scripture, the Buddha,
  Straightway, atop the Dharma-throne,
Crossing his legs, sat in a samādhi
  Named the Place of the Incalculable Doctrine.
The gods rained down māndārava-flowers,
  Divine drums resounded of their own accord,
And the gods, dragons, ghosts, and spirits
  Made offerings to the Supreme among Men.
All the Buddha-lands
  Straightway reverberated greatly.
The Buddha emitted from between his brows a ray,
  Displaying various rare things.
This ray illuminated to the east
  Eighteen thousand Buddha-lands,

Showing for all living beings
  The places of birth, death, and retribution for deeds.
There could be seen Buddha-lands
  Adorned with many jewels
The color of *vaiḍūrya* [cat's-eye gem] and *pārijāta* [coral tree];
  These were illuminated by the Buddha's ray.
Also visible were of gods, men,
  Dragons, spirits, and yakṣas a multitude,
And gandharvas and kinnaras
  Each making offerings to that Buddha.
There could also be seen Thus Come Ones,
  Of themselves achieving the Buddha Path,
Their bodies colored like a gold mountain,
  Erect, majestic, and very fine.
As within pure vaiḍūrya
  There is visible an image of true gold,
So in the great multitude, the World-Honored One
  Sets forth the doctrine of the profound Dharma.
One by one, in the Buddha-lands,
  Multitudes of voice-hearers without number
By virtue of the light of the Buddha's ray
  All make manifest their assemblies.
Now there are bhikṣus who,
  On mountains and in forests,
Exert themselves to keep to pure moral conduct,
  As if preserving a bright pearl [e.g., from theft].
Again, there can be seen bodhisattvas
  Who practice gift-giving, forbearance, and the like,
Their number like to Ganges' sands;
  These are illuminated by the Buddha's ray.
Again, there can be seen bodhisattvas
  Who have deeply entered into various
    dhyāna-concentrations,
Their bodies and minds quiet and unmoving,
  Thereby to seek the Unexcelled Path.
There are also seen bodhisattvas

Who know the mark of quiescence of the dharmas,*
Each in these lands
Preaching the Dharma and seeking the Buddha Path.
At that time the fourfold assembly,
Seeing the Buddha Sun-and-Moon-Glow
Demonstrate his great supernatural power,
Were all glad at heart,
Everyone asking his neighbor
For what reason this should be.
The Noble One, revered by gods and men,
At this very time arose from samādhi
And praised the bodhisattva Fine Luster:
"You are the eyes of the world,
He to whom all turn in faith,
The one who can reverently hold the treasure house of the Dharma.
The Dharma as I have preached it
Only you can know by direct witness."
The World-Honored One, having praised him
And having inspired joy in Fine Luster,
Preached this Scripture of the Dharma Flower,
Full sixty minor kalpas
Not rising from that seat.
The superior, fine Dharma that he preached
This Dharma-master Fine Luster
Was able to receive and keep whole.
The Buddha, having preached this Dharma Flower
And having caused the multitude to rejoice,
Then directly on that very day

* This is a reference to a controversy between the early Mahāyāna and the Sarvāstivāda school of the Hīnayāna, among whose adherents the Mahāyāna attempted to make its first converts. One of the cardinal Sarvāstivādin doctrines is that the 75 dharmas, the components of existence, are momentary, appearing and disappearing every instant. Attainment of nirvāṇa is contingent on the suppression (*nirodha*) of all 75. The Mahāyāna held that, if seen through enlightened eyes, the dharmas are in no contradiction with nirvāṇa, and are as quiescent as nirvāṇa itself. This is their "reality-mark" or "mark of quiescence."

Announced to the multitude of gods and men:
"The doctrine of the reality-marks of the dharmas
I have already preached to you.
Now I, at midnight,
Will enter into nirvāṇa.
With single-minded exertion, you
Must separate yourselves from self-indulgence,
For the Buddhas are very hard to encounter,
Happening upon men once in a million kalpas."
When the sons of the World-Honored One
Heard that the Buddha was entering nirvāṇa,
Each harbored grief and anguish, [saying]:
"Why must the Buddha's extinction be so swift?"
The sainted Lord, the King of the Dharma,
Comforted the incalculable multitude:
"When I cross to extinction,
Have neither care nor fear.
For this bodhisattva, Womb of Excellence,
Over the reality-marks without outflows
Has already attained mastery with his mind.
He shall next become a Buddha
Named Pure Body;
He, too, shall save an incalculable multitude."
The Buddha that night crossed to extinction
Like firewood utterly consumed by fire.
Distributing his śarīra,
They erected incalculable stūpas.
Bhikṣus and bhikṣuṇīs,
In number like to Ganges' sands,
Increased their exertions by severalfold,
Thereby seeking the Unexcelled Path.
This Dharma-master Fine Luster
Reverently held the treasure house of the Buddha's Dharma,
Throughout eighty minor kalpas
Broadly proclaiming the Scripture of the Dharma Flower.
These eight princes,

Enlightened and converted by Fine Luster,
Solidifying the Unexcelled Path,
Shall see numberless Buddhas.
After making offerings to various Buddhas,
They shall follow them in treading the Great Path.
In succession they shall be enabled to achieve Buddhahood,
By turns receiving prophecies.
The last of them, a god among gods,
Shall be called the Buddha Torch-Burner (Dīpaṃkara),
Guide of the seers (*ṛṣisaṃghapūjita*),
Savior of incalculable multitudes.
This Dharma-master Fine Luster
At that time had a disciple,
Whose mind constantly harbored indolence and sloth,
Who craved fame and advantage,
Whose desire for fame and advantage was insatiable,
Who often frequented the houses of the great clans,
Forsaking what he had repeated and committed to memory,
Relegating it to oblivion and deriving no profit from it.
For this reason
He was called Seeker of Fame.
He also, performing a multitude of good deeds,
Was able to see numberless Buddhas,
To make offerings to the Buddhas,
To follow them in treading the Great Path,
To acquire fully the six pāramitās,
And, now, to see the Lion Son of the Śākyas.
Hereafter he shall become a Buddha
Whose name shall be called Maitreya,
Broadly saving living beings
Whose number shall have no reckoning.
After that Buddha [Śākyamuni] shall have crossed to extinction,
That slothful, indolent one shall be you.
The Dharma-master Fine Luster
Is now indeed myself.

I saw how the Buddha Torch-Burner's (Dīpaṃkara)
  Former signal ray was of the same sort.
Thus do I know that the present Buddha
  Wishes to preach the Scripture of the Dharma Blossom.
The present signs are like the former portents;
  They are the Buddhas' devices.
The present Buddha emits a glow
  Which helps to set forth the doctrine of the reality-marks.
Men, the time has now come to know [the answers to all
    questions].
  Join palms and single-mindedly wait,
For the Buddha shall now precipitate a Dharma-rain
  That shall satisfy the seekers of the Path.
As for those who seek the rank of the three vehicles,
  If they have doubts or regrets,
For their sakes the Buddha shall remove them,
  Causing them to vanish without a trace.

Chapter Two: Expedient Devices

At that time, the World-Honored One rose serenely from his samādhi and proclaimed to Śāriputra: "The Buddhas' wisdom is profound and incalculable. The gateways of their wisdom are hard to understand and hard to enter, so that no voice-hearer or pratyekabuddha can know them. Why is this? In former times the Buddha, personally approaching hundreds of thousands of myriads of millions of innumerable Buddhas, performed exhaustively the dharmas of those Buddhas' incalculable paths. His fame for bold and earnest exertion having spread everywhere, he achieved profound dharmas that had never been before. What he preaches accords with what is appropriate, but the end point of its meaning is hard to understand. Śāriputra, since achieving Buddhahood I have, by a variety of means and by resort to a variety of parables, broadly set forth the spoken doctrine, by countless devices leading the living beings and enabling them to abandon their encumbrances. Why is this? The Thus Come One's expedient devices, his knowledge and insight, and his pāramitās have all been acquired to the fullest measure.

"Śāriputra, the Thus Come One's knowledge and insight are broad and great, profound and recondite, without measure and without obstruction. His might, his fearlessness, his dhyāna-concentration, his realease-samādhi have deeply penetrated the limitless. He has perfected all the dharmas that have never been before. Śāriputra, by making a variety of distinctions, the Thus Come One can skilfully preach the dharmas. His words are gentle, gladdening many hearts. Śariputra, to speak of the essential: as for the immeasurable, unlimited dharmas that have never been before, the Buddha has perfected them all. Cease, Śāriputra, we need speak no more. Why is this? Concerning the prime, rare, hard-to-understand dharmas, which the Buddha has perfected, only a Buddha and a Buddha can exhaust their reality, namely, the suchness of the dharmas, the suchness of their marks, the suchness of their nature, the suchness of their substance, the suchness of their powers, the suchness of their functions, the suchness of their causes, the suchness of their conditions, the suchness of their effects, the suchness of their retributions, and the absolute identity of their beginning and end."[1]

At that time the World-Honored One, wishing to restate this doctrine, proclaimed gāthās, saying:

The Hero of the World is incalculable.
  Among gods, worldlings,
And all varieties of living beings,
  None can know the Buddha.
As to the Buddha's strengths (*bala*), his sorts of fearlessness (*vaiśāradya*),
  His deliverances (*vimokṣa*), and his samādhis,
As well as the other dharmas of a Buddha,
  None can fathom them.
Formerly, following numberless Buddhas,
  He fully trod the various paths,
Those dharmas profound and subtle,
  Hard to see and hard to understand.
Throughout countless millions of kalpas
  He trod these various paths; [then]
On the platform of the Path he was able to achieve the Fruit:
  This I fully know.
As to such great fruits and retributions as these,
  Such varied doctrines of nature and marks,
I and the Buddhas of the ten directions
  Are the only ones who can know these things.
These dharmas cannot be demonstrated;
  Words, which are only signs, are quiescent in them.
Among the remaining kinds of living beings
  None can understand them,
Except for the multitude of bodhisattvas,
  Whose power of faith is firm.
The multitude of the Buddhas' disciples
  Formerly made offerings to the Buddhas.

All their outflows now exhausted,
  They inhabit this last body.
Men such as these,
  Their strength irresistible,
Even if they filled the world,
  If all were like Śāriputra,
And if, exhausting their thoughts, all calculated together,
  Could not fathom the Buddha's knowledge.
Even if they filled the ten directions,
  All of them like Śāriputra
And the remaining disciples,
  If, further, filling the *kṣetras* [Buddha-fields] of ten directions
And exhausting their thoughts, they were to calculate together,
  They still could not know it.
If pratyekabuddhas of keen intelligence (*tīkṣṇendriya*),
  Inhabiting a final body without outflows (*anāsravāṇām antimadehadhāriṇām*),
Were to fill even the spheres of the ten directions,
  In their number like bamboo groves,
And if, putting their minds together
  For millions of incalculable kalpas,
They wished to think on the real knowledge of the Buddha,
  None could know a slight portion thereof.
If bodhisattvas who have recently launched their thoughts*
  Who have made offerings to countless Buddhas,
Who understand completely the direction of the various doctrines,
  And who also can preach the Dharma well
Were, in the manner of stalks of hemp, bambo, and rice,
  To fill the kṣetras of the ten directions,
And if, with one mind and by resort to their subtle wisdom,
  For kalpas numerous as Ganges' sands

* *Ch'u fa hsin*, the recognized equivalent, if not a translation, of *navayānasaṃprasthita*, "set out on the new course." The reference is to a bodhisattva just recently embarked on his career, the first step of which is the resolve to attain Buddhahood.

They were all to think and calculate together,
Still they could not understand the Buddha's knowledge.
If bodhisattvas who do not backslide,
In number like to Ganges' sands,
Were with one mind to think and seek together,
They still could not know it.
I further proclaim to you, Śāriputra,
That that which is without outflows, beyond reckoning and discussion,
The extremely profound and subtle Dharma,
I have already gained completely.
[In this age] only I know its marks,
As do the Buddhas [of other ages] in the ten directions.
Śāriputra, let it be known
That the Buddhas' words are without discrepancy,
That toward the Dharma preached by the Buddha
One should display the strength of great faith.
After the World-Honored One's dharma has long been in effect,
He must preach the truth. [?][2]
I proclaim to the multitude of voice-hearers
And to those seeking the vehicle of condition-perceivers[3]
That I am the One who shall cause them to cast off the bonds of suffering
And attain nirvāṇa.
The Buddha, by the power of expedient devices,
Demonstrates the teaching of the three vehicles.
The living beings, attached to this object and that,
He attracts and thus enables to extricate themselves.

At that time, in the midst of the great multitude there were voice-hearers, their outflows exhausted, arhants, Ājñātakauṇḍinya and others, twelve hundred persons, as well as persons who had launched their thoughts toward the rank of pratyekabuddha and bhikṣus, bhiksuṇīs, upāsakas, and upāsikās, each of whom thought: "Now, why has the World-Honored One made this speech earnestly praising expedient devices? The Dharma which the Buddha has gained is very hard to understand. He has something to say, whose meaning is hard to know, and which no voice-hearer or pratyekabuddha can attain. The Buddha has preached the doctrine of unique deliverance, which means that we, too, gaining this Dharma, shall reach nirvāṇa. Yet now we do not know where this doctrine tends."

At that time, Śāriputra, knowing of the doubts in the minds of the fourfold assembly, and himself not yet fully understanding, addressed the Buddha, saying "World-Honored One, for what cause and through what conditions have you earnestly praised the Buddhas' prime device, their extremely profound and subtle Dharma, so hard to understand? In all this long time I have never before heard from the Buddha such a preaching as this. Now the fourfold assembly all have doubts. I beg the World-Honored One to expound this matter. World-Honored One, why have you earnestly praised this very profound and subtle Dharma, so hard to understand?"

At that time, Śāriputra, wishing to restate this idea, proclaimed gāthās, saying:

> The Sun of Wisdom, the Most Venerable of the Great Saints,
> After a long time indeed preaches this Dharma,
> Himself saying that he has gained such
> Strengths (*balā*), fearlessness, samādhis,
> Dhyāna-concentrations, releases (*vimokṣā*), and other such
> Inconceivable (*aprameyā*) dharmas.
> On the dharmas attained on the Platform of the Path,
> No one is able to put questions.
> "My mind [says the Buddha] is difficult to fathom,
> Nor is anyone able to question it."
> Unasked [O Buddha,] you preach it yourself,
> Praising the path you have trodden
> And that most subtle of wisdoms,
> Which the Buddhas have gained.
> The arhants without outflows
> And those who seek nirvāṇa
> Have now all fallen into a net of doubt,
> Asking themselves why the Buddha has preached this.

Those who seek to be condition-perceivers,
As well as bhikṣus, bhikṣuṇīs,
Gods, dragons, demons, spirits (*devā nāgāś ca yakṣāś ca*),
And gandharvas (*gandharvāś ca mahoragāḥ*),
Look at one another and harbor uncertainties,
Entreating the Most Venerable of Two-Legged Beings,
"Why is this?
We beg the Buddha to explain it to us."
Of the multitude of voice-hearers
The Buddha has said that I am the first.
Now, with respect to my own knowledge, I
Cannot resolve my doubts
As to whether this is the ultimate Dharma
Or whether it is [merely] a path to tread [toward that Dharma].
The sons born of the Buddha's mouth (*putra jinasya aurasā*),
Their palms joined and looking up in expectation,
Beg you to emit a subtle sound
And thus to make timely explanation in keeping with reality.
The gods, dragons, and spirits (*devāś ca nāgāś ca sayakṣarākṣasāḥ*),
In number like to Ganges' sands,
Bodhisattvas seeking to be Buddhas,
Their great number being eighty thousands,
And of several myriads of millions of realms
The wheel-turning sage-kings have arrived,
With palms joined and with thoughts deferential,
Wishing to hear of the Perfect Path.

At that time, the Buddha proclaimed to Śāriputra: "Cease, cease! There is no need to speak further. If I speak of this matter, gods and men in all the worlds shall be alarmed."

Śāriputra again addressed the Buddha, saying: "World-Honored One, I beg you to preach it, I beg you to preach it! What is the reason? In this assembly numberless hundreds of thousands of myriads of millions of *asaṃkhyeyas* of living beings, having seen Buddhas, their faculties (*indriya*) keen and their wisdom pellucid, if they hear the Buddha's preaching shall be able to put reverent faith in it." At that time Śāriputra, wishing to restate this meaning, proclaimed a gāthā, saying:

O King of the Dharma, Venerable One among the Unexcelled,
Do but preach! I beg you to have no second thoughts.
In this assembly the incalculable multitude
Includes those who can put reverent faith in you.

The Buddha again restrained Śāriputra: "If I preach this matter, all the gods, men, and asuras in all the worlds shall be alarmed, and the arrogant bhikṣus shall fall into a great trap." At that time the World-Honored One proclaimed a gāthā, saying:

Cease, cease! No need to speak.
My dharma is subtle and hard to imagine.
Those of overweening pride,
If they hear it, shall surely neither revere it nor believe in it.

At that time, Śāriputra again addressed the Buddha, saying: "I beseech you to preach, I beseech you to preach! In the present assembly, beings like me, numbering a hundred thousand myriads of millions, in successive incarnations have already been converted by Buddhas. Such men as these shall surely be able to revere and believe. Throughout the long night of time (*dīrgharātram*) they shall be secure, deriving much advantage therefrom."

At that time Śāriputra, wishing to restate this meaning, proclaimed gāthās, saying:

O You Supremely Venerable among Two-Legged Beings,
I beg you to preach the Prime Dharma!
I am the Buddha's eldest son:
Do but deign to preach explicitly.
Incalculable multitudes in this assembly
Can revere and believe this Dharma.
The Buddha has already, generation after generation,
Taught and converted many like these.

All of one mind, with palms joined,
  Wish to listen to the Buddha's Word.
We twelve hundred
  And the others who seek to be Buddhas
Beg that, for the sake of this multitude,
  You will but deign to preach explicitly.
If they hear this Dharma,
  Then they shall evince great joy.

At that time the World-Honored One declared to Śāriputra: "Since you have now thrice earnestly besought me, how can I not preach? Now listen with understanding and with careful thought, for I will state it to you explicitly."

While he was speaking these words, in the assembly bhikṣus, bhikṣuṇīs, upāsakas, and upāsikās to the number of five thousand straightway rose from their seats and, doing obeisance to the Buddha, withdrew. For what reason? This group had deep and grave roots of sin and overweening pride, imagining themselves to have attained and to have borne witness to what in fact they had not. Having such faults as these, therefore they did not stay. The World-Honored One, silent, did not restrain them.

At that time the Buddha declared to Śāriputra: "My assembly has no more branches and leaves, it has only firm fruit. Śāriputra, it is just as well that such arrogant ones as these have withdrawn. Now listen well, for I will preach to you."

Śāriputra said: "Very well, World-Honored One, for I am eager to hear."

The Buddha declared to Śāriputra: "A subtle Dharma such as this the Buddhas, the Thus Come Ones, preach but occasionally, as the *udumbara* [cluster fig] blossom appears but once in a while. You should believe that in what the Buddha says the words are not vain. Śāriputra, the Buddhas preach the Dharma appropriately; their purport is hard to understand. What is the reason? By resort to numberless devices and to various means, parables, and phrases do I proclaim the dharmas. This Dharma is not a thing that discursive or discriminatory reasoning can understand. Only Buddhas can know it. What is the reason?

The Buddhas, the World-Honored Ones, for one great cause alone appear in the world. Śāriputra, what do I mean by 'The Buddhas, the World-Honored Ones, for one great cause alone appear in the world?' The Buddhas, the World-Honored Ones, appear in the world because they wish to cause the beings to hear of the Buddha's knowledge and insight and thus enable them to gain purity. They appear in the world because they wish to demonstrate the Buddha's knowledge and insight to the beings. They appear in the world because they wish to cause the beings to understand. They appear in the world because they wish to cause the beings to enter into the path of the Buddha's knowledge and insight. Śāriputra, this is the one great cause for which the Buddhas appear in the world."

The Buddha declared to Śāriputra: "The Buddhas, the Thus Come Ones, teach the bodhisattvas merely that whatever they do is for one purpose, namely, to demonstrate and make intelligible the Buddha's knowledge and insight to the beings. Śāriputra, the Thus Come One by resort to the One Buddha Vehicle alone preaches the Dharma to the beings. There are no other vehicles, whether two or three. Śāriputra, the dharmas of the Buddhas in all ten directions are also of this sort. Śāriputra, the Buddhas of the past by resort to incalculable and numberless devices and to various means, parables, and phrases proclaimed the dharmas to the beings. These dharmas were all directed toward the One Buddha Vehicle. These beings, hearing the Dharma from the Buddhas, all attain thoroughly to knowledge of all modes (*sarvākārajñatā*).

"Śāriputra, future Buddhas shall come into the world, and they, too, by resorting to incalculable and numberless devices and to various means, parables, and phrases, shall proclaim the dharmas to the beings. These dharmas shall all be directed toward the One Buddha Vehicle. These beings, hearing the Dharma from the Buddhas, shall all attain thoroughly the knowledge of all modes.

"Śāriputra, the Buddhas, the World-Honored Ones, in the incalculable hundreds of thousands of myriads of millions of Buddha-lands in the ten directions of present time have many beings whom they benefit and put at their ease. These Buddhas also, by resort to incalculable and numberless devices and to various means, parables, and phrases, proclaim the dharmas to the beings. These dharmas are all directed toward the One Buddha Vehicle. These beings, hearing the Dharma from the Buddhas, shall all attain thoroughly to knowledge of all modes. Śāriputra, these Buddhas teach the bodhisattvas merely because they wish to demonstrate the Buddha's knowledge and insight to the beings, because they wish to enlighten the beings with the Buddha's knowledge and insight, because they wish to cause the beings to enter into the Buddha's knowledge and insight.

"Śāriputra, I, too, am like this. Knowing that the beings have various desires and objects to which their thoughts are profoundly attached, following their basic natures, by resort to the expedient power of various means, parables, and phrases, I preach the Dharma to them. Śāriputra, I do this only in order that they may gain the One Buddha Vehicle and knowledge of all modes. Śāriputra, in the worlds of the ten directions there are not even two vehicles. How much the less can there be three!

"Śāriputra, the Buddhas come into an evil world stained with five defilements, to wit, the defilement of the kalpa (*kalpakaṣāya*), the defilement of the agonies (*kleśakaṣāya*), the defilement of the beings (*sattvakaṣāya*), the defilement of views (*dṛṣtikaṣāya*), and the defilement of the life-span (*āyuṣkaṣāya*). When the kalpa is in chaos, Śāriputra, the stains of the beings run deep, and with greed and envy they complete unwholesome roots. Therefore, the Buddhas, with their expedient powers, make distinctions in the One Buddha Vehicle and speak of three.[4] Śāriputra, if a disciple of mine, thinking himself an arhant or a pratyekabuddha, neither has heard nor knows of these matters that the Buddhas, the Thus Come Ones, teach to bodhisattvas alone, he is no disciple of the Buddha, neither arhant nor pratyekabuddha. If such bhikṣus or bhikṣuṇīs say to themselves, 'I have already attained arhattva! This is my last body! I have perfected nirvāṇa!' and if then they resolve no further to seek anuttarasamyaksaṃbodhi, be it known that this lot are all persons of overweening pride. What is the reason? That a bhikṣu who had truly attained arhattva should not believe this Dharma—that is impossible, except when, after a Buddha's passage into extinction, no Buddha is present. What is the reason? After the Buddha's passage into extinction, persons who receive, keep, read, recite, and understand scriptures like this one shall be hard to find.[5] If they encounter other

Buddhas, they shall then get decisive instruction concerning this Dharma. Śāriputra, you must all single-mindedly believe, understand, receive, and keep the Buddha's Word; for in the Word of the Buddhas, the Thus Come Ones, there is nothing either vain or arbitrary. There are no other vehicles; there is only the One Buddha Vehicle."

At that time the World-Honored One, wishing to restate this meaning, proclaimed gāthās, saying:

Bhikṣus and bhikṣuṇīs
  Harboring arrogance,
Upāsakas with pride,
  And upāsikās of no faith—
In the fourfold assembly, the likes of these,
  Five thousand in number,
Not seeing their own faults,
  Having flaws in their discipline,
And jealously guarding their blemishes,
  These of slight wisdom have already left:
The chaff of the multitude,
  Thanks to the Buddha's imposing majesty, is gone.
These persons, ill-equipped with merit,
  Are not worthy to receive this Dharma.
This multitude has neither branches nor leaves,
  But has only firm fruits.
Śāriputra, listen well:
  The dharma that the Buddhas have gained
By resort to incalculable expedient powers
  They preach to the beings.
The thoughts thought by the beings,
  The sundry ways trodden by them,
The nature of their several desires,
  The good and evil deeds in their former incarnations—
The Buddha knows them thoroughly. Knowing them, and
  Resorting to various means and parables
And to their powers, and to the powers of phrases and other expedients,

He causes all to rejoice.
Now he preaches *sūtras* [sermons],
Gāthās and former matters (*itivṛttaka*),
Former lives (*jātaka*) and things that have never been before
[*adbhuta*, miracle tales]
Again, he preaches cause and condition (*nidāna*),
Parable (*aupamya*) and *geya* [verses repeating the prose],
And *upadeśa* [dialogue] scriptures.
Those of dull faculties, who desire lesser dharmas,
Who out of sheer greed cling to birth and death,
Who in the presence of incalculable Buddhas
Still fail to tread the profound and subtle Path,
And who are tormented by multitudinous woes—
For these I preach nirvāṇa.
Devising this expedient device, I
Enable them to enter into the Buddha's wisdom.
I never told them, "You all
Shall be able to achieve the Path of the Buddha."
The reason I never told them
Is that the time to tell it had not yet come.
Now is precisely the time
To preach the Great Vehicle definitively.
This Dharma of mine, in nine divisions,*
I preach by matching it to the beings,
Keeping the entry into the Great Vehicle as the basis:
This is why I preach this scripture.
There are sons of the Buddha whose thoughts are pure
And supple, and also whose faculties are keen,
Who in the presence of incalculable Buddhas
Have trodden the profound and subtle Path.
For these sons of the Buddha
I preach this scripture of the Great Vehicle.
I prophesy to such persons as these
That in a future age they shall achieve the Buddha's Path,

* In this context, the divisions are sūtra, gāthā, itivṛttaka, etc. just mentioned.

Because with profound thought they are mindful of the Buddha
  And because they practice and keep a pure discipline.
When they hear that they shall attain Buddhahood, these persons
  Have a great joy that permeates their bodies.
The Buddha, knowing the course of their thoughts,
  Therefore preaches the Great Vehicle to them.
A voice-hearer or a bodhisattva
  Who hears of the Dharma I preach
So much as a single gāthā
  Shall in every case achieve Buddhahood, of that there
    is no doubt.
Within the Buddha-lands of the ten directions
  There is the Dharma of only One Vehicle.
There are not two, nor are there yet three,
  Save where the Buddha, preaching by resort to expedients
And by merely borrowing provisional names and words,
  Draws the beings to him.
In order to preach Buddha-wisdom
  The Buddhas come into the world.
Only this one cause is true,
  For the other two are unreal.
To the very end he does not resort to the Lesser Vehicle
  To ferry the beings across.
The Buddha himself dwells in the Greater Vehicle;
  Whatever dharmas he acquires,
Adorned with the strength of concentration and wisdom,
  Through them does he rescue the beings.[6]
He himself bears witness to the Unexcelled Path,
  To the undifferentiating Dharma of the Great Vehicle.
If by resort to the Lesser Vehicle I were to convert
  So much as one person,
I should have fallen victim to greed,
  And this sort of thing would never do.[7]
A man in faith takes refuge in the Buddha, believing that
  The Thus Come One does not deceive,
Also that, having no thought of greed or malice,

He cuts off the evil in the dharmas;
It is for this reason that the Buddha in the ten directions
Alone is fearless.[8]
I, with marks adorning my body,
Radiantly give light to the world.
Being venerated by incalculable multitudes,
For them I preach the seal of reality-marks.[9]
Śāriputra, be it known
That formerly I took a vow,
Wishing to cause all multitudes
To be just like me, no different.
In keeping with my former vow,
All is now fulfilled,
For I have converted all living beings,
Causing them all to enter into the Buddha Path.
If, upon every encounter with the beings, I
Had taught them all the Buddha Path,
The ignorant, confused and
Gone astray, would not have accepted my teaching.
Because I knew that these beings
Had never cultivated wholesome roots;
That they were firmly attached to the five desires;
That, through delusion and greed, they were subject to agony;
That, by reason of their desires,
They fell into the three evil destinies;*
That they spun like wheels in the six destinies,
Receiving all manner of woe and harm;
That, receiving the frail form of a foetus,
For generation after generation they would constantly grow;
That men of slight virtue and little merit
Were attacked by multitudinous woes;
That, entering into the luxuriant forest of wrong views,
Whether of existence, or of nonexistence, or the like,

* Naraka, preta, and tiryagyonigata, the three lowest of the "six courses" defined in chapter 1 (see footnote to p. 5).

And relying on these views,
They fulfill sixty-two of them; *
That, profoundly attached to vain and arbitrary dharmas,
They firmly seize upon them and cannot cast them aside;
That their pride and arrogance are lofty,
Their sycophantic, crooked hearts insincere;
That for a thousand myriads of millions of kalpas
They neither hear the Buddha's name
Nor hear the right Dharma;
That men the likes of these are hard to save;
For these reasons, Śāriputra,
For their sakes I established an expedient device,

* The reference is probably to sixty-two views listed in chapter 48 of Kumārajīva's translation of the *Pañcaviṃśatisāhasrikā prajñāpāramitā sūtra*. Though they do not appear under that rubric, they are called by that very name in Kumārajīva's own commentary, a commentary that he modestly ascribes to Nāgārjuna, founder of the Mādhyamika school.

It will be recalled that the Sarvāstivāda posited 75 elements of existence (*dharma*). These were arranged in 5 groups (*skandha*), viz., (1) *rūpa*, visible matter (lit. 'form'), (2) *vedanā*, sensation, (3) *saṃjñā*, notion, (4) *saṃskāra*, acts, constituents of existence, (5) *vijñāna*, "connaissance." For each of these there are posited three tetrads (*catuṣkoṭi*) of views in the usual pattern of A, non-A, both A and non-A, neither A nor non-A. They are as follows:

A. the five skandhas are
1. permanent
2. transitory
3. both
4. neither

B. 1. finite
2. infinite
3. both
4. neither

C. 1. unchanging
2. finite in time, in the sense that they originate out of nothing, to endure for a time, then to vanish without a trace
3. imperishable (while the spirit alone perishes)
4. perishable (while the spirit alone is not)

A.B.C. are traditionally taken to refer to past, future, and present, respectively. By multiplying the twelve possibilities by the five skandhas, one arrives at the number 60. To this one adds the views that matter and spirit are (1) identical, (2) different.

Preaching ways that put an end to woe
And showing them nirvāṇa.
Though I preach nirvāṇa,
This is no true extinction.
The dharmas from their very origin
Are themselves eternally characterized by the marks of quiet extinction.
The Buddha's son, having trodden the Path,
In an age to come shall be able to become a Buddha.
I, having the power to devise expedients,
Set forth the dharma of the three vehicles.
All the World-Honored Ones,
All of them, preach the Way of the One Vehicle.
Now these great multitudes
Are all to purge their doubts and uncertainties.
The Buddhas say without differing
That there is only One Vehicle, not two.
For numberless kalpas in the past,
Incalculable Buddhas, since passed into extinction,
Of a hundred thousand myriads of millions of kinds,
Their number not to be reckoned—
World-Honored Ones in this manner,
By resort to various means and parables,
To the power of these and numberless other devices,
Expound the marks of the dharmas.
These World-Honored Ones,
All preaching the Dharma of the One Vehicle,
Convert incalculable beings
And cause them to enter into the Buddha Path.
Also, the Chiefs of the Great Saints,
Knowing all the worlds,
All the varieties of their gods, their men, and their living creatures,
The wishes in the deepest thoughts of all these beings,
By resort to yet other devices
Help to clarify the Prime Meaning.
If there are varieties of living beings

Who, having encountered Buddhas in the past,
Have heard the Dharma or dispensed gifts,
Or else kept the discipline or endured ignominy,
Or advanced with vigor, or cultivated dhyāna or wisdom—
Who, in short, have in various ways cultivated merit and wisdom,
Persons like these
Have all achieved the Buddha Path.
When the Buddhas have passed into extinction,
If a person is of good and gentle thought,
Living beings like him
Have all achieved the Buddha Path.
When the Buddhas have passed into extinction,
Persons who make offerings to their śarīra
Shall erect myriads of millions of kinds of stūpas,
[Using] gold and silver and *sphāṭika* [crystal],
Giant clam shell and agate,
Gems of carnelian (*mei kuei*)* and vaiḍūrya,
With which they brightly and extensively adorn and
With dignity accouter the stūpas.
Or there are those who erect stone mausoleums
Of *candana* [sandalwood] and aloeswood,
Of hovenia and other timbers,
Of brick, tile, clay, and the like.
Or there are those who in open fields,
Heaping up earth, make Buddha-shrines.
There are even children who in play

* See note 1 to chapter 11 for a list of the seven jewels in Skt. I have not been able to identify positively *mei kuei* or its Skt. counterpart, *lohitamukti*. They are red gems described differently by different authorities. *Lohita*, "red," is an epithet of the Brahmaputra river, which flows from Assam to the sea. A *lohitamukti* (lit. "red pearl") may conceivably be a pearl taken from an oyster of Indian Ocean waters by the mouth of the Brahmaputra (information furnished by A. N. Aklujkar). *Mei kuei* (also spelt *mei hui*) is identified by some with *huo ch'i chu*, which is said to be of purple gleam and to resemble mother-of-pearl. Elsewhere *mei kuei* is simply identified as a sparkling red gem. "Carnelian" was suggested by Professor Barbara Stoler Miller, as it is a gem common to northern India that resembles red jade.

Gather sand and make it into Buddha-stūpas.
Persons like these
Have all achieved the Buddha Path.
If any persons for the Buddha's sake
Erect images,
With carvings perfecting the multitudinous marks,
They have all achieved the Buddha Path.
Some fashion them completely with the seven jewels,
Or with nickel, or copper, or bronze,
Or with white tin, or with alloys of lead and tin [?],
Or with iron, or wood, or, again, with clay.
Some coat them with resin and lacquer,
With art creating Buddha images.
Persons like these
Have all achieved the Buddha Path.
Those who with many-colored designs create Buddha images,
Adorning them with the marks of hundredfold merit,
Making them themselves or having them done by others,
Have all achieved the Buddha Path.
Even children in play,
With grass, sticks, and brushes
Or with their fingernails,
Draw Buddha images.
Persons like these,
Gradually accumulating merit
And perfecting thoughts of great compassion,
Have all achieved the Buddha Path.
Or, merely converting bodhisattvas,
They may save incalculable multitudes.
If any persons, in stūpas and mausoleums,
To jeweled images and painted images.
With flowered and perfumed banners and canopies
And with deferential thoughts make offerings,
Or if they cause others to make music,
Beating drums and blowing horns and conchs,

Or sounding flutes, of many reeds or of only one, and lyres, mounted on stands or not,
And lutes and cymbals,
Producing many fine sounds like these
And holding them all up as offerings;
Or if with joyful thought
They sing hymns of praise to the excellences of the Buddha,
Producing so much as one tiny sound,
They have all achieved the Buddha Path.
If anyone, even with distracted thought,
And with so much as a single flower,
Makes offering to a painted image,
He shall at length see numberless Buddhas.
There will be some who prostrate themselves ceremoniously;
Others, again, who merely join palms;
Others yet who do no more than raise one hand,
Others yet again who incline their heads but slightly—
All, in these several ways, honoring the images.
They shall at length see incalculable Buddhas,
Themselves achieve the Unexcelled Path,
Broadly rescue numberless multitudes,
And enter into nirvāṇa without residue,
As, when the kindling wood is exhausted, the fire goes out.
If any, even with distracted thought,
Shall enter a stūpa or mausoleum
And recite *Namo Buddhāya* [Homage to the Buddha] but once,
They have all achieved the Buddha Path.
Under the tutelage of the Buddhas of the past,
Whether while they were in the world or after their extinction,
If any heard this Dharma,
They have all achieved the Buddha Path.[10]
The World-Honored Ones of the future
Shall be of number incalculable.
These Thus Come Ones
By resort to expedient devices also shall preach the Dharma.
All the Thus Come Ones,

By resort to incalculable expedient devices,
Save the living beings,
That they may enter into the Buddha's knowledge free of outflows.
Of any who hear the Dharma,
None shall fail to achieve Buddhahood.
Every Buddha's former vow [is as follows]:
"Whatever Buddha Path I may have trodden,
I wish universally to cause the beings
All alike to attain this Path as well."
The Buddhas of ages to come,
Though they shall preach hundreds of thousands of millions
Of numberless gateways to the Dharma,
Shall, in fact, be doing it for the sake of the One Vehicle.
The Buddhas, the Most Venerable of Two-Legged Beings,
Know that the dharmas are ever without a nature of their own.
By virtue of conditions is the Buddha-seed realized:
For this reason they preach the One Vehicle.[11]
The endurance of the dharmas, the secure position of the dharmas,
In the world ever abiding—
Having come to know these on the Platform of the Way,
The Guide-Teacher preaches them by resort to expedient devices.[12]
Recipients of offerings of gods and men,
The Buddhas of the present in the ten directions,
In number like to Ganges' sands,
Having appeared in the world
To put the beings at their ease,
Also preach a Dharma such as this.
They know the prime Quiet Extinction;
By resort to expedient devices
They may demonstrate various paths, but
They do so, in fact, for the sake of the Buddha Vehicle.[13]
I know the acts of the multitudinous beings,

That which they are mindful of in their deepest thoughts,
The deeds they have done repeatedly in the past,
The nature of their desires, their power of vigorous exertion,
And the keenness or dullness of their faculties.
By the use of [explanation of] a variety of causes and conditions,
Parables, also words and phrases,
And by resort to expedient devices, I preach in accord with what is appropriate.
Now I, too, am like them:
To put the beings at their ease,
By resort to various Dharma-gateways
I proclaim the Buddha Path.
With the power of wisdom
Knowing the natures and desires of the beings,
By resort to expedient devices I preach the dharmas,
Causing them all to gain joy.
Śāriputra, let these things be known:
I, with the eye of a Buddha,
See the beings on the six courses
Reduced to poverty's extreme, having neither merit nor wisdom;
Entered upon the steep highway of birth and death;
Their woes, in constant succession, knowing no interruption;
Profoundly attached to the five desires,
Like a long-tailed ox in love with [i.e., chasing] its own tail;
Covering themselves with lust and greed;
Blind and seeing nothing;
Seeking neither a Buddha of great might
Nor ways of cutting off woe;
Profoundly entered into wrong views;
By the use of woe wishing to cast off woe:
For the sake of these beings
I evince thoughts of great compassion.
When I first sat on the Platform of the Way,
Whether beholding the Tree or walking about,

Throughout three weeks
  I thought such thoughts as these:
"The wisdom I have gained
  Is the first among subtle things.
The beings, their faculties dull,
  Are attached to pleasure and blinded by delusion.
Being of such sort as this,
  How can they be saved?"
At that time the Brahmā kings
  And the chiefs of the gods, the Śakras,
The four god kings who protect the world
  And the great gods who are their own masters,
As well as the other multitudes of gods
  And their retinues, in the hundreds of thousands of myriads,
Reverently joining palms and doing obeisance,
  Begged me to turn the Dharma-wheel.
I then thought to myself:
  "If I merely praise the Buddha Vehicle,
The beings, sunk in woe,
  Shall not be able to believe this Dharma.
Reviling the Dharma and not believing it,
  They shall fall into the three evil courses.
I had rather not preach the Dharma,
  But enter speedily into nirvāṇa.
When I think back on the Buddhas of the past,
  On the power of the expedient devices put into practice by them,
I know that in the Way I have now gained
  I, too, must preach three vehicles."
When I had had these thoughts,
  The Buddhas of the ten directions all appeared,
Comforting and instructing me with Brahmā chant:
  "Good, Śakyamuni!
You, the First of Guide-Teachers,
  Having gained this unsurpassed Dharma,
Follow all the Buddhas

In using the power of expedient devices.
All of us, too, having gained
This most subtle prime Dharma,
For the sake of the varieties of living beings
Discriminated, preaching three vehicles.
Those of slight wisdom, desiring lesser dharmas,
Would not believe they could achieve Buddhahood.
For this reason, by resort to expedient devices,
We discriminated, preaching various fruits.
But, even though we preached three vehicles,
This was only for the purpose of teaching bodhisattvas."
Śāriputra, be it known
That, when I heard the Saintly Lions'
Deep, pure, and subtle voices,
Joyfully I proclaimed "*Namo Buddhebhyaḥ*!" [Homage to the Buddhas]
And that then I had this thought:
"Having come into a defiled and evil world,
As the Buddhas preach,
So must I, too, in obedience, act."
When I had had these thoughts,
Straightway I went to Vārāṇasī.
Since the quiet and extinct marks of the dharmas
Were not to be proclaimed in words,
By resort to the power of expedient devices
I preached to five bhikṣus.
This is called "turning the Dharma-wheel."
Then there was the sound "nirvāṇa,"
As well as "arhant,"
"Dharma," and "saṃgha"—several and distinct names such as these.
Since remote kalpas
I have set forth with praise the dharma of nirvāṇa;
"The woes of birth and death are forever terminated!"—
It is thus that I ever preached.
Śāriputra, be it known:

I see the Buddhas' sons,
Those who aspire to the Buddha Path,
In the incalculable thousands of myriads of millions,
All with deferential thought,
All coming before the Buddha,
Having formerly heard from the Buddhas
Dharmas preached by resort to expedient devices.
Then I had this thought:
"The reason a Buddha emerges
Is to preach Buddha-wisdom.
Now is the very time for it!"
Śāriputra, be it known that
Men of dull faculties and slight wisdom,
They who cling proudly to signs,
Cannot believe in this Dharma.
Now I, joyfully and fearlessly,
In the midst of the bodhisattvas
Frankly casting aside my expedient devices,
Merely preach the Unexcelled Path.
When the bodhisattvas hear this Dharma,
The network of their doubts is all cleared away:
[I have said] "A thousand two hundred arhants
Shall also become Buddhas, every one of them."[14]
As has been, for the Buddhas of the three ages,
The manner in which they preach the Dharma,
So I, too, now
Preach a Dharma without distinctions.
Buddhas emerge into the world
At remote intervals, and to encounter them is difficult.
Even when they do emerge in the world,
To preach this Dharma is also difficult.
Throughout incalculable and countless kalpas,
To hear this Dharma is no less difficult.
And, as for one who can listen to this Dharma,
Such a person, too, is rare.
The udumbara flower, for example,

Is loved and desired by all,
Regarded as rare by both gods and men,
Appearing only once at great intervals of time.
One who, hearing the Dharma, in joy and praise
Utters so much as a single word
Has already made offerings
To all the Buddhas in the three ages.
Such a person is very rare,
Rarer even than the udumbara flower.
Have no doubts:
I, being King of the Dharma,
Universally address the great multitudes,
Having recourse only to the Path of the One Vehicle,
Teaching and converting bodhisattvas,
And having no voice-hearing disciples.
All of you, Śāriputra,
Voice-hearers and bodhisattvas alike,
Are to know that this subtle Dharma
Is the secret essential to the Buddhas.
Since the beings of the age of the five defilements
Long for and cling to their desires alone;
Since beings the likes of these
Shall never seek the Buddha Path;
Since wicked men in ages to come,
Hearing the Buddha preach the One Vehicle
But gone astray and neither believing nor accepting,
Shall malign the Dharma and fall into evil destinies;
Since there shall be those who disgrace the pure
Aspirants to the Buddha Path;
I must for the likes of these
Broadly praise the Path of the One Vehicle.
Śāriputra, be it known that
The Buddhas' Dharma is like this:
By resort to myriads of millions of expedient devices
And in accord with what is appropriate for the situation, they preach the Dharma;

But they who have not practiced it
  Cannot understand this.
All of you, knowing now
  That the Buddhas, the Teachers of the Ages,
In accord with what is peculiarly appropriate have recourse to
    expedient devices,
  Need have no more doubts or uncertainties.
Your hearts shall give rise to great joy,
  Since you know that you yourselves shall become Buddhas.

Scripture of the Lotus Blossom of the Fine Dharma.
End of Roll the First.

Roll 2

Chapter Three: Parable

At that time Śāriputra danced for joy, then straightway rose and, joining his palms and looking reverently at the August Countenance, addressed the Buddha, saying: "Now that I have heard this Dharma-sound from the World-Honored One, I have in my heart the thought of dancing for joy. I have gained something I never had before. What is the reason? Formerly, when I heard such a Dharma as this from the Buddha, I saw the bodhisattvas receive the prophecy that they should become Buddhas; but we had no part in this. I was sore grieved that I was to miss the incalculable knowledge and insight of the Thus Come One. World-Honored One, in the past I have dwelt alone in mountain forests and at the foot of trees; and, whether sitting or walking, I always had this thought: 'We have all entered identically into Dharmahood. How is it that the Thus Come One shows us salvation by resort to the dharma of the Lesser Vehicle? This is our fault, not that of the World-Honored One. What is the reason? Had we waited for him to preach that on which the achievement of anuttarasamyaksaṃbodhi is based, then without fail we should have attained salvation through the Greater Vehicle. However, since we did not understand that the preaching had been based on expedient devices and accorded with what was appropriate to the particular circumstances, when we first heard the Buddha's dharma, directly we had encountered it we believed it, accepted it, had thoughts about it, and based conclusions on it.' World-Honored One, from of old, day long and into the night I have been reproaching myself. But now that I have heard from the Buddha what I had never heard before, a Dharma that has never been before, I have cut off my doubts and second thoughts; my body and mind are at ease, and happily I have gained peace. This day, at long last, I know that I am truly the Buddha's son, born of the Buddha's mouth, born of Dharma-transformation. I have gained a portion of the Buddha's Dharma."[1]

At that time Śāriputra, wishing to restate this meaning, proclaimed gāthās, saying:

Having heard this Dharma-sound, I
  Have gained that which I never had before.
My heart harbors a great joy,
  And the network of my doubt is completely cleared away.
From of old, having received the Buddha's doctrine,
  I have never lost the Greater Vehicle.[2]
The Buddha's voice is very rare,
  Able to clear away the agonies of the beings.
Having already gained the extinction of the outflows,
  Upon hearing this I also cleared away my cares and agonies.
Dwelling in mountains and valleys,
  Or being at the foot of trees in forests,
Whether seated or walking about,
  I constantly thought of these things.
"Ah!" said I in profound self-reproach,
  "How can I have so deceived myself?
Though all sons of the Buddha,
  Entered alike into dharmas without outflows,
We shall not all be able in the future
  To expound the Unexcelled Path.
The thirty-two [marks]*—the gold color,
  The ten strengths, and the various deliverances—
Are all together within one Dharma;
  Yet I have not gained these things.
The eighty kinds of the wondrously good,
  The eighteen unshared dharmas,
And such excellences as these though there be,
  Yet have I missed them all.
When I go about alone,
  I see the Buddha present in the great multitude,

* See Edward Conze, ed., *The Large Sutra on Perfect Wisdom* (London, Luzac, 1961), pp. 199–203, for a list of the thirty-two marks, and ibid., pp. 147–48, for the eighteen unshared dharmas. Chapter 16 of the book is a good reference for this whole section.

His Name being bruited about in all ten directions,
Broadly benefiting the beings.
I think to myself that I have lost this advantage,
For I imagine I have been deceiving myself.
I constantly, day and night,
Think repeatedly about these things.
I wish to question the World-Honored One about them,
Whether I have missed them or not.
I constantly see the World-Honored One
Praising the bodhisattvas:
Thus day and night
Do I constantly weigh and measure matters such as these.
Now I hear the Buddha's voice
Preaching the Dharma in accord with what is appropriate for the moment.
With what is free of outflows, hard to conceive or to discuss,
He causes the beings to reach the Platform of the Path.
Formerly I, attached to wrong views,
Was a teacher of Brahmans.
The World-Honored One, knowing my thoughts,
Uprooted the wrongs and preached nirvāṇa.
I, completely clearing away my wrong views,
Directly witnessed the empty dharmas.
At that time in my heart I said to myself
That I had contrived to reach the passage into extinction.
But now, at last, I am aware
That this is no real passage into extinction.[3]
When I contrive to become a Buddha,
When I am fully endowed with the thirty-two marks,
When a multitude of gods, men, and yakṣas,
As well as dragons, spirits, and the like, do me honor,
At that time and not before shall I be able to say
That I am forever and completely extinguished without residue.[4]
The Buddha, in the midst of the great multitude,
Says that I shall become a Buddha.

When I hear a Dharma-sound such as this,
  My doubts and second thoughts are completely cleared away.
When first I heard the Buddha's preaching,
  In my heart I was greatly alarmed:
"Surely Māra is playing Buddha,
  Confusing my thoughts!"
The Buddha by resort to various means,
  Parables, and cunning phrases preaches,
But his thought is as calm as the sea;
  When I hear him, my network of doubt is severed.[5]
The Buddha says that in ages gone by
  Incalculable Buddhas, now passed into extinction,
Dwelling securely in the midst of expedient devices,
  Also preached this Dharma, every one of them;
That the Buddhas of the present and the future,
  Their numbers past all reckoning,
Also, by resort to expedient devices,
  Set forth a Dharma such as this one,
Just as in the present the World-Honored One,
  Beginning with his birth and going through his departure from the household life,
His attainment of the Path, and his turning of the Dharma-wheel,
  Has also preached by resort to expedient devices.
The World-Honored One preaches the Real Path,
  While Pāpīyaṃs [the "More Evil One," Māra] has none of this.
By this token I know for a certainty
  That this is no Māra playing Buddha,
But that I, through having fallen into a net of doubt,
  Thought this was the work of Māra.
When I hear the Buddha's gentle voice,
  Profound, far removed from the ordinary understanding, and extremely subtle,
Setting forth the pure Dharma,
  My heart is overjoyed,
My doubts and second thoughts are cleared away forever,

And I dwell securely in the midst of real knowledge [saying]:
"Of a certainty I shall become a Buddha,
Revered by gods and men;
I shall turn the unexcelled Dharma-wheel,
Teaching and converting bodhisattvas."

At that time, the Buddha declared to Śāriputra: "I now speak in the midst of the great multitude of gods, men, śramaṇas, Brahmans, and the like. Formerly I, in the presence of two myriads of millions of Buddhas, for the sake of the Unexcelled Path was constantly teaching and converting you. And you, throughout the long night of time, following me, received my instruction. It is because I led you hither by resort to expedient devices that you have been born into my Dharma. Śāriputra, long ago I taught you to aspire to the Buddha Path. You have completely forgotten. Accordingly, you say to yourself that you have already gained passage into extinction. Now once again, wishing to cause you to recall the path you trod in keeping with your former vow, for the voice-hearers' sakes I preach this scripture of the Greater Vehicle, named the Lotus Blossom of the Fine Dharma, a Dharma preached to bodhisattvas, one which the Buddha keeps in mind.

"Śāriputra, you, in an age to come, beyond incalculable, limitless, inconceivable kalpas, having made offerings to several thousands of myriads of millions of Buddhas, having upheld the True Dharma and having acquired to perfection the Path trodden by bodhisattvas, shall be able to become a Buddha named Flower Glow (Padmaprabha), a Thus Come One, worthy of offerings, of right and universal knowledge, your clarity and conduct perfect, well gone, understanding the world, an unexcelled Worthy, a Regulator of men of stature, a Teacher of gods and men, a Buddha, a World-Honored One.

"That Buddha's realm shall be named Free of Defilements (Viraja). Its land shall be flat and even, clean, well-adorned, tranquil, rich, and abounding in gods and men. It shall have vaiḍūrya for soil in an eightfold network of highways, each bordered with cords of pure gold. At their sides shall be columns of seven-jeweled trees, constantly bearing blossoms and fruit.

"Flower Glow, the Thus Come One, shall furthermore by resort to the three vehicles teach and convert the beings. Śāriputra, though the time of that Buddha's emergence shall not be an evil age, by reason of his former vow he shall preach the dharma of the three vehicles. His kalpa shall be named Adorned with Great Jewels (Mahāratnapratimaṇḍita). Why shall it be named Adorned with Great Jewels? Because in that realm bodhisattvas shall be taken for great jewels. Those bodhisattvas shall be incalculable, limitless, past reckoning and discussion, beyond the reach of number or parable, such that, except with the power of Buddha-knowledge, none shall be able to know them.

"When they are about to walk, jeweled blossoms shall spring up to receive their feet (*ratnapadmavikrāmiṇo bhaviṣyanti*). These bodhisattvas shall not have just launched their thoughts, but all shall have long since planted the roots of excellence, and shall cultivate brahman-conduct purely, in the presence of incalculable hundreds of thousands of myriads of millions of Buddhas, being constantly the objects of the Buddhas' praise, ever cultivating Buddha-knowledge, acquiring thoroughly great spiritual penetration, knowing well the gateways of all the dharmas, straightforward and honest, without deception, firm in intent and mindfulness. Such bodhisattvas as these shall fill that realm.[6]

"Śāriputra, the life-span of the Buddha Flower Glow shall be twelve minor kalpas (*dvādaśāntarakalpā āyuṣpramāṇaṃ bhaviṣyati*), excluding the time during which he shall be a prince, having not yet become a Buddha. The life-span of the people of his realm shall be eight minor kalpas. Flower Glow, the Thus Come One, when twelve minor kalpas have passed, shall present a prophecy of anuttarasamyaksaṃbodhi to the bodhisattva Hard-Full (Dhṛtiparipūrṇa). I tell you bhikṣus that this bodhisattva Hard-Full shall in turn become a Buddha, who shall be called He Whose Feet Tread Securely on Blossoms (Padmavṛṣabhavikrāmin), a tathāgato 'rhan samyaksaṃbuddhaḥ. His Buddha-realm shall also be of the same sort.

"Śāriputra, after the passage into extinction of this Buddha Flower Glow, his True Dharma shall abide in the world for thirty-two minor kalpas, and his Counterfeit Dharma shall abide in the world also for thirty-two minor kalpas."

At that time, the World-Honored One, wishing to restate this meaning, proclaimed gāthās, saying:

Śāriputra, in an age to come
  You shall be venerated for your achievement of the universal wisdom of a Buddha.
Your name shall be called Flower Glow,
  And you shall save incalculable multitudes,
Having made offerings to numberless Buddhas;
  Having perfected bodhisattva conduct,
The ten strengths, and other such meritorious qualities;
  And having borne direct witness to the Unexcelled Path.
When incalculable kalpas have passed,
  The kalpa shall be named Adorned with Great Jewels.
The world shall be named Free of Defilement,
  Being pure and without blemish,
Having vaiḍūrya for its soil,
  Setting off its highways with golden cords,
Its particolored trees of seven jewels
  Constantly blooming and bearing fruit.
The bodhisattvas of that realm
  Shall be ever firm of intent and mindfulness,
Their supernatural penetrations and pāramitās
  All having been thoroughly perfected,
And they themselves, in the presence of numberless Buddhas, having
  Learned well the bodhisattva-path.
Great worthies such as these
  Shall have been converted by the Buddha Flower Glow.
When a prince, the Buddha,
  Forsaking his realm and setting aside his honors,
In his final body
  Shall leave the household life and achieve the Buddha Path.
The Buddha Flower Glow shall abide in the world
  For a life-span of twelve minor kalpas.
The people of his realm
  Shall have a life-span of eight minor kalpas.
After the Buddha shall have passed into extinction,
  His True Dharma shall abide in the world

For thirty-two minor kalpas,
Broadly saving the living beings.
When his True Dharma is completely extinct,
There shall be a Counterfeit Dharma for thirty-two minor kalpas.
His śarīra shall be spread far and wide,
And gods and men everywhere shall make offerings to it.
What the Buddha Flower Glow shall do
Shall all be as I have said.
That One Sainted and Venerable among Two-Legged Beings
Shall be most distinguished, without his like.
He shall be none other than you yourself:
You should and ought to be delighted.

At that time the fourfold multitude, bhikṣus, bhikṣuṇīs, upāsakas, and upāsikās, as well as a great multitude of gods, dragons, yakṣas, gandharvas, asuras, garuḍas, kinnaras, mahoragas, and the like, seeing Śāriputra receive in the Buddha's presence a prophecy of anuttarasamyaksaṃbodhi, danced endlessly for joy of heart and, each removing the uppermost garment he was wearing, presented it to the Buddha as an offering. Śakro Devānām Indraḥ and Brahmā, the king of the gods, together with numberless sons of gods, also made offerings to the Buddha of their fine divine garments and of divine māndārava and mahāmāndārava flowers. The divine garments they had scattered remained stationary in the open air, then turned about by themselves. Divine musicians all together at once made music of a hundred thousand myriads of kinds in the open air and, raining down many divine flowers, spoke these words: "The Buddha in former times in Vārāṇasī first turned the Dharma-wheel. Now, at long last, he is again turning the unexcelled and supremely great Dharma-wheel." At that time the sons of gods, wishing to restate this meaning, proclaimed gāthās, saying:

Formerly, in Vārāṇasī,
You turned the Dharma-wheel of the four truths,
With discrimination preaching the dharmas,

The origination and extinction of their five collections
(*skandhānām udayaṃ vyayam*).
Now again you are turning the most subtle,
Unexcelled great Dharma-wheel.
This Dharma is profound and recondite,
For few there are who can believe in it.
From of old we
Have often heard the World-Honored One preach,
But have never before heard such
A profound and subtle superior Dharma.
When the World-Honored One preaches this Dharma,
We are all delighted accordingly.
The greatly wise Śāriputra
Has now been able to receive an august prediction.
We also in this way
Shall certainly be able to become Buddhas,
In all the worlds
Most venerable and having none superior.
The Buddha Path, beyond reckoning and discussion,
We shall preach by resort to expedient devices and in accord with what is peculiarly appropriate.
What meritorious deeds are ours,
Whether in the present age or in ages gone by,
As well as the merit of having seen Buddhas,
We divert completely to the Buddha Path.

At that time, Śāriputra addressed the Buddha, saying: "World-Honored One! I now have no more doubts or second thoughts, since I have been personally enabled to receive in the Buddha's presence a prophecy of anuttarasamyaksaṃbodhi. These twelve hundred who freely control their own thoughts (*imāni bhagavan dvādaśa vaśībhūta-śatāni*) formerly dwelt on the level of learners. The Buddha constantly taught them, saying, 'My Dharma can separate one from birth, old age, sickness, and death, making possible the complete achievement of nirvāṇa.' These persons, the learners and those who had nothing more to learn, also thought, on the grounds that they had separated themselves from the view of 'I' and from the view of 'there is' and 'there is not,' that they had attained nirvāṇa. Yet now, in the presence of the World-Honored One having heard what they had never heard before, they have fallen into doubt and uncertainty. Very well, O World-Honored One! I beg you, for the sake of the fourfold multitude, to explain the causes and conditions, thus separating them from their doubts and second thoughts."

At that time the Buddha declared to Śāriputra: "Did I not say formerly that the Buddhas, the World-Honored Ones, by resort to a variety of [explanations of] causes and conditions, parables, words and phrases, and expedient devices preach the Dharma; that all is for the purpose of anuttarasamyaksaṃbodhi? This is because these preachings are all effected in order to convert bodhisattvas. However, Śāriputra, I shall now once again by resort to a parable clarify this meaning. For they who have intelligence gain understanding through parables.

"Śāriputra, imagine that a country, or a city-state, or a municipality has a man of great power, advanced in years and of incalculable wealth, owning many fields and houses, as well as servants. His house is broad and great; it has only one doorway, but great multitudes of human beings, a hundred, or two hundred, or even five hundred, are dwelling in it. The halls are rotting, the walls crumbling, the pillars decayed at their base, the beams and ridgepoles precariously tipped. Throughout the house and all at the same time, quite suddenly a fire breaks out, burning down all the apartments. The great man's sons, ten, or twenty, or thirty of them, are still in the house.[7]

"The great man, directly he sees this great fire breaking out from four directions, is alarmed and terrified. He then has this thought: 'Though I was able to get out safely through this burning doorway, yet my sons within the burning house, attached as they are to their games, are unaware, ignorant, unperturbed, unafraid. The fire is coming to press in upon them, the pain will cut them to the quick. Yet at heart they are not horrified, nor have they any wish to leave.'

"Śāriputra, this great man has the following thought: 'I am a man of great physical strength. I might, in the folds of my robe or on top of a table, take them out of the house.' He thinks: 'This house has only one doorway, which, furthermore, is narrow and small. The children are young and, as yet having no understanding, are in love with their playthings. They may fall victim to the fire and be burnt. I must explain the terror of it to them. This house is already on fire. They must make haste and get out in time. I must not let this fire burn them to death.' When he has had these thoughts, then in accord with his decision he says explicitly to the children, 'Get out quickly, all of you!' Though the father, in his compassion, urges them with explicit words, yet the children, attached as they are to their games, will not deign to believe him or to accept what he says. Unalarmed and unafraid, they have not the least intention of leaving. For they do not even know what a 'fire' is, or what a 'house' is, or what it means to 'lose' anything. All they do is run back and forth, looking at their father.

"At that time, the great man has this thought: 'This house is already aflame with a great fire. If we do not get out in time, the children and I shall certainly be burnt. I will now devise an expedient, whereby I shall enable the children to escape this disaster.' The father knows the children's preconceptions, whereby each child has his preferences, his feelings being specifically attached to his several precious toys and unusual playthings.[8]

"Accordingly, [the father] proclaims to them: 'The things you so love to play with are rare and hard to get. If you do not get them, you are certain to regret it later. Things like these, a variety of goat-drawn carriages, deer-drawn carriages, and ox-drawn carriages, are now outside the door for you to play with. Come out of this burning house quickly, all of you! I will give all of you what you desire.' The children hear what their father says. Since rare playthings are exactly what they desire, the heart of each is emboldened. Shoving one another aside in a mad race, all together in a rush they leave the burning house.

"At this time, the great man, seeing that his children have contrived to get out safely, and that all are seated in an open space at a crossroads, is no longer troubled. Secure at heart, he dances for joy. Then the children all address their father, saying: 'Father, the things you promised us a while ago—the lovely playthings, the goat-drawn carriages, deer-drawn carriages, and ox-drawn carriages—give us now, if you please.'

"Śāriputra, at that time the great man gives to each child one great carriage. The carriage is high and wide, adorned with a multitude of jewels, surrounded by posts and handrails, little bells suspended on all four sides. Also, on its top are spread out parasols and canopies. Further, it is adorned with an assortment of rare and precious jewels. Intertwined with jeweled cords and hung with flowered tassels, having heaps of carpets decorated with strips of cloth, as well as vermilion-colored cushions, it is yoked to a white ox, whose skin is pure white, whose bodily form is lovely, whose muscular strength is great, whose tread is even and fleet like the wind. [This ox] also has many attendants serving and guarding it.[9] What is the reason? Because this great man, of wealth incalculable, his various storehouses all full to overflowing, has this thought: 'My wealth being limitless, I may not give small, inferior carriages to my children. Now these little boys are all my sons. I love them without distinction. I have carriages such as these, made of the seven jewels, in incalculable numbers. I must give one to each of them with undiscriminating thought. I may not make distinctions. What is the reason? I take these things and distribute them to the whole realm, not stinting even then. How much the more should I do so to my own children!' At this time, the children, each mounting his great carriage, gain something they have never had before, something they have never hoped for. Śāriputra, what do you think? When this great man gives equally to all his children great carriages adorned with precious jewels, is he guilty of falsehood or not?"

Śāriputra said: "No, World-Honored One! This great man has but enabled his children to escape the calamity of fire, thus preserving their bodily lives. He is guilty of no falsehood. Why? Because the preservation whole of their bodily lives means that they have already received a lovely plaything. For what reason is that? All the [other] playthings, O Blessed One, were taken in exchange for their very lives. How much the more so when, by resort to an expedient device, he has rescued them from that burning house! World-Honored One! Had this great man given them not one tiny carriage, he would still be no liar. Why? Because this great man first thought: 'By resort to an expedient device I will enable the children to get out.' For this reason he is guilty of no falsehood. How much the more is this true when the great man, knowing that his wealth is incalculable and wishing to confer advantage on his children, gives to all equally a great carriage!"

The Buddha proclaimed to Śāriputra: "Good! Good! It is as you say! Śāriputra, the Thus Come One is also like this. That is, he is the Father of all the worlds. To fear, terror, debilitation, anguish, care, worry, ignorance, and obscurity he puts an absolute end. Also, completely achieving the might of incalculable knowledge and insight, as well as fearlessness; having great spiritual power and the power of wisdom; perfecting the pāramitās of practical expedients and of wisdom, as well as of great good will and great compassion; constantly unflagging; and constantly seeking the good, he benefits all. Thus he creates the old and rotten burning house of the three worlds and, in order to save the beings from the fires of birth, old age, sickness, death, worry, grief, woe, agony, folly, delusion, blindness, obscurity, and the three poisons,* he teaches and converts them, enabling them to attain anuttarasaṃyaksambodhi. He sees that the beings are scorched by birth, old age, sickness, death, care, grief, woe, and anguish. They also, thanks to a fivefold desire for wealth, suffer a variety of woes. Also, since they adhere greedily [to their views] and seek persistently [what they desire], they currently suffer many woes, and shall hereafter suffer the woes of hell, beasts, and hungry ghosts or, if they are born above the heavens or in the midst of men, suffer woe in the straits of destitution, or the woe of separation from what they love, or the woe of union with what they hate. It is in the midst of such various woes as these that the beings are plunged, yet they cavort in joy, unaware, unknowing, unalarmed, unafraid, neither experiencing disgust nor seeking release. In this burning house of the three worlds they run about hither and yon, and, though they encounter great woes, they are not concerned.[10]

"Śāriputra, having seen this, the Buddha then thinks: 'I am the Father of the beings; I must rescue them from their woes and troubles and give them the joy of incalculable and limitless Buddha-wisdom, thus causing them to frolic.'

* The "three poisons" are the three defilements of lust (*rāga*), sc. for the unwholesome; hatred (*dveṣa*), sc. for the wholesome; and delusion (*moha*), i.e., mistaking the one for the other.

"Śāriputra, the Thus Come One also has this thought: 'If merely by resort to my spiritual power and the power of my knowledge (*jñānabalo 'smīti kṛtvā ṛddhibalo 'smīti kṛtvā*), and casting aside expedient devices, for the beings' sake I praise the Thus Come One's power of knowledge and insight and his fearlessness, the beings cannot thereby attain salvation. What is the reason? These beings, who have not yet escaped from birth, old age, sickness, death, care, grief, woe, and anguish, are being burnt in the flaming house of the three worlds. How can they understand the Buddha's wisdom?'

"Śāriputra, just as that great man, though physically strong, did not use his strength, but, by resort to a gentle practical expedient, rescued his children from the troubles of the burning house, then gave each of them a great carriage adorned with precious jewels, just so does the Thus Come One in the same way, though he has various sorts of strength and fearlessness, refrain from using them, but merely, by resort to wisdom and practical expedients, rescue the beings from the burning house of the three worlds, preaching to them three vehicles—those of voice-hearer, of pratyekabuddha, and of Buddha—and saying to them: 'You all are to have no desire to dwell in the burning house of the three worlds. Have no lust for coarse and broken-down visible matter, sounds, smells, tastes, and tangibles! If, clinging to them greedily, you display lust for them, then you shall be burnt. Quick, get out of the three worlds! You shall get three vehicles, those of voice-hearer, pratyekabuddha, and Buddha. I now guarantee it, and I am never false. All you need do is strive earnestly with effort.' By such devices as this the Thus Come One attracts and urges the beings. He also says: 'You all are to know that the dharmas of these three vehicles are praised by the saints, [and they who mount them] are their own masters, unbound, depending on nothing and seeking nothing. Mounted on these three vehicles, one gains for oneself the pleasure of faculties, strengths, intuitive perceptions, paths, dhyāna-concentrations, deliverances, samādhis, and the like, all without outflows, then gets incalculable tranquil joys.'[11]

"Śāriputra, if there are beings who within are wise by nature; who, having heard the dharma from the World-Honored One, believe and accept it; who, earnestly striving and wishing to leave the three worlds, seek nirvāṇa for themselves; these are named [Those Who Mount] the Vehicle of the Voice-Hearers. They are like those children who left the burning house in quest of goat-drawn carriages. If there are beings who, having heard the dharma from the World-Honored One, believe and accept it; who, earnestly striving and seeking the knowledge which is so of itself (*anācāryakaṃ jñānam*), desire the quietude which is content with its own goodness (*damaśamatham ākāṅkṣamāṇāḥ*), and are deeply aware of the causes and conditions of the dharmas (*hetupratyayānubodhāya*), these are called [Those Who Mount] the Vehicle of the Pratyekabuddhas. They are like those children who left the burning house in quest of deer-drawn carriages. If there are beings who, having heard the Dharma from the World-Honored One, believe and accept it; who, vigorously practicing and striving, seek All-Knowledge, Buddha-Knowledge, the knowledge which is so of itself, knowledge without a teacher, the knowledge and insight of the Thus Come One, his strengths, and his fearlessness; who, mercifully recalling and comforting incalculable living beings and benefiting gods and men, convey all to deliverance; these are named [Those Who Mount] the Great Vehicle. It is because the bodhisattvas seek this Vehicle that they are named Mahāsattvas [great beings]. They are like those children who leave the burning house in quest of ox-drawn carriages. Śāriputra, just as that great man, seeing his children safely out of the burning house and in a place of safety, and thinking that he himself has wealth incalculable, presents his children equally with great carriages, just so in the same way does the Thus Come One, being the Father of all living beings, when he sees incalculable thousands of millions of beings going through the gateway of the Buddha's doctrine off the painful, fearful, and precipitous pathway of the three worlds, there to gain the joy of nirvāṇa—just so, I say, does the Thus Come One at that time have this thought: 'I have a treasure house of incalculable, limitless knowledge, strengths, various sorts of fearlessness, other such Buddhadharmas. These living beings are all my children.' Then he gives the Great Vehicle equally to all, not allowing any of them to gain passage into extinction for himself alone, but conveying them all to the extinction of the Thus Come One. To all these living beings who have escaped the three worlds he gives the Buddhas' dhyāna-concentration, their deliverances, and other devices of enjoyment, all of one appearance, of one kind, all praised by the saints (*sarvāṇy etāny ekavarṇāni*), all able to bring about the prime, pure, and subtle joy (*āryāṇi paramasukhāni krīḍanakāni ramaṇīyakāni*). Śāriputra, just as that great man, first having enticed his children with three carriages and then having given them only one great carriage, adorned with jewels and supremely comfortable, is yet not guilty of falsehood, just so in the same way is the Thus Come One free of falsehood, though he first preached the three vehicles in order to entice the beings, then conveyed them to deliverance by resort to only the One Great Vehicle. Why? Because the Thus Come One, having a treasure house of incalculable wisdom, strengths, various sorts of fearlessness, and other dharmas, is able to give the Dharma of the Great Vehicle to all living beings; but they are not all able to accept it. Śāriputra, for these reasons be it known that the Buddhas, by resort to the power of expedient devices, divide the One Buddha Vehicle and speak of three."

The Buddha, wishing to restate this meaning, proclaimed gāthās, saying:

Suppose that, for example, a great man
  Had a great house.
The house, since it was old,
  Was in a state of collapse:
The halls were lofty and precarious,
  The bases of the pillars crumbling and rotten,
The beams and ridgepoles aslant,
  The stairways and landings disintegrating,
The walls and partitions cracked,
  The clay and paint peeling off,
The thatch worn thin and in disarray,
  The rafters and eavepoles coming loose,
Totally misshapen
  And full of assorted filth.
There were five hundred persons
  Dwelling within.

Kites, owls, and eagles;
  Crows, magpies, pigeons, and doves;
Newts, snakes, vipers, and gribbles;
  Centipedes and millipedes;
Lizards and myriopods;
  Weasels, badgers, and mice,
And other malignant beings
  Milled back and forth in a crisscross.
Places stinking of faeces and urine
  Overflowed with their filth,
With May-bugs and other insects
  Clustered on them.
Foxes, wolves, and *yeh-kan**
  Gnawed at, trampled on,
And chewed up corpses,
  Leaving the bones and flesh a mess.
Thereupon bands of dogs,
  Racing to the spot, seized them,
Hungry, weak, and terrified,
  Seeking food here and there,
In their struggle snatching and pulling one another,
  Snarling, gnashing their teeth, and howling.
That house's terrors
  And strange sights were of this kind.
Here and there and all about
  Were ghosts and demons,
Yakṣas and evil spirits,
  Eating human flesh;
Varieties of poisonous insects
  And other malignant birds and beasts
Hatched from eggs,
  All defending themselves against one another.
The yakṣas would race to the spot,
  Vying with one another to seize and eat them.

* *Yeh kan*: a blind, emaciated tree-dweller somewhat resembling a fox.

When they had eaten their fill,
  Their wicked thoughts would be all the more intense.
The sound of their quarrels
  Was terrifying.
The *kumbhāṇḍa*-demons*
  Would squat on high ground,
Or at times would rise above the earth
  A foot or two,
Then would wander back and forth,
  Amusing themselves according to their own fancy,
Seizing two legs of a dog,
  Or beating it so that it lost its bark,
Or trampling on its neck,
  Terrifying the dog for their own amusement.
Again, there were demons
  Tall of body,
Naked, dark, and emaciated,
  Constantly dwelling there,
Emitting loud and baneful sounds,
  Howling in their quest for food.
Again, there were demons
  Whose throats were the shape of needles.
Again, there were demons
  Whose heads were the shape of ox-heads,
Who would now eat human flesh,
  And would then devour dogs,
The hair of their heads in a tousle,
  Harmful, malignant, and dangerous,
Hard pressed by hunger and thirst,
  Howling as they ran back and forth.
The yakṣas and hungry demons,
  The malignant birds and beasts,
Facing all four ways in their acute hunger,
  Would peer through windows.

* *Kumbhāṇḍa*: a kind of demon having testicles the shape of water jars.

The likes of these were the troubles
  And terrors incalculable.
This old and decayed house
  Belonged to one man.
The man had gone a short distance from the house
  When, before he had been gone very long,
In the rear apartments
  Suddenly a fire broke out,
From all four sides at once
  Raging in flame.
The ridgepoles and beams, the rafters and pillars,
  Shaking and cracking with a sound of explosion,
Broke asunder and fell,
  While the walls and partitions collapsed.
The ghosts and demons
  Raised their voices in a scream.
The eagles and other birds,
  As well as the kumbhāṇḍas,
Milled about in a panic,
  Unable to get out.
The malignant beasts and poisonous insects
  Hid in crevices;
While the *piśāca*-demons [kind of ogre],
  Who also dwelt therein,
Being of slight merit,
  When they were hard pressed by the fire,
Wrought harm on one another,
  Drinking blood and devouring flesh.
Since the bands of yeh-kan
  Were already dead,
The great malignant beasts,
  Racing to the spot, devoured them.
Stinking smoke, with its foul odor,
  Filled the place on all four sides.
Centipedes and millipedes,
  As well as varieties of poisonous snakes,

Being burnt by the fire,
  Vied with one another to get out of their holes,
And the kumbhāṇḍaka-demons,
  Seizing them at will, devoured them.
Also, the hungry demons,
  The tops of their heads aflame,
And tormented by hunger, thirst, and heat,
  Ran about in agonized panic.
In this way that house was
  Extremely frightening,
With calamities, conflagrations,
  And many other troubles, hardly just the one.
At that time the householder,
  Standing outside the door,
Heard someone say,
  "Your children
A while ago, in play,
  Entered this house.
Being little and knowing nothing,
  They are enjoying themselves and clinging to their
    amusements."
Having heard this, the great man
  Entered the burning house in alarm,
To save them
  From the catastrophe of burning.
He uttered a warning to his children,
  Explaining the many calamities:
"Malignant demons, poisonous insects,
  And conflagrations are rampant.
A multitude of woes, in succession,
  Shall follow one another unceasingly.
The poisonous snakes, the newts and vipers,
  As well as the yakṣas
And kumbhāṇḍa-demons
  The yeh-kan, the foxes and dogs,
The eagles, the kites, and the owls,

And the varieties of centipedes,
Beside themselves with hunger and thirst,
Are most frightening.
This is a woeful and troublesome place;
How much the more so with a great fire!"[12]
The children, knowing nothing,
Though they heard their father's admonitions,
Still, addicted as before to their pleasures,
Amused themselves ceaselessly.
At that time, the great man
Had this thought:
"The children, being this way,
Make my cares even more acute.
Now this house
Has not one pleasant feature,
Yet the children,
Steeped in their games
And not heeding my instructions,
Will surely be injured by the fire."
Then straightway, intentionally
Devising some expedients,
He announced to the children:
"I have various
Precious playthings,
Lovely carriages adorned with fine jewels,
Goat-drawn carriages, deer-drawn carriages,
And carriages drawn by great oxen,
Now outside the door.
Come out, all of you!
For your sakes I
Have made these carriages,
Following the desire of your own thoughts.
You may amuse yourselves with them."
When the children heard him tell
Of carriages such as these,
Straightway, racing one another,

They ran out at a gallop,
Reaching an empty spot
And getting away from woes and troubles.
The great man, seeing his children
Able to get out of the burning house
And abiding at a crossroads,
Sat on his lion throne
And joyfully said to himself,
"Now I am happy!
These children
Were very hard to bring into the world and raise.
Foolish, and little, and knowing nothing,
They entered a dangerous house,
Where there were many poisonous insects,
Frightful spirits,
And raging flames of great fires
Rising up together from all four sides.
Yet these children
Were addicted to their games.
I have already saved them,
Enabling them to escape trouble.
It is for this reason, O men,
That I am now happy."
At that time the children,
Knowing that their father was serenely seated,
All went before their father
And addressed him, saying:
"We beg you to give us
The three kinds of jeweled chariots
That you promised us a while ago, saying,
'Children, come out!
I will use three kinds of carriages
To accord with your wishes.'
Now is the right time.
Please give them to us!"

The great man, being very rich,
  And having treasure houses filled with
Gold, silver, and vaiḍūrya,
  Giant clam shells and agate,
From many precious objects
  Had several carriages made,
Decked with ornaments,
  Surrounded with handrails and shielding,
With little bells hanging from all four sides
  And golden cords intertwined;
With pearl-studded netting
  Stretched out over the top,
And gold-flowered tassels
  Dropping down here and there;
With assorted ornaments in many colors
  Encircling them all around;
With soft and fine silk and cotton
  Made into cushions;
With superbly fine mats,
  Their value in the thousands of millions,
Pure white and spotlessly clean,
  Covering them;
With great white oxen,
  Fat, and in the prime of life, and endowed with great strength,
Their physical form lovely,
  Yoked to the jeweled carriages;
With many footmen, fore and aft,
  Attending them.
These lovely carriages
  He gave equally to all the children.
The children at this time,
  Dancing for joy
And mounting these jeweled carriages,
  Cavorted in all four directions,
Playing and enjoying themselves,

Completely at ease and feeling no encumbrances.
I tell you, Śāriputra:
I, too, am like this,
Being the Most Venerable among many saints,
The Father of the World.
All the living beings,
All my children,
Are profoundly addicted to worldly pleasure
And have no wise thoughts.
The three spheres, completely insecure,
Are just like a house afire,
Being full of many woes
Most frightful,
Constantly marked by birth, old age,
Sickness, death, and care—
Fires such as these,
Raging without cease.
The Thus Come One, having already left
The burning house of the three spheres,
Is quiet and unperturbed,
Dwelling securely in forest and field.
Now these three spheres
Are all my possession.
The living beings within them
Are all my children.
Yet, now these places
Have many cares and troubles,
From which I alone
Can save them.
Even though I teach and command,
Yet they neither believe nor accept,
But to their tainting desires
Are so profoundly addicted that I,
By resort to an expedient device,
Preach the three vehicles to them,
Causing the beings

To know the woes of the three spheres
And demonstrating and setting forth
The Supramundane Way.
If these children
With fixed thought
Acquire fully the three wisdoms
And the six supernatural penetrations,
They shall include among them those who can be
cause-perceivers
And nonbacksliding bodhisattvas.
O, Śāriputra!
For the beings' sake, I,
By resort to this parable,
Preach the One Buddha Vehicle;
All of you, if you can
Believe and accept these words,
Shall without exception
Completely attain to the Buddha Path.[13]
This Vehicle is fine,
Supremely pure,
In all the worlds
Having not its master.
It is a thing which they whom the Buddha gladdens,
All living beings,
Should praise,
To which they should make offerings and do obeisance.
It is incalculable thousands of millions
Of strengths and deliverances,
Dhyāna-concentrations and modes of knowledge,
And other dharmas of the Buddhas.
If they can gain this kind of Vehicle,
I enable those children
Night and day, for a number of kalpas,
Ever to amuse themselves,
With bodhisattvas
And the multitude of voice-hearers

To mount this jeweled Vehicle
  And to arrive directly at the Platform of the Way.[14]
For these reasons,
  Seek as you will in all ten directions:
There is no other vehicle,
  Apart from the expedient devices of the Buddhas.
I tell you, Śāriputra,
  You men
Are all my children,
  And I am your Father.
For kalpa upon kalpa, you
  Have been scorched by multitudinous woes,
And I have saved you all,
  Causing you to leave the three spheres.
Although earlier I said
  That you would pass into extinction,
This was to be a mere end to birth and death,
  And no true extinction.
What you should now achieve
  Is nothing other than Buddha-wisdom.
If there are bodhisattvas
  In the midst of this multitude,
They can listen single-mindedly
  To the Buddhas' real Dharma.
Even though the Buddhas, the World-Honored Ones,
  Resort to expedient devices,
The living beings whom they convert
  Are all bodhisattvas.[15]
If there are persons of slight understanding (*bālabuddhayaḥ*),
  Profoundly addicted to lust and desire,
For their sakes
  I preach the Truth of Suffering,
And the beings rejoice at heart
  That they have gained something they never had before.
The Buddha's preaching of the Truth of Suffering
  Is reality without falsehood.

If there are beings
  Who, not knowing the origin of woe,
Are profoundly addicted to the causes of woe,
  Unable to cast them off even for a moment,
For their sakes,
  By resort to an expedient device, I preach the Path:
That the origin of all woes
  Is desire; which is their basis.
If one extinguishes desire,
  They have nothing on which to rest.
The extinction of woes
  Is called the Third Truth.
For the sake of the Truth of Extinction
  One cultivates the Path.
Separation from the bonds of woe
  Is called the attainment of deliverance.
As for these [ignorant] men, whereby
  Do they attain deliverance?
It is the mere separation of self from falsehood
  That is called "deliverance."
In fact, however, they have not yet attained
  Total deliverance.
The Buddha says that these men
  Are not yet truly extinguished,
For these men have not yet attained
  The Unexcelled Path.
At heart I have no wish
  To cause them to attain passage into extinction.
I am the Dharma King,
  With respect to the Dharma acting completely at will.
To bring the gift of tranquillity to the beings
  Is why I have appeared in the world.[16]
You, Śāriputra!
  As for this Dharma-seal of mine,
I wish to benefit the world,
  And therefore I preach it.[17]

Wherever you go,
  Do not propagate it recklessly.
If there is a listener
  Who with due rejoicing receives it upon the crown of his head,
You are to know that that man
  Is an *avivartika* ["not to be turned back"].
If there is one who believes and accepts
  This Scripture-Dharma,
That man has already, in times gone by,
  Seen Buddhas of the past,
Deferentially made offerings to them,
  And also heard this Dharma.
If among men there is one who can
  Believe what you preach,
Then it means that he sees me
  And also sees you
And the *bhikṣusaṃgha* [company of monks],
  As well as the bodhisattvas.
This Scripture of the Dharma Blossom
  Is preached for those of profound knowledge;
Those of shallow perception, if they hear it,
  Shall go astray and not understand.
For all voice-hearers
  And pratyekabuddhas,
The content of this scripture
  Is beyond the reach of their faculties.
You, Śāriputra,
  Even you, where this scripture is concerned,
Gained entry through faith.
  How much the more so the other voice-hearers!
Those other voice-hearers
  By virtue of their belief in the Buddha's Word
Accept this scripture;
  It does not fall within the range of their own knowledge.
Also, Śāriputra,
  To the proud, arrogant, lazy, and indolent,

To those who reckon in terms of "I,"
  Do not preach this scripture.
To the ordinary fellow of shallow perception,
  Profoundly addicted to the five desires,
Hearing yet unable to understand,
  Also do not preach.
If a man, not believing,
  Maligns this scripture,
Then he cuts off all
  Worldly Buddha-seeds.
Or, again, he may, with contorted face,
  Harbor doubts and uncertainties.
You are now to hear me tell
  Of that man's retribution for his sins:[18]
Whether the Buddha be in the world,
  Or whether it be after his passage into extinction,
There shall be those who malign
  Such scriptures as this one
And who, seeing that there are readers, and reciters,
  And copiers, and keepers of this scripture,
Shall, in disparagement, deprecation, hatred, and envy of them,
  Harbor grudges against them.
The retribution for these men's sins
  You are now to hear:
These men, at life's end,
  Shall enter the Avīci hell,
Where they shall fulfill one kalpa.
  When the kalpa is ended, they shall be reborn there.
In this way, spinning around
  Throughout kalpas unnumbered, [and then]
From hell emerging,
  They shall fall into the rank of beasts.
If they are dogs or yeh-kan,
  Their forms shall be hairless and emaciated,
Spotted and scabbed,
  Things from which men shrink.

They shall also by men be
  Detested and despised,
Ever suffering from hunger and thirst,
  Their flesh and bones dried out and decayed.
While living, they are pricked by poisonous thistles;
  When dead, they are covered with tiles and stones.
It is because they have cut off the Buddha-seed
  That they suffer these retributions for their sins.
If they become camels,
  Or if they are born among asses,
On their bodies they shall ever carry heavy loads
  And suffer the blows of rods and whips,
Thinking only of water and grass
  And knowing nothing else.
For maligning this scripture
  They shall suffer punishments such as these.
If they are those who become yeh-kan,
  They shall enter human settlements,
Their bodies spotted and scabbed,
  Also missing one eye,
By the children
  Beaten,
Suffering all manner of woe and pain,
  At times to the point of death.
Having died in this form,
  They shall then be endowed with the bodies of monster serpents,
Their forms long and huge,
  To the extent of five hundred yojanas,
Deaf, stupid, and legless,
  Writhing about on their bellies,
By little insects
  Pecked at and eaten,
Day and night suffering woe
  And enjoying no respite.
For maligning this scripture

They shall suffer punishments such as these.
If they contrive to become humans,
They shall be obscure and dull of faculties,
Short, mean, bent over, and crippled,
Blind, deaf, and hunched.
If they have anything to say,
Men shall neither believe nor accept it.
The breath of their mouths ever stinking,
They shall be possessed by ghosts,
Poor and lowly,
Doing men's bidding,
Much plagued by headache and emaciation,
Having nothing on which to rely.
Though they may personally attach themselves to men,
Men do not have them in their thoughts.
If they gain something,
Shortly afterward they shall leave it behind.[19]
If they practice the Way of medicine,
Tending disease in accord with prescription,
They shall but aggravate the illnesses of others,
At times bringing them even to the point of death.[20]
If they themselves have diseases,
No man shall be able to save them;
Even if they take good medicine,
The sickness shall be all the more acute.[21]
Or others may attack them,
Snatching, pillaging, stealing, or robbing.[22]
Such are the sins
Into whose misfortune they shall fall by their own willful acts.
Sinners such as these
Shall never see the Buddha,
The King of the many saints,
Preaching the Dharma, teaching, and converting.
Sinners such as these
Shall ever be born in places of trouble.
Mad, deaf, and confused of thought,

They shall never hear the Dharma.
For kalpas as numberless
As Ganges' sands,
Whenever born, they shall be deaf and dumb,
Of defective faculties,
Ever dwelling in hell
As if amusing themselves in a pleasure garden
Or being in other evil paths
As if in their own homes.
Camels, asses, pigs, and dogs—
These shall be their companions. [?]
For maligning this scripture
They shall suffer punishments such as these.
If they contrive to become human beings,
They shall be deaf, blind, and dumb,
Poor, destitute, and in general decrepit,
Yet adorning themselves withal.
Swollen with water or dried out and wizened,
Scabs, boils,
And ills like these
They shall have for their dress.
Their bodies a constant stench,
Filthy and unclean,
Profoundly addicted to the view of "I,"
They shall magnify their anger.
Their lust being acute,
There shall be nothing to choose between them and birds or beasts.
For maligning this scripture
They shall suffer punishments such as these.[23]
I say to you, Śāriputra,
Of those who malign this scripture
That, if I were to tell their punishments,
Even if I should exhaust a kalpa, I should not finish them.
For this reason
I expressly tell you,

[When you are] in the midst of ignorant men,
Do not preach this scripture.
If there are those of keen faculties,
Of knowledge clear and bright,
Of much learning and strong memory,
Who seek the Buddha Path,
For men like these,
And only for them, may you preach.
If a man, having formerly seen
Hundreds of thousands of millions of Buddhas,
Has planted seeds of goodness,
His profound thought being firm,
For a man like this,
And only for him, may you preach.
If a man strives,
Constantly cultivating thoughts of good will
And not begrudging his own body or his own life,
Then for him alone may you preach.
If a man is deferential
And has no other thoughts,
Separating himself from common fools
And dwelling alone in mountains and marshes,
For men like him,
And only for them, may you preach.
Also, Śāriputra,
If you see that there is a man
Who rejects evil acquaintances
And clings to good friends,
For men like him,
And only for them, may you preach.
If you see a son of the Buddha
Keeping a discipline as pure
As a bright jewel
And seeking the scriptures of the Great Vehicle,
For men like him,
And only for them, may you preach.

If a man, having no anger,
  Is honest and gentle,
Ever pitying all
  And venerating the Buddhas,
For men like him,
  And only for them, may you preach.
Again, there may be a son of the Buddha
  In the midst of the great multitude
Who, with pure thought
  And by resort to various means,
Parables, and phrases,
  Preaches the Dharma, unobstructed.
For men like him,
  And only for them, may you preach.
If there is a bhikṣu
  Who for the sake of All-Knowledge
Seeks the Dharma in all four directions,
  With joined palms receiving it on the crown of his head,
Desiring merely to receive and keep
  The scriptures of the Great Vehicle,
Not accepting so much
  As a single gāthā from the other scriptures,
For men like him,
  And only for them, may you preach.
As a man wholeheartedly
  Seeks the Buddhaśarīra,
So may one seek the scriptures
  And, having found them, receive them on the crown of one's head.
Such a person shall never again
  Wish to seek other scriptures,
Nor has he ever before thought
  Of the books of the unbelievers.
For men like him,
  And only for them, may you preach.
I say to you, Śāriputra,

That I, in telling of this sort
Of seekers of the Buddha Path,
Could spend a whole kalpa and still not finish.
If they are men of this sort,
Then they can believe and understand,
And for their sakes you may
Preach the Scripture of the Fine Dharma Flower.[24]

Chapter Four: Belief and Understanding

At that time, the wise and long-lived Subhūti, Mahākātyāyana, and Mahāmaudgalyāyana, in view of the unprecedented Dharma they had heard from the Buddha, in which the World-Honored One had conferred upon Śāriputra a prophecy of anuttarasamyaksaṃbodhi, displayed the thought that this was something rare and danced for joy (*āścaryaprāptā adbhutaprāptā audbilyaprāptāḥ*). Then they rose from their seats, adjusted their garments, bared their right shoulders, knelt to the ground on their right knees, single-mindedly joined palms, inclined their bodies in veneration, looked up at the August Countenance, and addressed the Buddha, saying: "We, who were at the head of the saṃgha, all of us advanced in years, and who told ourselves that we had already attained nirvāṇa and could be charged with nothing further, made no effort to seek anuttarasamyaksaṃbodhi. The time is now long since the World-Honored One, of old, began preaching the Dharma. All this time, we, sitting in our seats, our bodies tired, were mindful merely of emptiness, signlessness, and deedlessness; and in bodhisattva-dharmas, sport, supernatural penetrations, the cleansing of Buddha realms, and the perfection of the beings our hearts took no pleasure. What is the reason? The World-Honored One had caused us to leave the three spheres and made us able to bear direct witness to nirvāṇa. Furthermore, we are now well advanced in years, and, when the Buddha instructed bodhisattvas in anuttarasamyaksaṃbodhi, this did not arouse in us the least thought of desire. Now, however, since in the Buddha's own presence we have heard a prophecy of anuttarasamyaksaṃbodhi conferred on voice-hearers, our hearts are very glad, having gained something they had not had before. For we did not think that now suddenly we should be able to hear a rare Dharma. Profoundly we rejoice, having received this great good advantage. An incalculable precious treasure, unsought by us, of itself has come into our possession.

"World-Honored One! We now wish to speak a parable, with which to clarify this meaning. Suppose there were a man who was young in years and who also, forsaking his father and running off, dwelt long in another country, whether ten, or twenty, or as much as fifty years. Not only did he grow old, but he was also reduced to destitution, running about in all four directions in quest of food and clothing. At length, in his wanderings, he accidentally headed toward his native land. His father, who had preceded him, and who had sought his son without finding him, had stopped midway in a certain city. The father's house was great and rich, with treasure and jewels immeasurable, gold and silver, vaiḍūrya and coral, amber and sphāṭika and other jewels. His treasure houses were all filled to overflowing. He had many servants, assistants, vassals, elephants and horses, carriages and chariots, oxen and sheep without number. The profits that flowed in and out would fill the whole realm, and also merchants and itinerant traders were very numerous.[1]

"At that time, the poor son, having visited various settlements and passed through kingdoms and metropolises, at length reached the city where his father was staying. The father and mother were thinking of their son, for it had already been more than fifty years since they had parted with him. Yet, without ever mentioning such matters to others [?], they merely thought to themselves, their hearts harboring regret and resentment: 'Old and decrepit, we have much gold and silver and many precious gems, with which our treasure houses are filled to overflowing; but we have no son. One day we shall die, and our riches shall be scattered, for we shall have no one to whom to bequeath them. For this reason we are earnestly and constantly recalling our son.' Again, they thought: 'If we should get a son to whom to bequeath our riches, we should be calmly happy, and have no further cares.'

"World-Honored One! At that time, the poor son, hiring himself out as a laborer in his wanderings, by chance reached his father's house, where, stopping by the side of the gate, he saw in the distance his father seated on a lion throne, his feet resting on a jeweled footstool; Brahmans, *Kṣatriyas* [the governing or military class], and householders all deferentially surrounding him; his body adorned with pearl necklaces valued in the thousands of myriads; attended on his left and right by vassals and servants holding white feather dusters in their hands; covered by a jeweled canopy, from which flowered banners were hanging down; the ground round about him sprinkled with scented water and strewn with many outstanding flowers; with rows of precious objects that were given and received upon entering and leaving [?]: having, in short, various adornments of this sort, whereby he appeared most majestic and distinguished. As soon as the poor son had seen his father with this great power, straightway, harboring great fear, he regretted having come to that place, and privately thought: "This is either a king or the equal of a king; but at any rate, this is no place for me to hire out my labor and earn anything. The best thing for me to do is to go to a poor village, where there will be room for me to use my strength to the fullest and where food and clothing will be easy to obtain. If I stay long in this place, I may be coerced to work.'

"When he had had this thought, he quickly ran off. At that time, the great and wealthy man, from his lion throne seeing his son, instantly recognized him and, greatly pleased at heart, straightway thought: 'My treasures and treasure houses now have someone to whom they can be bequeathed! I constantly thought of this son but had no way of seeing him. Then, quite suddenly, he came of his own accord, fulfilling my hopes. Though I was decrepit and aged, still I was eager [for an heir] and reluctant [to die without one].'

"Accordingly, he dispatched an attendant to follow the young man and bring him back. The messenger, running quickly, went and overtook him. The poor son was alarmed, and cried out resentfully, 'I have committed no offense! Why have I been seized?' The messenger, grasping him all the more firmly, forced him to return with him. At that time, the poor son thought to himself: 'I am guiltless and yet have been seized. This surely means that I must die!' All the more terrified, and helpless with agony, he fell to earth. Seeing this from afar, the father said to the messenger, 'I do not want this man. Do not force him to come with you!' Then, sprinkling him with cool water, he brought him to, but spoke to him no more. What is the reason? The father knew that his son's ambitions were mean, and he knew that he himself, being rich and powerful, would be a source of trouble to his son.

"He knew perfectly well that this was his son, but for reasons of expediency would not tell others, 'This is my son.' The messenger said to the son, 'I am now letting you go wherever you wish!' The poor son rejoiced, having gained something he had never had before. Rising from the ground, he went to a poor village, there to seek food and clothing. At that time the great man, wishing to entice his son, devised an expedient: he secretly dispatched two men, whose appearance was miserable and who had no dignity of bearing, saying to them: 'You may go to that place and say gently to that poor fellow, "There is a work place here, to which we will accompany you." If the poor fellow agrees, bring him along and put him to work. If he asks what you wish him to do, then you may say to him, "You are being hired to sweep away dung. We two shall also work with you."' At that time, the two messengers sought out the poor son directly. When they had found him, they told him the above in detail. The poor son first took his pay, then swept the dung with them. The father, seeing his son, was struck by both pity and amazement.

"Then, on another day, through a window he saw the figure of his son, weak and emaciated, wasted away, grimy and soiled with dung, dirt, and dust. Straightway he removed his necklaces, his fine outer garments, and his ornaments, and put on instead a rough, torn, dirty, tar-stained garment and, smearing dust over his body, took in his right hand a dung-shovel. Now frightful in appearance, he addressed his workmen: 'You men, work! You may not slacken!' by this means contriving to approach his son. Then he addressed him, saying: 'Ah, my man! Work here always, and do not go anywhere else! I will increase your wages. Whatever you need, whether pots or vessels, rice or noodles, salt or vinegar, or that sort of thing, do not trouble yourself about it. For I have other servants, aged and decrepit, whose needs I supply and who can well afford to put their minds at ease. I am like your father: have no more cares! What is the reason? I am old, my years are great, while you are young and vigorous. Whenever you work, you are never guilty of lying or cheating, of anger or resentment, or of hateful words. I have never seen you guilty of these evils, as are the other workmen. From now on you shall be like my own son!'

"Straightway the great man gave him a new name and called him his son. The poor son, though delighted by this treatment, continued as before to call himself a lowly workman from elsewhere. For this reason, for twenty years he was kept constantly at work clearing away dung. At the end of this time he had complete confidence in himself, and came and went without anxiety [?]. Yet he was lodged in the same place as before.[2]

"World-Honored One! At that time, the great man was taken ill, and knew himself that he was to die before long. He addressed his poor son, saying: 'I now have much gold and silver and many precious jewels, with which my treasure houses are filled to overflowing. You are to find out whether there is much or little in those [houses], what is to be taken in, what to be given out. Such are my thoughts, and you are to understand my meaning. What is the reason? Is is that you and I are now to be no different. You are to exercise care and to let nothing get lost.'

"At that time, the poor son, straightway receiving his instructions, took charge of the multitude of things, the gold and silver, the precious jewels and the several treasure houses. Yet he had no craving for so much as a single meal, but continued to live as before in the same place, still unable to put off his lowly thoughts.

"Then, when some time had passed, the father knew that his son had at length become more at ease, that, having achieved a great ambition, he was ashamed of his former state of mind. When facing his end, the old man commanded his son to gather his kinsmen, as well as kings, great ministers, Kṣatriyas, and householders, who were all to gather together. Then he himself proclaimed to them: 'Sirs! Know that this is my son, begotten by me. Having forsaken me in such-and-such a city and run off, he suffered loneliness and hardship for more than fifty years. His original name was so-and-so. My own name is thus-and-so. Formerly, in my native city, affected by grief, I sought him. Some time ago, I suddenly encountered him by accident and got him back. He is really my son. I am really his father. Now all the treasure I have belongs to my son. What was formerly paid out and taken in, my son knows it all.'

"World-Honored One! At this time, the poor son, hearing his father's words, straightway rejoiced greatly, having gained something he had never had before. Then he thought: 'Formerly I had no thought of seeking or expecting anything, and now these treasure houses have come to me of themselves!'

"World-Honored One! The great rich man is the Thus Come One. We are all alike the Buddha's sons. The Thus Come One constantly tells us that we are his sons. World-Honored One! By reason of the three kinds of woe, in the midst of birth and death we suffer various annoyances. Erring and ignorant, we cling in desire to lesser dharmas. This day the World-Honored One commands us to take thought and to clear away the dung of frivolous assertions concerning the dharmas. In the course of this we, striving all the more earnestly, contrive to arrive at nirvāṇa. Having earned one day's wages, we rejoice greatly at heart, imagining this to be enough. Then we say to ourselves that in the Buddhadharma, thanks to our increased efforts, what we have gained is broad and plentiful. Yet the World-Honored One, knowing beforehand that our thoughts are addicted to base cravings and that we desire lesser dharmas, makes a show of permissiveness, and does not specify to us, 'You are all to have a portion in the treasure house of the Thus Come One's knowledge and insight!' The World-Honored One by resort to the power of expedient devices preaches the wisdom of the Thus Come One. We, having earned from the Buddha one day's wages in nirvāṇa, imagine that we have gained a great thing, and have no ambitions with regard to this Great Vehicle. Also, since the Thus Come One's wisdom is set forth for the bodhisattvas, we ourselves had no expectations regarding it. What is the reason? The Buddha, knowing that in our thoughts we craved the lesser dharmas, by resort to the power of expedient devices preached in a manner appropriate to us, and we did not know that we are truly the Buddha's children. Now, at last, we know. With regard to Buddha-knowledge the World-Honored One is unstinting. What is the reason? From of old we have been the Buddha's children, yet we have craved only lesser dharmas. If we had had a craving for the greater, then the Buddha would have preached for us the Dharma of the Greater Vehicle. In this sermon he preaches only the One Vehicle. Also, in former times, in the presence of bodhisattvas, he maligned the voice-hearers who crave the lesser dharmas. Yet the Buddha teaches and converts by recourse to the Greater Vehicle. This is why we say that, whereas formerly we had no thought of seeking or expecting anything, now the great jewel of the Dharma King has come to us of its own accord. What the Buddha's children should gain, that we have already gained."[3]

At that time, Mahākāśyapa, wishing to restate this meaning, proclaimed gāthās, saying:

This day we,
  Having heard the Buddha's spoken teaching,
Dance for joy
  That we have gained something we had never had before.
For the Buddha says that voice-hearers
  Shall be able to become Buddhas,
And a cluster of unexcelled gems,
  Unsought by us, has come into our possession of its own accord.
For example: suppose that a boy,
  Young and knowing nothing,
Forsaking his father and running away,
  Arrived far off in another land,
Then went about through several countries
  For more than fifty years.
His father, tormented by grief,
  Sought him in all four directions;
Then, when weary with the search,
  He settled in a city,
Where he built himself a house
  In which he amused himself with the objects of the five desires.
The house was great and rich,
  Having much gold and silver,
Giant clam shell and agate,
  Pearl and vaiḍūrya,
Elephants and horses, cattle and sheep,
  Hand-carts and palanquins, carriages and chariots,
Workmen to tend the fields,
  And many dependent people.
The profits that flowed out and in

Extended to other countries as well.
Merchants and traders
Were everywhere; there was no place without them.
Multitudes in the thousands of myriads of millions
Surrounded him in deference,
And by kings he was constantly
Loved and cherished.
Assembled ministers and powerful clans
Alike all revered and valued him.
For this reason
Those who came and went were numerous.
Such were his power and wealth.
Having great power,
But being of advanced and decrepit age,
He was all the more grief-stricken in recalling his son.
Morn and night he thought:
"When my time to die was about to arrive,
My stupid son left me,
Now more than fifty years since.
My treasure houses and everything in them—
What shall I do with them?"
At that time, the poor son,
In quest of food and clothing,
Was going from metropolis to metropolis,
From kingdom to kingdom,
Now getting something,
Now not.
Hungry, weak, and emaciated as he was,
He developed scabs on his body.
Eventually, in his passage,
He reached the city in which his father dwelt
And, going about for hire,
At length arrived at his father's house.
At that time, the great man
Within his gateway
Had erected a great jeweled tent,

91

Where he was seated on a lion throne,
Surrounded by dependents
And attended by various persons.
Among them were those who reckoned the quantity of
Gold, silver, and gems
And of the goods given out and taken in,
Who recorded them in ledgers.[4]
The poor son, seeing his father
Rich and powerful, stern and majestic,
Thought, "This is a king,
Or the equal of a king." (*rājā ayaṃ bheṣyati rājamātraḥ*)
In his consternation he wondered
Why he had come hither.
Repeatedly he thought,
"If I stay long,
I may be driven
Or coerced to work."
When he had had these thoughts,
He ran off in haste,
Inquiring about poor villages,
For he wished to go to one to work for hire.
The great man, at this time
Seated on his lion throne,
And seeing his son in the distance,
Silently recognized him.
Accordingly, he commanded messengers
To overtake him and bring him back.
The poor son cried out in alarm,
In sore distraction falling to the ground;
"If these men have seized me,
It must mean that I am going to be killed.
Of what use are food and clothing,
If they bring me to this?"
The great man knew his son
To be foolish and mean:
"He will not believe my words,

He will not believe this is his father."
Accordingly, resorting to an expedient device,
He sent other men,
Squint-eyed and crouched over,
Persons of no imposing appearance
[And told them]: "You may talk to him,
Saying, 'We will hire you
To clear away dung and other filth,
Giving you a double wage.'"
The poor son, hearing this
And following them joyfully,
At their behest cleared away dung and filth
And cleaned the rooms and apartments.
The great man through his window
Constantly saw his son,
And was mindful that the son, being foolish and inferior,
Enjoyed doing menial work.
Thereupon the great man,
Putting on torn and filthy garments
And taking in hand a dung-shovel,
Went to his son's work place,
Where, by resort to an expedient device approaching him
And talking to him, he caused him to work with diligence:
"I have already increased your wage
And anointed your feet with oil.
Your food and drink suffice,
And your bedding is thick and warm."
He spoke to him sternly:
"You must work hard!"
He also used gentle words:
"You are like my son."[5]
The great man, being wise,
Eventually permitted him to enter and leave,
Throughout twenty years
Having charge of the great man's household affairs.
He showed him his gold and silver,

His pearls and sphāṭika,
The income and expenditure of his various things,
Making him responsible for them all.
Yet, the son still lived outside the gate,
Dwelling in a grass hut
And thinking of his own poor state:
"I have none of these things."
The father, knowing that his son's thoughts
Were at last broad and great,
And wishing to give him his treasure,
Straightway assembled his kin,
The king and his ministers,
Kṣatriyas and householders,
And in this great multitude
Said, "This is my son![6]
Since he forsook me and went away,
Fifty years have passed;
Since I saw my son come back,
It has already been twenty years.
Formerly, in such-and-such a city,
I lost this son.
Going in search of him,
At length I came to this place.
Everything I have,
My houses and my vassals,
I make over entirely to him,
To do with as he pleases."
The son, who still had in mind his former poverty
And his lowly ambitions,
And who now, in his father's presence,
Was the great recipient of precious gems,
As well as of houses, apartments,
And all manner of treasure,
Was overjoyed,
Having gained something he had never had before.

The Buddha also in this way,
  Knowing our fondness for the petty,
Has never before told us,
  "You shall become Buddhas!"
On the contrary, he told us
  To achieve freedom from outflows,
To achieve the Lesser Vehicle,
  To be voice-hearing disciples.
The Buddha commanded us
  To say of the Unexcelled Path
That they who cultivate it
  Shall be able to achieve Buddhahood.
We, receiving the Buddha's instructions,
  For the great bodhisattvas' sakes,
By invoking causes and conditions,
  A variety of parables,
And divers words and phrases,
  Preached the Unexcelled Path.
The Buddha's sons,
  Hearing the Dharma from us
And day and night taking thought,
  Engaged in cultivated practice.
At that time the Buddhas
  Straightway conferred on them this prophecy:
"In an age to come, you
  Shall be able to become Buddhas."
Of all Buddhas
  This is the Dharma of the secret treasure house.
Merely for the bodhisattvas' sakes
  Did we set forth these matters,
Not for our own sakes
  Preaching these essentials.
Just as that poor son
  Was able to approach his father
And, though responsible for his father's things,

Had no thought of taking them,
So we, though we preached
The jewel cache of the Buddhadharma,
Had ourselves no hope for it
In the same way.
For us, personal extinction
Was thought to suffice.
We understood only this,
Having no hold on anything else.
Had we heard
Of cleansing Buddha-lands, and
Of teaching and converting the beings,
We should have taken absolutely no pleasure therein.
What is the reason?
All dharmas
Without exception are empty and quiescent,
Having no birth and no extinction,
Neither great nor small,
Having no outflows and no ado.*
With this in mind,
We experienced no pleasure.
Throughout the long night of time,
For Buddha-knowledge
We had no craving and no attachment,
Nor yet any hope.
On the contrary, where Dharma is concerned, to ourselves
We said: "This is the ultimate!
Throughout the long night of time
Having practiced and cultivated the dharma of emptiness,
We have contrived to shake off the three spheres
And their ills of woe and anguish.
We occupy our final bodies,
Nirvāṇa with residue.

* See footnote to p. 256.

The Buddha teaches
  That the attainment of the Path is no vain matter;
Yet we have already contrived [by our practice]
  To repay the Buddha's munificence."[?][7]
Although we, for the sake of
  The Buddha's sons,
Preached the Bodhisattvadharma,
  Wherewith the Buddha Path was to be sought,
Yet, with respect to this Dharma,
  We never had any hopes.
The Teacher made a show of indifference,
  For he knew our thoughts.
He never urged us on
  By telling us that we should gain a real advantage.
Just as the great rich man,
  Knowing that his son's ambitions were lowly,
By resort to the power of an expedient device
  Mollified his feelings,
And only then bequeathed to him
  All his treasure,
The Buddha also in the same way
  Demonstrates rare things
But, understanding those who crave the petty,
  By resort to the power of expedient devices
Tames their thoughts
  And only then teaches them great wisdom.
We this day
  Have gained something we had never had before,
Something which, though never before hoped for,
  Yet now has come into our possession of its own accord.
As that poor son
  Gained incalculable gems,
So, O World-Honored One, have we now
  Gained the Path and the Fruit,
For dharmas without outflows

Having attained a pure eye.
Throughout the long night of time, we
Have kept the Buddha's pure discipline,
But only this day
Have we gained its fruit, its retribution.
In the midst of the dharmas of the Dharma King
Long having cultivated brahman-conduct,
Now we have gained something without outflows,
A great unexcelled fruit.
We now
Are truly voice-hearers,
Taking the voice of the Buddha Path
And causing all to hear it.[8]
We now
Are true arhants,
Since among the various worlds'
Gods, men, Māras, and Brahmās,
Everywhere in their midst,
We are entitled to receive offerings.
The World-Honored One in his great lovingkindness
Uses a rare thing,
Teaching and converting us with compassion,
To afford us profit.
In incalculable millions of kalpas
Who could repay this?
Were he to sacrifice his hands and feet,
Do obeisance with his head bowed,
And make sundry offerings,
No one could repay this.
Were one to receive him on the crown of one's head,
Carry him on both shoulders
For kalpas numerous as Ganges' sands,
Exhausting one's thoughts in deference;
Were one, further, to make use of lovely delicacies,
Of garments adorned with incalculable gems,
And of various kinds of bedding

And assorted broths and medicines;
Were one with ox-head candana*
And precious gems
To erect a stūpa-shrine,
Spreading jeweled garments on the ground;
Were one to take such things as these
And use them to make offerings
For kalpas numerous as Ganges' sands:
Still one could not repay him.
The Buddhas have the rare,
Incalculable, limitless,
Inconceivable, and ineffable
Power of great supernatural penetrations.
Free of outflows and with no ado,
The King of the dharmas
Can, for the sake of the inferior [beings],
Patiently endure these things. [?]
For ordinary fellows, taken with signs,
He preaches in accord with what is peculiarly appropriate.
The Buddhas, with respect to the dharmas,
Have achieved the utmost in self-mastery.
Knowing the beings'
Varied desires and predilections,
As well as their strength of will,
And in accord with what they can bear,
By resort to incalculable parables
He preaches the Dharma to them.
In accord with the beings'
Wholesome roots from former ages,
Also knowing who is ripe
And who unripe,
When, as a result of varied weighings and measurings,

* *Niu t'ou chan-t'an* (*gośīrṣacandana*): according to the folk etymology given by several lexicographers, the wood is named for its most famous source, a mountain shaped like an ox's head. Monier-Williams says merely that it is a copper-colored and very fragrant sandalwood, and cites, among other references to the word, one in the *Rāmāyaṇa*.

He knows [these things] with discrimination,
Then, for the Path of the One Vehicle,
In accord with what is peculiarly appropriate, he preaches three.[9]

Scripture of the Lotus Blossom of the Fine Dharma.
End of Roll the Second.

Roll 3

Chapter Five: Medicinal Herbs

At that time, the World-Honored One proclaimed to Mahākāśyapa and the great disciples: "Good! Good! Kāśyapa has well stated the Thus Come One's real merits. Truly it is as he has said. The Thus Come One also has incalculable, limitless asaṃkhyeyas of merit. If you were to tell of them for incalculable millions of kalpas you could not finish. Kāśyapa, know that the Thus Come One is King of the dharmas. If he has anything to say, it is never vain. He sets forth all dharmas by resort to wisdom and practical expedients. Without exception, the dharmas he preaches all reach to the ground of All-Knowledge. The Thus Come One sees and knows that to which all dharmas tend, that to which they are reduced. He also knows what the profound thoughts of all living beings can do, penetrating them without obstruction. Furthermore, with respect to the dharmas he is perfectly clear, demonstrating all manner of wisdom to the beings.[1]

"Kāśyapa, consider the grasses, trees, shrubs, and forests, as well as the medicinal herbs, in their several varieties, and their different names and colors, that the mountains and rivers, the dales and vales of the thousand-millionfold world produce. A thick cloud spreads out, covering the whole thousand-millionfold world and raining down on every part of it equally at the same time, its infusions reaching everywhere. The grass and trees, the shrubs and forests, and the medicinal herbs—whether of small roots, stalks, branches, and leaves, or of middle-sized roots, stalks, branches, and leaves, or of large roots, stalks, branches, and leaves—and also all trees, great and small, whether high, intermediate, or low, all receive some of it. Everything rained on by the same cloud in keeping with its nature gains in size, and its blossoms and fruit spread out and bloom. Though produced by the same earth, and moistened by the same rain, yet the grasses and trees all have their differences. Kāśayapa, know that the Thus Come One is also like this: he appears in the world as the great cloud rises. With the sound of his great voice he pervades the world, with its gods, its men, and its asuras, just as that great cloud covers the lands of the thousand-millionfold world. In the midst of a great multitude he proclaims these words: 'I am the Thus Come One, worthy of offerings, of right and universal knowledge, whose clarity and conduct are perfect, well gone, understanding the world, the unexcelled Worthy, the Regulator of men of stature, the Teacher of gods and men, the Buddha, the World-Honored One. Those who have not yet crossed over I enable to cross. Those who do not yet understand I cause to understand. Those not yet at ease I put at their ease. Those not yet in nirvāṇa I enable to attain nirvāṇa. For this age and for later ages, I know things as they are. I am the one who knows all, the one who sees all, the one who knows the Path, the one who opens up the Path, the one who preaches the Path. You multitude of gods, men, and asuras should all come here in order to listen to the Dharma!' At that time, numberless thousands of myriads of millions of kinds of living beings come before the Buddha and hear the Dharma. The Thus Come One at this time observes these beings, their keenness or dullness, their exertion or laxity, and in accord with what they can bear, preaches the Dharma to them in an incalculable variety of modes, each causing them to rejoice and enabling them speedily to gain good advantage. These beings, having heard this Dharma, in the present age are tranquil and are later born in a good place; they enjoy pleasure consonant with the Path and also are enabled [again] to hear the Dharma. When they have heard the Dharma, they are separated from obstacles, and in the midst of the dharmas, in keeping with their powers, gradually contrive to enter upon the Path.

"Just as that great cloud rains down on all grasses and trees, shrubs and forests, and medicinal herbs, and just as they all, in accord with their nature and kind, derive the full benefit of the moisture, each gaining in growth, just so is the Dharma preached by the Thus Come One of a single mark and a single flavor, namely, the mark of deliverance, the mark of disenchantment, the mark of extinction, arriving completely at knowledge of all modes. Whenever there are beings who hear the

Dharma of the Thus Come One, if they hold to it, read it, recite it, and act according to his preachings, then the merit they gain thereby shall be unknown and unnoticed even by themselves. What is the reason? Only the Thus Come One knows these beings, their kinds, their signs, their substance, their nature, what things they think back on, what things they think ahead to, what things they cultivate, how they think back, how they think ahead, how they practice, by resort to what dharmas they think back, by resort to what dharmas they think ahead, by resort to what dharmas they practice, what dharma they gain and by resort to what dharma they gain it. The living beings dwell on a variety of grounds. Only the Thus Come One sees them for what they are and understands them clearly and without obstruction. Those grasses and trees, shrubs and forests, and medicinal herbs do not know themselves whether their nature is superior, intermediate, or inferior; but the Thus Come One knows this Dharma of a single mark and a single flavor, namely, the mark of deliverance, the mark of disenchantment, the mark of extinction, the mark of ultimate nirvāṇa, of eternally quiescent nirvāṇa, finally reducing itself to Emptiness. The Buddha, knowing this, observes the heart's desire of each of the beings, and guides them protectively. For this reason he does not immediately preach to them the knowledge of all modes. All of you, Kāśyapa, are very rare, in that you are able to know that the Thus Come One preaches the Dharma in accord with what is peculiarly appropriate, and in that you are able to believe and accept this. What is the reason? The Buddhas', the World-Honored Ones' preaching of the Dharma in accord with what is peculiarly appropriate is difficult to understand and hard to know."[2]

At that time, the World-Honored One, wishing to restate this meaning, proclaimed gāthās, saying:

The Dharma King who demolishes being
  Appears in the world and,
In accord with the desires of the beings,
  Preaches the Dharma in various ways.
The Thus Come One, being venerable,

His wisdom profound and far-reaching,
Long kept silence on this essential matter
And was in no haste to tell of it.
Those having intelligence, if they hear of it,
Can then believe and understand it;
While those of no intelligence, having doubts and second thoughts,
Will then, on that account, lose it forever.
For this reason, O Kāśyapa,
I preach for you in accord with your powers,
By resort to a variety of means
Enabling you to see properly.
Kāśyapa, know that,
For example, it is as if a great cloud
Were to arise in the world,
Universally covering everything,
A beneficent cloud containing enriching moisture,
Its lightning flashes bright and illuminating,
Its thunder sounds far-reaching and shattering,
Causing the multitudes to rejoice.
The light of the sun is covered by it,
And the surface of the earth is clear and cool.
The cloud is spread out, and hangs down
As if one could actually touch it.
Its rain, everywhere equal,
Descends equally on all four sides,
Infusing without measure,
So that the whole earth is filled.
The mountains', rivers', steep valleys',
And cavernous recesses' products of
Grass, trees, and medicinal herbs,
Of trees great and small,
Of a hundred grains, of shoots and plants,
Of sweet potatoes and grapes,
Infused by the rain,
Do not fail to prosper.

Dry earth is everywhere moistened,
  Herbs and trees flourish together.
From the product of that cloud,
  Water of a single flavor,
The grass, the trees, the shrubs, and the forests,
  Each in due portion, receive infusions.
All trees,
  High, intermediate, and low,
In accordance with their size
  Are each enabled to grow,
Their roots, their stalks, their branches, and their leaves,
  Their blossoms and their fruits having luster and color.
What the one rain reaches
  All gains a fresh gloss,
According as its substance, its signs,
  And its natural portion are great or small.
What is infused into all these is one and the same,
  Yet they flourish and prosper severally.
In this way, the Buddha also
  Appears in the world,
As if he were a great cloud
  Universally covering all.
Once having emerged into the world,
  For the sake of living beings
With discrimination he sets forth
  The reality of the dharmas.[3]
The Great Saint, the World-Honored One,
  Among gods and men and
In the midst of all multitudes
  Proclaims these words:
"I am the Thus Come One,
  Venerable among Two-Legged Beings.
Emerging into the world
  Just like a great cloud,
I fully infuse all
  The dried-out beings,

Causing them all to be separated from woe
  And to gain the pleasure of tranquillity,
Worldly pleasure,
  And the pleasure of nirvāṇa.
The multitudes of gods and men,
  Well and single-mindedly listening,
Should all come hither
  To behold the Unexcelled Venerable One.
I am the World-Honored One,
  He whom none can reach.
To put the living beings at their ease,
  For that have I appeared in the world.
For the great multitude I preach
  The Dharma pure as sweet dew,
The Dharma having a single flavor,
  That of deliverance and nirvāṇa.
With a single subtle sound
  I set forth this meaning,
Constantly for the Greater Vehicle's sake
  Giving causes.
I, in viewing all,
  Regard all without exception as equal,
Since I have neither "that" nor "this,"
  Nor any thought of love or hatred.
I have no greed or attachment,
  Nor have I any limitations or encumbrances.
Constantly, and for the sake of all
  Equally, I preach the Dharma,
As for one person,
  So for many.
Constantly I have proclaimed the Dharma,
  Never having any other business,
Going or coming, sitting or standing,
  Never feeling fatigue or disgust.
I have filled the world,
  Just as the rain moistens everything,

Noble and base, superior and inferior,
  Those who keep the discipline and those who violate it,
Those whose bearing is perfect
  And imperfect,
Those of right views and those of wrong views,
  Those of keen faculties and those of dull faculties,
Sending down the Dharma-rain equally
  And never wearying.
Among the living beings
  Those who hear my Dharma,
In accordance with what they are strong enough to accept,
  Dwell on their several grounds.
Some dwell among men, gods,
  Wheel-turning sage-kings,
Śakra, Brahmā, and their several kings:
  These are the lesser medicinal herbs.
Those who know dharmas without outflows,
  Who can attain nirvāṇa,
Who can raise up the six supernatural penetrations
  And attain the three clarities,
Who can dwell alone on mountains and in forests,
  Who constantly practice dhyāna-concentration,
And who contrive to bear direct witness as condition-perceivers—
  These are the intermediate medicinal herbs.[4]
Those who seek the Place of the World-Honored One—
  "We will become Buddhas!"—
Who carry out concentration with earnest striving,
  These are the superior medicinal herbs.
Also, the Buddhas' sons
  Who devote their thoughts exclusively to the Buddha Path,
Who constantly practice good will and compassion,
  Who know that they themselves shall become Buddhas
Decidedly and without any doubt—
  These are called "small trees."
Those who dwell secure in supernatural penetrations,
  Who turn the wheel that does not backslide,

Who ferry across incalculable millions
  Of hundreds of thousands of living beings—
Such bodhisattvas as these
  Are called by the name, "great trees."
The Buddha's undifferentiating preaching
  Is, like the rain, of a single flavor,
In accord with the beings' natures
  Differently received,
Just as what those grasses and trees
  Receive is in every case different.
The Buddha's use of these parables
  And expedient devices to demonstrate
And of a variety of words and phrases
  To set forth the One Dharma
Is to the Buddha's wisdom
  Like one drop of water to the ocean.
I send down the Dharma-rain,
  Filling the world,
And the Dharma of a single flavor
  They put into practice, in accord with their powers,
Just as those shrubs and forests,
  Medicinal herbs and several trees,
In accord with their size
  Gradually increase in florescence and loveliness.
The Dharma of the Buddhas
  By the constant use of a single flavor
Causes the several worlds
  Universally to attain to perfection,
By gradual practice
  All to obtain the Fruit of the Way.
The voice-hearers and condition-perceivers,
  Dwelling on mountains and in forests,
Occupying their final bodies,
  Hearing the Dharma and gaining the fruits—
These are called by the name of medicinal herbs

Which severally gain in growth.
If the bodhisattvas,
Their wisdom firm,
Penetrating the three spheres in their understanding,
Seek the Supreme Vehicle,
These are called "small trees,"
Which gain in growth.
Again, there are those who dwell in dhyāna;
Who gain the strength of supernatural penetration;
Who, hearing of the emptiness of the dharmas,
At heart are overjoyed;
Who, emitting numberless rays,
Ferry across the living beings.
These are called "great trees,"
Which gain in growth.
In this way, O Kāśyapa,
Is the Dharma preached by the Buddha
To be likened to a great cloud,
Which with the rain of a single flavor
Moistens human flowers,
Enabling each to perfect its fruit.
Kāśyapa, let it be known
That, when by invoking causes and conditions
And a variety of parables
I demonstrate the Buddha Path,
This is my expedient device.
The other Buddhas are also this way.
Now, for your sakes,
I preach the most true Reality:
The multitude of voice-hearers
Have in no wise crossed over to extinction.
What you are now treading
Is the bodhisattva-path.
By the gradual cultivation of learning,
You shall all achieve Buddhahood.

[*What has appeared above in chapter 5 is a translation based on Kumārajīva's version. That version, however, lacks the latter half of this chapter, and what appears immediately below is translated directly from the Sanskrit.*]

"Again, O Kāśyapa, the Thus Gone One, in his guidance of the beings, is equitable, not inequitable. O Kāśyapa, just as the light of the sun and the moon illuminates the whole world, both him who does well and him who does ill, both him who stands high and him who stands low, the good-smelling and the bad-smelling, just as that light falls everywhere equally, not unequally, in just that way, O Kāśyapa, does the light of the thought of the knowledge of the All-Knowing, of the Thus Gone Ones, the Worthy Ones, the Properly and Fully Enlightened Ones, the demonstration of the True Dharma, function equally among all beings in the five destinies according to their predispositions, be they persons of the Great Vehicle, persons of the Vehicle of the Individually Enlightened, or persons of the Vehicle of the Auditors. Nor in the light of the knowledge of the Thus Gone One is there either deficiency or superfluity, for the light conduces to knowledge in accord with merit. O Kāśyapa, there are not three vehicles. There are only beings of severally different modes of conduct, and for that reason three vehicles are designated."

When this had been said, the long-lived Mahākāśyapa said to the Blessed One: "If, O Blessed One, there are not three vehicles, what is the reason for the present designation of auditors, individually enlightened, and bodhisattvas?"

When this had been said, the Blessed One said to the long-lived Mahākāśyapa: "It is just as the potter, O Kāśyapa, makes pots with the same clay. Among them, some become pots for sugar lumps, some pots for clarified butter, some pots for curds or milk, while some become pots for inferior and filthy things; and just as there is no difference in the clay, but rather a supposed difference in the pots based solely on the things put into them, in just this way, O Kāśyapa, is there this one and only one vehicle, to wit, the Buddha Vehicle. There exists neither a second nor a third vehicle."

When this had been said, the long-lived Kāśyapa said to the Blessed One: "But if, O Blessed One, the beings who have extricated themselves from the triple sphere are of assorted predispositions, is their nirvāṇa one, or two, or three?"

The Blessed One said: "Nirvāṇa, you see, Kāśyapa, comes from an understanding of the sameness of all dharmas. And it is one, not two and not three. For this reason, you see, Kāśyapa, I will fashion a parable for you. By a single parable men of discernment understand the meaning of what is said.

"Suppose, O Kāśyapa, that there is a man born blind. He speaks as follows: 'There are no sightly or unsightly shapes, nor are there any viewers of sightly or unsightly shapes. There are no sun and moon, there are no stars, there are no planets, nor are there any viewers of planets.'

"Then other men speak as follows in the presence of that congenitally blind man: 'There *are* sightly and unsightly shapes, there are viewers of sightly and unsightly shapes, there are sun and moon, there are stars, there are planets, there are viewers of planets.' But the man born blind does not believe those men, nor does he accept what they say.

"Now there is a certain physician, who knows all ailments. He sees that man born blind. The following occurs to him: 'This man has fallen victim to an ailment thanks to a former evil deed. Whatever ailments arise, they are all of four kinds: rheumatic, bilious, phlegmatic, or due to a derangement of the humors.' Then the physician thinks again and again of a means to put an end to that ailment. The following occurs to him: 'Whatever drugs are current, with them this ailment cannot be treated. But on the Snowy King of Mountains there are four herbs. Which four? The first is named The One Possessed of All Colors, Flavors, and States of Being [?] (*sarvavarṇarasasthānānugatā*); the second is named The One That Brings Release from All Ailments; the third is named The One That Destroys All Poisons; the fourth is named The One That Confers Happiness on Those Standing in the Right Place: these four herbs.' Then the physician, showing compassion for that man born blind, thinks of a device by means of which he is able to go to the Snowy King of Mountains and, having gone, ascend it, then descend it, and also search through it thoroughly. Searching in this way, he finds the four herbs. And, having found them, he gives the blind man one chewed with his teeth, one he gives him pounded, one he gives him cooked in a mixture with other things, one he gives him mixed with other things raw, one he gives him after piercing his body with a lancet, one he gives him after burning it in fire, one he gives him mixed with a variety of things, including even such things as food, drink, and the like.

"Then that man born blind, through the application of those devices, regains his sight. Having regained his sight, he sees externally and internally, far and near, the light of the sun and the moon, the stars, the planets, and all shapes. And he speaks as follows: 'Oh, what a fool I was in not believing those who spoke to me earlier, in not accepting what they said! I now see everything. I am released from blindness! I have regained my sight! There is now no one superior to me.'

"Then at that time there are seers endowed with the five kinds of superknowledge, skilled in the heavenly eye, in the heavenly ear, in the knowledge of the thoughts of others, in the knowledge consisting of recollection of former states of being, in supernatural power, and in the achievement of deliverance. They address that man as follows: 'Sir, you have merely regained your sight, but you do not know anything. Whence comes your arrogance? For you have no wisdom, and you are not learned.' They speak to him in this way: 'When you, Sir, seated in your inner house, neither see nor know other forms outside, nor which beings are well disposed to you, nor which ill disposed; and when you cannot discern, or understand, or hear the sound of a man standing five leagues away and talking, or of a drum, or of a conch shell, or the like; and when you cannot go more than a league without lifting your feet; and when you were born and grew in your mother's womb, and remember none of these acts: in what sense are you wise? And how can you say, "I see everything!?" Very well, Sir! Take darkness for light and light for darkness, if that is what you wish!'

"Then that man addresses those seers as follows: 'By resort to what device, by doing what good deed, may I acquire such wisdom, by your favor acquire these qualities?'

"Then those seers tell the man the following: 'If you wish them, live in the forest; or think of the Dharma, seated in mountain caves! And your defilements are to be forsaken. In that way, endowed with pure qualities, you shall acquire the various kinds of superknowledge.'

"Then that man, having received that meaning, goes forth. Dwelling in the forest, his mind concentrated on a single object, and forsaking his worldly cravings, he gains the five kinds of superknowledge. And, having acquired the various kinds of superknowledge, he thinks: "Whatever other deed I might have done formerly, no good quality ever accrued to me because of it. Now I go wherever I think to go, whereas formerly I was a person of slight wisdom and slight experience, a blind man.' [?] (*pūrvaṃ cāham alpaprajño 'lpapratisaṃvedī andhabhūto 'smy āsīt* //)

"This parable has been fashioned thus, O Kāśyapa, in order to set forth the following meaning; this, moreover, is the point to be seen in it: by those 'born blind,' O Kāsyapa, are meant the beings dwelling in the round of the six destinies, who do not know the True Dharma and who augment the darkness of their own impurities. For they are blind with ignorance, and, being blind with ignorance, heap up predispositions (*saṃskāra*) and, going back to predispositions, name and form, and so on until this whole great mass of suffering has taken shape. In this way the beings, blinded by ignorance, stand in the round of transmigration. But the Thus Gone One, having himself escaped the triple sphere, generates compassion, showing compassion as would a father for a dear and only son; and as he leaves the triple sphere he beholds the beings tumbling about in the round of transmigration. Nor are they aware of an exit from the round. Then the Blessed One sees them with the eye of wisdom. And, seeing them, he knows: 'These beings, having formerly done some good, are of slight hatred and of strong lust, or of slight lust and of strong hatred, some wise, some mature in purity, some of wrong views.' To these beings the Thus Gone One, through his skill in devising expedients, demonstrates the three vehicles. Thereupon, as did those seers with the five kinds of superknowledge and the pure vision, so, too, the bodhisattvas intuit with the intuition of unexcelled and proper enlightenment, producing thoughts of enlightened intuition and accepting [the doctrine of] unproduced dharmas.*

"Therein, just as that great physician was, so is the Thus Gone One to be viewed. Just as was that congenitally blind man, so are the beings, blinded by delusion, to be viewed. Just as were wind, bile, and phlegm, so are lust, hatred, and delusion, as well as the products of the sixty-two views, to be regarded. As were the four herbs, so is the gateway to nirvāṇa, that of the empty, the signless, and the wishless, to be viewed. Whenever medicines are applied, then are the ailments assuaged. In the same way, by realizing the entries into deliverance of emptiness, signlessness, and wishlessness, do the beings suppress ignorance.† From the suppression of ignorance comes the suppression of predispositions, and so on until the suppression of this whole great mass of suffering is achieved. And in this way the thought of the practitioner stands neither in good nor in evil.

"As the blind man who regained his vision was viewed, so should be the person in the vehicle of the auditor or of the individually enlightened. He severs the bonds of the defilements of the round of transmigration. Released from the bond of defilement, he is freed from the triple sphere with its six destinies. In this way the person in the vehicle of the auditor knows and voices the following: 'There are no more dharmas to be intuited! I have attained extinction!'

"Then, indeed, the Thus Gone One demonstrates the Dharma to him: 'Since you have not attained to all the dharmas, whence comes your extinction?' The Blessed One encourages him toward enlightened intuition. The thought of enlightened intuition having been excited within him, he neither stands in the round of transmigration nor attains to extinction. Having understood, he sees the world of the triple sphere

* As was noted earlier, the Sarvāstivāda school asserted that the dharmas emerge and submerge every second, while the Mādhyamikas said that this could no more be asserted than could anything else. Concerning the latter idea the Mahāyāna practioner must reach an intuitive knowledge or gnosis (*jñāna*), but before he can do this he must achieve "acquiescence" (*kṣānti*), i.e., accept the idea on faith.

† Emptiness means the absence of dharmahood in the dharmas; signlessness refers to the lack of significance in what are commonly regarded as signs, specifically in the dharmas; *apraṇihita*, "wishlessness" means that there is nothing in the dharmas on which to premise anything.

in its ten directions as empty, a fabrication, a mock creation, a dream, a mirage, an echo. He sees all dharmas as unoriginated, unsuppressed, unbound, unreleased, not dark, not bright. Whoever sees the profound dharmas in this way, he, with nonvision, sees the whole triple sphere as full, assigned as an abode to a variety of beings." [?]

Then, indeed, the Blessed One, demonstrating this meaning on a larger scale, at that time spoke these verses:

As the light of the sun and the moon falls alike on all men, /
The virtuous as well as the evil, and as in their glow there is no deficiency [for some] or fullness [for others], //45//

So the glow of the Thus Gone One's wisdom, as equitable as the sun and the moon, /
Guides all beings, being neither deficient nor yet excessive. //46//

As a potter may be making clay pots, the pieces of clay being quite the same, /
Yet there take shape in his hand containers of sugar, milk, clarified butter, and water, //47//

Some for filth, while yet others take shape as containers of curds; /
As that potter takes one clay, making pots of it; //48//

And as, whatever thing is put into it, by that thing the pot is designated: /
So to match the distinction among the beings, because of the difference in their inclinations, the Thus Gone Ones //49//

Tell of a difference in vehicles, whereas the Buddha Vehicle is the true one./
Out of ignorance of the wheel of transmigration they do not understand the Blessed Rest. //50//

However, he who understands the dharmas as empty, as devoid of self, /
He understands in its very essence the intuition of the Fully Enlightened Blessed Ones. //51//

The individually victorious is so called because of his middle position in wisdom, /
While the auditor is so called because he lacks knowledge of Emptiness. //52//*

The Perfectly Enlightened, however, is so called because of his understanding of all dharmas; /
Thanks to it, and by resort to hundreds of means, he constantly demonstrates the Dharma to the beings. //53//

For, just as a certain man, born blind and thus of the sun, the moon, the stars, and the planets /
Having no vision, might say, "There are no shapes at all!"; //54//

And as, a great physician, taking pity on that congenitally blind man /
And going across, up, and down the Snowy Range, //55//

Might take herbs from the mountain, The One Possessed of All Colors, Flavors, and States of Being /
And other such, four in all, and put them to use; //56//

As, chewing one with his teeth, pounding another, then yet another, /
Inserting them into a limb on the point of a needle, he might apply them to the man born blind; //57//

And as the latter, regaining his sight, might see the sun, the moon, the stars, and the planets, /
And this might occur to him: "Formerly, I uttered that out of ignorance!": //58//

Just so do the beings, greatly ignorant and congenitally blind, wander about, /

* That is, by "auditor" *is meant* one who lacks knowledge of Emptiness. The *śrāvaka* symbolizes the Hīnayāna, a system in which, according to the Mahayanists, the substancelessness ("emptiness") of the dharmas was not understood. In other words, while the earlier schools, like all Buddhists, denied the existence of a self, except in the most conventional terms, they insisted that the dharmas were real. This latter view was, in fact, nuanced far more than the Mahayanists were willing to admit.

Trapped in woe by their ignorance of the wheel of conditioned production; //59//

Just so, in a world deluded by ignorance, has the Supreme All-Knower, /
The Thus Gone One, the Great Physician, arisen, he of compassionate nature. //60//

A Teacher skilled in means, he demonstrates the True Dharma, /
He demonstrates the Buddha's unexcelled enlightened intuition to those in the Supreme Vehicle. //61//

The Leader reveals the middle [intuition] to the one of middle wisdom, /
While to the one who fears transmigration he describes yet another enlightened intuition. //62//

To the discerning auditor, [who has] escaped from the triple sphere, /
The following occurs: "I have attained spotless, auspicious extinction!" //63//

Thereupon, it is to them that I declare: "This is not the thing called extinction, /
Rather from the understanding of all dharmas is immortal extinction attained!" //64//

Just as the great seers, evincing compassion for him, /
Say to him, "You are a fool! Do not think, 'I am wise.' //65//

When you are within your house, /
You cannot know what happens outside with your slight intelligence. //66//

What is to be known without, whether done or not done, he who is within /
To this day does not know. Whence can *you* know it, O you of slight intelligence? //67//

Whatever sound may be produced about five leagues from here, /

That you are unable to hear, to say nothing of one from far off! //68//

Which men are ill disposed to you, which ones well disposed, /
These it is impossible for you to know. Whence comes your overweening pride? //69//

When but one league is to be walked, there can be no walking without a beaten track. /
Whatever happened in your mother's womb has been forgotten by you, every bit of it. //70//

He who has the five kinds of superknowledge, he is called 'all-knowing,' /
Yet you, ignorant as you are from delusion, say, 'I am all-knowing!' //71//

If you seek All-Knowledge, you should achieve superknowledge. /
Think on this achievement as a forest-dweller. /
You shall gain pure Dharma and, through it, the various kinds of superknowledge"; //72//

And just as he, grasping the meaning and going, quite collected, to the forest, reflects, /
Then, having gained the five kinds of superknowledge, is in no great time endowed with superior qualities: //73//

Just so are all the auditors possessed of the notion that they have attained extinction, /
And then the Victorious One tells such persons that this is mere repose, not Blessed Rest. //74//

It is an expedient device of the Buddhas that they speak in this manner, /
For, apart from All-Knowledge, there is no extinction. Undertake it! //75//

The infinite knowledge of the three periods, and the six pure perfections, /

And emptiness and the signless, and that devoid of plans,*
//76//

And the thought of enlightened intuition, and what other
dharmas lead to extinction, /
Dharmas both with outflows and without, tranquil, all
resembling open space, //77//

The four kinds of brahman-conduct, and what has been much
bruited as methods of attraction: /
For the guidance of the beings these have been proclaimed by
the Supreme Seers. //78//

And he who discerns the dharmas as similar in nature to
dreams and illusions, /
As being as devoid of a core as a bunch of plantains, as being
similar to an echo, //79//

And he who knows that that, too, without exception, is the
nature of the triple sphere, /
And who discerns the Blessed Rest as being neither bound nor
free, //80//

And by whom all dharmas, being the same, and being devoid
of a variety of appearances and natures, /
Are not looked to, nor is any dharma perceived, //81//

He, in his great wisdom, sees the whole Dharma-body, /
For there is no triad of vehicles, but only the One Vehicle.
//82//

"All dharmas are the same, all the same, ever quite the same."
Knowing this, one understands auspicious and immortal
extinction. //83//

The above is the fifth chapter in the Dharma-circuit of the Exalted White Lotus of the True Dharma, the one called the Chapter of Herbs.

* "Devoid of plans" renders *praṇidhānavivarjita*, lit. "devoid of anything on which anything else might be premised or posited." This is another way, dictated by metrical considerations, of saying *apraṇihita*, rendered above with "wishless."

Chapter Six: Bestowal of Prophecy

At that time, having spoken these gāthās, the World-Honored One addressed the great multitude, proclaiming words like these: "This disciple of mine, Mahākāśyapa, in time to come shall have audiences with three hundred myriads of millions of world-honored Buddhas, shall make offerings to them, shall revere, honor, and praise them, shall broadly propagate the Buddhas' great incalculable Dharma, and, in his final body, shall be able to become a Buddha named Ray Glow (Raśmiprabhāsa), a Thus Come One, worthy of offerings, of right and universal knowledge, his clarity and conduct perfect, well gone, understanding the world, an unexcelled Worthy, a Regulator of men of stature, a Teacher of gods and men, a Buddha, a World-Honored One. His realm shall be named Glow Power (Prabhāsaprāptā) his kalpa shall be named Magnificently Accoutered (Mahāvyūha). The Buddha's life-span shall be twelve minor kalpas, his True Dharma shall abide in the world twenty minor kalpas, and his Counterfeit Dharma shall also abide twenty minor kalpas. The territories of his realm shall be well adorned, having no filth or evil, no tiles or pebbles, no thorns or thistles, no excrement or other impurities. Its soil shall be flat and even, having no high or low, no hills or crevices. It shall have vaiḍūrya for earth and jeweled trees in rows. With cords made of gold shall its highways be bordered. It shall be everywhere clean and pure, with jeweled flowers scattered about. The bodhisattvas of that realm shall exist in incalculable thousands of millions, and the multitude of voice-hearers shall also be innumerable. Māra shall have no business there. Though Māra and the subjects of Māra shall be there, they shall all protect the Buddhadharma."

At that time, the World-Honored One, wishing to restate this meaning, proclaimed gāthās, saying:

I declare to the bhikṣus:
  With my Buddha-eye, I
See that this Kāśyapa,
  In ages to come,
Beyond innumerable kalpas,
  Shall be able to become a Buddha:
To wit, that in an age to come,
  Having made offerings to and had audiences with
Three hundred myriads of millions
  Of world-honored Buddhas,
And having, for the sake of Buddha-knowledge,
  Purely cultivated brahman-conduct
And made offerings to the Supremely
  Venerable among Two-Legged Beings,
He shall cultivate and practice all
  Unexcelled knowledge,
And shall, in his last body,
  Be able to become a Buddha.
His land shall be pure,
  With vaiḍūrya for soil,
With many jeweled trees
  In rows by the roadsides,
And with gold cord bordering the highways,
  So that they who see shall rejoice.
It shall ever produce goodly scents
  And be strewn with a multitude of outstanding flowers
Of many varieties and of rare and wonderful beauty,
  With which it shall be adorned.
Its soil shall be flat and even,
  Having no mounds or crevices.
Its multitude of bodhisattvas
  Shall be impossible to reckon,
Their thoughts being tamed and gentle,
  And they themselves having reached great supernatural penetration,
Reverently upholding the Buddhas'

Canon of the Great Vehicle.
The multitude of voice-hearers
In their final body, free of outflows,
Sons of the Dharma King,
Shall also be unreckonable,
For even by resort to a divine eye
It shall not be possible to know their number.
That Buddha shall live
Twelve minor kalpas,
His True Dharma shall abide in the world
Twenty minor kalpas,
And his Counterfeit Dharma shall also abide
Twenty minor kalpas.
As for Ray Glow, the World-Honored One,
This shall be the manner of him.

At that time, the great Maudgalyāyana, Subhūti, and Mahākātyāyana, all greatly agitated, joined palms and, looking up at the World-Honored One, not taking their eyes off him for a moment, straightway together with a single voice proclaimed gāthās, saying:[1]

The greatly fierce and heroic World-Honored One,
The Dharma King of the Śākyas,
Because he took pity on us
Conferred on us the sound of the Buddha's voice.
If, knowing our deepest thoughts
And perceiving that we are the recipients of this prophecy,
He sprinkles sweet dew on us,
He will thereby rid us of oppressive heat, and we shall be cool.[2]
As if, coming from a famished land
And suddenly encountering a great king's feast,
One still harbored doubts and fears in one's thoughts,
Not yet daring to eat without further ado,
Or as if, again, one had to get the king's permission,
And then and only then would dare to eat,

We, too, in the same way,
  Ever thinking of the errors of the Lesser Vehicle,
Do not know how we are
  To gain the Buddha's unexcelled knowledge.
Though we hear the sound of the Buddha's voice
  Saying that we shall become Buddhas,
In our thoughts we still harbor cares and fears,
  As if we dared not yet eat.
If we receive the Buddha's gift of his prophecy,
  Only then shall we be quickly put at ease.
O greatly fierce and heroic World-Honored One,
  Who constantly desire to put the world at ease,
We beg you to confer this prophecy upon us,
  As if we were hungry men awaiting permission to eat!

At that time, the World-Honored One, knowing what the great disciples were thinking at heart, declared to the bhikṣus: "This Subhūti in ages to come shall have audiences with three hundred myriad millions of *nayutas* [a *nayuta* is 100 million] of Buddhas, shall make offerings to them and venerate them, shall honor and praise them, and shall ever cultivate brahman-conduct and perfect the bodhisattva-path, in his final body contriving to become a Buddha named Name Sign, [*sic*; Skt. has Śaśiketu, "moon sign"], a Thus Come One, worthy of offerings, of right and universal knowledge, his clarity and conduct perfect, well gone, understanding the world, an unexcelled Worthy, a Regulator of men of stature, a Teacher of gods and men, a Buddha, a World-Honored One. His kalpa shall be named Having Jewels (Ratnāvabhāsa), and his realm shall be named Birthplace of Jewels (Ratnasaṃbhava). Its soil shall be flat and even. It shall have sphāṭika for earth and shall be adorned with jeweled trees. It shall have no mounds or crevices, no pebbles or thorns, no filth or excrement. Its soil covered with jeweled flowers, it shall be everywhere clean and pure. The people of that land shall all dwell in rare and wondrous towers on jeweled terraces. Its voice-hearing disciples shall be incalculable and limitless, such as cannot be known by resort to either number or parable. Its multitude of bodhisattvas shall be in the numberless thousands of myriads of millions of nayutas. That Buddha's life-span shall be twelve minor kalpas. His True Dharma shall abide in the world twenty minor kalpas, and his Counterfeit Dharma shall also abide twenty minor kalpas. That Buddha shall ever dwell in empty space, preaching the Dharma for the multitude, saving incalculable bodhisattvas and multitudes of voice-hearers."

At that time, the World-Honored One, wishing to restate this meaning, proclaimed gāthās, saying:

O multitude of bhikṣus,
  I now inform you;
You must all single-mindedly
  Listen to what I say:
My great disciple
  Subhūti
Shall be able to become a Buddha,
  Whose name shall be Name Sign.
He shall make offerings to countless
  Myriads of millions of Buddhas.
Following the Buddha's course of conduct,
  He shall at length perfect the Great Path,
In his final body gaining
  The thirty-two marks,
Becoming straight, upright, and of wondrous beauty,
  Quite like a jeweled mountain.
His Buddha-land
  Shall be first among the purely adorned,
And, of the living beings who see him,
  None but shall love and desire him.
Within his Buddhadharma,
  Many bodhisattvas,
All without exception being of keen faculties,
  Shall turn the wheel that has no backsliding.
That realm shall ever be with
  Bodhisattvas adorned.
The multitude of voice-hearers
  Shall be innumerable,

All having gained the three clarities,
  Having perfected the six supernatural penetrations,
Dwelling in the eight deliverances,
  And having great and imposing excellences.
In his preaching of the Dharma that Buddha
  Shall display incalculable
Supernatural penetrations and magical powers,
  Not to be conceived or discussed.
The gods and human subjects,
  In number like to Ganges' sands,
Shall all, together joining palms,
  Listen receptively to the Buddha's words.[3]
That Buddha shall live
  Twelve minor kalpas,
His True Dharma shall abide in the world
  Twenty minor kalpas,
And his Counterfeit Dharma shall also abide
  Twenty minor kalpas.

At that time, the World-Honored One again declared to the bhikṣus: "I now tell you that in an age to come, with divers implements this Great Kātyāyana shall make offerings to and reverently serve eight thousand millions of Buddhas, doing them deference and honor. After the Buddhas' extinction, for each he shall erect a stūpa-shrine, whose height shall be a thousand yojanas, whose length and breadth shall be each five hundred yojanas, and which shall be filled with gold, silver, vaiḍūrya, giant clam shell, agate, pearl, and carnelian, these precious seven. With a multitude of flower garlands, paint-scent, powdered scent, burnt incense, cotton canopies, and banners shall he make offerings to those stūpa-mausoleums.[4] When that [time] is past, he shall again make offerings to two myriads of millions of Buddhas, in the same way. Having made offerings to these Buddhas, he shall perfect the bodhisattva-path, and shall be able to become a Buddha named Jāmbūnada Gold* Glow

* See footnote to page 252.

(Jāmbūnadaprabhāsa), a Thus Come One, worthy of offerings, of right and universal knowledge, his clarity and conduct perfect, well gone, understanding the world, an unexcelled Worthy, a Regulator of men of stature, a Teacher of gods and men, a Buddha, a World-Honored One. His land shall be flat and even, with sphāṭika for soil, adorned with jeweled trees, with cords made of gold bordering its highways, its ground covered by lovely flowers, so that it is everywhere clean and pure, and so that they who see it shall rejoice. It shall have none of the four evil destinies, to wit, hell, hungry ghosts, beasts, or asuras. It shall have many gods and men; and multitudes of voice-hearers, as well as bodhisattvas, in the incalculable myriads of millions shall adorn that realm. The Buddha's life-span shall be twelve minor kalpas, his True Dharma shall abide in the world twenty minor kalpas, and his Counterfeit Dharma shall also abide twenty minor kalpas."

At that time, the World-Honored One, wishing to restate this meaning, proclaimed gāthās, saying:

You multitude of bhikṣus,
  Listen, all of you, with a single mind!
As is what I preach,
  So is the truth, no different.
This Kātyāyana
  Shall, with a variety
Of wondrously fair implements,
  Make offerings to Buddhas.
After the Buddhas' extinction,
  He shall erect stūpas of the seven jewels,
And also with flowers and scents
  Make offerings to their śarīra.
In his last body
  He shall gain Buddha-knowledge
And achieve undifferentiating and right intuition,
  His land being clean and pure.
He shall save incalculable
  Myriads of millions of living beings,
From all of whom from all ten sides he shall

Receive offerings.
That Buddha's radiance
None shall be able to exceed.
That Buddha's name shall be called
Jāmbū Gold Glow.[5]
Bodhisattvas and voice-hearers
Who have severed all being,
Incalculable and innumerable, shall
Adorn his realm.

At that time, the World-Honored One again declared to the great multitude: "I now tell you that this Great Maudgalyāyana with divers implements shall make offerings to eight thousand Buddhas, doing them deference and honor. After the Buddhas' extinction, for each he shall erect a stūpa-mausoleum, whose height shall be a thousand yojanas, whose length and breadth shall be each five hundred yojanas, and which shall be filled with gold, silver, vaiḍūrya, giant clam shell, agate, pearl, and carnelian, these precious seven. With a multitude of flower garlands, paint-scent, powdered scent, burnt incense, cotton canopies, and banners he shall make offerings. When that [time] is past, he shall again make offerings to two hundred myriads of millions of Buddhas, in the same way, and shall be able to achieve Buddhahood. His name shall be Tamālapatracandana [garcinia and sandalwood] Fragrance (Tamālapatracandanagandha), a Thus Come One, worthy of offerings, of right and universal knowledge, his clarity and conduct perfect, well gone, understanding the world, an unexcelled Worthy, a Regulator of men of stature, a Teacher of gods and men, a Buddha, a World-Honored One. His kalpa shall be named Full of Joy (Ratipūrṇa), and his realm shall be named Mind-Pleasing (Manobhirāma). Its ground shall be flat and even, with sphāṭika for soil, adorned with jeweled trees, strewn with pearl flowers, everywhere clean and pure, so that they who see it shall rejoice. It shall have many gods and men, and its bodhisattvas and voice-hearers shall be of incalculable number. The Buddha's life-span shall be twenty-four minor kalpas, his True Dharma shall abide in the world forty minor kalpas, and his Counterfeit Dharma shall also abide forty minor kalpas."

At that time, the World-Honored One, wishing to restate this meaning, proclaimed gāthās, saying:

This my disciple,
  Great Maudgalyāyana,
Having shed this body,
  Shall be enabled to see eight thousand
Two hundred myriads of millions
  Of world-honored Buddhas,
For the sake of the Buddha Path
  Making them offerings and doing them honor.
Before the Buddhas
  He shall ever cultivate brahman-conduct,
And for incalculable kalpas
  Reverently uphold the Buddhadharma.
After the Buddhas' extinction
  He shall erect stūpas of the seven jewels,
Making long displays of golden *chattras* [parasols],
  Flowers, incense, and skillfully played music,
Therewith to make offerings
  To the Buddhas' stūpa-shrines.
Having at length perfected
  The bodhisattva-path,
In the realm Mind-Pleasing
  He shall be able to become a Buddha
Named Tamāla-
  Candana's Fragrance.
That Buddha's life-span
  Being twenty-four kalpas,
Ever for gods and men
  Shall he set forth the Buddha Path.
Voice-hearers as incalculable
  As Ganges' sands,
With the three clarities and six penetrations
  And with great imposing excellence,
And bodhisattvas innumerable,

Of firm resolve and earnest effort,
With respect to Buddha-knowledge shall
All be nonbacksliders.
After the Buddha's passage into extinction,
His True Dharma shall abide
Forty minor kalpas,
And his Counterfeit Dharma the same.
My disciples,
Their imposing excellence perfect,
Their number five hundred,
Shall all be granted prophecies
That in ages to come
They shall all be able to achieve Buddhahood.
My own and all your
Causes and conditions from former ages
I now will tell:
All of you, listen well!

Chapter Seven: Parable of the Conjured City

The Buddha declared to the bhikṣus: "Long ago, beyond incalculable, limitless, inconceivable and unutterable asaṃkhyeyakalpas, at that time there was a Buddha named Victorious through Great Penetrating Knowledge (Mahābhijñājñānābhibhū), a Thus Come One, worthy of offerings, of right and universal knowledge, his clarity and conduct perfect, well gone, understanding the world, an unexcelled Worthy, a Regulator of men of stature, a Teacher of gods and men, a Buddha, a World-Honored One. His realm was named Goodly City (Saṃbhavā). His kalpa was named Great Appearance (Mahārūpa). Bhikṣus! Since that Buddha passed into extinction in a remote age, the time has been great and long indeed. For example, suppose a hypothetical man took all the kinds of earth there are in the thousand-millionfold world and ground them to ink powder, and after carrying the powder through a thousand lands at last deposited a bit the size of a particle of dust, then after passing through another thousand lands deposited another particle, and so on depositing them a bit at a time until all the particles had been exhausted. In your opinion, how would it be? Where these lands are concerned, could an abacus master or his disciple ever reach the limit of these lands and know their number, or could he not?"

"He could not, O World-Honored One."

"O bhikṣus! If the lands this man passed through, whether he made a deposit in them or not, were all ground to dust, and if each grain of dust were to equal one kalpa, the time since that Buddha's passage into extinction would still exceed their full number by incalculable, limitless hundreds of thousands of myriads of millions of asaṃkhyeya-kalpas. Thanks to the Thus Come One's power of knowledge and insight, I see that time in the remote and distant past as if it were this very day."

At that time, the World-Honored One, wishing to restate this meaning, proclaimed gāthās, saying:

I recall that in an age gone by,
  Incalculable, limitless kalpas ago,
There was a Buddha, One Venerable among Two-Legged
    Beings,
  Whose name was Victorious through Great Penetrating
    Knowledge.
If with all his might a man were to grind
  The soil of the thousand-millionfold world,
Using up all kinds of earth
  And reducing them all without exception to powdered ink,
Then to pass through a thousand lands
  And only then deposit a single grain,
In this way going from place to place and making deposits
  Until he had exhausted all these grains of powdered ink,
And if lands equal in number to these,
  Those in which deposits both were and were not made,
Were, further, to be completely reduced to dust,
  One grain of dust to equal one kalpa,
These grains of dust would in number
  Be exceeded by the kalpas
Since that Buddha's passage into extinction;
  It has been kalpas incalculable as those.
The Thus Come One, in his unobstructed wisdom,
  Knows that Buddha's passage into extinction
And his voice-hearers and bodhisattvas
  As if seeing a passage into extinction but now.
Let the bhikṣus know
  That Buddha-knowledge is pure and subtle,
Without outflows and unobstructed,
  Penetrating incalculable kalpas.

The Buddha declared to the bhikṣus: "The Buddha Victorious through Great Penetrating Knowledge had a life-span of five hundred and forty myriad millions of nayutas of kalpas. When that Buddha was seated on the Platform of the Way, after having smashed Māra's army, just as he was about to gain anuttarasamyaksaṃbodhi, still the Buddhadharmas did not appear before him. In this way, from one minor kalpa up through ten minor kalpas he sat cross-legged, body and mind immobile; yet the Buddhadharmas still did not appear before him.

"At that time, the Trāyastriṃśa gods [Indra and his thirty-three] prepared for that Buddha, under the bodhi tree, a lion throne, one yojana in height; for on that throne the Buddha was to attain anuttarasamyaksaṃbodhi. Just when he sat on that throne, the Brahmā god kings rained down a multitude of divine flowers, the surface of each being a hundred yojanas. A fragrant wind sprang up at that time, blew away the wilted flowers, and rained down new ones, for full ten minor kalpas ceaselessly making offerings to the Buddha in this way, raining down these flowers until the very moment of his passage into extinction. The gods in the train of the Four Kings as an offering to the Buddha constantly beat divine drums, while the other gods in the very same way played skillful divine music for full ten minor kalpas, until his passage into extinction.

"O bhikṣus! Only after the Buddha Victorious through Great Penetrating Knowledge had passed ten minor kalpas [in this way] did the Dharma of the Buddhas appear before him, and only then did he achieve anuttarasamyaksaṃbodhi. Before that Buddha left his household he had had sixteen sons, of whom the first was named Knowledge Accumulation (Jñānākara). The children each had a variety of rare, precious, excellent playthings. When they heard that their father had been able to achieve anuttarasamyaksaṃbodhi, they all cast aside the things to which they had attached such great value and went before the Buddha. Their mothers, shedding tears, accompanied them. Their grandfathers, wheel-turning sage-kings, with a hundred great ministers and a hundred thousand myriads of millions of subjects all together surrounding them, accompanied them to the Platform of the Path, wishing personally to approach the Thus Come One Victorious through Great Penetrating Knowledge to make offerings and do honor to him, to revere and praise him. When they arrived, with heads bowed they did obeisance to his feet, and having circumambulated him, single-mindedly and with palms joined they looked up at the World-Honored One and praised him with gāthās, saying:

O World-Honored One of great imposing might!
  In order to save the living beings,
Only after incalculable millions of years had run their course
  Did you achieve Buddhahood.
Your vows have now been fulfilled.
  Excellent, O Supremely Fortunate One!
World-Honored One, you are very rare!
  For, once you are seated, for ten minor kalpas
Your body, your arms and legs,
  Quiet and calm, do not move;
Your thought, ever serene,
  Never suffers any disturbance;
Quiet and extinct to absolute eternity,
  You dwell securely in the Dharma free of outflows.
Now that we see the World-Honored One
  Serenely achieve the Buddha Path,
We have gained good advantage;
  Proclaiming our delight, we are overjoyed.
The living beings, ever tormented by pain,
  Blind and without a guide,
Do not recognize the Path wherein pain is terminated,
  Nor do they know enough to seek deliverance.
Throughout the long night of time they gain in evil destinies
  And reduce the ranks of the gods.*
From darkness proceeding to darkness,
  They never hear the Buddha's name.
Now that the Buddha has gained the supremely
  Serene Dharma free of outflows,
We and the gods and men,
  In order to gain the greatest advantage,

* That is, they are reincarnated into the lower destinies and thus reduce the number of beings reborn as gods.

For this purpose, all bowing our heads,
  Submit to the Supremely Venerable One.

"At that time, the sixteen princes, having praised the Buddha with gāthās, urgently pleaded with the World-Honored One to turn the Dharma-wheel, all saying: 'World-Honored One! Preach the Dharma, and thus calm, have pity on, and benefit many subjects, divine and human.'[1] Repeating it, they proclaimed gāthās, saying:

Hero of the World, who have no equal,
  Self-adorned with a hundred merits,
Who have gained unexcelled knowledge,
  We beg you, for the world's sake, to preach,
To ferry to salvation us
  And the several species of living beings,
For all our sakes to make explicit revelation,
  Thus enabling us to gain this knowledge.
For, if we can attain Buddhahood,
  Then so can other living beings.
The World-Honored One knows the beings'
  Deepest constant thoughts;
He also knows the paths they tread;
  He knows as well the power of their knowledge,
Their desires and the merits they cultivate,
  And also the deeds they did in former lives.
The World-Honored One, knowing all this,
  Should turn the Unexcelled Wheel."

The Buddha declared to the bhikṣus: "When the Buddha Victorious through Great Penetrating Knowledge attained anutta-samyaksaṃbodhi, in each of the ten directions five hundred myriads of millions of Buddha-worlds trembled in six different ways, and in the intervals between those lands, dark and obscure places that the glorious light of the sun and moon could not illuminate were all very bright. The living beings within them were all enabled to see one another, and all said: 'Why has this place suddenly produced living beings?' Also, the palaces of the gods within the territories of those realms, up through the Brahmā palaces, shook in six different ways, and a great light, shining everywhere, filled the world, exceeding the glow of the gods themselves.

"At that time, in five hundred myriads of millions of lands to the east, the palaces of the Brahmā gods were aglow with twice their usual splendor, and the Brahmās, the god kings, each had this thought: 'Now the palaces glow as they never have before. For what reason do they show this portent?' At this time, the Brahmās, the god kings, visited one another and discussed this matter together.

"At that time, there was a great Brahmā god king named Rescuing All (Sarvasattvatrātṛ), who for the sake of the Brahmā multitudes proclaimed gāthās, saying:

Our palaces
  Are aglow as never before.
What the reason for this may be,
  Each of us should seek to learn.
Is it because a god of great power has been born,
  Or because a Buddha has emerged into the world,
That this great glow
  Shines everywhere, in all ten directions?

"At that time, the Brahmā god kings of five hundred myriads of millions of lands, together with their palace retinues, each god king putting divine flowers atop a cloth spread, went together to the west to seek this portent. They saw the Thus Come One Victorious through Great Penetrating Knowledge on the Platform of the Path under the bodhi tree, seated on a lion throne, the gods, dragon kings, gandharvas, kinnaras, mahoragas, humans and nonhumans deferentially surrounding him. And they saw the sixteen princes begging the Buddha to turn the Dharma-wheel. Straightway the Brahmā god kings with heads bowed worshiped the Buddha, circumambulated him a hundred thousand times, then scattered divine flowers over him, the [mound of] flowers being like Mount Sumeru. They also made offerings therewith to the Buddha's bodhi tree, the bodhi tree being ten yojanas in height. When they had made flower offerings, each presented a palace to that Buddha, and said: 'Do but show us compassion and favor! Deign, we pray you, to accept these and to occupy them!'

"At that time the Brahmā god kings straightway in the Buddha's presence with a single thought and with a common voice praised him, saying:

The World-Honored One is very rare;
  Only with difficulty can he be encountered.
Fully endowed with incalculable merits,
  He can rescue and preserve all.
The great teacher of gods and men,
  He takes pity on the world,
And living beings in the ten directions
  All everywhere receive his favors.
Whence we have come,
  In those five hundred myriads of millions of lands,
We have abandoned the joys of deep dhyāna-concentration
  In order to make offerings to the Buddha.
With our merits of former ages
  Are these palaces much adorned.
Now we present them to the World-Honored One,
  And beg him mercifully to accept them.[2]

"At that time, all the Brahmā god kings, having praised the Buddha with gāthās, said: 'We beg the World-Honored One to turn the Dharma-wheel, to rescue the beings, and to open the Way to nirvāṇa!' At that time the Brahmā god kings with a single thought and with a common voice proclaimed gāthās, saying:

Hero of the World, Venerable among Two-Legged Beings!
  We beg you to set forth the Dharma,
By the might of your great good will and compassion
  Saving the woe-beset, agonized living beings!

"At that time, the Thus Come One Victorious through Great Penetrating Knowledge consented silently. O bhikṣus, the great Brahmā kings in five hundred myriads of millions of lands in the southeast, every one of them seeing the palaces radiant with glow, as they had never been before, danced for joy, evincing the thought that this had never been before. Then, straightway visiting one another, they discussed this matter together. At that time, there was in that multitude a great Brahmā god king named Greatly Compassionate, who for the sake of the Brahmā multitudes proclaimed gāthās, saying:[3]

> In this matter, for what reason
> Are these signs revealed?
> Our palaces
> Glow as never before.
> Is it that a god of great merit has been born?
> Or is it that a Buddha has emerged in the world?
> Never before have we seen such signs!
> We must trace them together, with a single thought,
> Crossing a thousand myriads of millions of lands,
> Seeking the glow and investigating it together.
> It is most likely that a Buddha has emerged in the world
> To convey woe-smitten living beings to deliverance.

"At that time, the Brahmā god kings of five hundred myriads of millions of lands, together with their palace retinues, each putting divine flowers atop a cloth spread, went together to the northwest to seek this portent. They saw the Thus Come One Victorious through Penetrating Knowledge on the Platform of the Path under the bodhi tree, seated on a lion throne, the gods, dragon kings, gandharvas, kinnaras, mahoragas, humans and nonhumans deferentially surrounding him. And they saw the sixteen princes begging the Buddha to turn the Dharma-wheel. Straightway the Brahmā god kings with heads bowed worshiped the Buddha, circumambulated him a hundred thousand times, then scattered divine flowers over him, the [mound of] flowers being like Mount Sumeru. They also made offerings therewith to the Buddha's bodhi tree. When they had made flower offerings, each presented a palace to that Buddha, and said: 'Do but show us compassion and favor! Deign, we pray you, to accept these and to occupy them!' Then in the Buddha's presence with a single thought and with a common voice they praised him in gāthās, saying:

O Sainted Lord! O God among gods!
  O you with the voice of a *kalaviṅka!* [Indian cuckoo]
O you who take pity on the beings!
  We now salute you!
The World-Honored One is very rare,
  For only in long intervals of time does he appear, and then but once.
One hundred and eighty
  Kalpas have gone by empty, without a Buddha,
The three evil courses being full,
  The multitude of gods few and decreasing.
Now a Buddha has emerged into the world,
  Acting as eyes for the living beings,
One to whom the world turns,
  One who rescues and preserves all,
A Father to the living beings,
  Who bestows pity and advantage on them.
As a blessing on our former merit,
  Now we have been enabled to encounter a World-Honored One.

"At that time, all the Brahmā god kings, having praised the Buddha in gāthās, said: 'We beg the World-Honored One, out of pity for all, to turn the Dharma-wheel, to convey the beings to deliverance.'

"At that time, the Brahmā god kings with a single thought and with a common voice proclaimed gāthās, saying:[4]

O Great Saint! Turn the Dharma-wheel,
  Displaying the marks of the dharmas,
Saving the woe-smitten, agonized beings,
  And causing them to gain great joy!
If the beings hear this Dharma,
  Gaining the Path, they may be reborn as gods. [?]

The evil destinies shall diminish,
  And those of good forbearance shall increase. [?]

"At that time, the Thus Come One Victorious through Great Penetrating Knowledge consented silently. O bhikṣus, the great Brahmā kings in five hundred myriads of millions of lands in the south, every one of them seeing the palaces radiant with glow, as they had never been before, danced for joy, evincing the thought that this had never been before. Then, straightway visiting one another, they discussed this matter together: 'For what reason do our palaces have this glow?' Then, there was in that multitude a great Brahmā god king named Fine Dharma, who for the sake of the Brahmā multitude proclaimed gāthās, saying:[5]

Our palaces,
  Aglow, have a most imposing luster.
This cannot be without a cause.
  This is a portent we should trace.
In more than a hundred thousand kalpas
  We have never seen such a portent.
Is it that a god of great power has been born,
  Or that a Buddha has emerged in the world?

"At that time, five hundred myriads of millions of Brahmā god kings, together with their palace retinues, each putting divine flowers atop a cloth spread, went together to the north to seek this portent. They saw the Thus Come One Victorious through Great Penetrating Knowledge on the Platform of the Path under the bodhi tree, seated on a lion throne, the gods, dragon kings, gandharvas, kinnaras, mahoragas, humans and nonhumans deferentially surrounding him. And they saw the sixteen princes begging the Buddha to turn the Dharma-wheel. Straightway the Brahmā god kings with heads bowed worshiped the Buddha, circumambulated him a hundred thousand times, then scattered divine flowers over him, the [mound of] flowers being like Mount Sumeru. They also made offerings therewith to the Buddha's bodhi tree. When they had made flower offerings, each presented a palace to that Buddha, and said: 'Do but show us compassion and favor! Deign, we pray you, to accept the palaces we offer.'

"At that time, the Brahmā god kings straightway in the Buddha's presence with a single thought and with a common voice praised him in gāthās, saying:

> The World-Honored One, so very difficult to see,
>   Him who demolishes the agonies,
> After the passage of a hundred and thirty kalpas
>   We have now, at last, contrived to see but once.
> The hungry and thirsty beings
>   O satiate with Dharma-rain!
> Him whom we had never before seen,
>   The One of incalculable wisdom,
> Who is like an udumbara flower,
>   This day, at last, we have met.
> Our palaces,
>   Adorned by the glow they have received,
> O World-Honored One, O you of great good will and compassion,
>   We beg you to deign to accept.

"At that time, all the Brahmā god kings, having praised the Buddha, in gāthās, said: 'We beg the World-Honored One to turn the Dharma-wheel, enabling the gods, Māras, Brahmās, śramaṇas, and Brahmans in all the worlds to achieve serenity and to gain passage to deliverance.'

"At the time, the Brahmā god kings with a single thought and with a common voice praised him in gāthās, saying:

> We beg the Venerable One among Gods and Men
>   To turn the wheel of the unexcelled Dharma,
> To beat the drum of the great Dharma,
>   And to blow the conch shell of the great Dharma,
> Everywhere sending down great Dharma-rain
>   And saving incalculable living beings.

We all submissively beg
  That you utter a profound and far-reaching sound!

"At that time, the Thus Come One Victorious through Great Penetrating Knowledge silently assented.

"So it was in all directions, from the southwest down through the lower quarter.

"At that time, the great Brahmā god kings in five hundred myriads of millions of lands in the upper quarter, all without exception seeing with their own eyes that the palaces in which they dwelt were radiant with glow as they had never been before, danced for joy, evincing a rare feeling. Straightway visiting one another, they discussed this matter together: 'For what reason do our palaces have this glow?'

"Then in that multitude was a great Brahmā god king whose name was Śikhin. For the sake of the Brahmā multitude he proclaimed gāthās, saying:

Now for what reason
  Do our palaces
Shine with a radiant glow,
  Adorned as never before?
Wondrous portents like these
  Are such as formerly we neither saw nor heard.
Is it that a god of great power has been born,
  Or is it that a Buddha has emerged in the world?

"At that time, five hundred myriads of millions of Brahmā god kings, together with their palace retinues, each putting divine flowers atop a cloth spread, went together to the lower quarter to seek this portent. They saw the Thus Come One Victorious through Great Penetrating Knowledge on the Platform of the Path under the bodhi tree, seated on a lion throne, the gods, dragon kings, gandharvas, kinnaras, mahoragas, humans and nonhumans deferentially surrounding him. And they saw the sixteen princes begging the Buddha to turn the Dharma-wheel. At that time the Brahmā god kings with heads bowed worshiped the Buddha, circumambulated him a hundred thousand times, then scattered divine flowers over him, the [mound of] flowers being like Mount Sumeru. They also made offerings therewith to the Buddha's bodhi tree. When they had made flower offerings, each presented a palace to that Buddha, and said: 'Do but show us compassion and favor! Deign, we pray you, to accept and occupy the palaces we offer.'

"At that time, the Brahmā god kings straightway in the Buddha's presence with a single thought and with a common voice praised him in gāthās, saying:

How good to see the Buddhas,
  The venerable Saints who save the world,
And who can from the prison of the three spheres
  Release the living beings!
The Venerable One among Gods and Men, he of all-encompassing wisdom,
  In his pity for the many varieties of buds,
Is able to open the ambrosial gates
  And broadly save all.
For incalculable kalpas since antiquity,
  Time has passed vainly without a Buddha.
Before the World-Honored One emerged,
  The ten directions were constantly obscured by darkness,
The three evil courses were growing,
  Also the asuras were thriving,
And the multitudes of gods were ever decreasing,
  Most of them descending after death into evil destinies.
Not hearing the Dharma from the Buddha,
  They were ever doing unwholesome deeds.
Their physical strength, their wisdom,
  And things of this sort were all diminishing. [?]
By reason of their sinful deeds
  They lost pleasure and the idea of pleasure.
Dwelling in the dharma of wrong views,
  They did not recognize the rules of wholesomeness.
Not being party to the Buddha's conversion,

They were constantly descending into evil destinies.
But the Buddha is the Eye of the World;
Only at long intervals does he emerge.
It is out of pity for the living beings
That he appears in the world,
Then transcends it, achieving right, enlightened intuition.[6]
We are exceeding glad,
We and all the other multitudes.
We sigh in joy at this which has never been before.
Our palaces
Are adorned by the glow bestowed up on them.
Now we present them to the World-Honored One:
Deign, out of kindness, to accept them.
We beg to take this merit
And spread it universally to all,
We with the living beings
All together achieving the Buddha Path.

"At that time, all the five hundred myriads of millions of Brahmā god kings, having praised the Buddha in gāthās, addressed the Buddha, saying: 'We beg the World-Honored One to turn the Dharma-wheel, putting many at their ease and conveying many to deliverance.'

"At that time the Brahmā god kings proclaimed gāthās, saying:

O World-Honored One! Turn the Dharma-wheel!
Beat the drum of the Dharma that is like sweet dew!
Save the woe-beset and agonized living beings!
Reveal the Path of nirvāṇa!
We beg you to accept our entreaty,
With great, fine sounds
To favor us, and to set forth
The Dharma you have perfected through incalculable kalpas.

"At that time, the Thus Come One Victorious through Great Penetrating Knowledge, entertaining the entreaties of the great Brahmā god kings of the ten directions, as well as those of the sixteen princes, at that very time thrice turned the Dharma-wheel of twelve spokes, which neither śramaṇas nor Brahmans, nor gods, nor Māras, nor Brahmās, nor inhabitants of other worlds can turn, namely: this is woe, this is the collection of woe, this is the extinction of woe, this is the road to that extinction; also the dharma of the twelve causes and conditions: Inclarity conditions actions, actions condition cognition, cognition conditions name and visible form, name and visible form condition the six entries, the six entries condition contact, contact conditions sensation, sensation conditions greed, greed conditions seizure, seizure conditions being, being conditions old age, death, care, grief, woe, and anguish. When inclarity is extinguished, then actions are extinguished; when actions are extinguished, then cognition is extinguished; when cognition is extinguished, then name and visible form are extinguished; when name and visible form are extinguished, then the six entries are extinguished; when the six entries are extinguished, then contact is extinguished; when contact is extinguished, then sensation is extinguished; when sensation is extinguished, then greed is extinguished; when greed is extinguished, then seizure is extinguished; when seizure is extinguished, then being is extinguished; when being is extinguished, then birth is extinguished; when birth is extinguished, then old age, death, care, grief, woe, and anguish are extinguished.

"When the Buddha, in the midst of a great multitude of gods and men, was preaching this Dharma, six hundred myriads of millions of nayutas of human beings, because they would not accept any dharmas, had their thoughts freed from all outflows, and all gained profound and subtle dhyāna-concentration, the three clarities, and the six penetrations, and were fully endowed with the eight deliverances.

"When he delivered the second, third, and fourth Dharma sermons, living beings equal in number to a thousand myriads of millions, times the number of sands in the Ganges, times a nayuta, because they would not accept any dharmas, also had their thoughts freed from all outflows. Thereafter the multitude of voice-hearers was incalculable, limitless, not to be counted.

"At that time, the sixteen princes, all as boys, left their household and became *śrāmaṇeras* [Buddhist novices], their faculties keen and penetrating, their wisdom pellucid, having already made offerings to a hundred thousand myriads of millions of Buddhas, purely cultivated brahman-conduct, and sought anuttarasamyaksaṃbodhi. All addressed the Buddha, saying: 'O World-Honored One! For our sakes, too, you should preach the anuttarasamyaksaṃbodhi-dharma. When we have heard it, we shall all cultivate learning together. World-Honored One! We aspire to the World-Honored One's knowledge and insight. What our deep thoughts are pondering, of that the Buddha himself has direct knowledge.'

"At that time, within a multitude led by the wheel-turning sage-king, eight myriads of millions of men, seeing that the sixteen princes had left their household, also sought to leave their households. The king straightway allowed them to do so.[7]

"At that time, that Buddha, entertaining the śrāmaṇeras' entreaty, when twenty thousand kalpas had passed, in the midst of the fourfold multitude finally preached this scripture of the Great Vehicle named the Lotus Blossom of the Fine Dharma, a Dharma taught to bodhisattvas, one which Buddhas keep in mind.

"When he had preached this scripture, the sixteen śrāmaṇeras, for anuttarasamyaksaṃbodhi's sake, all together received and held it, committed it to memory and recited it, and sharply penetrated its meaning.

"When he preached this scripture, the sixteen bodhisattva-śrāmaṇeras all received it with faith. Among the voice-hearers also were some who were inclined to it. But the remainder of the multitudinous beings, in their thousands of myriads of millions of varieties, all evinced doubts.

"That Buddha preached this scripture for eight thousand kalpas, never resting or tiring. When he had finished preaching this scripture, straightway he entered a quiet room, where he remained in dhyāna-concentration for eighty-four thousand kalpas.

"At that time, each of the sixteen bodhisattva-śrāmaṇeras, knowing that the Buddha had entered his room, where he was quietly concentrated in dhyāna, ascended a Dharma-throne, where he also, throughout eighty-four thousand kalpas and for the sake of the four assemblies, broadly explained and set forth distinctly the Scripture of the Blossom of the Fine Dharma, each conveying to salvation living beings equal in number to the sands of six hundred myriads of millions of nayutas of Ganges rivers, demonstrating and teaching, giving profit and joy, and enabling the beings to evince the anuttarasamyaksaṃbodhi-mind.

"When the Buddha Victorious through Great Penetrating Knowledge had passed through eighty-four thousand kalpas, he arose from his samādhi and approached his Dharma-throne, where he sat in composure. Then he declared equally to all the great multitude: 'These sixteen bodhisattva-śrāmaṇeras are exceeding rare, their faculties penetrating and keen and their wisdom pellucid, they themselves having already in times past made offerings to countless thousands of myriads of millions of Buddhas, in whose presence they were constantly cultivating brahman-conduct, receiving and keeping Buddha-knowledge, manifesting it to living beings and causing them to enter into it. You must all time and again approach them and make offerings to them. Why is this? Because if any voice-hearer, or pratyekabuddha, or bodhisattva, able to believe in the scripture-dharmas preached by these sixteen bodhisattvas, can receive and hold them without maligning them, that person shall in every case attain anuttarasamyaksaṃbodhi, the wisdom of the Thus Come One.' "

The Buddha declared to the bhikṣus: "These sixteen bodhisattvas constantly wished to preach this Scripture of the Lotus Blossom of the Fine Dharma, and the living beings equal in number to the sands of six hundred myriads of millions of nayutas of Ganges rivers, converted by each and every one of these bodhisattvas and born in these numbers in each and every age, together with the bodhisattvas and having heard the Dharma from them, all felt inclined to it, and by reason of this were able to encounter four myriads of millions of world-honored Buddhas, and to this very moment have not stopped doing so.

"O bhikṣus! I now declare this to you: those disciples of that Buddha, the sixteen śrāmaṇeras, now having all gained anuttarasamyaksaṃbodhi, are at present preaching the Dharma in the lands of the ten directions, having incalculable hundreds of thousands of myriads of millions of bodhisattvas and voice-hearers for their retinue. Two of the śrāmaṇeras have become Buddhas in the east, one named Akṣobhya dwelling in the Land of Joy (Abhiratir lokadhātuḥ), the second named Sumeru Peak (Sumerukūṭa). In the southeast there are two Buddhas, one named Lion Sound (Siṃhaghoṣa), the second named Lion Sign (Siṃhadhvaja). The south has two Buddhas, one named Space-Dweller (Ākāśapratiṣṭhita), the second named Ever Extinguished (Nityaparinirvṛta). The southwest has two Buddhas, one named Sovereign Sign (Indradhvaja), the second named Brahmā Sign (Brahmadhvaja). The west has two Buddhas, one named Amitāyus, the second named Savior of All Worlds from Pain and Woe.[8] The northwest has two Buddhas, one named Supernatural Penetration of the Fragrance of Tamālapatra and Candana (Tamālapatracandanagandhābhijña), the second named Sumeru Sign [Merukalpa, "Meru-like"]. The north has two Buddhas, one named Cloud Self-Master, the second named King of the Cloud Self-Masters.[9] The northeast has a Buddha named He Who Demolishes the Fears of All the Worlds (Sarvalokabhayacchambhitatvavidvaṃsanakara). The sixteenth is I myself, Śākyamunibuddha, who in the Sahā land have achieved anuttarasamyaksaṃbodhi.

"O bhikṣus! Of the living beings, as numerous as the sands of incalculable hundreds of thousands of myriads of millions of Ganges rivers, who, having heard the Dharma from me, achieved anuttarasamyaksaṃbodhi—of those beings, I say, to those who dwell on voice-hearers' ground I teach anuttarasamyaksaṃbodhi. Those persons shall, by virtue of this Dharma, at length enter into the Buddha's Path. Why is this? Because the Thus Come One's wisdom is hard to believe and hard to understand. The living beings who were converted at that time, as numerous as the sands of incalculable Ganges rivers, are you yourselves, O bhikṣus, and the voice-hearing disciples who shall be in time to come, after my extinction.[10]

"After my extinction there shall again be disciples who, not having heard this scripture and not knowing, nor being aware of, bodhisattva-conduct, shall entertain the notion of extinction with regard to the merits attained by themselves and shall enter nirvāṇa. I will become a Buddha in another realm, having again a different name. Though these persons may evince the notion of extinction and enter nirvāṇa, yet in that land, seeking Buddha-wisdom, they shall be able to hear this scripture, to hear that it is only with the Buddha Vehicle that one can gain extinction; that there is no other vehicle, except for the dharmas preached by the Thus Come Ones as a matter of expedient device. O bhikṣus! When the Thus Come One of himself knows that his time of nirvāṇa has arrived, and also that his multitude is pure, that their inclinations are firm, and that, having arrived at an understanding of the Dharma of emptiness, they have profoundly entered into dhyāna-concentration, he then assembles the bodhisattvas and the multitude of voice-hearers and for their sakes preaches this sermon: 'There are not in the world two vehicles by which one can gain extinction. There is only one Buddha Vehicle by which one can gain extinction, and that is all. O bhikṣus, know that the Thus Come One's skill at the use of expedient devices is such that he profoundly enters into the beings' natures, and that, knowing that they aspire to a lesser dharma and that they are profoundly attached to the five desires, for their sakes he preaches nirvāṇa. These persons, when they hear the preaching, then believe and accept it.'

"All this may be likened to the following: There is a steep, difficult, very bad road, five hundred yojanas in length, empty and devoid of human beings—a frightful place. There is a great multitude wishing to traverse this road to arrive at a cache of precious jewels. There is a guide, perceptive and wise, of penetrating clarity, who knows the hard road, its passable and impassable features, and who, wishing to get through these hardships, leads the multitude. The multitude being led get disgusted midway and say to the guide, 'We are exhausted, and also frightened; we cannot go on. It is still a long way off, and we now wish to turn back.' The guide, being a man of many skillful devices, thinks: 'These wretches are to be pitied! How can they throw away a fortune in jewels and wish instead to turn back?' When he has had this thought, with his power of devising expedients he conjures up on that steep road, three hundred yojanas away, a city, then he declares to the multitude, 'Have no fear! There is no need to turn back! Here is this great city. You may stop in it and do as you please. If you enter the city, you can quickly regain your composure. If you then feel able to proceed to the jewel cache, you will also be free to leave.'

"At that time, the exhausted multitude, overjoyed at heart, sigh as at something they have never had before, saying, 'We have escaped that bad road, and shall quickly regain our composure.' Thereupon the multitude proceed to enter the conjured city, having the notion that they are saved and evincing a feeling of composure. At that time, the guide, knowing that the multitude have rested and are no longer fatigued, straightway dissolves the conjured city and says to the multitude, 'Come away! The jewel cache is near. The great city of a while ago was conjured up by me for the purpose of giving you a rest, nothing more.'

"O bhikṣus! The Thus Come One is also like this. He now functions as a Great Guide for you all. He knows that the bad road of the agonies of birth and death is steep and hard, long and far-reaching, but that it must be crossed over and left behind, knowing also that, if the beings do but hear of the single Buddha Vehicle, they will have no wish to see the Buddha or to approach him, thinking, 'The Buddha Path is long and far off. It is only by long submission to suffering that one can achieve it.' The Buddha, knowing this state of mind to be cowardly and mean, by resort to his power to devise expedients preaches two nirvāṇas midway for the purpose of giving them rest. When the beings take up residence in these two lands, then the Thus Come One preaches to them, 'What you had to do is not yet done. The lands in which you dwell are near to Buddha-knowledge. You must observe and consider, weigh and measure. The nirvāṇa you have gained is not the real one.' This is simply the Thus Come One's power to device expedients: within the one Buddha Vehicle he speaks of a threefold distinction. He is like that guide, who, to give the travelers rest, conjured up a great city, but who, when he knew they were rested, declared to them, 'The jewel cache is near. This city is not real, being nothing more than a magical creation of mine.'"

At that time, the World-Honored One, wishing to restate this meaning, proclaimed gāthās, saying:

The Buddha Victorious through Great Penetrating Knowledge
  For ten kalpas sat on the Platform of the Path,
Yet no Buddhadharma came to the fore,
  Nor was he able to achieve the Buddha Path.
Gods, demons, dragon kings,
  A multitude of asuras, and others

Constantly rained divine flowers on him,
  Thus making offerings to that Buddha.
The gods beat divine drums
  And made many kinds of music;
Then a fragrant wind blew away the withered flowers
  And rained down new and lovely ones in their stead.[11]
When ten minor kalpas had passed,
  At length he was able to achieve the Buddha Path,
And gods and worldlings
  All danced for joy of heart.
That Buddha's sixteen sons,
  All accompanied by retinues
In the thousands of myriads of millions, who surrounded them,
  Together went before that Buddha.
With heads bowed doing obeisance to the Buddha's feet,
  They begged him to turn the Dharma-wheel:
"May the Dharma-rain of the Sainted Lion
  Fill us and all!
A World-Honored One is very hard to meet with,
  In a long time appearing only once and,
For the purpose of enlightening all living beings,
  Agitating everything."
In the world-spheres to the east,
  In five hundred myriads of millions of lands,
The Brahmā palaces gleamed
  In a way they had never done before.[12]
The Brahmās, seeing these signs,
  Then came before the Buddha,
Where they made him an offering of scattered flowers
  And presented palaces to him as well.
They begged the Buddha to turn the Dharma-wheel,
  With gāthās praising him;
But the Buddha, knowing the time had not yet come,
  Received their entreaties seated in silence.
In three principal and four intermediate directions,
  Also upward and downward in the same way,

They scattered flowers as offerings to the palaces,
Begging the Buddha to turn the Dharma-wheel:
"A World-Honored One is very hard to meet with.
We beg you with your great compassion
To open wide the ambrosial gates
And turn the unexcelled Dharma-wheel."
The World-Honored One, being of incalculable wisdom,
Received the entreaties of that multitude
And for their sakes preached a variety of dharmas,
Namely, the four truths and the twelve conditions:
"From nescience through old age and death,
All exist through the cause of birth.
In this way the multitude of faults and griefs
You all should know."[13]
When he pronounced this Dharma,
Six hundred myriads of millions of billions
Were enabled to exhaust the limits of sundry woes
And all to become arhants.
At the second time of the preaching of the Dharma
A multitude as numerous as the sands of a thousand myriads of Ganges rivers,
Without receiving the dharmas,
Yet attained arhattva.[14]
After them, of those who found the Way
The number was incalculable,
For one could count them throughout myriads of millions of kalpas
And still be unable to reach their limit.
At that time, the sixteen princes
Left their household and became śrāmaṇeras,
And all together besought that Buddha
To preach the Dharma of the Great Vehicle:
"May we and our following
All achieve the Buddha Path!
We beg to gain, like the World-Honored One,
An eye of wisdom, supremely pure."

The Buddha, knowing the minds of the young men
And their deeds in former ages,
By resort to incalculable means
And varieties of parables
Preached the six pāramitās
And the matters of the various supernatural penetrations,
Defining the real Dharma,
The Way trodden by the bodhisattva,
And preaching, of this Scripture of the Dharma Blossom,
Gāthās as numerous as Ganges' sands.
That Buddha, having preached the scripture,
In a quiet room entered into dhyāna-concentration,
Single-mindedly sitting in one place
For eighty-four thousand kalpas.[15]
These śrāmaṇeras,
Knowing that the Buddha had not yet emerged from his dhyāna,
For the sake of the multitude of incalculable millions
Preached the Buddha's unexcelled wisdom.
Each seated on a Dharma-throne,
They preach this scripture of the Great Vehicle,
After the Buddha's serene quiescence
Propagating and thus aiding conversion through the Dharma.[16]
Each and every śrāmaṇera
Conveyed to salvation living beings
Who numbered as many as six hundred myriad million
Ganges rivers' sands.[17]
After that Buddha's passage into extinction,
These persons who heard the Dharma,
In whatever Buddha-land they might happen to be,
Were born together with their Teacher.
These sixteen śrāmaṇeras,
Having perfectly trodden the Buddha Path,
Now in the ten directions have each been able to achieve right intuition.[18]

At such time, those who hear the Dharma,
Each before a different Buddha,
And who have taken the stand of the voice-hearer
Shall be taught at length by recourse to the Buddha Path.
I, numbering among the sixteen,
In time past did also preach for you.
Thus, by resort to devices
I drew you toward Buddha-wisdom.
It is through these former causes and conditions
That I now preach the Scripture of the Dharma Blossom,
Causing you to enter the Buddha Path.
Be on your guard against fear and alarm.
For example, suppose that there were a bad, steep road,
Remote and with many harmful beasts,
Also without water or grass,
A place feared by men.
A multitude of innumerable thousands of myriads
Wish to traverse this steep road,
But the roadway is vast,
Extending for five hundred yojanas.
At that time there is a guide,
Firm of memory and endowed with wisdom,
A man of clarity whose mind is fixed,
And who in the midst of dangers can save men from many troubles.
The multitude, all tired and disgusted,
Address the guide, saying,
"We are now quite exhausted,
And at this point wish to turn back."
The guide has this thought:
"This lot is much to be pitied.
How can they wish to turn back
And lose these most precious jewels?"[19]
At that moment he thinks of an expedient device,
Whereby, through resort to the power of supernatural penetration,

He conjures up a great city, with inner and outer walls,
One whose houses are beautifully adorned,
Surrounded by parks and groves,
By moats and pools,
By layered gates and tall towers,
Full of men and women.
When he has conjured up this creation,
He comforts the multitude, saying, "Fear not!
When you enter this city,
Each may do as he pleases."
These persons, having entered the city,
Are all delighted at heart,
All realizing composure
And saying to themselves that they have been saved.
The guide, knowing that they are at rest,
Assembles the multitude and announces,
"You are now to go forward.
This is only a magically created city.
When I saw how exhausted you were,
How you wished to turn back midway,
Then, by resort to my power of devising expedients,
In the emergency I conjured up this city.
You are now to make every effort
To reach the jewel cache together."
I, too, am like this,
For I am the Guide of all.
Since I see the seekers of the Way
Exhausted and disgusted in mid-course,
Unable to transcend birth and death
Or the steep road of agony,
Therefore by resort to the power of expedient devices,
In order to give them rest, I preach nirvāṇa to them,
Saying, "Your suffering is at an end.
What was to be done you have already achieved."[20]
When I know that, having reached nirvāṇa,
They have all attained arhattva,

Only then do I gather the multitude
And for them preach the real Dharma:
"The Buddhas, by their power of devising expedients,
Create distinctions, preaching three vehicles,
But there is in fact only One Buddha Vehicle,
And it is to provide a resting place that the other two are preached.
Now for your sakes I preach the reality,
For what you have gained is not extinction.
For the sake of Buddha-omniscience
You must put forth great and vigorous effort,
For only when you are directly aware of All-Knowledge
And of the ten strengths, of the Buddhadharmas comprising these and other things,
Only when you are in full possession of the thirty-two marks,
Shall you have real extinction.
The Guides among the Buddhas
Preach nirvāṇa in order to give rest.
Once they know that the beings are at rest,
They lead them into Buddha-knowledge.

Scripture of the Lotus Blossom of the Fine Dharma.
End of Roll the Third.

Roll 4

Chapter Eight: Receipt of Prophecy by Five Hundred Disciples

At that time, Pūrṇa, the son of Maitrāyaṇī, who had heard about this wisdom from the Buddha and about these preachings in accord with what is appropriate and by resort to expedient devices, who had heard him confer on the great disciples a prophecy of anuttarasamyak-saṃbodhi, who had heard further the matter of the causes and conditions of bygone ages, and who had heard that the Buddhas have powers of supernatural penetration, powers over which they have perfect mastery, gained something he had never had before, and his heart danced with unsullied joy. Then he rose from his seat, went into the Buddha's presence, and with head bowed did obeisance before his feet. Then he stood off to one side, looking up at the August Countenance, never removing his eyes, and thought: "The World-Honored One is most unique! His deeds are rare! In accord with the varied natures of worldlings and by resort to knowledge and insight, being skilled in the use of expedients, for their sakes he preaches the Dharma, extricating the living beings from their attachments, wherever they happen to be. In the face of the Buddha's merits, we have not the words with which to express ourselves. Only the Buddha, the World-Honored One, is able to know the vows we once took with deep thought."[1]

At that time, the Buddha proclaimed to the bhikṣus: "Do you see this Pūrṇa, the son of Maitrāyaṇī, or do you not? I constantly declare him to be the first among those who preach Dharma. I am also constantly sighing in admiration of his manifold merits, of how with pure effort he keeps and helps to propagate my Dharma; of how, in the midst of the fourfold assembly, he demonstrates and teaches, thereby affording advantage and joy; of how perfectly he interprets the True Dharma of the Buddha, thereby greatly benefiting those united in brahman-conduct (*alam anugrahītā sabrahmacāriṇā*). Apart from the Thus

Come One, none can do perfect justice to his talent with words.[2] Do not think that Pūrṇa is able to keep and help to propagate my Dharma alone. For before ninety million Buddhas of the past he also kept and helped to propagate the Buddhas' True Dharma, and was the first among their Dharma-preachers as well. Also, with respect to the empty dharmas preached by the Buddhas, he has clearly penetrated this teaching, having gained the four kinds of unobstructed knowledge, constantly being able to understand precisely and to preach Dharma with purity, having no doubts, having perfected the bodhisattva's strength of supernatural penetration and constantly throughout his life having cultivated brahman-conduct.[3] That Buddha's contemporaries all thought that he was in fact a voice-hearer. For by this expedient device Pūrṇa benefited incalculable hundreds of thousands of living beings. He also converted incalculable asaṃkhyeyas of humans, causing them to stand on anuttarasamyaksaṃbodhi. In order to purify Buddha-lands, he constantly did Buddha-deeds, teaching and converting living beings.[4] O bhikṣus! Pūrṇa also received first place among those who preached Dharma in the presence of the seven Buddhas, and now also is first among those who preach Dharma in my presence.

In the kalpa Worthy, he shall also be first among the Dharma-preachers of Buddhas to come, and shall in every case keep and help to propagate the Dharma of incalculable, limitless Buddhas, teaching, converting, and benefiting incalculable living beings and causing them to stand on anuttarasamyaksaṃbodhi.[5] In order to purify his Buddha-land, he shall constantly persevere with vigor, shall teach and convert the beings, and shall at length perfect the bodhisattva-path. After the passage of incalculable asaṃkhyeyakalpas, in this land he shall attain anuttarasamyaksaṃbodhi and shall be called Dharma Glow (Dharmaprabhāsa) a Thus Come One, worthy of offerings, of right and universal knowledge, his clarity and conduct perfect, well gone, understanding the world, an unexcelled Worthy, a Regulator of men of stature, a Teacher of gods and men, a Buddha, a World-Honored One.

"That Buddha shall have thousand-millionfold worlds equal in number to Ganges' sands for a single Buddha-land, the seven jewels for earth, land as flat as the palm of the hand, without mountains or hills, vales or dales, river basins or hollows, the midst of the land filled with terraces and palaces of the seven jewels, the residences of its gods in the nearby skies, where men and gods may consort, each able to see the other, with no evil destinies, also without women, all living things being born by transformation (*sarve ca te sattvā aupapādukā bhaviṣyanti*),* there being no lewd desires, all having gained great supernatural penetration, their bodies giving off a bright glow, all flying through space at will, their intentions and resolutions firm, all endowed with vigor and wisdom, all without exception adorned with the thirty-two marks in gold. The living beings of that realm shall constantly subsist on two kinds of food, the one being the food of Dharma-joy, the other the food of dhyāna-joy. There shall be a bodhisattva-multitude numbering incalculable asaṃkhyeyas of thousands of myriads of millions of nayutas, who shall gain great supernatural penetration and the four kinds of unobstructed knowledge, and who shall be able well to teach and convert all varieties of living beings. Its multitude of voice-hearers shall be such that no count or numeration, no measure or calculation, may know it, all of them having gained to perfection the six penetrations, the three clarities, and the eight deliverances. Such shall be the number of the incalculable merits of that Buddha's land, with which it shall be adorned to perfection. The kalpa's name shall be Jewel Glow (Ratnāvabhāsa), the name of the realm Well Purified (Suviśuddhā). That Buddha's life-span shall be incalculable asaṃkhyeyakalpas, and his Dharma shall persist a very long time. After that Buddha's passage into extinction, there shall be erected a stūpa of the seven jewels, which shall fill the realm."

At that time, the World-Honored One, wishing to restate this meaning, proclaimed gāthās, saying:

O bhikṣus, listen with discernment
  To the Path trodden by the Buddha's son,
Which, because he was well schooled in expedient devices,

* Birth "by transformation" (*aupapādukā jātiḥ*) means, in effect, birth by magic; in other words, there will be no sexual intercourse in that land, nor even sexual desire. This is one of the four kinds of birth, the others being from a womb (*jarāyujā*), from an egg (*aṇḍajā*), and from moisture (*saṃsvedajā*); the last-named is the supposed source of maggots and other such things.

Was beyond reckoning and discussion![6]
Knowing that the multitude craves the lesser Dharma
And fears great wisdom,
For this reason the bodhisattvas
Become voice-hearers and cause-perceivers.
By resort to numberless expedient devices
They convert varieties of living beings,
Saying of themselves that they are voice-hearers,
Far removed from the Buddha Path.
They rescue an incalculable multitude,
All of whom they enable to achieve perfection,
For even those of limited desires and of no effort
Shall eventually be enabled to become Buddhas.
Inwardly concealing their bodhisattva-conduct
And outwardly showing themselves to be voice-hearers,
Though of slight desires and disgusted with birth-and-death,
They are in fact, and of their own accord, purifying Buddha-lands.
Showing the multitude that they [themselves] have the three poisons,
And also displaying the signs of wrong views,
My disciples, too, in the same way,
By resort to expedient devices rescue the beings.
If I should fully explain
My various transformed manifestations,
The living beings who heard it
In their hearts would harbor doubts.[7]
Now, this Pūrṇa,
In the presence of a thousand millions of former Buddhas,
Cultivated with diligence the Path that he was to traverse,
And propagated and kept the Buddhadharmas.[8]
In order to seek unexcelled knowledge,
In the presence of several Buddhas
He made a show of being at the head of the disciples,
Where he heard much and acquired wisdom.
In what he preached he was fearless,

Being able to cause the multitude to rejoice,
Never experiencing fatigue or disgust,
And thus aiding the Buddhas' enterprise.
Having already crossed over into great supernatural penetration,
Being fully endowed with the four kinds of unobstructed knowledge,
And knowing the keenness and dullness of the multitude's faculties,
He constantly preached the pure Dharma.
Propagating such doctrine as this,
He taught thousands of millions of multitudes,
Causing them to dwell in the Dharma of the Great Vehicle,
And also cleansed his own Buddha-land.[9]
In time to come he shall also make offerings
To incalculable, innumerable Buddhas,
Guarding and assisting them in their propagation of the True Dharma,
And he shall also purify his own Buddha-land.
By resort to expedient devices, ever
Shall he preach the Dharma without fear,
Saving an incalculable multitude
And achieving omniscience for them.
Making offerings to Thus Come Ones
And keeping their treasure houses of Dharma,
He shall thereafter be able to achieve Buddhahood,
Being called by the name of Dharma Glow.
His realm shall be named Well Purified,
Composed of the seven jewels.
The kalpa shall be named Jewel Glow,
The multitude of bodhisattvas being very great.[10]
Their number shall be in the incalculable millions,
All having crossed over into great supernatural penetration,
And the perfect might of their imposing majesty
Shall fill the land.

The voice-hearers also shall be numberless,
With their three clarities and eight deliverances,
And having attained the four kinds of unobstructed knowledge:
The religious community shall consist of these.
The beings of that realm
Shall already have detached themselves from their lewd desires.
Born purely of transformation,
With perfect marks they shall adorn their bodies.[11]
Joy in Dharma and joy in dhyāna shall be their food,
And they shall have no thought of any other nourishment.
There shall be no women,
Nor shall there be any evil destinies.
Pūrṇabhikṣu,
His merit perfect in every way,
Shall gain a Pure Land such as this,
With a multitude of saints, and sages most numerous.
Incalculable as these things are,
I have now spoken of them but briefly.

At that time, the twelve hundred arhants, masters of their own thoughts, thought: "We are overjoyed, having gained something we have never had before! If the World-Honored One would confer on each of us a prophecy, as he has done for the other great disciples, would that not be cause for joy?"

The Buddha, knowing the thoughts in their minds, declared to Mahākāśyapa: "On these twelve hundred arhants I will now manifestly and in order confer a prophecy of anuttarasamyaksaṃbodhi. Of this multitude, my disciple, Kauṇḍinyabhikṣu, shall make offerings to sixty-two thousands of millions of Buddhas and, having done so, shall be able to achieve Buddhahood, being called Universally Lustrous, a Thus Come One, worthy of offerings, of right and universal knowledge, his clarity and conduct perfect, well gone, understanding the world, an unexcelled Worthy, a Regulator of men of stature, a Teacher of gods and men, a Buddha, a World-Honored One. His five hundred arhants,

Urubilvākāśyapa, Gayākāśyapa, Nadīkāśyapa, Kālodāyin, Udāyin, Aniruddha, Revata, Kapphiṇa, Bakkula, Cunda, Svāgata, and others, shall all attain anuttarasamyaksaṃbodhi, all of them called by the same name, Universally Lustrous."[12]

At that time, the World-Honored One, wishing to restate this meaning, proclaimed gāthās, saying:

Kauṇḍinyabhikṣu
  Shall see incalculable Buddhas and,
Only after having traversed an asaṃkhyeyakalpa,
  Shall achieve undifferentiating, right, enlightened intuition.
Ever emitting a great glow,
  He shall perfect the supernatural penetrations.
His name, bruited about in all ten directions,
  Shall be honored by all.
He shall ever preach the Unexcelled Way,
  and hence shall be called Universally Lustrous.
His land shall be pure.
  His bodhisattvas, all courageous and mighty,
Shall all mount wondrous towers
  And frolic in the realms of the ten directions,
Of unexcelled offerings
  Making presents to the Buddhas.
When they have made these offerings,
  Their hearts shall harbor great joy,
And briefly they shall return to their original realm:
  Such are the supernatural powers they shall have.
That Buddha's life-span shall be sixty thousand kalpas,
  His True Dharma shall last twice that long,
And his Counterfeit Dharma shall, in turn, last twice the length of that.
  When that Buddha becomes extinct, gods and men shall mourn.
The five hundred bhikṣus
  Shall in turn become Buddhas,

Identically named Universally Lustrous.
  They shall confer prophecies, each on his successor:
"After my passage into extinction,
  Such-a-one shall become a Buddha,
The world that he shall convert
  Being like this of mine today.
The chaste purity of his land,
  As well as his powers of supernatural penetration,
His multitudes of bodhisattvas and voice-hearers,
  His True Dharma and Counterfeit Dharma,
And the number of kalpas in his life-span
  Shall all be as I have just said."
Kāśyapa, you now know
  The five hundred self-masters.
The multitude of remaining voice-hearers
  Shall also be like this.
As for those not in this assembly,
  You must explain it to them.[13]

At that time, the five hundred arhants, having received a prophecy in the Buddha's presence, danced for joy, then, rising from their seats, went into the Buddha's presence, where with head bowed they did obeisance to his feet, repented of their transgressions, and reproached themselves, saying: "O World-Honored One! We have been constantly having this thought, saying to ourselves, 'We have already gained the ultimate passage into extinction.' Now that at last we understand it, we know we have been like ignoramuses. What is the reason? We should have gained the Thus Come One's wisdom, yet we were content with petty knowledge. We are to be likened to the following case: There is a man who arrives at the house of a close friend, where he gets drunk on wine, then lies down. At that time, his friend, having official business, is on the point of going away, when he sews a priceless jewel into the interior of the first man's garment and departs, leaving it with him. The first man, laid out drunk, is unaware of anything. When he has recovered, he sets out on his travels, then reaches another country, where he devotes every effort to the quest for food and clothing. He suffers such hardship that he is content with however little he may get. Then his friend, encountering him by chance, speaks these words to him: 'Alas, Sir! How can you have come to this for the sake of mere food and clothing? Once I, wishing to afford you comfort and joy, as well as the natural satisfaction of your five desires, in such-and-such a year, on a certain day of a certain month, sewed a priceless jewel into the inside of your garment. Surely it is still there. Yet you, not knowing of it, have suffered pain and grief in quest of a livelihood. How foolish you have been! Now you need only take this jewel, exchange it for what you need, and have things always as you wish, suffering neither want nor shortage.'

"The Buddha is also thus. When he was a bodhisattva, he taught and converted us, inspiring in us the thought of All-Knowledge, but later we forgot, and thus neither understood nor were aware of anything. Having achieved the way of the arhant, we said to ourselves that this was passage into extinction. We were so hard-pressed to support life that we were satisfied with what little we got, though the vow concerning All-Knowledge, still there, had never lost its effect. Now the World-Honored One, to make us aware, says to us: 'Bhikṣus! What you have gained is not ultimate extinction. I have long caused you to plant the roots favorable to Buddhahood, and [recently] by resort to an expedient device I made a display of the signs of nirvāṇa. You have been imagining, however, that you had in fact achieved the passage into extinction.' World-Honored One! We now know at last that we are in fact bodhisattvas, that we have gained a prophecy of anuttarasamyaksaṃbodhi. For this reason we are very greatly overjoyed, having gained something we had never had before."

At that time, Ājñātakauṇḍinya and his fellows, wishing to restate this meaning, proclaimed gāthās, saying:

Having heard the unexcelled
  Sound of the prophecy of tranquillity
And being delighted at something we have never had before,
  We do obeisance before the Buddha of incalculable wisdom.
Now, in the presence of the World-Honored One,
  We freely repent our transgressions and faults,

For in the midst of incalculable Buddha-jewels
We had acquired but a slight share of nirvāṇa.
Like ignorant, foolish men,
We imagined we had enough.
It may be likened to this case: A destitute man
Goes to the house of a close friend.
The house, very great and rich,
Is fully stocked with delicacies.
Taking a priceless jewel,
[The rich man] attaches it to his friend's garment inside,
Then, leaving it in silence, he goes away,
While his friend, lying down at the time, is aware of nothing.[14]
The latter, having arisen,
Travels to another country,
Where, seeking food and clothing, he supports himself,
But the maintenance of life is very hard.
He is satisfied with the little he gets,
And has no wish at all for good things.
He is unaware that inside his garment
There is a priceless jewel.
The close friend who gave him the jewel
Later sees this poor man and,
Having sternly rebuked him,
Shows him the jewel tied to the garment.
The poor man, seeing this jewel,
Is overjoyed at heart.
In his wealth, he comes to own various precious objects,
Able to satisfy his five desires at will.
We also are thus,
For the World-Honored One throughout the long night of time,
Ever in his pity teaching and converting,
Has caused us to plant the seeds of the Unexcelled Vow.[15]
Because we were ignorant,
Imperceptive and also unknowing,

Having gained a trifling portion of nirvāṇa
  We were satisfied, and sought no further.
Now the Buddha has made us aware,
  Saying that this is no real passage into extinction.
We have gained the Buddha's unexcelled wisdom,
  Which now for the first time we take to be true extinction.
Now, having heard from the Buddha
  The matter of the adornment by prophecy,
As well as of the successive prophecies of each [Buddha] to his successor,
  We are thoroughly delighted in body and mind.

Chapter Nine: Prophecies Conferred on Learners and Adepts

At that time, Ānanda and Rāhula thought: "We are constantly thinking how pleasant it would be if we were to receive a prophecy." Then straightway, rising from their seats and going into the Buddha's presence, with heads bowed they did obeisance to the Buddha's feet and together adressed the Buddha, saying, "World-Honored One! We should also have a share in this, for only in the Buddha do we take our refuge. Also, we are seen and recognized by the gods, men, and asuras of all the worlds. Ānanda is in constant attendance, guarding and keeping the treasure house of the Dharma. Rāhula is the Buddha's son. If the Buddha grants us a prophecy of anuttarasamyaksaṃbodhi, then not only shall our wishes be fulfilled, but also the hopes of the multitude shall be satisfied."[1]

At that time, there were voice-hearing disciples, both those who were learning and those who had nothing more to learn, to the number of two thousand, all of whom rose from their seats, bared only their right shoulders, went before the Buddha and, single-mindedly joining palms, looked up at the World-Honored One, expressing prayerful wishes as had Ānanda and Rāhula. Then they stood to one side.[2]

At that time, the Buddha declared to Ānanda: "In an age to come, you shall succeed in becoming a Buddha called Consummate King and Master of the Wisdom of Mountains and Sea, a Thus Come One, worthy of offerings, of right and universal knowledge, your clarity and conduct perfect, well gone, understanding the world, an unexcelled Worthy, a Regulator of men of stature, a Teacher of gods and men, a Buddha, a World-Honored One.[3] You shall make offerings to sixty-two millions of Buddhas and guard and keep their treasure houses of Dharma. Thereafter you shall attain anuttarasamyaksaṃbodhi and teach and convert bodhisattvas equal in number to the sands of twenty thousand myriads of millions of Ganges rivers, causing them to achieve anuttara-samyaksaṃbodhi. Your realm shall be named the Ever-Raised Banner of Victory (Anavanāmitavaijayantī). Its land shall be pure, having vaiḍūrya for soil. The kalpa shall be named Subtle Sound All-Pervading (Manojñaśabdābhigarjita).[4] That Buddha's life-span shall be incalculable thousands of myriads of millions of asaṃkhyeyakalpas. If a man should reckon by thousands of myriads of millions of incalculable asaṃkhyeyakalpas, he still would not be able to know the sum.* His True Dharma shall abide in the world twice as long as his life-span, and his Counterfeit Dharma shall abide in the world twice as long again. Ānanda! This Buddha, Consummate King and Master of the Wisdom of Mountains and Sea, shall be praised in unison by Buddhas, Thus Come Ones, in each of the ten directions equal in number to the sands of countless thousands of myriads of millions of Ganges rivers, who shall praise his merits."

At that time, the World-Honored One, wishing to restate this meaning, proclaimed gāthās, saying:

Now in the saṃgha's midst I tell you
  That Ānanda, who bears the Dharma,
Shall make offerings to Buddhas
  And thereafter achieve right, enlightened intuition.[5]
He shall be called of the Wisdom of Mountains and Sea
  The Buddha, the Consummate King.
His realm, perfectly pure,
  Shall be named the Ever-Raised Banner of Victory.[6]
He shall teach and convert bodhisattvas
  In numbers like to Ganges' sands.
That Buddha shall have a great imposing majesty,
  His name and renown filling the ten directions.

* If I understand correctly, this means that a person could not reckon that Buddha's life-span even by taking a million millions of asaṃkhyeyakalpas as a single unit, i.e., as equal to the number one. The original merely says that Buddha's life-span shall be measureless *kalpas* in length, *yeṣāṃ kalpānāṃ na śakyaṃ gaṇanayā paryanto 'dhigantum*, "whose limit cannot be comprehended by counting."

His life-span shall have no measure,
  Since he shall have pity on the multitude of living beings.
His True Dharma shall be double his life-span,
  And his Counterfeit Dharma double that again.
Equal in number to Ganges' sands,
  Countless living beings
Within this Buddha's Dharma
  Shall plant the causes and conditions of the Buddha Path.

At that time, those within the assembly who had just launched their thoughts, eight thousand persons, all thought: "We have not heard even a great bodhisattva get such a prophecy as this. What reason can there be for the voice-hearers now to receive such assurances?" At that time, the World-Honored One, knowing the thoughts in the bodhisattvas' minds, said to them: "Good men, I shared a place with Ānanda in the presence of the Buddha King of Emptiness, and at the same time [as Ānanda] experienced the thought of anuttarasamyaksaṃbodhi. [However,] Ānanda constantly wished to be a hearer of much [*bahuśruta*, very learned person], while I constantly strove with vigor [for the enlightenment of all]. This is why I have already contrived to achieve anuttarasamyaksaṃbodhi, while Ānanda guards and keeps my Dharma, teaching, converting, and perfecting a multitude of bodhisattvas. Such having been his former wish [i.e., to guard the Dharma], he has now received this prophecy [as his reward]."[7]

When Ānanda, himself facing the Buddha, heard this prophecy and the description of the adornments of his land, his wishes were fulfilled and his heart was overjoyed, since he had gained what he had never had before. In that instant he recalled the Dharma-store of incalculable thousands of myriads of millions of past Buddhas and their unobstructed attainments, just as he was hearing them now. He also recalled his own original vow.

At that time, Ānanda proclaimed gāthās, saying:

O World-Honored One, it is exceeding rare,
  How you cause me to recall past
Incalculable Buddhadharmas

Just as I am hearing them today![8]
Now, no longer in doubt, I
Dwell securely in Buddha's Path,
By expedient means having become his attendant,
Guarding and keeping the Buddhas' Dharma.

At that time, the Buddha declared to Rāhula: "In an age yet to come, you shall become a Buddha called the One Who Treads on Flowers of Seven Jewels (Saptaratnapadmavikrāntagāmin), a Thus Come One, worthy of offerings, of right and universal knowledge, your clarity and conduct perfect, well gone, understanding the world, and unexcelled Worthy, a Regulator of men of stature, a Teacher of gods and men, a Buddha, a World-Honored One. You shall make offerings to Buddhas, to Thus Come Ones, equal in number to the grains of dust in ten worlds. You shall ever be an eldest son to those Buddhas, just as you are now. The description of the land of the Buddha One Who Treads on Flowers of Seven Jewels, the number of kalpas in his life-span, the number of disciples converted by him, his True Dharma and his Counterfeit Dharma shall all be the same as those of the Thus Come One the Consummate King and Master of the Wisdom of Mountains and Sea, there being no difference. You shall also be an eldest son to this Buddha as well, and thereafter you shall attain anuttarasamyaksaṃbodhi."

At that time, the World-Honored One, wishing to restate this meaning, proclaimed gāthās, saying:

When I was a crown prince,
Rāhu[la] was my eldest son.
Now that I have perfected the Buddha Path,
He, having received the Dharma, is my Dharma-son.
In an age yet to come,
You shall see incalculable millions of Buddhas,
To all of whom you shall be an eldest son,
Single-mindedly seeking the Buddha Path.
[This,] Rāhula's secret conduct,
Only I can know.[9]

Now he is my eldest son,
  And shows this to the living beings.
His incalculable millions of thousands of myriads
  Of merits cannot be counted.
He dwells secure in the Buddhadharma,
  And thus seeks the Unexcelled Path.[10]

At that time, the World-Honored One saw the learners and those who had nothing more to learn, all two thousand of them, their minds pliant, quietly calm, single-mindedly observing the Buddha. The Buddha declared to Ānanda: "Ānanda! Do you see these, both learners and those who have nothing more to learn, all two thousand of them? Or do you not?"

"Yes. I do see them."

"Ānanda! These men shall make offerings to Buddhas, to Thus Come Ones, equal in number to the grains of dust in fifty worlds. They shall honor and revere them, guard and keep their treasure of Dharma, and at the latter end, at the same time and in [all] the realms of the ten directions, shall each be enabled to achieve Buddhahood, all being called by the same name, Jewel Sign (Ratnaketu) the Thus Come One, worthy of offerings, of right and universal knowledge, his clarity and conduct perfect, well gone, understanding the world, an unexcelled Worthy, a Regulator of men of stature, a Teacher of gods and men, a Buddha, a World-Honored One. Their life-span shall be one kalpa. Their lands, [the number of] their voice-hearers and bodhisattvas, their True Dharma and Counterfeit Dharma, shall all be exactly equal to one another."

At that time the World-Honored One, wishing to restate this meaning, proclaimed gāthās, saying:

These two thousand voice-hearers
  Now in my presence stand,
And on them all I confer a prophecy
  That in time yet to come they shall achieve Buddhahood.
The Buddhas to whom they shall make offerings
  Shall be like grains of dust, as I have already said.

They shall guard and keep those Buddhas' Dharma-treasure,
  Then achieve right, enlightened intuition.[11]
Each [dwelling] in the realms of the ten directions,
  They shall all have the same name.
At the same time, they shall sit on the Platform of the Path
  And thus bear direct witness to unexcelled Knowledge.
All shall be named Jewel Sign,
  And their lands and disciples,
True Dharma and Counterfeit Dharma,
  Shall be absolutely the same, with no differences.
All, by resort to the same supernatural penetrations,
  Shall save living beings in the ten directions.
Their names shall be universally renowned,
  And they shall enter into nirvāṇa.[12]

At that time, the learners and those who had nothing more to learn, all two thousand of them, having heard the Buddha's prophecy and dancing for joy, proclaimed a gāthā, saying:

O World-Honored One! O lamp of wisdom!
  Since we have heard the sound of prophecy,
Our hearts are full of joy,
  As if we had been infused with sweet dew.[13]

Chapter Ten: Preachers of Dharma

At that time, through the bodhisattva Medicine King (Bhaiṣajya-rāja), the World-Honored One addressed the eighty thousand great worthies: "Medicine King, do you see within this great multitude incalculable gods, dragon kings, yakṣas, gandharvas, asuras, garuḍas, kinnaras, mahoragas, humans and nonhumans, as well as bhikṣus, bhikṣuṇīs, upāsakas, upāsikās, seekers after the rank of voice-hearers, seekers after the rank of pratyekabuddhas, and seekers after the rank of Buddhas? If any like these in the Buddha's presence hears a single gāthā or a single phrase of the Scripture of the Blossom of the Fine Dharma, or devotes to it a single moment of rejoicing, I hereby confer on him a prophecy that he shall attain anuttarasamyaksaṃbodhi." The Buddha declared to Medicine King: "Further, if after the Thus Come One has passed into extinction there is a man who, having heard of the Scripture of the Blossom of the Fine Dharma a single gāthā or a single phrase, devotes to it a single moment of rejoicing, on him, too, I confer the prophecy of anuttarasamyaksaṃbodhi. Again, if there is a man who shall receive and keep, read and recite, explain, or copy in writing a single gāthā of the Scripture of the Blossom of the Fine Dharma, or who shall look with veneration on a roll of this scripture as if it were the Buddha himself, or who shall make to it sundry offerings of flower perfume, necklaces, powdered incense, perfumed paste, burnt incense, silk canopies and banners, garments, or music, or who shall even join palms in reverent worship of it, O Medicine King, be it known that this man or any other like him shall have already made offerings to ten myriads of millions of Buddhas in former time, and in those Buddhas' presence taken a great vow. It is by virtue of the great pity he shall have had for living beings that he shall be born here as a human being.

"Medicine King! If a person shall ask which living beings in an age yet to come shall succeed in becoming Buddhas, you must show him that these very men in an age yet to come shall without fail contrive to become Buddhas. For what reason? The reason is this: if a good man or good woman shall receive and keep, read and recite, explain, or copy in writing a single phrase of the Scripture of the Dharma Blossom, or otherwise and in a variety of ways make offerings to the scriptural roll with flower perfume, necklaces, powdered incense, perfumed paste, burnt incense, silk banners and canopies, garments, or music, or join palms in reverent worship, that person is to be looked up to and exalted by all the worlds, showered with offerings fit for a Thus Come One. Let it be known that that person is a great bodhisattva who, having achieved anuttarasamyaksaṃbodhi, taken pity on the living beings, and vowed to be reborn here, is preaching the Scripture of the Blossom of the Fine Dharma with breadth and discrimination. How much the more may this be said of one who, receiving and keeping this scripture in its entirety, makes sundry offerings to it! O Medicine King, be it known that this person, rejecting the reward due his own pure deeds, out of pity for living beings after my passage into extinction shall have been reborn in the evil world, where he shall broadly preach this scripture. If this good man or good woman, after my passage into extinction, can secretly for a single person preach so much as a single phrase of the Scripture of the Dharma Blossom, be it known that that person is an emissary of the Thus Come One, sent by the Thus Come One, doing the Thus Come One's business. How much the more may this be said of one who in the midst of a great multitude broadly preaches it for men in general!

"O Medicine King! If there is an evil man who with unwholesome thought shall appear before the Buddha in the midst of a kalpa and constantly malign him, his guilt shall be comparatively light. If there is a person who with a single malicious word shall denigrate those who read and recite the Scripture of the Dharma Blossom, be they within the household or already out of the household, his guilt shall be very grave. O Medicine King! If there is a person who shall read and recite the Scripture of the Dharma Blossom, be it known that that person shall be of himself adorned with the adornments of a Buddha; borne about on the Buddha's shoulders; to be greeted with obeisance and worshiped single-mindedly with joined palms wherever he may go; to be humbly venerated and showered with offerings; to be held in solemn esteem and sung with praise; to be celebrated with music along with flower perfume, necklaces, powdered incense, perfumed paste, burnt incense, silk banners and canopies, garments and sweetmeats; to be showered with men's choicest offerings; to have divine jewels carried about and scattered over him; to have clusters of divine jewels presented to him. What is the reason? When this man preaches Dharma with joy, anyone who hears it for a moment shall straightway achieve ultimate anuttarasamyaksaṃbodhi."[1]

At that time, the World-Honored One, wishing to restate this meaning, proclaimed gāthās, saying:

If one wishes to dwell in the Buddha Path
  And achieve the knowledge born of itself,
One must ever strive to make offerings
  To those who receive and keep the Dharma Blossom.
If there is anyone who wishes quickly to attain
  Knowledge of all modes,
He must receive and keep this scripture
  And make offerings to its bearers.
If there is anyone who can receive and keep
  The Scripture of the Blossom of the Fine Dharma,
Be it known that he was dispatched by the Buddha
  In his merciful mindfulness of the living beings.
Those who can receive and keep
  The Scripture of the Blossom of the Fine Dharma,
Having forsaken their pure lands,
  Have been reborn here out of pity for the multitude.[2]
Be it known that a man such as this,
  Having the power to be reborn wherever he chooses,
Is able in this evil age
  To preach broadly the unexcelled Dharma.
One must with the perfume of divine flowers
  And with garments adorned with divine jewels,
As well as with clusters of the divine jewels themselves,
  Make offerings to one who preaches Dharma.
One who after my extinction, in an evil age,

Is able to bear this scripture
Is to be worshiped with palms joined,
As if offerings were being made to a World-Honored One.
With supreme delicacies and many sweetmeats,
As well as varieties of garments,
Shall [the beings] make offerings to this Buddha's son,
Hoping to be able to hear him even for a moment.
If there is one who in the latter age can
Receive and keep this scripture,
I will send him into the midst of men,
Where he shall do the Thus Come One's business.
If anyone throughout one kalpa,
Ever harboring unwholesome thoughts
And flushed in color, shall malign the Buddha,
He shall incur incalculably grave guilt.[3]
If there be any who read, recite. and keep
This Scripture of the Dharma Blossom
Anyone who for a moment heaps abuse on them
Shall incur guilt exceeding even this.
If there is a man who, in his quest for the Buddha Path,
Shall throughout one kalpa,
Joining palms in my presence,
Praise me with numberless gāthās,
By reason of this praise of the Buddha
He shall gain incalculable merit;
But he who shall praise the bearers of this scripture
Shall have merit that exceeds even that.
One who throughout eighty millions of kalpas'
With the finest colors and sounds,
As well as scents, flavors, and touches,
Makes offerings to the bearers of the scripture—
Having made offerings in this way,
If he can hear it for but a moment,
Shall himself experience delight,
Thinking, "I have now gained a great advantage!"[4]
Medicine King, I now proclaim to you

The scriptures that I preach;
And among these scriptures
The Dharma Blossom is foremost.

At that time, the Buddha again declared to Medicine King, the bodhisattva-mahāsattva: "The scriptural canons I preach are in the incalculable thousands of myriads of millions, whether already preached, now being preached, or still to be preached. Yet among them this Scripture of the Dharma Blossom is the hardest to believe, the hardest to understand. Medicine King! This scripture is the treasure house of the Buddhas' secret essentials. It may not be distributed, then given at random to men. What the Buddhas, the World-Honored Ones, have kept has never, since ancient times, been explicitly stated. This scripture has many enemies even now, when the Thus Come One is present. How much the more so after his passage into extinction![5]

"O Medicine King, be it known that after the extinction of the Thus Come One, those who can write it, hold it, read and recite it, make offerings to it, or for others preach it the Thus Come One shall cover with garments.* They shall also benefit from the protective mindfulness of Buddhas now in other quarters. These persons shall have the power of great faith, as well as the power of will and of good faculties. Be it known that these persons shall have dwelt together with the Thus Come One, and shall have had their heads caressed by the hand of the Thus Come One.

"O Medicine King! Wherever it may be preached, or read, or recited, or written, or whatever place a roll of this scripture may occupy, in all those places one is to erect a stūpa of the seven jewels, building it high and wide and with impressive decoration. There is no need even to lodge śarīra in it. What is the reason? Within it there is already a whole body of the Thus Come One. This stūpa is to be showered with offerings, humbly venerated, held in solemn esteem, and praised with all manner of flowers, scents, necklaces, silk banners and canopies, music skillfully sung and played. If there are persons who can see this stūpa

* That is, protect them. Skt. has *tathāgatacīvaracchanna*, they shall be "covered with the Buddha's cloak."

and worship and make offerings to it, be it known that these persons are all close to anuttarasamyaksaṃbodhi. O Medicine King! There are many persons, both in the household and gone forth from it, who tread the bodhisattva-path. Be it known that if they cannot contrive to see and hear, read and recite, write and keep, or make offerings to this Scripture of the Dharma Blossom, these persons have not yet well trodden the bodhisattva-path. If there are any who do contrive to hear this scriptural canon, they alone can well tread the bodhisattva-path. If there are living beings who in quest of the Buddha Path see or hear this Scripture of the Dharma Blossom and who, having heard it, believe and understand, receive and keep it, be it known that these persons have contrived to approach anuttarasamyaksaṃbodhi.[6]

"O Medicine King! Suppose, for example, there were a man hard pressed by thirst and in need of water. Though on yon high plain he digs in his search, still he sees only dry earth, and knows that the water is yet far off, that his efforts will be to no avail. Turning, he sees moist earth, then at length reaches mud. His mind is then assured, for he knows that water must be near. The bodhisattva is also like this. If he has not yet heard, nor understood, nor been able to put into practice this Scripture of the Dharma Blossom, be it known that this person is still far from anuttarasamyaksaṃbodhi. What is the reason? The reason is that the anuttarasamyaksaṃbodhi of all bodhisattvas in every case belongs to this scripture. This scripture opens the door of expedient devices; it shows the marks of reality. This treasure house of the Scripture of the Dharma Blossom is profound, firm, obscure, and remote from the ordinary. No man could arrive at it, except that now the Buddha, in teaching, converting, and perfecting the bodhisattvas, reveals it for their sakes. O Medicine King! If there is a bodhisattva who, upon hearing this Scripture of the Dharma Blossom, is alarmed, or in doubt, or in fear, be it known that this is a bodhisattva who has but newly launched his thought. If a voice-hearer, upon hearing this scripture, is alarmed, or in doubt, or in fear, be it known that this is a person of overweening pride.

"O Medicine King! If a good man or good woman after the extinction of the Thus Come One wishes to preach this Scripture of the Dharma Blossom to the fourfold assembly, how is he or she to preach it? This good man or good woman is to enter the room of the Thus Come One, don the cloak of the Thus Come One, sit on the throne of the Thus Come One, and only then preach this scripture broadly to the fourfold assembly. The room of the Thus Come One is the thought of great compassion toward all living beings. The cloak of the Thus Come One is the thought of tender forbearance and the bearing of insult with equanimity. The throne of the Thus Come One is the emptiness of all dharmas. It is only by dwelling securely among these that he or she can with unabating thought broadly preach this Scripture of the Dharma Blossom to the bodhisattvas and the fourfold assembly. O Medicine King! Into other countries I will send magically conjured men as multitudes gathered to listen to Dharma. I will also send magically conjured bhikṣus, bhikṣuṇīs, upāsakas, and upāsikās, who shall listen to the preaching of Dharma.[7] These magically conjured persons shall hear the Dharma, receive it in faith, and obey it without violation. If the preacher of Dharma is in an empty and idle place, at that time I will send large numbers of gods and dragons, ghosts and demons, gandharvas and asuras to hear him preach the Dharma. Though I may be in another land, from time to time I will enable the preacher of Dharma to see my body. If he forgets or otherwise loses a single period of this scripture, I will simply tell it to him, thus enabling him to achieve perfection."

At that time the World-Honored One, wishing to restate this meaning, proclaimed gāthās, saying:

If one wishes to reject all slackness,
  One must listen to this scripture,
For this scripture may not be heard easily,
  And those who receive it in faith are also rare.
Suppose there is a man who is thirsty and in need of water,
  Who, though he digs on a high plain,
Still sees only dry earth,
  And thus knows that the water is yet far off.
At length he sees moist earth and mud,
  Thus knowing of a certainty that water is near.
O Medicine King, you are to know
  That, in this way, men

Who do not hear the Scripture of the Dharma Blossom
  Are very far removed from Buddha-knowledge.
If they hear this profound scripture,
  Which determines precisely the dharma of the voice-hearer,
This king of scriptures,
  And, having heard it, think on it with understanding,
Let it be known that these persons
  Are close to Buddha-wisdom.
If a man is to preach this scripture,
  He should enter the room of the Thus Come One,
Don the cloak of the Thus Come One,
  And sit on the throne of the Thus Come One,
Taking his place in the multitude fearlessly
  And preaching to them with breadth and discrimination.
Great compassion is the room,
  Tender harmony and endurance of insult the cloak,
While the emptiness of the dharmas is the throne:
  Making these his home, he preaches to [the multitude].
If when he is preaching this scripture
  A person reviles him with a foul mouth,
Or hits him with knife, staff, tile, or stone,
  In his mindfulness of the Buddha let him endure this.
In a thousand myriads of millions of lands, I,
  Displaying a body pure and firm,
For incalculable millions of kalpas
  Preach Dharma for living beings.
If after my passage into extinction
  Anyone can preach this scripture,
I will send him a magically conjured fourfold assembly,
  Bhikṣus and bhikṣuṇīs,
As well as gentlemen and ladies of pure faith,
  To make offerings to the Dharma-master.
Attracting various living beings
  And collecting them there, I will cause them to listen to Dharma.
If any man should wish to do ill to the Dharma-master

With knife or staff, or with tile or stone,
Then I will send a person magically conjured,
Who shall be his protection.
If a man preaching Dharma
Is alone in a quiet and idle place,
Lonely, without a human sound,
There reading or reciting this scriptural canon,
At that time I will appear to him, displaying
A body of pure radiance.
If he forgets chapter or verse,
I will tell it to him, thus enabling him to get it out with ease.
If a man, fully endowed with these excellences,
Should preach for the fourfold assembly,
In a deserted place reading or reciting scripture,
They would all be enabled to see my body.
If a man is in an empty and idle place,
I will send him gods and dragon kings,
Yakṣas, ghosts, and demons,
To compose a multitude to listen to his Dharma.[8]
This man takes pleasure in preaching Dharma,
In setting it forth with discrimination and without obstacles.
Because the Buddhas have him protectively in mind,
He is able to cause great rejoicing in the multitude.
If anyone can be close to the Dharma-master,
He can quickly gain the bodhisattva-path.
One who studies under the guidance of this master
Shall contrive to see Buddhas numerous as Ganges' sands.

Chapter Eleven: Apparition of the Jeweled Stūpa

At that time, there appeared before the Buddha a seven-jeweled stūpa, five hundred yojanas in height and two hundred and fifty yojanas in breadth, welling up out of the earth and resting in mid-air, set about with sundry precious objects. It had five thousand banisters, a thousand myriads of grotto-like rooms, and numberless banners to adorn it. Jeweled rosaries trailed from it, and ten thousand millions of jeweled bells were suspended from its top. Tamālapatracandana scent issued from all four of its surfaces and filled the world; its banners were made of the seven jewels, to wit, gold, silver, vaiḍūrya, giant clam shell, coral, pearl, and carnelian; and its height extended to the palaces of the four god kings. The thirty-three gods rained down on it divine māndārava flowers, with which they made offerings to the jeweled stūpa. The other gods, dragons, yakṣas, gandharvas, asuras, garuḍas, kinnaras, mahoragas, humans and nonhumans, numbering a thousand myriads of millions, made offerings to the jeweled stūpa of all manner of flower perfumes, necklaces, banners, and skillfully played music, reverently worshiping it, holding it in solemn esteem, and singing its praises. At that time, from the midst of the jeweled stūpa issued forth the sound of a mighty voice, praising and saying, "How excellent! How excellent, O Śākyamuni, O World-Honored One, that with great undifferentiating wisdom you can teach the bodhisattva-dharma, that you can preach to the great multitude the Scripture of the Blossom of the Fine Dharma, which Buddhas keep protectively in mind! Verily, verily, O Śākyamuni, O World-Honored One! Whatever you preach is all true reality."[1]

At that time, the fourfold assembly, seeing the great jeweled stūpa fixed in mid-air and also hearing the sound of the voice issuing forth from inside the stūpa, all attained Dharma-joy, amazed at what had never been before. They rose from their seats, humbly worshiping with palms joined, and then stood off to one side.

At that time there was a bodhisattva-mahāsattva named Great Joy in Preaching (Mahāpratibhāna), who, understanding the doubts in the minds of the gods, men, and asuras of all the worlds, addressed the Buddha, saying, "O World-Honored One! From what causes and conditions comes this jeweled stūpa, welling up out of the earth and producing from its midst the sound of this voice?"

At that time, the Buddha declared to the bodhisattva Great Joy in Preaching: "Within this jeweled stūpa is the whole body of a Thus Come One. That is to say, in the distant past, incalculable thousands of myriads of millions of asaṃkhyeyas of world-spheres to the east, there was a realm named Jewel-Pure (Ratnaviśuddhā). In it was a Buddha called Many Jewels (Prabhūtaratna). Earlier, when that Buddha was treading the bodhisattva-path, he took a great vow: 'If I achieve Buddhahood, and if, after my passage into extinction, in any of the lands of the ten directions there is a place in which the Scripture of the Dharma Blossom is preached, in order that that scripture may be heard, may my stūpa-shrine well up before it and bear witness to it by praising it, saying "Excellent!"' When that Buddha had achieved the Way, when he was on the point of passing into extinction, in the midst of a great multitude of gods and men he declared to the bhikṣus: 'After my passage into extinction, anyone who wishes to make offerings to my whole body must erect a great stūpa.' Such are that Buddha's supernatural penetrations, such the force of his vow that in the worlds of all ten directions, wherever anyone preaches the Scripture of the Dharma Blossom, his jeweled stūpa invariably wells up before that person, his whole body in the stūpa giving praise with the words, 'Excellent! Excellent!' Great Joy in Preaching! Now, because he has heard the Scripture of the Dharma Blossom being preached, the stūpa of the Thus Come One Many Jewels has welled up out of the earth with the words of praise, 'Excellent! Excellent!'"

At this time, the bodhisattva Great Joy in Preaching, with the aid of the supernatural power of the Thus Come One,* addressed the

* The Skt. has Mahāpratibhāna asking the Buddha for the spiritual strength required to see Prabhūtaratna, while the Ch. has him making the request with the aid of the Buddha's spiritual strength. The Chinese copyist must have misplaced the words *yi ju lai shen li ku* (corresponding to *bhavagato 'nubhāvena*).

Buddha, saying "World-Honored One! We pray, we wish to see this Buddha's body." The Buddha declared to the bodhisattva-mahāsattva Great Joy in Preaching: "This Buddha, Many Jewels, took a profound and solemn vow: 'When my jeweled stūpa appears in the Buddhas' presence in order that the Scripture of the Dharma Blossom may be heard, if there is anyone who wishes to show my body to the fourfold assembly, then may the Buddhas who are emanations* of that Buddha's body, when they have finished preaching the Dharma in the world-spheres of the ten directions, again gather in one place, for then and only then shall my body appear.'[2] Great Joy in Preaching! The Buddhas who are emanations of my body, who in the world-spheres of the ten directions preach Dharma, are now to gather."

Great Joy in Preaching addressed the Buddha, saying, "O World-Honored One! We also pray and wish to see the Buddhas who are emanations of the body of the World-Honored One, to worship them and make offerings to them!"

At that time, the Buddha emitted a single glow from his white hair-tuft, by which straightway were seen the Buddhas of lands in the eastern quarter equal in number to the sands of five hundred myriads of millions of nayutas of Ganges rivers. All those lands had sphāṭika for soil, and were adorned with jeweled trees and jeweled garments. Within, they were full of numberless thousands of myriads of millions of bodhisattvas. Jeweled flags were hoisted within them, and a jeweled net spread over them. The Buddhas of those lands preached the dharmas with a great, subtle sound. Also seen were incalculable thousands of myriads of millions of bodhisattvas, who filled the lands everywhere, preaching Dharma to the multitudes. To the south, the west, and the north, to the four intermediate directions as well as upward and downward, wherever the glow of the white hair-tuft reached, it was also thus.[3]

* *Ātmabhāvavigraha* in the Skt. There is a difficulty with the precise meaning of this word. I take it to mean a partial or separate manifestation (*vigraha*) of the essence (*ātmabhāva*, "self-being") of the Universal Buddha. The Ch. *fen shen* ("divided body" of the Buddha's body) seems to be getting at the same thing. In popular Mahāyāna lore, a Buddha can divide his own body into an infinite number of Buddha-bodies. The Skt. (see note 2 for a translation of this passage) seems to be stressing Many Jewels's power to appear anywhere at will, while Kumārajīva's version seems to be saying that he can divide himself up into a great number of Buddhas, any one of whom can appear anywhere.

At that time, the Buddhas in the ten directions all addressed their multitudes of bodhisattvas, saying "Good men! We are now to go to the Sahā world-sphere, to the place of Śākyamunibuddha, there to make offerings at the same time to the jeweled stūpa of the Thus Come One Many Jewels." Then the Sahā world-sphere was straightway transformed into something pure: with vaiḍūrya for soil; adorned with jeweled trees; having golden cords to set off its eight highways; having no villages, towns, or cities, no oceans or rivers, no mountains or streams, no forests or thickets; burning incense made of great jewels; having māndārava flowers spread all over its earth surface; having jeweled nets and banners spread over it; and holding only this assembled multitude, having moved gods and men away, to place them in other lands. At this time, the several Buddhas, each bringing with him one great bodhisattva as an attendant, reached the Sahā world-sphere, each going to the foot of a jeweled tree. Each jeweled tree was five hundred yojanas in height, adorned with branches, leaves, blossoms, and fruits in due order, the several trees each having at its base a lion throne five hundred yojanas in height, and each adorned with great jewels. At that time the Buddhas sat cross-legged, each on his own throne.[4]

In this way, by turns, the [lands of the] thousand-millionfold world were filled, and still there was no limit to the emanations of Śākyamunibuddha in even one quarter. At that time, Śākyamunibuddha, wishing accommodation for the Buddhas who were emanations of his body, conjured up in all eight directions two hundred myriads of millions of nayutas of realms, making them all pure, free of hells, hungry ghosts, beasts, and asuras, and moving gods and men away, placing them in other lands. These magically conjured realms also had vaiḍūrya for soil and were adorned with jeweled trees, each tree being five hundred yojanas in height, decked with branches, leaves, blossoms, and fruits in due order, each tree having at its base a jeweled lion throne five yojanas high and adorned in turn with a variety of jewels. There were also no oceans, rivers, or streams, or Mucilinda or Mahāmucilinda mountains, or Iron-Rimmed or Great Iron-Rimmed mountains, or Sumeru mountains, or indeed any other kings of mountains. Throughout, these realms were a single Buddha-land, its jeweled earth flat and even, covered by banners on which jewels were mingled with dew, hung with flags and canopies, burning incense made of great jewels, having divine jeweled flowers spread all over its earth surface.*[5]

At that time, Śākyamunibuddha's emanations in the eastern quarter, Buddhas of lands equal in number to the sands of a hundred thousand myriads of millions of Ganges rivers, each Buddha preaching Dharma, assembled in this place, Buddhas of ten directions all gathering in order and sitting in the eight quarters. In the four hundred myriads of millions of nayutas of lands in every quarter, the Buddhas, the Thus Come Ones, filled every direction. At this time, the Buddhas, each seated on a lion throne under a jeweled tree, all sent attendants to make courteous inquiry of Śākyamunibuddha, each attendant carrying jeweled flowers enough to fill both hands, and said to them, "Good men! Go now to Mount Gṛdhrakūṭa, to the place of Śākyamunibuddha, and say to him for me, 'Are you in good health and free of pain? Are your humours in good order? Is your strength unimpaired? And your multitude of bodhisattvas and voice-hearers, are they well or not?' Scatter these jeweled flowers before the Buddha as an offering and say, 'The Buddha So-and-so wishes to open this jeweled stūpa with you.' " The other Buddhas also sent messengers in the same way.

At that time, Śākyamunibuddha, seeing that the Buddhas who were emanations of his body had all arrived, and seeing how each, seated on a lion throne, was hearing that the Buddhas together wished to open the jeweled stūpa, straightway rose from his seat and rested in mid-air. All the four assemblies, rising with palms joined, single-mindedly beheld the Buddha. Thereupon with his right finger Śākyamunibuddha opened the door of the seven-jeweled stūpa, which made a great sound as of a bar being pushed aside to open the gate of a walled city. At that very moment all the assembled multitude saw the Thus Come One Many Jewels in the jeweled stūpa, seated on a lion throne, his body whole and undecayed, as if [he were] entered into dhyāna-concentration. They also heard his words: "Excellent! Excellent, O

* The preceding paragraph, except for the first sentence, is here repeated in both the Chinese and the Sanskrit texts.

Śākyamunibuddha! Happily have you preached this Scripture of the Dharma Blossom. It is to listen to this scripture that I have come here."

At that time, the four assemblies, seeing a Buddha passed into extinction for incalculable thousands of myriads of millions of kalpas speaking such words as these, sighed in admiration at something that had never been before, and scattered clusters of divine jeweled flowers over the Buddha Many Jewels and Śākyamunibuddha. The Buddha Many Jewels, in his jeweled stūpa, then gave half his seat to Śākyamunibuddha, speaking these words: "O Śākyamunibuddha, will you take this seat?" At that very moment Śākyamunibuddha, entering that stūpa, sat on half that seat, his legs crossed.[6]

At that time, the great multitude, seeing the two Thus Come Ones in the seven-jeweled stūpa on the lion throne, seated with legs crossed, all thought: "The Buddhas sit high up and far off. We wish that the Thus Come One, with his power of supernatural penetration, would enable the lot of us together to dwell in open space." At that very moment Śākyamunibuddha, with his power of supernatural penetration, touched the great multitudes, so that they were all in open space, and with a great voice proclaimed universally to the fourfold assembly: "Who can broadly preach the Scripture of the Blossom of the Fine Dharma in this Sahā land? Now is the very time! Not long hence, the Buddha shall enter nirvāṇa. The Buddha hopes for someone to whom this Scripture of the Blossom of the Fine Dharma may be assigned."

At that time, the World-Honored One, wishing to restate this meaning, proclaimed gāthās, saying:

The Sainted Lord, the World-Honored One,
  Though long since passed into extinction,
Yet into the jeweled stūpa's midst
  Has come for Dharma's sake.
O men! How may one
  Not strive for Dharma's sake?
This Buddha, though passed into extinction
  Unnumbered kalpas ago,
Yet in place after place listens to Dharma,

For it is hard to encounter.
That Buddha's former vow was,
"After my passage into extinction,
Wherever I am, wherever I go,
There may my purpose be to listen to Dharma."[7]
Also, the emanations of my body,
Incalculable Buddhas,
Equal in number to Ganges' sands,
Have come, wishing to listen to Dharma
And to see him who has passed into extinction,
The Thus Come One Many Jewels.
Each abandoning his fine land,
As well as the multitude of his disciples,
Gods, men, dragons, and demons
And their several offerings,
To cause Dharma long to endure
Have they all come hither.
In order to seat the Buddhas,
By the powers of my supernatural penetration
I have moved incalculable multitudes,
Causing the realms to be purified.
The Buddhas, each severally,
Proceed to the foot of their [respective] jeweled trees.
As in a cool, clear pond,
Lotus blossoms decorate
At the foot of those jeweled trees
The several lion thrones.[8]
The Buddhas, sitting atop them,
Are radiant in their splendour,
As if, in the midst of a dark night,
Kindling a great torch.
Their bodies emit a fine scent
That pervades the realms in all ten directions.
The living beings favored with the scent
Experience unbearable joy,
As if from a great wind

Blowing on the branches of small trees.
For by this expedient device
They enable Dharma long to endure.[9]
Each Buddha declares to the great multitudes:
"After my passage into extinction,
Who can guard and keep,
Read and recite this scripture?
Now, in the Buddha's presence,
Let him speak his own vow!"
The Buddha Many Jewels,
Though long since passed into extinction,
Through his great vow
Utters a lion's roar.[10]
The Thus Come One Many Jewels,
As well as I myself
And the magically conjured Buddhas here assembled,
Will know this meaning.
O sons of the Buddhas!
Who can keep the Dharma?
Let him utter a great vow
And thus enable it long to endure.
If there is one who can keep
This Scripture-Dharma,
Then thereby he shall have made offerings
To me and to Many Jewels.
This Buddha Many Jewels,
Dwelling within the jeweled stūpa,
Ever travels in the ten directions
For this scripture's sake.
Moreover, those who, as an offering
To the magically conjured Buddhas who have come hither,
Decorate with splendor
The various world-spheres,
If they only preach this scripture,
Shall then, on that account, see me,

The Buddha Many Jewels,
  And the magically conjured Buddhas.
O good men!
  Think carefully, each of you!
This is a difficult matter,
  And for it a great vow should be taken.[11]
The other scriptural canons
  Are in number like to Ganges' sands,
But if one were to preach these,
  Still this should not be thought difficult.
If one were to take hold of Sumeru
  And fling it into another quarter
Over untold Buddha-lands,
  That also would not be difficult.
If with a toe
  One were to move the thousand-millionfold world,
Flinging it far off to another realm,
  That also would not be difficult.
If one were to stand on the Pinnacle of Existence
  And for the multitude set forth
Other incalculable scriptures,
  That also would not be difficult.
But if after the Buddha's extinction,
  In the midst of an evil age
One can preach this scripture,
  That is difficult.
If there should be a man
  Who, holding open space in his hand,
Were to walk about with it,
  Even that would not be difficult.
After my extinction,
  If one can write and keep it oneself,
Or cause another to write it,
  That is difficult.[12]
If one should take the Great Earth

And, placing it on one's toenail,
Mount with it to the Brahmā gods,
That, too, would not be difficult.
After the Buddha's passage into extinction,
In the midst of an evil age,
To read this scripture for but a moment—
That is difficult.[13]
Even if in the kalpa's holocaust
One should carry dry grass on one's back
And enter the flame, yet not be burnt,
That, too, would not be difficult.
After my extinction,
If one can hold this scripture
And preach it to even one person,
That is difficult.
If one were to carry eighty-
Four thousand treasure houses
Of the twelvefold scriptural canon
And preach them to men,
Causing the listeners
To gain the six supernatural penetrations—
Even if one could do this,
It would still not be difficult.
If after my extinction
One can accept this scripture by listening to it,
Inquiring into its purport,
This is difficult.[14]
If a man, preaching Dharma,
Causes the equal of a thousand myriads of millions
Of incalculable, innumerable
Ganges rivers' sands of living beings
To attain the rank of arhant
And to perfect the six supernatural penetrations,
Though he were to confer this benefit,
Still it would not be difficult.
After my extinction,

If one can reverently hold aloft
Scriptural canons like this one,
That will be difficult.
For the sake of the Buddha Path, I,
In incalculable lands,
From the beginning until now,
Have broadly preached the scriptures,
But among them
This scripture is first.
If there is anyone who can hold it,
Then he holds the Buddha-body.
O good men!
After my extinction,
Who can receive and keep,
Read and recite this scripture?
Now, in the Buddha's presence,
Let him speak a vow himself!
This scripture is hard to hold.
If anyone can hold it for but a moment,
Then I will be delighted,
As shall the other Buddhas also.
A person like this
Shall be praised by the Buddhas:
"This fellow, you know, is doughty.
This fellow, you know, moves forward with sincerity.
He is called a keeper of the precepts,
A performer of *dhūta* [ascetic] practices.
Thus he shall quickly attain
To the unexcelled Buddha Path."[15]
If in future ages he can
Read and keep this scripture,
Then he is a true son of Buddha,
Dwelling in a pure, good land.
After the Buddha's passage into extinction,
If they can understand its meaning,
Then such gods and men

Shall be the eyes of the world.
If in a terrifying age
They can preach for but a moment,
Then all gods and men
Must make offerings to them.[16]

Scripture of the Lotus Blossom of the Fine Dharma.
End of Roll the Fourth.

Roll 5

Chapter Twelve: Devadatta

At that time, the Buddha declared to the bodhisattvas and to the fourfold assembly of gods and men: "In time past, throughout incalculable kalpas I sought the Scripture of the Dharma Blossom, throughout many kalpas being neither negligent nor impatient. I was ever king of a realm, [and as king] I vowed to seek unexcelled bodhi, my thought never receding. Wishing to fulfill the six pāramitās, I strove to confer gifts, in my mind never begrudging elephants, horses, or the seven jewels; nor realms or walled cities; nor wife and children, slaves and servants; nor head, eyes, marrow, trunk and flesh, arms and legs; not begruding bodily life itself. At that time, the people of the age had incalculable length of life. For Dharma's sake, I abandoned realm and title, leaving the government to my heir, and to the beat of a drum I announced to the four quarters that I was seeking Dharma: 'Whoever can preach the Great Vehicle to me, for him I will render service and run errands for the rest of my life!' At that time there was a seer (*ṛṣi*) who came and reported to the king, saying, 'I have a great vehicle; its name is the Scripture of the Lotus Blossom of the Fine Dharma. If you can obey me, I will set it forth for you.' When the king heard the seer's words, he danced for joy, then straightway followed the seer, tending to whatever he required: picking his fruit, drawing his water, gathering his firewood, preparing his food, even making a couch of his own body; feeling no impatience, whether in body or in mind. He rendered him service for a thousand years, bending all efforts to menial labor for Dharma's sake and seeing to it that he lacked nothing."[1]

At that time, the World-Honored One, wishing to restate this meaning, proclaimed gāthās, saying:

I recall past kalpas,
When, in quest of Great Dharma,

Though I was lord of the realm for the age,
I did not crave the pleasures of the five desires.
I beat a drum, declaring to the four quarters:
"Whosoever is in possession of the Great Dharma,
If he can explain it to me,
In person I will be his slave!"
At the time there was an ṛṣi-seer,
Who came and reported to the great king,
"I have a fine and subtle dharma,
Rarely to be had in the world.
If you can practice it,
Then I will preach it to you."
At the time the king, hearing the seer's words,
At heart was overjoyed.
Then straightway, following the seer,
He rendered him whatever service he required,
Gathering his firewood, his fruits and melons,
Presenting them to him respectfully at the appropriate times.
Because my heart cherished the Fine Dharma,
My body and mind knew neither sloth nor impatience.
For the living beings' sakes, universally,
I strove in quest of Great Dharma,
Neither for myself
Nor for the pleasures of the five desires.
Thus I became the lord of a great realm,
Strove to gain and keep this Dharma,
Contrived at length to achieve Buddhahood,
And now expressly preach to you.[2]

The Buddha declared to the bhikṣus: "The king at that time was myself. The seer was he who is at present Devadatta.[3] It is thanks to my good friend Devadatta that I have been enabled to perfect the six pāramitās; tenderness, compassion, sympathetic joy, and indifference to self; the thirty-two marks and the eighty beautiful features; the color of polished red-gold; the ten strengths; the four kinds of fearlessness; the four inclusive dharmas; the eighteen kinds of uniqueness; the power of the Way of the supernatural penetrations. The achievement of undifferentiating, right, enlightened intuition and the broad conveyance of living beings to salvation I owe to my good friend Devadatta. I declare this to the fourfold assembly: hereafter Devadatta, following the passage of incalculable kalpas, shall contrive to achieve Buddhahood, and shall be called God King (Devarāja) the Thus Come One, worthy of offerings, of right and universal knowledge, his clarity and conduct perfect, well gone, understanding the world, an unexcelled Worthy, a Regulator of men of stature, a Teacher of gods and men, a Buddha, a World-Honored One; and his world-sphere shall be named Highway of the Gods [Devasopānā, "Stairway of the Gods"]. At that time, the Buddha God King shall dwell in the world twenty intermediate kalpas, broadly preaching the Fine Dharma to the living beings. Beings equal in number to Ganges' sands shall gain the fruit of the arhant. Incalculable living beings shall display the mind of the perceiver of conditions. Beings equal in number to Ganges' sands shall open up their thought to the unexcelled Way and, gaining acceptance of [the doctrine of] the unborn, dwell where there is no backsliding. At that time, after the parinirvāṇa of the Buddha God King, his True Dharma shall abide in the world twenty intermediate kalpas; and a stūpa of the seven jewels shall be erected to house the śarīra of his whole body, sixty yojanas in height, forty yojanas in length and breadth. Gods and men with assorted flowers, powdered incense, burnt incense, perfumed paint, clothing and necklaces, banners and parasols, and music skillfully sung and played shall all make offerings to that fine stūpa of the seven jewels. Incalculable living beings shall gain the fruit of the arhant. Numberless beings shall have the enlightened intuition of the pratyekabuddha. Living beings whose number shall be beyond reckoning and discussion shall open up their thoughts to bodhi and reach the point from which there is no backsliding."

The Buddha declared to the bhikṣus: "In ages yet to come, if there is a good man or a good woman who, hearing the Devadatta Chapter of the Scripture of the Blossom of the Fine Dharma, with a pure heart believes and reveres it, evincing no doubts or uncertainties, he shall not fall to the level of hell, hungry ghosts, or beasts, but shall be reborn in the presence of the Buddhas of all ten directions, constantly hearing this scripture wherever he may be born. If he is reborn among men or gods, he shall enjoy superior subtle pleasures. If he is in the presence of a Buddha, he shall be magically reborn in a lotus blossom."[4]

At that time, in the nether region there was a bodhisattva in the train of Many Jewels the World-Honored One whose name was Wisdom Accumulation (Prajñākūṭa). He reported to the Buddha Many Jewels that he was about to return to his original land. Śākyamunibuddha addressed Wisdom Accumulation, saying, "Good man, wait a bit! There is here a bodhisattva named Mañjuśrī whom you would do well to meet, for he will preach the Fine Dharma to you, and then you may return to your original land."

At that time, Mañjuśrī was seated on a lotus blossom with a thousand leaves, the size of a carriage wheel, and the bodhisattvas who had come with him were also seated on jeweled lotus blossoms, which were welling up of themselves out of the great sea, from the dragon palace of Sāgara, and resting in mid-air. Thence he went to the Mount of the Numinous Eagle (Gṛdhrakūṭa), where, descending from the lotus blossom, he went into the Buddha's presence, with head bowed did obeisance before both feet of the World-Honored One, and, having attended to all courtesies, went before Wisdom Accumulation. There, having questioned him solicitously, he sat off to one side.[5] The bodhisattva Wisdom Accumulation asked Mañjuśrī, "You have been to the dragon palace. How great is the number of the beings converted by you there?" Mañjuśrī said, "The number is beyond dimension, it is incalculable, not a thing the mouth can proclaim, nor anything the mind can fathom. Just wait a bit, for you shall have proof yourself." Before his speech was finished, numberless bodhisattvas, seated on jeweled lotus blossoms, welled up out of the sea and went to the Mount of the Numinous Eagle, where they rested in mid-air. These bodhisattvas had all been converted and conveyed to salvation by Mañjuśrī, all had perfected bodhisattva-conduct, and all were discussing together the six pāramitās. Those who had formerly been voice-hearers were in mid-air preaching the conduct of the voice-hearer. But now all were putting into practice the Great Vehicle's doctrine of emptiness. Mañjuśri spoke to Wisdom Accumulation, saying, "Such is the manner of teaching and conversion within the sea!"

At that time, the bodhisattva Wisdom Accumulation praised him with gāthās, saying:

O most excellently wise, most courageous and vigorous,
You have converted and conveyed to salvation an incalculable multitude.
Now this great assembly
And I myself have all seen you
Setting forth the doctrine of the true marks,
Laying open the Dharma of the One Vehicle,
Broadly guiding multitudinous living beings,
And enabling them quickly to achieve bodhi.[6]

Mañjuśrī said, "I have never preached in the sea's midst anything but the Scripture of the Blossom of the Fine Dharma." The bodhisattva Wisdom Accumulation questioned Mañjuśrī, saying, "That scripture is very profound and subtle, a gem among the scriptures, a thing rarely to be found in the world. Are there any beings who, putting this scripture into practice by the strenuous application of vigor, speedily gain Buddhahood, or are there not?"

Mañjuśrī said, "There is the daughter of the dragon king Sāgara, whose years are barely eight. Her wisdom is sharp-rooted,* and well she knows the faculties and deeds of the beings. She has gained dhāraṇī. The profound treasure house of secrets preached by the Buddhas she is able to accept and to keep in its entirety. She has profoundly entered into dhyāna-concentration, and has arrived at an understanding of the dharmas. In the space of a *kṣaṇa* [moment] she produced bodhi-thought, and has attained the point of nonbacksliding. Her eloquence has no obstructions, and she is compassionately mindful of the beings as if they were her babies. Her merits are perfect.[7] What she

* That is, her capacity for intuitive understanding is supported by keen faculties (*li ken*, Skt. *tīkṣṇendriya*). There are 32 *indriyas*, or faculties, among them the six sense-faculties. The first five are fancied to be invisible, impalpable, weightless substances covering the respective sense organs, while the sixth, *mana'indriya*, is any sensual sensation of a moment (*kṣaṇa*) before. The *indriyas* are the "base" of sense perception, and the Ch. accordingly renders the word as *ken*, "root."

recollects in her mind and recites with her mouth is subtle and broad. She is of good will and compassionate, humane and yielding. Her will and thought are harmonious and refined, and she is able to attain to bodhi."

The bodhisattva Wisdom Accumulation said, "I have seen the Thus Come One of the Śākyas throughout incalculable kalpas tormenting himself by doing what is hard to do, piling up merit and heaping up excellence, seeking the Path of the bodhisattva and never resting. When I look at the thousand-millionfold world, there is no place, not even the size of a mustardseed, where the bodhisattva did not cast away body and life for the beings' sakes, and only then did he achieve the Way of bodhi. I do not believe that this girl in the space of a moment directly and immediately achieved right, enlightened intuition."

Before he had finished speaking, at that very time the daughter of the dragon king suddenly appeared in front [of them], and, doing obeisance with head bowed, stood off to one side and spoke praise with gāthās, saying:

Having profoundly mastered the marks of sin and merit,
  Universally illuminating all ten directions,
The subtle and pure Dharma-body
  Has perfected the marks thirty-two,
Using the eighty beautiful features
  As a means of adorning the Dharma-body.
The object of respectful obeisance for gods and men,
  It is reverently honored by all dragons and spirits.
Of all varieties of living beings,
  None fails to bow to it as an object of worship.
I have also heard that, as for the achievement of bodhi,
  Only the Buddha can know it by direct witness.
I, laying open the teachings of the Great Vehicle,
  Convey to release the suffering beings.[8]

At that time, Śāriputra spoke to the dragon girl, saying, "You say that in no long time you shall attain the unexcelled Way. This is hard to believe. What is the reason? A woman's body is filthy, it is not a

Dharma-receptacle. How can you attain unexcelled bodhi? The Path of the Buddha is remote and cavernous. Throughout incalculable kalpas, by tormenting oneself and accumulating good conduct, also by thoroughly cultivating the perfections, only by these means can one then be successful. Also, a woman's body even then has five obstacles. It cannot become first a Brahmā god king, second the god Śakra, third King Māra, fourth a sage-king turning the Wheel, fifth a Buddha-body. How can the body of a woman speedily achieve Buddhahood?"

At that time, the dragon girl had a precious gem, whose value was the [whole] thousand-millionfold world, which she held up and gave to the Buddha. The Buddha straightway accepted it. The dragon girl said to the bodhisattva Wisdom Accumulation and to the venerable Śāriputra, "I offered a precious gem, and the World-Honored One accepted it. Was this quick or not?"

He answered, saying, "Very quick!"

The girl said, "With your supernatural power you shall see me achieve Buddhahood even more quickly than that!"

At that time, the assembled multitude all saw the dragon girl in the space of an instant turn into a man, perfect bodhisattva-conduct, straightway go southward to the world-sphere Spotless, sit on a jeweled lotus blossom, and achieve undifferentiating, right, enlightened intuition, with thirty-two marks and eighty beautiful features setting forth the Fine Dharma for all living beings in all ten directions. At that time, in the Sahā world-sphere bodhisattvas, voice-hearers, gods, dragons, the eightfold assembly, humans and nonhumans, all from a distance seeing that dragon girl achieve Buddhahood and universally preach Dharma to the men and gods of the assembly of that time, were overjoyed at heart and all did obeisance from afar. Incalculable living beings, hearing the Dharma and understanding it, attained to nonbacksliding. Incalculable living beings were enabled to receive a prophecy of the Path. The Spotless world-sphere trembled in six different ways, and in the Sahā world-sphere three thousand living beings dwelt on the ground from which there is no backsliding. Three thousand living beings opened up the thought of bodhi and were enabled to receive prophecies. The bodhisattva Wisdom Accumulation, as well as Śāriputra and all the assembled multitude, silently believed and accepted.[9]

Chapter Thirteen: Fortitude

At that time, the bodhisattva-mahāsattva Medicine King (Bhaiṣajya-rāja) and the bodhisattva-mahāsattva Great Joy in Preaching (Mahā-pratibhāna), together with a retinue of two myriads of bodhisattvas, in the Buddha's presence took this oath, saying:[1] "We beg you, O World-Honored One, not to be concerned, for after the Buddha's extinction, we will reverently exalt, read and recite, and preach this scriptural canon. Though the beings of the latter evil age shall be of ever slighter wholesome faculties, though they shall have much over-weening pride and shall covet offerings, though their unwholesome faculties shall increase and they shall be hard to teach and convert, yet we, rousing the strength of great forbearance, will read and recite this scripture, bear and preach it, write and copy it, and in a variety of ways make offerings to it, not begrudging even bodily life."

At that time, five hundred arhants within the multitude who had received prophecies addressed the Buddha, saying, "O World-Honored One! We, too, vow to preach this scripture broadly in other lands." Again, there were learners and those who had nothing more to learn, eight thousand in number, who had received prophecies, and who, rising from their seats and facing the Buddha with hands clasped, took this vow, saying: "O World-Honored One! We, too, will preach this scripture broadly in other lands. What is the reason? In the midst of this Sahā realm, most men are evil, harboring thoughts of overweening pride, their merit shallow and thin, irascible, muddied, sycophantic, and crooked, their hearts not true."

At that time, with learning bhikṣuṇīs and those who had nothing more to learn, six thousand in number, the Buddha's maternal aunt, the bhikṣuṇī Mahāprajāpatī, rose from her seat and single-mindedly and with hands clasped looked up at the August Countenance, her eyes not turning aside even for a moment. At that time, the World-Honored One asked Gautamī, "Why do you look upon the Thus Come One with such a troubled mien? You are surely saying to yourself that I did not mention your name when conferring prophecies of anuttarasamyaksaṃbodhi, are you not? Yet, in an age to come, with respect to the Dharma of sixty-eight thousands of millions of Buddhas, you shall be a great Dharma-teacher. Together with six thousand bhikṣunīs, learners and those who have nothing more to learn, you shall be a Dharma-teacher. In this way, little by little you shall perfect the Path of the bodhisattva, and shall succeed in becoming a Buddha named Seen with Joy by All Living Beings, a Thus Come One, worthy of offerings, of right and universal knowledge, his clarity and conduct perfect, well gone, understanding the world, an unexcelled Worthy, a Regulator of men of stature, a Teacher of gods and men, a Buddha, a World-Honored One. Gautamī! This Buddha, Seen with Joy by All Living Beings, on* six thousand bodhisattvas, one by one, shall confer a prophecy of the attainment of anuttarasamyaksambodhi."[2]

At that time, Rāhula's mother, the bhikṣuṇī Yaśodharā, thought: "In the course of his prophecies the World-Honored One failed to mention only my name." The Buddha declared to Yaśodharā, "In time to come, you shall perform bodhisattva-conduct with respect to the Dharma of a hundred thousand myriads of millions of Buddhas and become a Dharma-teacher. At length you shall perfect the Buddha Path, and in the realm Goodly shall contrive to become a Buddha named He Who Has Perfected a Thousand Myriads of Glowing Marks, a Thus Come One, worthy of offerings, of right and universal knowledge, his clarity and conduct perfect, well gone, understanding the world, an unexcelled Worthy, a Regulator men of stature, a Teacher of gods and men, a Buddha, a World-Honored One. That Buddha's life-span shall be incalculable asaṃkhyeyakalpas."[3]

At that time, the bhikṣuṇī Mahāprajāpatī and the bhikṣuṇī Yaśodharā, together with their retinues, were overjoyed, having gained

* Instead of "on," Kumarajiva's version has "and" (*chi*), which makes no sense, and which also conflicts with the Sanskrit, where the verb is in the third singular: *vyākariṣyaty anuttarāyāṃ samyaksaṃbodhau* //

something they had never had before, and straightway in the Buddha's presence proclaimed a gāthā, saying:

> O World-Honored One, O Guide, O Teacher!
> You put gods and men at their ease.
> Having heard your prophecy, we
> Are perfectly at ease in our hearts.

Having proclaimed this gāthā, the bhikṣuṇīs addressed the Buddha, saying, "O World-Honored One! We, too, can proclaim this scripture broadly in other lands."

At that time, the World-Honored One looked at the eighty myriads of millions of nayutas of bodhisattva-mahāsattvas. These bodhisattvas were all avaivartikas, turning the unreceding Wheel of the Dharma and having attained the dhāraṇīs. Straightway, rising from their seats, they went into the Buddha's presence, single-mindedly joined palms, and thought: "If the World-Honored One should command us to hold this scripture, then in obedience to the Buddha's instructions, we should propagate this scripture broadly." Then they thought: "The Buddha is now silent, issuing no commands. What should we now do?" At the time the bodhisattvas were respectfully obedient to the Buddha's intentions, and at the same time wished to fullfil their own former vows. Then in the Buddha's presence, with a lion's roar they uttered a vow, saying, "O World-Honored One! After the extinction of the Thus Come One, we shall go round and about and back and forth in the world-spheres of all ten directions and shall be able to cause living beings to write and copy this scripture, to accept and keep it, to read and recite it, to explain its meaning, to put it into practice in accordance with Dharma, and to be rightly mindful of it—and all this shall be thanks to the majestic might of the Buddha. We beg that the World-Honored One, while dwelling in another quarter, may grant us his protection from afar."[4]

Directly, then, the bodhisattvas, raising their voices in unison, proclaimed gāthās, saying:

> We beg you not to be concerned,
> For after the Buddha's passage into extinction,

In a frightful and evil age,
  We will broadly preach.
Those ignorant men, whoever they may be,
  That revile us with foul mouths,
Or attack us with knives and staves,
  We will all endure.
The bhikṣus in an evil age,
  Men of twisted wisdom, their hearts sycophantic and crooked,
Say they already have attained what in fact they have not yet
    attained,
  Their hearts being full of pride.
Or there are *āraṇyakas* [forest-dwelling hermits],
  Clothed in patched rags and living in the wilderness,
Who say of themselves that they are treading the True Path,
  Holding mankind cheaply.
Because they covet profit and nourishment,
  They preach Dharma to white-robed laymen,
And are held in humble reverence by the world,
  As though they were arhants of the six penetrations.
These men, harboring evil thoughts,
  Constantly mindful of the affairs of the world,
Borrow the name of āraṇyakas
  Because they love to display our faults.
Then they make such talk as this:
  "These bhikṣus,
Out of greed for profit and nourishment,
  Preach the arguments of external paths.*
Having themselves created this scriptural canon
  To deceive worldlings and lead them astray,
In the quest for name and renown
  They preach this scripture with much discrimination."[5]
Since within the great multitude they ever
  Wish to ruin us,
Turning to kings and great ministers,

* *Wai tao* (*tīrthika*), standard term for all non-Buddhist schools of thought in India.

To Brahmans and householders,
And to multitudes of other bhikṣus,
They slanderously speak evil of us,
Saying, "These fellows of wrong views
Preach arguments of external paths."
Out of veneration for the Buddha, we
Will endure all these evils.
By them we shall be addressed with derision,
"You fellows are all Buddhas!"
Such words of derision as these
We will all endure with patience.[6]
In a muddied kalpa, in an evil age,
Many shall be the frightful
Evil demons that enter their bodies
To malign and disgrace us.
We, venerating and believing the Buddha,
Will don the armor of forbearance
And, to preach this scripture,
Will endure these troubles.[7]
We do not covet bodily life,
We do but regret the Unexcelled Path.
In an age to come, we
Will guard and keep what the Buddha has assigned.
The World-Honored One himself must know
That in the muddied age the evil bhikṣus
Shall not know the Buddha's expedient devices,
The Dharma he preaches in accord with what is appropriate.
Foul language and wry faces,
Repeated banishment [from the Order],
Separation from stūpas and monasteries—
Such shall the many evils be;
But, mindful of the Buddha's commands,
We will all endure these things.[8]
In villages, cities, and towns,
If there is a person who seeks Dharma,
We will all go to that place

To preach the Dharma assigned by the Buddha.
We are the messengers of the World-Honored One,
Dwelling in the multitude without fear.
Well will we preach the Dharma:
We beg the Buddha to remain tranquil.[9]
In the presence of the World-Honored One,
To the Buddhas who have arrived from the ten quarters
We utter such an oath as this,
And the Buddha himself knows our thoughts.

Chapter Fourteen: Comfortable Conduct

At that time, Mañjuśrī the Dharma-prince, the bodhisattva-mahāsattva, addressed the Buddha, saying, "O World-Honored One! Very rarely do there exist such bodhisattvas as these, who out of respectful obedience to the Buddha utter a great vow to keep and hold, to read and recite this Scripture of the Dharma Blossom in the latter evil age! O World-Honored One! How can a bodhisattva-mahāsattva preach this scripture in the latter evil age?"

The Buddha declared to Mañjuśrī: "If in the latter evil age a bodhisattva-mahāsattva wishes to preach this scripture, he must dwell securely in four dharmas. First, by dwelling securely in the place where the bodhisattva acts, in the place that he approaches with familiarity, he shall be able to set forth this scripture for the sake of living beings. Mañjuśrī! What is meant by 'the place where the bodhisattva-mahāsattva acts'? If a bodhisattva-mahāsattva dwells on the ground of forbearance; if he is gentle, agreeable, good, and acquiescent, not given to fits of violence, nor at heart becoming alarmed; if, further, he performs no act with respect to the dharmas, but views the dharmas in keeping with their true marks; if, also, he performs no act and commits no discrimination, this is called 'the place where the bodhisattva-mahāsattva acts.' What is meant by 'the place that the bodhisattva-mahāsattva approaches with familiarity?' The bodhisattva-mahāsattva does not approach with familiarity kings or princes of realms, nor ministers or senior officials. He does not approach with familiarity the followers of external paths, nor Brahmans, nor Nirgranthas [heretical monks, esp. Jain], nor those who compose worldly letters, nor those who sing the praises of external writings, nor Lokāyatas [materialists], nor those who oppose the Lokāyatas. Nor does he approach with familiarity those who, to provide wicked amusement, beat one another with fists or knock one another down, nor *naṭas* [dancers, actors], nor [practitioners of] any of a variety of magical games. He also does not approach with familiarity *caṇḍālas* [outcastes] or those who raise pigs, sheep, chickens, and dogs; nor those who hunt, or fish, or cultivate other evil practices. If such persons on some chance occasion come to him, then he preaches Dharma to them but hopes for nothing. Also, he does not approach with familiarity bhikṣus, bhikṣuṇīs, upāsakas, or upāsikās who seek to be voice-hearers, nor does he ask after their well-being. Whether in a room, or in a thoroughfare, or in a hall for public speaking, he does not stay with them. If on some chance occasion they come to him, he preaches Dharma appropriately, but seeks and hopes for nothing.

"Nor should a bodhisattva-mahāsattva take a woman's body as the mark of something that can produce thoughts of desire; but even when preaching Dharma to her, he should have no desire to see her. If he enters another's house, he does not talk with little girls, or maidens, or widows. Nor does he approach the five kinds of unmanly men* in order to be friendly with or close to them. He does not enter another's house alone. When there is a condition under which he absolutely must enter alone, he single-mindedly recalls the Buddha. If he preaches the Dharma to a woman, he does not bare his teeth when smiling, nor show his chest. Not even for Dharma's sake does he become familiar or close. How much the less for anything else! He has no desire to rear a young disciple or a śrāmaṇera-boy, nor does he wish to share the same master with him; but he ever loves to sit in dhyāna, improving and collecting

* The Skt. simply says *paṇḍaka*, "impotent"; the Ch. specifies the number five, without identifying them. They are as follows: (a) *jātipaṇḍaka*, a male congenitally devoid of sexual impulses or feelings; (b) *pakṣapaṇḍaka*, a male potent only part of the time, lit. half of every month; (c) *āsaktaprādurbhāvī paṇḍakaḥ*, a male who becomes impotent through premature ejaculation; (d) *īrṣyāpaṇḍaka*, one who can become sexually aroused only by seeing others having intercourse; (e) *āpatpaṇḍaka*, a male who has lost his potency through illness or accident. The source for this is *Mahāvyutpatti* §§8769–73. The canonical source is the *vinaya* (monastic code). The reason for the concern is that the saṃgha did not want anyone joining the order as an escape. It barred from membership married men who did not have their wives' permission, fathers who did not have the permission of their adult children, debtors reneging on their debts, deserters from military service, fugitives from justice, persons in arrears in taxes, novices who did not have the permission of both parents (when the parents were alive), homosexuals, hermaphrodites, and men who, for whatever reason, were sexually not quite normal.

his thoughts in a quiet place. Mañjuśrī! This is called the first place which he approaches with familiarity.

"Again, the bodhisattva-mahāsattva views all dharmas as empty, in accord with their true marks, not inverted, nor moving, nor receding, nor revolving, devoid of character as empty space, inaccessible of approach by any words, not born, nor coming out, nor arising, nameless, signless [markless?], having in truth no being, incalculable and unlimited, unimpeded and unobstructed, existing solely by virtue of causes and conditions, [their "reality"] born of inverted notions. That is why he preaches, ever wishing to see such dharma-marks as these. This is called the second place that the bodhisattva-mahāsattva approaches with familiarity."[1]

At that time, the World-Honored One, wishing to restate this meaning, proclaimed gāthās, saying:

If there is a bodhisattva
  In the latter evil age
Who, with heart free of fear,
  Wishes to preach this scripture,
He should enter the place of action
  And the place of familiar approach,
Ever separating himself from the lords of realms
  And from their heirs,
As well as great ministers and senior officials,
  Those who play dangerous games,
And caṇḍālas,
  Adherents of external paths, and Brahmans.[2]
Nor is he to approach with familiarity
  Men of overweening pride,
Who cling with craving to the Lesser Vehicle,
  Students of the three storehouses (*tripiṭaka*),
Bhikṣus who violate the precepts,
  Arhants in name only,
Or bhikṣuṇīs
  Who love to play and laugh,
Profoundly attached to the five desires,

Or those who seek to display passage into extinction,
To wit, upāsikās:
Let him approach none of these with familiarity.[3]
If such persons as these
Come in good heart,
Arriving in the bodhisattva's presence
In order to hear of the Buddha Path,
May the bodhisattva then, with
A heart free of fear,
Cherishing no hopes,
Preach Dharma to them.
Widows, maidens,
And unmanly men,
None of these is he to approach with familiarity,
To be intimate with or close to them.
Nor is he to approach with familiarity
Butchers or meat-cutters,
Hunters or fishermen,
Or any who kill for profit,
Selling meat for their livelihood,
Or those who advertise and sell female flesh:
Of the likes of these,
He is to approach none with familiarity.[4]
Those who play foolish and dangerous games, such as knocking one another down [?],
Or engage in any other of such sundry amusements,
Or prostitutes—
Let him approach none of these with familiarity.
He is never alone in a secluded place
To preach Dharma to women.
When he does preach Dharma to them,
He is never to joke or laugh.
When he enters a village to beg for food,
Let him take a bhikṣu with him.
If there is no bhikṣu,
He is single-mindedly to recollect the Buddha.

This, then, is called
  "The place of action," "the place of approach."
By resort to these two places,
  One can comfortably preach.[5]
Nor, again, does he course
  In superior, mediate, and inferior dharmas,
Or in constituted and unconstituted,
  Or real and unreal, dharmas.
Nor does he make the distinction,
  "This is a man; this, a woman."
He does not gain the dharmas,
  Nor know, nor see them.[6]
This, then, is called
  The bodhisattva's place of action.
All the dharmas
  Are empty, having nothing,
Neither any permanency
  Nor any arising or perishing.
This is called the wise man's
  Place of familiar approach.[7]
It is only through inverse discrimination
  That the dharmas exist or do not exist,
That they are real or unreal,
  Born or unborn.
If in a quiet place
  One perfects and collects one's thoughts,
Dwelling securely and unmoving
  As if one were Mount Sumeru itself,
Observing that all dharmas
  Have nothing whatsoever,
Being quite like empty space;
  That they have nothing firm or solid,
Being unborn, unemerging,
  Unmoving, unreceding,[8]
Ever dwelling in one mark,
  This is called the place of approach.

When a bhikṣu,
 After my passage into extinction,
Enters this place of action
 And place of familiar approach,
When preaching this scripture,
 He experiences no panic.
The bodhisattva, at times,
 Shall enter into a quiet room
And with right mindfulness
 View the dharmas in keeping with the doctrine,
Then, rising from dhyāna-concentration,
 For lords of realms,
Princes and subjects,
 Brahmans, and the like,
Enlighten, convert, and set forth,
 Preaching this scriptural canon,
His heart tranquil
 And subject to no panic.
O Mañjuśrī!
 Such is the bodhisattva
Who, dwelling securely in the first Dharma,
 Shall be able in the latter age
To preach the Scripture of the Dharma Blossom.[9]

"Also, O Mañjuśrī, if after the extinction of the Thus Come One, and in the final Dharma, one wishes to preach this scripture, one must dwell in comfortable activity. Whether setting forth explication by word of mouth or reading the scripture itself, one is to have no wish to mention the faults of men or of the scriptural canon. Nor is one to hold other Dharma-masters lightly or in contempt, or to talk of the good and bad, the advantages and deficiencies of others. With respect to voice-hearing men, one is also not to talk of their faults mentioning them by name. Nor, for that matter, is one to laud their virtues, mentioning them by name. Nor, again, is one to give rise to a heart of resentment and suspicion. It is because one is skilled at cultivating such comfortable thoughts as these that one's listeners shall not oppose one's intentions. If there are objections or queries, one is not to answer them by resort to the dharma of the Lesser Vehicle, but one is to explain only in terms of the Greater Vehicle, causing persons to gain knowledge of all modes."[10]

At that time, the World-Honored One, wishing to restate this meaning, proclaimed gāthās, saying:

The bodhisattva ever wishes
  In tranquil security to preach Dharma,
On pure soil
  Arranging his chair.
Smearing his body with oil
  And washing away the impurities,
Let him don a new, clean garment,
  Clean both within and without.
Resting securely on his Dharma-seat,
  Let him preach in answer to questions.[11]
If there be bhikṣus
  And bhikṣuṇīs,
Upāsakas
  And upāsikās,
Kings and princes,
  Sundry ministers, gentlemen, and commoners,
Let him, by resort to subtle doctrine,
  Preach to them with harmonious countenance.
If there be objections or queries,
  Let him answer them in keeping with Doctrine,
By resort to causes and conditions, as well as parables,
  Expounding and making distinctions:
Through such devices as these
  Enabling all to open up their thought, and
Gradually and increasingly
  To enter into the Buddha Path.
Ridding himself of slothful intentions,
  As well as of notions of idleness,
And freeing himself from care and agony,
  With a compassionate heart let him preach the Dharma,

Day and night ever preaching
  The doctrine of the Unexcelled Path,
By resort to causes and conditions,
  As well as to incalculable parables,
Opening up and demonstrating to living beings,
  Causing them all to rejoice;
And as to clothing and bedding,
  Food, drink, and medicine,
With respect to these
  Having no hopes,
But, single-mindedly recollecting
  The reasons for preaching Dharma,
Desiring to achieve the Buddha Path
  And to cause the multitude to do the same.
This, then, is the great [source of] profit,
  The offering that brings comfort.
After my passage into extinction,
  If there is a bhikṣu
Who can expound this
  Scripture of the Fine Dharma Blossom,
His thought free of envy and anger,
  And of the obstructions of assorted agonies,
He shall also have no care
  For detractors,
Nor be in fear
  Of wielders of knives or staves,
Nor shall he ever be banished,
  For he shall dwell securely in forbearance.
If in this way a wise man,
  Skillfully collecting his thoughts,
Can dwell securely in comfort,
  As I have just said,
That man's merit shall be such
  That in a thousand myriads of millions of kalpas
Number or parable
  Cannot fully tell its tale.

"Also, O Mañjuśrī, the bodhisattva-mahāsattva who in the age of the latter end, when the Dharma is about to perish, receives and keeps, reads and recites this scriptural canon shall harbor no thought of envy, flattery, or deceit, nor shall he make light of or malign those who study the Buddha Path, seeking their virtues and shortcomings, be they bhikṣus, bhikṣuṇīs, upāsakas, or upāsikās, be they seekers after the rank of voice-hearer, seekers after the rank of pratyekabuddha, or seekers after the Path of the bodhisattva. He shall not permit himself to torment them, causing them to have doubts, by saying to them, 'You fellows are very far from the Path! You shall never contrive to attain knowledge of all modes! What is the reason? It is that you are careless men, lax in the Path.' Nor should he resort to frivolous assertions about the dharmas, as if there were anything to dispute. But he should think on all living beings with great compassion, feel that the Thus Come One is a benign Father, feel that the bodhisattvas are great masters. To the bodhisattvas of the ten directions he should ever do obeisance reverently and with deep thought. By being in perfect accord with Dharma, to all living beings he is to preach Dharma consistently, neither exceeding it nor falling short of it. Even to a person who deeply loves Dharma he is not to preach overmuch.

"O Mañjuśrī! In the age of the latter end, when the Dharma is about to perish, there shall be those among these bodhisattva-mahāsattvas who shall achieve this third form of comfortable conduct, and whom it will not be possible to dismay or to confuse when they are preaching this Dharma. They shall get good fellow-scholars, who together shall read and recite this scripture. They shall also obtain great multitudes who shall come to listen and accept: who, when they have listened, shall be able to keep; when they have kept, shall be able to recite; when they have recited, shall be able to preach; and, when they have preached, shall be able to write or to cause others to write; who shall make offerings to the scriptural roll, venerating it with humility and holding it in solemn esteem."

At that time, the World-Honored One, wishing to restate this meaning, proclaimed gāthās, saying:

If one wishes to preach this scripture,
  One should cast aside jealousy, anger, pride,

Flattery, deception, crookedness, and dishonesty from one's heart,
Ever cultivating conduct of substance and honesty.
One should not make light of men nor hold them in contempt,
Nor is one to discourse frivolously on the dharmas,
Or cause others to have doubts
By saying to them, "You shall never attain Buddhahood!"
When this son of the Buddha preaches Dharma,
He is ever gentle and agreeable, able to forbear,
Benevolent and compassionate toward all,
Producing no lax thoughts, [thinking],
"To the great bodhisattvas in all ten directions,
Who out of compassion for the multitude tread the Path,
I owe thoughts of humble respect,
For they are my great teachers."
Toward the Buddhas, the World-Honored Ones,
His attitude is as if they were his supreme Fathers;
He demolishes his thoughts of overweening pride
And preaches Dharma without obstacles.
The third dharma, in this way,
The wise person is to keep,
For, if he performs it comfortably and single-mindedly,
He shall be revered by an incalculable multitude.[12]

"Again, O Mañjuśrī, the bodhisattva-mahāsattva who in the age of the latter end, when the Dharma is about to perish, holds this Scripture of the Dharma Blossom, thinking with great good will of persons in the household and of those gone forth from the household, with great compassion of those who are not bodhisattvas—let him form this thought: 'Persons like these have simply missed the Thus Come One's expedient devices, his exposition of Dharma in accord with what is appropriate, not hearing it, nor knowing it, nor being aware of it, nor inquiring into it, nor believing it, nor understanding it. Although those persons do not inquire into, nor believe, nor understand this scripture, when I attain anuttarasamyaksaṃbodhi, then wherever they may happen to be, with my power of supernatural penetration and my power of wisdom I will draw them to me, enabling them to dwell in this Dharma.'

"O Mañjuśrī! If after the extinction of the Thus Come One there is any among these bodhisattva-mahāsattvas who achieves this fourth dharma, then when preaching this Dharma he shall commit no faults, but ever by bhikṣus, bhikṣuṇīs, upāsakas, upāsikās, kings, princes, great ministers, commoners, Brahmans, and householders he shall be showered with offerings, humbly revered, held in solemn esteem, and lauded. The gods of open space also shall ever follow in his retinue in order to listen to the Dharma. If in settlements, cities and towns, open spaces, or forests, anyone comes who wishes to query with objections, then day and night, for Dharma's sake, the gods shall ever protect him, having the power to enable the listeners all to gain joy. What is the reason? It is that this scripture is protected by the supernatural power of all Buddhas, past, present, and future. O Mañjuśrī! This Scripture of the Dharma Blossom is such that in incalculable realms it is not possible even to hear its name; how much the less to see it, to receive and keep it, to read and recite it!

"O Mañjuśrī! Suppose, for example, there is a wheel-turning sage-king of great strength, who wishes with his imposing might to subdue all realms, yet whose commands the lesser kings will not obey. At that time, the wheel-turning king raises a varied force and goes to chastise them. When the king sees in his multitude of soldiers those who fight successfully, straightway he is delighted, and rewards them in accord with their merit. To some he gives fields and houses, settlements, cities and towns; to some he gives clothing and accouterments for bodily adornment; to some he gives a variety of precious jewels, gold, silver, vaiḍūrya, giant clam shell, agate, coral, amber, elephants, horses, carriages, slaves and subjects. The bright pearl in his top-knot is the only thing he will not give them. What is the reason? Only on top of the king's head is such a gem to be found. If he gives it away, the king's retainers assuredly will be greatly alarmed. O Mañjuśrī! The Thus Come One is also like this. Having gained the Dharma-realm with the power of dhyāna-concentration and wisdom, he reigns over the three spheres, yet the Māra kings will not consent to obey him. The wise and saintly generals of the Thus Come One do battle with them. With those who are successful he is also delighted at heart, and among the fourfold multitude it is to them that he preaches the scriptures, causing their hearts to rejoice. He confers upon them the precious Dharma-gifts of dhyāna-concentration, deliverance, faculties without outflows, and powers. He also confers upon them as a gift the city of nirvāṇa, telling them they shall gain passage into extinction. He guides their thoughts, causing them to rejoice, but does not preach to them this Scripture of the Dharma Blossom. O Mañjuśrī! Just as the wheel-turning king, seeing among the multitude of soldiers those who have had great success, is overjoyed at heart, and this incredible pearl, long in his top-knot, which he would not recklessly give away, he now gives, just so is the Thus Come One. Being the great Dharma King within the three spheres, with Dharma he teaches and converts all living beings. When he sees his army of saints and sages do battle with the Māras of the five *skandhas*,* the Māras of the agonies, and the Māra of death, achieving great success, annihilating the three poisons, leaving the three spheres, and tearing apart Māra's net, at that time the Thus Come One is greatly overjoyed, and this Scripture of the Dharma Blossom, which can enable the beings to reach omniscience, which all the worlds much resent with incredulity, and which he has never preached before, he now preaches. O Mañjuśrī! This Scripture of the Dharma Blossom is the supreme preaching of the Thus Come One, among the various preachings the most profound, the one he confers at the very end. As that very powerful king long kept his bright pearl and only now gives it away, so, O Mañjuśrī, this Scripture of the Dharma Blossom, the secret treasure house of the Thus Come Ones, among the sundry scriptures placed on the very top, which through the long night of time he kept, but did not merely forget to expound, today for the first time he expounds to you."

At that time, the World-Honored One, wishing to restate this meaning, proclaimed gāthās, saying:

Let one ever practice forbearance toward insult,
  Having compassion on all,

* The Sarvāstivāda school, almost certainly the one at issue here, divided existence into 75 dharmas, of which 3 were *asaṃskṛta*, "unconditioned," i.e., not subject to the pattern of cause and condition. The other 72 were grouped into five "masses" (*skandha*), viz., (1) *rūpa*, visible matter; (2) *vedanā*, sensation; (3) *saṃjñā*, (false) perception or notion; (4) *saṃskāra*, "constituent forces" leading to actions; (5) *vijñāna*, cognition-cum-consciousness.

For it is only thus that one can expound
　A scripture lauded by the Buddha.[13]
At the time of the latter end,
　For those who keep this scripture,
Whether in the household or gone forth from the household,
　And for those who are not bodhisattvas
One should produce good will and compassion [saying]:
　"If these do not hear
Nor believe this scripture,
　Then they shall suffer a great loss.[14]
When I have attained the Buddha Path,
　By recourse to expedient devices
I will preach this Dharma to them,
　Enabling them to dwell within it."
Suppose, for example, there is a mighty
　Wheel-turning king
Who on soldiers successful in battle
　Confers gifts of various things,
Elephants, horses, carriages,
　Accouterments for bodily adornment,
And fields and houses,
　Settlements, cities, and towns.
Or he may give clothing,
　Sundry gems,
Slaves and valuables,
　Conferring the gifts with joy.
If there is a brave and stout fellow
　Able to do difficult things,
The king separates from his top-knot
　A bright pearl, which he gives to him.
The Thus Come One is also thus:
　Being king of the dharmas,
Who of the great force of forbearance
　And of wisdom is the treasure house,
With his great good will and compassion,
　In keeping with Dharma, he converts the world.

When he sees all men
  Suffering all manner of bitterness and agony,
Wishing to find deliverance,
  And fighting with the Māras,
To these living beings
  He preaches sundry dharmas,
As a great expedient device
  Preaching these scriptures.
Once he knows that the living beings
  Have gained the appropriate strength,
At the end, then and only then, to them
  He preaches this Dharma Blossom,
As the king, separating from his top-knot
  The bright pearl, gives it away.
This scripture is venerable,
  Supreme among the multitude of scriptures.
I, who have ever kept it,
  Would not set it forth recklessly.
Now, however, is just the very time
  To preach it to you all.
After my passage into extinction,
  Those who seek the Buddha Path,
If they wish to gain tranquillity
  And at the same time to expound this scripture,
Should approach with familiarity
  Four dharmas such as these.*
One who reads this scripture
  Shall ever be without care or agony,
Also without sickness or pain,
  His color a fresh white,
Nor shall he be born into poverty, want,
  Lowliness, degradation, ugliness, or restriction.[15]

* The four dharmas are (a) keeping away from the wrong people, (b) understanding the dharmas from the Mahāyāna point of view, (c) preaching a consistent message, and (d) preaching the *Lotus* when the time is ripe, not before. The dharmas are set forth in the prose but not in the verse.

Living beings shall desire to see him
  As they would aspire to see a sage or a saint.
The children of the gods
  Shall be his servants and messengers.
Knife and staff shall not touch him,
  Nor can poison harm him.
If any man hatefully reviles him,
  That man's mouth shall then be stopped up.
He shall travel fearlessly
  Like a king of lions,
His wisdom as radiant
  As the light of the sun.[16]
Or, in a dream
  He may simply see wondrous sights.
He shall see the Thus Come Ones
  Seated on their lion thrones,
A multitude of bhikṣus
  Surrounding them as they preach the Dharma.
He shall also see dragons and demons,
  Asuras and the like,
In number like to Ganges' sands,
  Their palms joined in humble reverence,
To whom, showing his body,
  He preaches the Dharma.
He shall also see Buddhas,
  One of their marks being their gold color,
Emitting incalculable rays,
  Wherewith they illuminate all,
And with a voice of Brahmā sound
  Expounding the dharmas.
While to the fourfold assembly the Buddha
  Preaches the unexcelled Dharma,
[This man,] displaying his body in their midst,
  With palms joined lauds the Buddha.
Hearing the Dharma, he is delighted,
  Then performs offerings,

Gains dhāraṇī,
And bears direct witness to unreceding knowledge.
The Buddha, knowing that his thought
Is deeply entered upon the Buddha Path,
Straightway confers upon him the prophecy
That he shall achieve supremely right, enlightened intuition:
"You, O good man,
In an age to come shall
Gain incalculable knowledge,
The Buddha's Great Path.
Your land shall be adorned and pure,
Broad and great without equal.
You shall also have a fourfold assembly
Who shall listen to Dharma with palms joined."
He also sees himself
In the midst of mountains and forests
Cultivating and practicing good dharmas,
Bearing direct witness to the marks of Reality,
Deeply entering into dhyāna-concentration,
And seeing Buddhas in all ten quarters.
The Buddhas' bodies, of golden hue,
With a hundred happy marks shall be adorned.
He hears the Dharma and preaches it to others:
Such shall ever be this lovely dream.
He also dreams of becoming lord of a realm,
Of forsaking palace and retinue,
As well as the supremely wondrous objects of the five desires.
He goes to the Platform of the Path;
Under the bodhi-tree,
Seated on a lion throne,
His quest for the Path having passed the seventh day,
He gains the knowledge of the Buddhas.
Having achieved the Unexcelled Path,
He rises, and turns the Dharma-wheel,
To the fourfold assembly preaching Dharma
Throughout a thousand myriads of millions of kalpas.

Preaching the Fine Dharma without outflows
  And conveying to salvation incalculable living beings,
Thereafter he is to enter into nirvāṇa,
  As smoke stops when the candle is extinguished.
If in the latter evil age
  He preaches this prime Dharma,
This man shall achieve great profit,
  Such as the merits told above.[17]

Chapter Fifteen: Welling Up out of the Earth

At that time, the bodhisattva-mahāsattvas who had come from lands in other quarters, exceeding in number the sands of eight Ganges rivers, rose up in the midst of the great multitude and, doing obeisance with palms joined, addressed the Buddha, saying, "O World-Honored One! If you will allow us, then after the Buddha's extinction, in this Sahā world-sphere, by striving to devote vigorous effort to keep, read and recite, write down and copy and make offerings to this scriptural canon, we will broadly preach it in this land."

At that time, the Buddha declared to the bodhisattva-mahāsattvas, "Stop! Good men, there is no need for you to keep this scripture. What is the reason? My Sahā world-sphere itself has bodhisattva-mahāsattvas equal in number to the sands of sixty thousand Ganges rivers, each of whom has in turn a retinue equal in number to the sands of sixty thousand Ganges rivers. After my extinction, these men shall be able to keep, read and recite, and broadly preach this scripture."

When the Buddha had said this, in the thousand-millionfold lands of the Sahā world-sphere[1] the earth trembled and split, and from its clefts there welled up simultaneously incalculable thousands of myriads of millions of bodhisattva-mahāsattvas. These bodhisattvas all had bodies of golden hue, [displaying] the thirty-two marks and incalculable rays of light. They all had been under this Sahā world-sphere, in an open space belonging to this sphere. When these bodhisattvas heard the sound of Śākyamunibuddha's preaching voice, they emerged from below, each bodhisattva at the head of, and commanding, a great multitude, each leading a retinue equal in number to the sands of sixty thousand Ganges rivers. How much the more numerous, then, were those leading retinues equal in number to the sands of fifty, forty, thirty, twenty, or ten thousand Ganges rivers! How much the more numerous those leading retinues equal in number from any of these down to the sands of one Ganges river, or half a Ganges river, or one-quarter of a Ganges river, or anything down to one-thousand-myriad-million-nayutath of a Ganges river! How much the more numerous those whose retinues numbered a thousand myriads of millions of nayutas! How much the more numerous those whose retinues numbered a million myriads! How much the more numerous those whose retinues numbered a thousand myriads, a hundred myriads, anything down to one myriad! How much the more numerous those whose retinues numbered a thousand, a hundred, or ten! How much the more numerous those who brought with them five, four, three, two, or one disciple! How much the more numerous those who came alone, desiring the practice of self-isolation! The likes of these were incalculable, endless, such as neither numeration nor parable could know.[2]

When these bodhisattvas had emerged from the earth, they all went to the fine seven-jeweled stūpa situated in open space, where were the Thus Come One Many Jewels and Śākyamunibuddha. When they had arrived, turning toward the two World-Honored Ones, they worshiped their feet with heads bowed, then did obeisance to everything up through the places prepared for the Buddhas on the lion throne under the bodhi-tree of sundry gems. Doing three turns of rightward circumambulation and paying humble respects with palms joined, they lauded them with varied bodhisattva-praises, then stood off to one side, with joyful expectation looking up at the two World-Honored Ones.[3]

These bodhisattva-mahāsattvas, welling up out of the earth, by resort to bodhisattvas' sundry devices of praise lauded the Buddha, such time persisting fifty minor kalpas. During this time, Śākyamunibuddha was seated in silence, and the fourfold assemblies were also seated in silence. The fifty minor kalpas, thanks to the Buddha's supernatural power, were made to appear to the great multitudes as if they were half a day. At that time, the fourfold assembly, thanks to the Buddha's supernatural power, also saw bodhisattvas fill the open air of incalculable hundreds of thousands of myriads of millions of lands. Within this multitude of bodhisattvas were four leaders, the first named Superior Conduct (Viśiṣṭacāritra), the second named Limitless Conduct (Anantacāritra), the third named Pure Conduct (Viśuddhacāritra), the fourth named Conduct Standing Firm (Supratiṣṭhitacāritra). These four bodhisattvas were the supreme chiefs among that multitude, the masters who commanded and led. At the head of his respective great multitude, each of them, together with the others, joined palms and, gazing at Śākyamunibuddha, inquired after him, saying, "O World-Honored One! Are you in good health and free of pain? Are you conducting yourself in comfort or not? Do those worthy of conveyance to salvation accept your doctrine easily, or do they not? Are they not causing the World-Honored One to suffer fatigue and labor?"

At that time, the four great bodhisattvas proclaimed gāthās, saying:

O World-Honored One! Are you in comfort?
  Are you in good health, free of pain?
When teaching and converting living beings,
  Do you contrive to do so without fatigue or disgust?
Also, do the living beings
  Accept conversion with ease, or do they not?
Are they not causing the World-Honored One
  To experience fatigue or labor?[4]

At that time, in the midst of the great bodhisattva-multitude the World-Honored One said: "Verily, verily, good men, the Thus Come One is comfortable, in good health and free of pain. The sundry living beings are easy to convert and to convey to salvation. I have neither fatigue nor labor. What is the reason? These living beings, for ages now, have been ever accepting conversion by me. Also, in the presence of past Buddhas, humbly honoring them and holding them in solemn esteem, they have planted wholesome roots. When these living beings first saw my body and heard my preachings, they straightway accepted me with faith, entering into the knowledge of the Thus Come One. Except for those whose previous repeated practice was devoted to learning the Lesser Vehicle, such persons as these I now enable to hear this scripture as well and thus to enter into Buddha-knowledge."[5]

At that time, the great bodhisattvas proclaimed gāthās, saying:

How excellent, how excellent,
  O Great Hero, O World-Honored One,
That the sundry living beings
  Can be so easily converted and conveyed to salvation,
That they can inquire into the Buddhas'
  Profound knowledge
And, having heard about it, carry it out with faith!
  We rejoice accordingly!

At that time, the World-Honored One lauded the chief bodhisattvas: "How excellent, how excellent, O good men, that you all can produce for the thus Come One thoughts of appropriate joy!"

At that time, the bodhisattva Maitreya and a multitude of bodhisattvas equal in number to the sands of eight thousand Ganges rivers all thought: "From of old we have never seen nor heard of such a great multitude of bodhisattva-mahāsattvas welling up out of the earth, remaining in the presence of the World-Honored One, making offerings to the Thus Come One, and inquiring after him with palms joined."[6]

At that time, the bodhisattva-mahāsattva Maitreya, knowing what the bodhisattvas equal in number to the sands of eight thousand Ganges rivers were thinking inwardly, and also wishing to resolve his own doubts, faced the Buddha with palms joined, then questioned him in gāthās, saying:

The incalculable thousands of myriads of millions
  Of bodhisattvas, in a great multitude
Such as has never before been seen,
  Beg you, O Venerable among Two-Legged Beings, to explain!
Whence have come,
  For what reason are gathered,
Those of huge bodies and great supernatural penetrations,
  Their wisdom beyond reckoning and discussion,
Their resolve firm,
  Who have the great power of withstanding humiliation,

Whom the beings desire to see?
  Whence come they?[7]
Each bodhisattva's
  Retainers, whom he brings in tow,
Are in number incalculable,
  Equal to the sands of the river Ganges.
There are some great bodhisattvas
  Leading retainers as numerous as the sands in sixty thousand Ganges':
Such are their great multitudes,
  Single-mindedly seeking the Buddha Path.
These great masters'
  Retinues, equal in number to the sands of sixty thousand Ganges rivers,
Have come together to make offerings to the Buddha
  And to guard and keep this scripture.
Those bringing in tow retinues equal in number to the sands of fifty thousand Ganges
  Are in number in excess of these,
While those whose retinues number forty or thirty thousand,
  From twenty to ten thousand,
One thousand, one hundred, or
  Anything down to one Ganges' sands,
Or a half, or a third, or a quarter,
  Or one-myriad-millionth,
Or a thousand myriads of nayutas,
  Or a myriad millions of disciples,
Or anything down to half a million,
  Are again in number superior to them.
Those who bring from a hundred myriads down to one myriad,
  Or a thousand or a hundred,
Or fifty or ten,
  Or anything down to three, two, or one,
Or who, alone and without retinue,
  Desiring to remain in isolation,
Come together before the Buddha

Are in number yet again in excess of these.[8]
Great multitudes like these,
If a man should count them on an abacus
For kalpas numbering more than Ganges' sands,
Still could not be fully known.
These great, imposingly majestic,
Vigorously persevering multitudes of bodhisattvas—
For whose sake are they preaching Dharma,
Teaching, converting, and achieving successes?
As whose followers did they first launch their thoughts,
And to exalt the Dharma of which Buddha?
Whose scriptures do they accept, bear, and put into practice?
Which Buddha's Path do they cultivate by repeated practice?
Such is these bodhisattvas'
Power of supernatural penetration, and such their great wisdom,
That the earth in all four quarters trembles and splits
As they all well up out of its midst.
O World-Honored One! From of old I
Have never before seen such a thing!
I beg you to state its origin,
The name of the land.
I am ever traveling through various realms,
Yet have never before seen such a thing.
Within this multitude I
Do not recognize a single person,
Yet here, of a sudden, they emerge from the earth.
I beg you to explain the cause!
Now, in this great assembly
Of incalculable hundreds of thousands of millions,
The bodhisattvas
All wish to know these things,
This bodhisattva-multitude's
Causes and conditions from first to last.
O World-Honored One, of incalculable excellences!
We beg you to resolve our manifold doubts![9]

At that time, the Buddhas who were emanations of the body of Śākyamuni, coming from incalculable thousands of myriads of millions of lands in different quarters, sat cross-legged on lion thrones under jeweled trees in the eight directions. Those Buddhas' attendants, seeing these great multitudes of bodhisattvas in the four quarters of the thousand-millionfold world welling up out of the earth and dwelling in open space, each addressed his Buddha, saying, "O World-Honored One! Whence come these great multitudes of incalculable, limitless asaṃkhyeyas of bodhisattvas?" At that time, the Buddhas declared each to his attendants, "Good men! Wait a bit. There is a bodhisattva-mahāsattva named Maitreya, on whom Śākyamunibuddha has conferred the prophecy that he shall be the next Buddha, directly following him. He has already inquired into this matter, and the Buddha will now answer him. Of course, you all should hear it, through his intercession."

At that time Śākyamunibuddha declared to the bodhisattva Maitreya, "How excellent, how excellent, O Ajita, that you are able to question the Buddha on such a great matter as this! You should all together with a single mind don the armor of vigorous perseverance and launch a firm resolve. For the Thus Come One now wishes to lay open and to proclaim the Buddhas' wisdom, the Buddhas' powers of self-mastery and supernatural penetration, the Buddhas' power to move with the resolute speed of a lion, the Buddhas' power of imposing, frighteningly great strength."[10]

At that time, the World-Honored One, wishing to restate this meaning, proclaimed gāthās, saying:

You should strive vigorously for single-mindedness,
  For I wish to state this matter.
Allow yourselves no doubts or regrets,
  For the Buddha's knowledge is beyond reckoning or
    discussion.
Put forward now the power to believe,
  Dwelling in the midst of the tolerant and the good,
For a Dharma never before heard
  You shall all now be able to hear.[11]
I am now reassuring you:

Do not allow yourselves to harbor doubts or fears,
For the Buddha speaks no falsehoods,
And his knowledge is incalculable.
The prime Dharma that I have gained
Is profound, not subject to discrimination.
As such I will now preach it:
All of you, listen single-mindedly!

At that time, the World-Honored One, having proclaimed these gāthās, declared to the bodhisattva Maitreya, "Now in this great multitude I will make a declaration to you all. O Ajita! These incalculable, numberless asaṃkhyeyas of great bodhisattva-mahāsattvas who have welled up out of the earth, and whom you have never before seen, I taught and converted in this Sahā world-sphere, once I had attained anuttarasamyaksaṃbodhi. I guided and showed the way to these bodhisattvas. I tamed their minds, causing them to launch thoughts of the Path. These bodhisattvas all dwell beneath this Sahā world-sphere, in the midst of the open space of this sphere. Where this scripture is concerned, they read and recite it, gaining fluency and advantage, they think about it with discrimination, and are rightly mindful of it. O Ajita! These good men have no desire to be in a multitude, there to have much talk, but they ever desire a quiet place, for they strive to practice vigorous perseverance, never allowing themselves to rest. Nor do they take up residence among men and gods, for they ever desire profound knowledge without obstacles. They also constantly desire the Dharma of the Buddhas, vigorously and single-mindedly persevering in their quest of unexcelled knowledge."

At that time, the World-Honored One, wishing to restate this meaning, proclaimed gāthās, saying:

Ajita! Know
That these great bodhisattvas
For numberless kalpas
Have been practicing and perfecting Buddha-knowledge.
All were converted by me
And enabled to open up their thought to the Great Path.
These are my sons,

Abiding in this world-sphere.
Ever performing dhūta-deeds,
They aspire to quiet places,
Rejecting the hustle-bustle of great multitudes,
And having no desire for much talk.
It is such sons as these
Who study and practice the Dharma of my Path.[12]
Day and night ever persevering,
In order to seek the Buddha Path,
On the Sahā world-sphere's
Under side, in open space, they dwell.
Hard and firm of resolve and mindfulness,
Ever do they strive in their quest for wisdom,
Preaching a variety of fine dharmas,
Their hearts knowing no fear.
In Gayā city, I,
Seated under the bodhi-tree,
Was able to achieve supremely right, enlightened intuition
And to turn the wheel of the Unexcelled Dharma.
Only then did I teach and convert them,
Enabling them for the first time to open their thought to the Path.
Now all, dwelling in the unreceding,
Shall without fail achieve Buddhahood.
I now preach the true Word:
Do you all single-mindedly believe it.
For, since time long past, I
Have been teaching and converting these multitudes.

At that time, the bodhisattva-mahāsattva Maitreya and the innumerable other bodhisattvas, at heart doubtful and confused, suspicious of what had never been before, thought: "In [such] a short space of time, how can the World-Honored One have taught and converted such incalculable, limitless asaṃkhyeyas of great bodhisattvas, causing them to dwell in anuttarasamyaksaṃbodhi?" Straightway they addressed the Buddha, saying, "O World-Honored One! The Thus

Come One, when he was a prince, left the Śakya palace and, in a place not far from Gayā city, sat on the Platform of the Path and contrived to achieve anuttarasamyaksaṃbodhi. From that time to this is only a bit more than forty years. O World-Honored One! How in that little time could you accomplish so much of the business of a Buddha, with the might of a Buddha and the merits of a Buddha teach and convert so many incalculable multitudes of great bodhisattvas, destining them to achieve anuttarasamyaksambodhi? O World-Honored One! The great bodhisattva-multitudes are such that, were a man to count them for a thousand myriads of millions of kalpas, he could not finish doing so, nor reach their limit. Since remote time, in the presence of incalculable, limitless Buddhas, they have been planting wholesome roots, achieving the bodhisattva-path, ever practicing brahman-conduct. O World-Honored One! Such a thing as this the world finds hard to believe!

"It is as if there were a man, his natural color fair and his hair black, twenty-five years of age, who pointed to men a hundred years of age and said, 'These are my sons!' The hundred-year-old men likewise point to the youngster and say, 'This is our father! He begot and reared us.' This thing would be hard to believe. So also is the Buddha. It is in fact no long time since his attainment of the Path. Now the bodhisattvas in this great multitude for incalculable thousands of myriads of millions of kalpas, for the sake of the Buddha Path, have already striven to practice with vigorous perseverance; have skillfully entered, or left, or remained in incalculable hundreds of thousands of myriads of millions of samādhis; have attained great supernatural penetration; have long perfected brahman-conduct; well and ably by degrees have practiced sundry wholesome dharmas; and have acquired skill in questioning and answering. In short, they are veritable gems of mankind, such that all the worlds regard them as very rare. This day the World-Honored One tells us that it was only upon his own attainment of the Buddha Path that he caused them to open up their thought; that he taught and converted them, showed them and guided them; that he caused them to turn to anuttarasamyaksaṃbodhi. Since the World-Honored One's attainment of Buddhahood it is no long time, yet he has been able to do these very meritorious things! Although we for our own part believe that the Buddha's preachings in keeping with what is appropriate, the words uttered by the Buddha, have never been false, and that what the Buddha knows is all thoroughly penetrating, yet the bodhisattvas who have but newly launched their thought, if after the Buddha's extinction they hear these words, may not accept them in faith, but may on the contrary produce the causes and conditions of the sinful act of attacking the Dharma. Very well, O World-Honored One! We beg you to explain, both in order to remove our own doubts and in order that good men of ages yet to come, when they hear these things, may also experience no doubt."[13]

At that time, the bodhisattva Maitreya, wishing to restate this meaning, proclaimed gāthās, saying:

At one time, the Buddha, issuing from the Śakya seed,
  Left his household, and near Gayā
He sat by a bodhi-tree,
  Since when it is still no long time.
These sons of the Buddhas,
  Their number incalculable,
Long ago having trodden the Buddha Path,
  Dwell in the power of supernatural penetration.
They have well learned the bodhisattva-path, and
  They are untainted by worldly dharmas,
Like the lotus blossom in the water.
  Out of earth welling up,
They all produce the thought of humble veneration,
  Remaining in the presence of the World-Honored One.[14]
This thing is hard to reckon or to discuss.
  How may it be believed?
The Buddha's attainment of the Path is very recent,
  Yet his achievements are very many.
We beg you, in order to dispel a multitude of doubts,
  To explain with discrimination in accord with Reality.
It is as if there is a young man in the prime of life,
  His years only just twenty-five,
Who points to men of a hundred years,
  Their hair white, their faces wrinkled,

Saying, "These are my begotten sons!"
The sons also say, "This is our father!"
That the father is young and the sons old
Is a thing the whole world will refuse to believe.
So also is the World-Honored One,
For his attainment of the Path is still very recent,
While these bodhisattvas,
Of firm resolve and fearing nothing,
For incalculable kalpas have
Been treading the bodhisattva-path,
Skilled in objection, in question and answer,
Their hearts fearless,
Enduring humiliation with minds made up,
Standing erect with imposing majesty,
Praised by the Buddhas of the ten quarters,
Well able to preach with discrimination,
Having no desire to be in a human multitude,
Ever loving to be in dhyāna-concentration,
In order to seek the Buddha Path
Dwelling in the open space below.[15]
For our own part, we, having heard it from the Buddha,
Have no doubts regarding this matter,
But we beg the Buddha, for the future's sake,
To expound, causing clear understanding.
If with regard to this scripture
Anyone engenders doubt and disbelief,
Straightway he shall fall into an evil course.
We beg you now, on this account, to explain,
With regard to these incalculable bodhisattvas,
How in little time
You taught and converted them, enabling them to open up their thought
And to dwell on the ground from which there is no backsliding.

Scripture of the Lotus Blossom of the Fine Dharma.
End of Roll the Fifth.

Roll 6

Chapter Sixteen: The Life-span of the Thus Come One

At that time, the Buddha declared to the bodhisattvas and all the great multitude: "Good men! Believe and understand the true speech of the Thus Come One!" Again he declared to the great multitude: "Believe and understand the true speech of the Thus Come One!" Again he declared to the great multitude: "Believe and understand the true speech of the Thus Come One!" At this time, the great multitude of bodhisattvas, Maitreya at their head, with palms joined addressed the Buddha, saying, "O World-Honored One! We beg you to speak it! We will accept with faith the words of the Buddha." When they had thus spoken three times, they again said, "We beg you to speak it! We will accept with faith the words of the Buddha."[1]

At that time, the World-Honored One, knowing that the bodhisattvas' plea, now thrice repeated, would not be stilled, declared to them, "All of you now listen with understanding to the power of the secret supernatural penetrations of the Thus Come One! In all the worlds, gods, men, and asuras all say that the present Śākyamunibuddha left the palace of the Śakya clan and at a place not far removed from the city of Gayā, seated on the Platform of the Path, attained anuttarasamyaksaṃbodhi. And yet, O good men, since in fact I achieved Buddhahood it has been incalculable, limitless hundreds of thousands of myriads of millions of nayutas of kalpas. For example, one might imagine that in the five hundred thousand myriads of millions of nayutas of asaṃkhyeyas of thousand-millionfold worlds there is a man who pounds them all to atoms, and then, only after passing eastward over five hundred thousand myriads of millions of nayutas of asaṃkhyeyas of realms, deposits one atom, in this way in his eastward movement exhausting all these atoms. Good men! In your thinking, how would it be? Could these world-spheres be conceived of and counted? Could one know their number, or could one not?"

The bodhisattva Maitreya and the others together addressed the Buddha, saying, "O World-Honored One! These world-spheres are incalculable, limitless, such as number cannot know nor the power of thought reach. No voice-hearer or pratyekabuddha, with the aid of his knowledge-without-outflows, can think on or know their limit or their number. We, too, dwelling as we do on the soil of the *avaivartya* [point of non-backsliding], cannot arrive at anything where this matter is concerned. O World-Honored One! So incalculable and limitless are these world-spheres!"

At that time, the Buddha declared to the great multitude of bodhisattvas, "Good men! Now I will declare it to you plainly. If these world-spheres, whether an atom was deposited in them or not, were all reduced to atoms, and if each atom were a kalpa, the time since my achievement of Buddhahood would exceed even this. For a hundred thousand myriads of millions of nayutas of asaṃkhyeyakalpas I have been constantly dwelling in this Sahā world-sphere, preaching the Dharma, teaching and converting; also elsewhere, in a hundred thousand myriads of millions of nayutas of asaṃkhyeyas of realms [I have been] guiding and benefiting the beings. Good men! In this interval, I preached of the Buddha Torch-Burner and others (*Dīpaṃkaratathāgataprabhṛtayaḥ*), and I also said of them that they had entered into nirvāṇa. Things like this are all discriminations made as an expedient device. O good men! If living beings come before me, I, with my Buddha-eye, observe the keenness or dullness of their faith and other faculties and, in keeping with their degrees of receptiveness to salvation, ascribe to myself names that are not the same and an age in years that is now great, now small. I also declare openly that I will enter into nirvāṇa. Further, by resort to sundry expedient devices I preach a subtle Dharma, being thus able to cause the beings to open their thoughts to joy. O good men! The Thus Come One, seeing the beings' desire for a lesser dharma, their qualities thin and their defilements grave, preaches to such persons, saying, 'In my youth I left my household and attained anuttarasamyaksaṃbodhi.' However, since in fact I achieved Buddhahood it has been as long a stretch of time as this. It is merely by resort to an expedient device, in order to teach and convert living beings, to enable them to enter upon the Buddha Path, that I speak such words as these. O good men! The scriptural canon preached by the Thus Come One is all for the purpose of conveying living beings to deliverance. At times he speaks of his own body, at times of another's body; at times he shows his own body, at times another's body, at times his own affairs, at times another's affairs. Everything he says is Reality, not vanity. What is the reason? The Thus Come One in full accord with Reality knows and sees the marks of the triple sphere. There is no birth-and-death, whether withdrawal from or emergence into the world, nor is there any being in the world nor anyone who passes into extinction. [The triple sphere] is neither Reality nor vanity, neither likeness nor difference. Not in the manner of the triple sphere does he view the triple sphere. Such matters as these the Thus Come One sees clearly, without confusion or error. Since the living beings have sundry natures, sundry desires, sundry actions, sundry recollections, notions, and discriminations; wishing to enable them to produce wholesome roots, by resort to divers parables and expressions in sundry ways he preaches the Dharma. The Buddha-deeds that he does he has never stopped doing. In this way, since my attainment of Buddhahood it has been a very great interval of time. My life-span is incalculable asaṃkhyeyakalpas, ever enduring, never perishing. O good men! The life-span I achieved in my former treading of the bodhisattva path even now is not exhausted, for it is twice the above number. Yet even now, though in reality I am not to pass into extinction, yet I proclaim that I am about to accept extinction. By resort to these expedient devices the Thus Come One teaches and converts the beings. What is the reason? If the Buddha were to dwell long in the world, men of thin qualities would not plant wholesome roots, while the lowly and the poor would crave the objects of the five desires and enter into the net of recollections, notions, and unwarranted views. If they were to see that the Thus Come One is ever present and unperishing, then they would conceive pride and willfulness and harbor impatience and negligence, unable to produce notions of something difficult to encounter or thoughts of humble reverence. It is for this reason that the Thus Come One preaches by resort to expedient devices, 'Bhikṣus! Know that a Buddha's emergence into the world is a thing difficult to encounter.' What is the reason? Men of thin qualities may pass through incalculable hundreds of thousands of myriads of millions of kalpas, some having occasion to see a Buddha, others not. For just this reason I say to them, 'O bhikṣus! A Thus Come One cannot easily be seen!' These beings, hearing such words, will invariably produce the notion of something difficult to encounter, and they will harbor longing in their hearts, looking up with thirst to the Buddha; then they will plant wholesome roots. It is for this reason that the Thus Come One, though in fact he is never extinct, yet speaks of passage into extinction. Also, O good men, the Dharma of the Buddhas, of the Thus Come Ones, having the sole purpose of conveying the beings to salvation, is in every case Reality, not vanity.

"For example, suppose there is a good physician, wise and of penetrating sensitivity, who intelligently refines medical herbs and skillfully heals many sicknesses. That man has many sons—ten, or twenty, or as many as a hundred or more. On an affair of business, he goes far off to another realm. His sons, left behind, drink some other, poisonous medicines and show agonized pain and confusion, rolling about on the earth. At this time their father returns home. The sons, having drunk poison, and some of them having lost their sanity, though others have not, are all overjoyed at seeing their father from afar. They kneel worshipfully and inquire after him, saying, 'Welcome back to peace and security! We in our folly have made the mistake of taking poisonous medicine. We beg you to heal us and restore our lives to us!' The father, seeing how acute were the agonies of his sons, searched for good medicinal herbs, colorful, fragrant, and tasty, perfect in every way, guided by the prescriptions in his treatises. He pounded, sifted, and blended them, then gave them to his sons, ordering them to take them, speaking these words: 'Take these great and good herbs, colorful, fragrant, and tasty, perfect in every way, for you shall then quickly be rid of your agonies, and shall never again be subject to a host of torments.' Among the sons, those who had not lost their sanity, seeing that these herbs were good in both color and fragrance, straightway took them, and their sickness was completely removed and healed.

The others, who had lost their sanity, though when they saw their father coming they, too, inquired after him joyfully and sought a cure for their sickness, yet, when given the medicine, still would not take it. What is the reason? It is that through the deep entry of the poisonous vapors they had lost their sanity. They said that this lovely, colorful, fragrant medicine was no good. The father thought: 'These children are to be pitied! Their thoughts, having been affected by poison, are all topsy-turvy. Though when they saw me they rejoiced and sought relief, fine medicine like this they will not consent to take! I must now devise an expedient with which to induce them to take this medicine.' Straightway he spoke these words: 'You all should know that I am now aged and infirm, and that my time of death is already at hand. This fine and good medicine I now leave here for you to take. Have no concern about not recovering!' When he had given these instructions, he went again to another realm and then sent a messenger back to declare, 'Your father is dead!' At this time, the sons, hearing that their father had forsaken them, felt much anguish in their hearts, and thought: 'If our father were here, he would take pity on us, and we could be saved and protected; but now he has forsaken us, having gone far off to die in another country!' Thinking themselves forsaken and exposed, having nothing further on which to rely, they ever harbored feelings of sadness. It is only when at length their thoughts were awakened that they understood that the medicine was colorful, fragrant, and tasty. Then straightway they took it, and the poisons and the sickness were all healed. The father, hearing that his sons had all achieved a cure, then came back, enabling all to see him. O good men! In your thinking, how is it? Is there any man who can say that this good physician is guilty of the sin of willfully false speech, or is there not?"

"There is not, O World Honored One."

The Buddha said, "So, too, am I. Since my achievement of Buddhahood it has been incalculable, limitless hundred thousands of myriads of millions of nayutas of asaṃkhyeyakalpas. For the beings' sake, by resort to my power of expedient devices I say that I shall pass into extinction. Still there is no one who can, in keeping with the Dharma, say that I am guilty of the sin of willfully false speech."

At that time, the World-Honored One, wishing to restate this meaning, proclaimed gāthās, saying:

Since I attained Buddhahood,
  Throughout the number of kalpas that have passed,
Incalculable hundred thousands of myriads
  Of million times asaṃkhyeyas,
Ever have I been preaching Dharma, teaching and converting.
  Countless millions of living beings
Have I caused to enter into the Buddha Path,[2]
  Since which time it has been incalculable kalpas.
For the beings' sake,
  And as an expedient device, I make a show of nirvāṇa;
Yet in fact I do not pass into extinction,
  But ever dwell here and preach Dharma.
I, ever dwelling here,
  By the power of my supernatural penetrations,
Cause the topsy-turvy living beings,
  Though they are near, not to see.[3]
The multitude, seeing me passed into extinction,
  Broadly make offerings to my śarīra,
All harboring feelings of longing
  And conceiving the thought of looking up in thirst.
The beings, bowed down in faith,
  Straightforward and honest, their minds gentle and pliant,
Single-mindedly desiring to see the Buddha,[4]
  Do not begrudge their own bodily lives.
At that time I, together with my multitudinous saṃgha,
  Emerge on the Mount of the Numinous Eagle.
I then tell the beings
  That I will ever be here, not becoming extinct,
And that it was by resort to the power of an expedient device
  That I made a show of extinction or nonextinction.
Other realms possess living beings
  Humbly reverent and with faith desiring,
In whose midst also

And for whose sakes I preach the Unexcelled Dharma.
Not hearing this, you all
Did but imagine that I should pass into extinction.
I, seeing the beings
Sunk in a sea of woe,
And for that reason not displaying my body to them,
Caused them to look up in thirst.
When their thoughts aspired with longing,
Only then did I appear and preach Dharma to them:
Such is the power of my supernatural penetrations.
Throughout asaṃkhyeyakalpas
Ever am I on the Mount of the Numinous Eagle
And in my other dwelling places.
When the beings see the kalpa ending
And being consumed by a great fire,
This land of mine is perfectly safe,
Ever full of gods and men;
In it are gardens and groves, halls and towers,
Variously adorned with gems,
As well as jeweled trees with many blossoms and fruits,
Wherein the beings play and amuse themselves;
Where the gods beat their divine drums,
Making melodies most skillfully played,
And rain down māndārava-flowers,
Scattering them on the Buddha and his great multitude.[5]
My Pure Land is not destroyed,
Yet the multitude, seeing it consumed with flame,
Are worried, and fear the torment of pain;
The likes of these are everywhere.
These sin-ridden beings,
By reason of their evil deeds,
Throughout asaṃkhyeyakalpas
Do not hear the Name of the Three Jewels.*
Those who have cultivated merit,

* Buddha, Dharma (in the sense of enunciated doctrine), and saṃgha.

Who are gentle and agreeable, straightforward and honest,
All do, however, see my body
Dwelling here and preaching Dharma.[6]
At times to this multitude
I preach that the Buddha's life-span is incalculable;
Then, at length, to those who finally see the Buddha,
I preach that the Buddha is hard to encounter.
Such is the power of my knowledge,
The rays of my wisdom having an incalculable glow,
My life-span being of numberless kalpas,
Gained after cultivation of long practice.
All of you, who have knowledge,
Entertain no doubts in this regard!
You must cut them off and forever banish them,
For the Buddha's Word is not vain.
As a physician skilled in expedient devices,
In order to heal a son gone mad,
Is in fact living but says he is dead,
Yet none can say he tells a willful lie,
So I, too, Father of the World that I am,
Savior from woe and suffering,
Because ordinary fellows are set on their heads,
Though I really live, say I am in extinction.
Otherwise, because they constantly see me,
They would conceive thoughts of pride and arrogance,
Recklessly clinging to the objects of the five desires
And falling into evil destinies.
I, ever knowing the living beings
Who tread the Path and those who do not,
In response to those who may be saved
Preach to them a variety of dharmas,
Each time having this thought:
"How may I cause the beings
To contrive to enter the Unexcelled Path
And quickly to perfect the Buddha-body?"[7]

Chapter Seventeen: Discrimination of Merits

At that time, after the great assembly had heard the Buddha speak of the great length of his life-span, incalculable, limitless asaṃkhyeyas of living beings gained a great advantage. At that time, the World-Honored One declared to the bodhisattva-mahāsattva Maitreya: "O Ajita! When I preached on the great length of the life-span of the Thus Come One, living beings to the number of sands in six hundred and eighty myriads of millions of nayutas of Ganges rivers gained acceptance of [the doctrine of] the unborn dharmas. Again, a thousand times this number of bodhisattva-mahāsattvas heard and were enabled to take hold of the gateway of the dhāraṇīs. Again, bodhisattva-mahāsattvas equal to the number of the atoms in one world-sphere gained joy in preaching and unimpeded eloquence. Again, bodhisattva-mahāsattvas equal in number to the atoms in one world-sphere gained the dhāraṇī that can be turned to a hundred thousand myriads of millions of incalculable [uses]. Again, bodhisattva-mahāsattvas equal in number to the atoms in the thousand-millionfold world were enabled to turn the unreceding Wheel of the Dharma. Again, bodhisattva-mahāsattvas equal in number to the atoms in two thousand middle lands were enabled to turn the pure Wheel of the Dharma. Again, bodhisattva-mahāsattvas equal in number to the atoms in a minor thousand of lands were destined after eight rebirths to gain anuttarasamyaksaṃbodhi. Again, bodhisattva-mahāsattvas equal to four times the number of atoms under four heavens were destined after four rebirths to gain anuttarasamyaksaṃbodhi. Again, bodhisattva-mahāsattvas equal in number to three times the number of atoms under four heavens were destined after three rebirths to gain anuttarasamyaksaṃbodhi. Again, bodhisattva-mahāsattvas equal in number to twice the atoms under four heavens were destined after two rebirths to gain anuttarasamyaksaṃbodhi.

Again, bodhisattva-mahāsattvas equal in number to the atoms under four heavens were destined after one rebirth to gain anuttarasamyaksaṃbodhi. Again, living beings equal in number to the atoms in eight world-spheres opened up their thoughts to anuttarasamyaksaṃbodhi."

When the Buddha said that these bodhisattva-mahāsattvas had gained a great Dharma-advantage, in open space there was a rain of māndārava and mahāmāndārava flowers, scattered over the Buddhas seated on lion thrones at the foot of incalculable hundred thousands of myriads of millions of jeweled trees; scattered at the same time on Śākyamunibuddha and on the Thus Come One Many Jewels, long passed into extinction, both seated on the lion throne within the stūpa of the seven jewels; scattered also on all the bodhisattvas and fourfold assemblies. There was also a rain of finely powdered candana and of incense that sinks in water (*agurusya cūrāṇi ca*). In open space the divine drums sounded of themselves, their sound being fine, deep, and far-reaching. There also rained down a thousand varieties of divine garments, hung with laces of jewels, laces of pearls, laces of maṇi-jewels, laces of wish-granting jewels, filling the nine directions. A great number of jeweled censers were burning priceless incense, whose scent of itself reached everywhere as an offering to the great assembly. Above each Buddha were bodhisattvas holding banners and parasols, reaching in ascending order up to the Brahmā-gods. With fine sounds these bodhisattvas sang incalculable hymns of praise, lauding the Buddhas.

At that time, the bodhisattva Maitreya, rising from his seat, bared his right shoulder and, facing the Buddha with palms joined, proclaimed gāthās, saying:

The Buddha preaches a rare Dharma,
  One that we have never heard before,
That the World-Honored One has great power,
  And that his life-span cannot be measured.
Countless sons of the Buddha,
  Hearing the World-Honored One with discrimination
Preach of those who shall gain profit from the Dharma,
  Rejoice in a joy that fills the whole body.

Some dwell on the ground from which there is no turning
back,
Some have gained dhāraṇīs;
Some, gaining unimpeded joy in preaching,
[Master the] all-protective [charm] that can be turned to
myriads of millions [of uses] (*koṭīsahasrāya ca dhāraṇīye*);
Or, as many as are the thousand-millionfold world's
Atoms, so many are the bodhisattvas
Every one of whom can [now] turn
The unreceding Dharma-wheel.
Again, as many as are the millionfold world's
Atoms, so many are the bodhisattvas
Every one of whom can turn
The pure Dharma-wheel.
Again, as many as are the thousandfold world's
Atoms, so many are the bodhisattvas
Who in eight rebirths more
Shall contrive to achieve the Buddha Path.
Or, as many as in four, three, two,
And the like times the worlds under heaven
There are atoms, so many are the bodhisattvas
Who, after a respective number of rebirths, shall achieve
Buddhahood.
Or, as many as in one world under the four heavens there are
Atoms, so many are the bodhisattvas
Who, after one rebirth more,
Shall achieve omniscience.
Beings such as these,
Hearing of the great length of the Buddha's life-span,
Shall gain incalculable, outflow-free,
Pure fruits and retributions.[1]
Again, as many as are eight world-spheres'
Atoms, so many are the living beings
Who, hearing the Buddha preach of his life-span,
Produced unexcelled thoughts.
The World-Honored One preaches incalculable

Dharmas, beyond reckoning and discussion,
From which many derive benefits
As limitless as open space.[2]
There rain down heavenly māndāravas
And mahāmāndāravas;
And Śakras and Brahmās, like Ganges' sands
In their numberlessness, come from the Buddha-lands.
Candana and incense that sinks in water rain down
In a jumble, falling in confusion
Like birds flying down from the sky,
Scattered as offerings over the Buddhas.
In the midst of open space divine drums
Of themselves produce subtle sounds,
While divine garments in the thousands of myriads
Come whirling down.
Fine censers made of a variety of gems
And burning priceless incense
Of themselves move about everywhere,
Making offerings to the World-Honored Ones.
The great bodhisattva-multitude
Grasps banners and parasols of the seven jewels,
Lofty and fine and of a myriad millions of kinds,
Which by degrees reach to the Brahmā-gods;
And before every Buddha
Are jeweled banners from which hang the pendants of victory.
Also, in a thousand myriads of gāthās
The praises of the Thus Come Ones are sung.
All these many things
Are such as have never been before.
Hearing that the Buddha's life-span is incalculable,
All are delighted.
The Buddha's Name, bruited in ten directions,
Broadly benefits the beings,
And all are fully endowed with wholesome roots,
Which serve to further the unexcelled thought
[of perfect enlightened intuition].[3]

At that time the Buddha declared to the bodhisattva-mahāsattva Maitreya, "O Ajita! Whatever living beings, hearing that the Buddha's life-span is as long as this, can produce as much as a single moment of faith and understanding shall gain merit that shall have no limit, no measure. A good man or good woman for anuttarasamyaksaṃbodhi's sake throughout eighty myriads of millions of nayutas of kalpas may practice the five pāramitās, to wit, *dānapāramitā*, *śīlapāramitā*, *kṣāntipāramitā*, *vīryapāramitā*, and *dhyānapāramitā*, all except *prajñāpāramitā*,* but if one compares his or her merit with the former, it does not come to the hundredth part, not to the thousandth, nor the hundred-thousand-myriad-millionth, nor, for that matter, can it be known by resort to count or even to parable. That a good man or good woman having this sort of merit should recede from anuttarasamyaksaṃbodhi is simply not possible."

At that time, the World-Honored One, wishing to restate this meaning, proclaimed gāthās, saying:

If a man should seek Buddha-knowledge
  Throughout eighty myriads of millions
Of nayutas, yea, of kalpas in that number,
  Practicing the five pāramitās
Throughout all those kalpas,
  Making gifts and presenting offerings to Buddhas
And to condition-perceiving disciples,
  As well as to multitudes of bodhisattvas,
Gifts and offerings of rare and unusual food and drink,
  Of superior clothing and bedding,
Using candana to build monasteries
  Adorned with gardens and groves,
Gifts of this kind and others,
  All of them fine in sundry ways,
Throughout this number of kalpas,
  Diverting them [i.e., the good deeds] to the Buddha Path;
If, again, he should hold to the prohibitions

* For definitions of these, see *pāramitā* in the glossary.

Purely, without omission or neglect,
Seeking the Unexcelled Path,
The one praised by the Buddhas;
If, again, he should practice forbearance in the face of humiliation,
Dwelling on the soil of conciliation and gentleness,
So that, even if numerous evildoers should come and inflict themselves upon him,
His thought would not be shaken,
And if those who possess Dharma
Should cherish overweening pride,
Even then the insult and torment he should receive at their hands,
As well as all things of that sort, he could bear with equanimity;
If, again, he could strive to persevere with vigor,
Ever hard and firm of will and presence of mind,
Throughout incalculable millions of kalpas
Single-minded and not slackening,
Also throughout numberless kalpas
Dwelling in an empty, idle place
And, whether sitting or walking,
Ridding himself of drowsiness and ever collecting his thoughts;
If then, thanks to these causes and conditions,
He should be able to produce dhyāna-concentrations,
For eighty millions of myriads of kalpas,
Dwelling secure, his thought undisturbed,
Holding to this single-minded happiness,
Praying to find the Unexcelled Path—
"May I obtain omniscience,
Exhausting the limits of dhyāna-concentration!";
If this person throughout a hundred thousand
Myriads of millions of kalpas, yea, throughout kalpas in that number,
Should put into practice these merits

Just preached;
And if there should be good men and women
Who, hearing me preach about my life-span,
Should believe for but a single moment,
The happiness of these would exceed even that.
If a person should have absolutely no
Doubts or second thoughts whatever,
Believing with profound thought for a single instant,
Such should be his happiness.[4]
Whatever bodhisattvas there are
Who, having trodden the path for incalculable kalpas,
Hear me preach about my life-span
Shall be able thereby to accept it with faith.
Persons such as these
Shall receive this scriptural canon on the crown of their heads,
Praying, "May I in time to come,
Throughout a long life, convey living beings to salvation!
Just as this day the World-Honored One,
King among the Śākyas,
On the Platform of the Path, with his lion's roar,
Preaches Dharma fearlessly,
May we in time to come,
Objects of veneration on the part of all,
When seated on the Platform of the Path,
Preach of our life-span also in the same way."
If there are persons of profound thought,
Pure, substantial, and straightforward,
Having heard much and able to hold all,
Who understand the Buddha's Word in accord with its meaning,
Then persons such as these
Concerning this shall have no doubts.

"Further, O Ajita, if there is anyone who, hearing of the great length of the Buddha's life-span, understands the import of the words, the merit gained by that man shall have no limit or measure, for he shall be able to produce the unexcelled knowledge of the Thus Come One. How much the truer shall this be of one who broadly hears this scripture, or causes others to hear it, or holds it himself, or causes others to hold it, or writes it down himself, or causes others to write it, or who makes offerings to the scriptural roll of flower perfume, necklaces, banners, parasols, fragrant incense, and candles made of wax scented with fragrant wood! For this man's merit shall be incalculable and limitless, able to produce knowledge of all modes.

"O Ajita! If a good man or good woman, hearing me preach of the great length of my life-span, with profound thought believes and understands, then he or she thereby shall ever see the Buddha on Gṛdhrakūṭa Mountain, with his great multitude of bodhisattvas and voice-hearers surrounding him as he preaches Dharma. He or she shall also see this Sahā world-sphere, its soil made of vaiḍūrya; flat and even; highways in eight directions bordered with Jāmbūnada* gold[5] and rows of jeweled trees; its terraces, towers, and halls all fashioned from gems; a multitude of bodhisattvas all dwelling in its midst. Be it known that if a person is able to take such a view as this, this ability is a mark of profound faith and understanding.

"Again, if after the extinction of the Thus Come One anyone hears this scripture and without maligning it raises up thoughts of appropriate joy, be it known that this is a mark of his having already achieved profound faith and understanding. How much truer is this of one who reads and recites, accepts and keeps it! For such a man thereby carries the Thus Come One on his head. O Ajita! Such a good man or good woman need not ever erect stūpa or monastery, build cells for the saṃgha, or make the four kinds of offerings to the saṃgha-multitude for my sake. What is the reason? Such a good man or good woman, by accepting and holding, by reading and reciting this scriptural canon, thereby shall already have erected stūpas, built saṃgha-cells,

* *Jāmbūnada* is the adjective derived from *Jambūnadī*, the river Jambū (or Jambu), alleged to be formed of the juice of the *jambu* fruit and to flow down from Mount Sumeru into our continent, which thus bears the name Jambudvīpa, "*jambu* island." In Kumārajīva's version, *jāmbūnada* bears the deceptive appearance of *yen-fou-t'an* (ancient pronunciation approximately *yem-bu-dan*), while the Sanskrit, as we have it, does not have the word at all (see note 5).

and made offerings to the saṃgha-multitude. That is, he or she shall have erected with the Buddhaśarīra stūpas of the seven jewels, tapering both vertically and horizontally and reaching to the Brahmā-gods; hung with banners, parasols, and a multitude of jeweled tinkling bells; fitted out with flower perfume, necklaces, powdered incense, perfumed paint, burnt incense, a multitude of drums and musical instruments, pipes, flutes, reeds, and sundry dancers, who shall sing praise with fine-sounding song. That is, he shall have made these offerings throughout incalculable thousands of myriads of millions of kalpas. O Ajita! If after my extinction there be among the hearers of this scriptural canon any who can accept and keep it, or write it down themselves, or instruct others to write it, then they shall thereby have erected saṃgha-cells; also with red candana they shall have fashioned palatial halls, thirty-two in number, the height of eight *tala*-trees [fan-palm, palmyra],[6] high and wide, imposing and lovely, a hundred thousand bhikṣus dwelling within them; with gardens, groves, and bathing ponds, with walks and dhyāna-caves filled with clothing, food and drink, sitting mats and bedding mats, potions and medicines, and all manner of musical instruments; such saṃgha-cells, halls, and towers being in several hundred thousands of myriads of millions, the number being in fact incalculable: so shall they appear, making offerings to me and to the bhikṣu-saṃgha. For that reason I say: if after the extinction of the Thus Come One there is anyone who accepts and keeps, reads and recites, preaches to others, or writes down himself, or instructs others to write, and thus honors the scriptural roll, he need not go further and erect stūpa or monastery or build saṃgha-cells as offerings to the multitudinous saṃgha. If, then, there is a man who can keep this scripture and at the same time practice the spreading of gifts, the keeping of the prohibitions, forbearance in the face of humiliation, vigorous perseverance, single-mindedness, and wisdom, how far superior his excellences shall be, how incalculable, how limitless! Just as open space, eastward, westward, southward, and northward, as well as in the four intermediate directions, upward, and downward, is incalculable and limitless, so shall this man's merit, too, be incalculable and limitless, leading quickly to Knowledge of All Modes. If a person shall read and recite, accept and keep, this scripture and preach it to others, or write it down himself, or instruct another to write it; if, again, he can erect stūpas and build saṃgha-cells, making offerings and singing hymns of praise to the multitudinous saṃgha of voice-hearers; if also, having recourse to a hundred thousand myriads of millions of modes of praise, he lauds the merits of the bodhisattvas; if he also, by various means, preaches to others, in accord with its meaning, this Scripture of the Dharma Blossom; if, again, he can purely keep the prohibitions and dwell with gentle and agreeable persons, enduring humiliation without anger, his will and presence of mind hard and firm, ever attaching great weight to sitting in dhyāna, attaining to the deep concentrations, persevering vigorously and with heroic courage, gathering all good dharmas to himself, being of keen faculties and wisdom, skilled at answering queries and objections: if, O Ajita, after my extinction the good men and good women who accept and keep, read and recite this scriptural canon also have good merits like these, be it known that these persons have already turned toward the Platform of the Way, that they are close to anuttarasamyaksaṃbodhi and seated under the Tree of the Path. O Ajita! Wherever these good men and good women sit, or stand, or walk, there one should erect a stūpa, and all gods and men should make offerings to it, as if it were a stūpa of the Buddha himself."

At that time, the World-Honored One, wishing to restate this meaning, proclaimed gāthās, saying:

> If after my passage into extinction
>   Anyone can exalt this scripture,
> That person's happiness (*puṇyaskandha*) shall be incalculable,
>   As has just been stated.
> He shall thereby have completed
>   All manner of offerings
> And with śarīra have erected a stūpa
>   Adorned with the seven jewels,
> Displaying a chatra very high and wide,
>   Gradually tapering till it reaches the Brahmā-gods,
> And jeweled tinkling bells in the thousands of myriads of millions
>   That give forth a subtle sound when shaken by the wind.

He also throughout incalculable kalpas
  Shall have made offerings to this stūpa
Of flower perfume and necklaces,
  Of divine garments and the music of a host of instruments,
And burnt candles of scented wax,
  Ever shining brightly all around.
In an evil age, at the time of the final Dharma,
  Whoever can keep this scripture
Thereby, as just said, shall already
  Have perfected sundry offerings.
If one can keep this scripture,
  Then it shall be as if, in the very presence of the Buddha,
With ox-head candana
  He had erected saṃgha-cells as an offering,
With halls thirty-two,
  The height of eight tala-trees,
And presented superior sweetmeats and fine garments,
  As well as mats and beds, all perfect,
A dwelling-place for a multitude of a hundred thousand,
  Gardens and goves, bathing ponds,
Walks, and dhyāna-caves,
  All variously imposing and lovely.
If there are any who with the thought of faith and
    understanding
  Accept and keep, read and recite, write,
Or, again, instruct others to write;
  Also make offerings to the scriptural roll,
Scattering flower perfume and powdered incense;
  Or take *sumanā* [large-flowered jasmine], *campaka* [champac
    tree]
And *atimuktaka* [*Gaertneria racemosa*]
  And, extracting their fragrant oil, ever burn it:
He who makes offerings like these
  Shall gain incalculable merit;
As open space is limitless,
  So shall his happiness be.

How much truer shall this be of one who keeps this scripture
  And who at the same time spreads gifts all round, keeps the
    prohibitions,
Endures humiliation, desires dhyāna-concentration,
  Neither angry nor foul-mouthed,
Humbly reveres the stūpa-shrines,
  Defers to the bhikṣus,
Puts arrogant thoughts far from himself,
  Ever aspires to wisdom,
And is not angry when there are queries or objections
  But explains himself acquiescently!
If one can perform these acts,
  One's merit shall be incalculable.
If one sees this Dharma-master
  Perfect such excellences as these,
One must strew him with divine flowers,
  Cover his body with divine garments,
Touch one's face and head to his feet in obeisance,
  And produce thoughts of him as if of a Buddha.
One should also think:
  "In no long time he shall arrive at the Platform of the Way,
Gaining the no-ado that has no outflows*
  And broadly benefiting men and gods."
Wherever he may have dwelt,
  Or walked, or sat or lain,
Wherever, for that matter, he may have uttered a single gāthā,
  Therein one is to erect a stūpa,

* The "no-ado that has no outflows" is supreme enlightenment that leads to nirvāṇa. It has "no outflows" in the sense that it does not conduce to reincarnation. "No-ado" (*wu wei*) is a Taoist term taken over by the Ch. Buddhists, first to mean nirvāṇa, later to mean *asaṃskṛta*. Here, I believe, Kumārajīva's Ch. amanuenses, without his knowledge, were harking back to an earlier usage, or rather to a kindred sense, not *nirvāṇa* but *bodhi*, "enlightened intuition" (which is what the Skt. has). *Wu wei* implied for the Taoists that all action is bad, that the Sage who really understands Heaven's will can sit perfectly motionless and let things take care of themselves. There can be little doubt that the first Chinese to be attracted to Buddhism misunderstood nirvāṇa to mean just that.

Adorning it, making it fine and lovely,
  And making sundry offerings to it.
If the Buddha's son dwells in this land,
  Then the Buddha gains the advantage thereof,
Ever being within it,
  Whether walking, sitting, or lying.[7]

Chapter Eighteen: The Merits of Appropriate Joy

At that time, the bodhisattva-mahāsattva Maitreya addressed the Buddha, saying, "O World-Honored One! If there is a good man or good woman who, hearing this Scripture of the Dharma Blossom, rejoices appropriately, how much happiness shall he or she obtain?" Then he proclaimed a gāthā, saying:

> After the World-Honored One's passage into extinction,
> If there is one who hears this scripture
> And if he can rejoice appropriately,
> How much happiness shall he obtain? (*kiyantaṃ kuśalaṃ bhavet* //)

At that time, the Buddha declared to the bodhisattva-mahāsattva Maitreya, "O Ajita! After the Thus Come One's passage into extinction, if bhikṣu, bhikṣuṇī, upāsaka, upāsikā, or any other wise person, old or young, having heard this scripture and rejoiced appropriately, leaves the assembly of the Dharma and, going to another place, whether saṃgha-cells, empty and idle places, walled cities, towns, alleyways, footpaths, settlements, or rustic villages, expounds it to the limit of his ability to father and mother, close kin, or good friends and acquaintances, and if these persons, having heard it, rejoice appropriately and go in turn and teach it to others who likewise, having heard it, rejoice in their own turn, and if it goes on in this way until it reaches the fiftieth person, then, O Ajita, I will now tell of the merits of the appropriate joy of that good man or good woman. Listen well!

"Suppose that in the hundred myriads of millions of asaṃkhyeyas of world-spheres, among living beings of the six destinies and the four kinds of birth—to wit, birth from eggs, birth from a womb, birth from moisture, and birth from transformation—whether shaped or shapeless, whether conscious, unconscious, not conscious, or not unconscious, whether legless, two-legged, four-legged, or many-legged, and the like, suppose that among these many living beings there is a man who, seeking happiness,[1] gives them whatever enjoyable things they desire, to every being giving a whole Jambudvīpa full of gold, silver, vaiḍūrya, giant clam shell, agate, coral, amber, and other fine and precious gems, as well as elephants, horses, carriages, and palaces, halls, and towers fashioned of the seven jewels. If this great donor, having spread gifts about in this way full eighty years, then thinks: 'I have already given to the beings whatever playthings they desired. Yet these beings are all old and decrepit, their years in excess of eighty, their hair white, their faces wrinkled, and in no long time they will die. I must teach and guide them by recourse to the Buddhadharma'; if then he straightway assembles these beings, expounding conversion through Dharma, demonstrating and teaching, benefiting and delighting them, so that at once all gain the path of the *srota'āpanna* [the first-stage śrāvaka], the path of the *sakṛdāgāmin* ["once-returner"] the path of the *anāgāmin* ["nonreturner"], the path of the arhant, exhausting whatever outflows there may be, all acquiring the self-mastery [to enter] profound dhyāna-concentration [at will], and perfecting the eight deliverances, in your thinking how shall it be? Shall the merits gained by this great donor be many or not?"

Maitreya addressed the Buddha, saying, "O World-Honored One! This man's merit shall be very great, incalculable and limitless. If this donor were but to give the beings all manner of playthings, his merit would be incalculable. How much the more if he were to enable them to gain the fruit of the arhant!"

The Buddha declared to Maitreya, "I now tell you plainly: the merit gained by this man for giving all manner of playthings to living beings of the six destinies in four hundred myriads of millions of asaṃkhyeyas of world-spheres, and also enabling them to obtain the fruit of the arhant, does not equal one-hundredth, not one-thousandth, not one-hundred-thousand-myriad-millionth part of the merit of that fiftieth person for appropriately rejoicing at hearing a single gāthā of the Scripture of the Dharma Blossom, for it is something that cannot be known through number or parable. O Ajita! The merit of this fiftieth person for having rejoiced at hearing, albeit indirectly, the Scripture of the Dharma Blossom shall even so be incalculable, limitless, asaṃkhyeya. How far superior, how much the more incalculable, limitless, and asaṃkhyeya shall be the happiness of him who hears it among the first in the assembly and rejoices appropriately! For the two cannot be compared.[2]

"Further, O Ajita, if a man for this scripture's sake goes to a saṃgha-cell and, whether seated or standing, listens and accepts for but a moment, then, by virtue of this merit, the body into which he is reborn shall acquire lovely, superior, and fine elephants, horses, and carriages, as well as palanquins fitted with precious gems, and shall ascend to divine palaces.[3] If, again, a person is seated in a place where Dharma is expounded, and if yet another man comes, and the former urges the latter to sit and listen, or offers him a share of his own seat, through his merit this former man upon the rebirth of his body shall gain the seat of the great god Śakra, or the seat of the Brahmā-king, or the place where sits a wheel-turning sage-king. O Ajita! If, again, there is a man who says to others, 'There is a Scripture named Dharma Blossom. Let us go together and listen to it!'; and if straightway they accept his advice and hear it for but a moment, this man's merit shall be such that upon the his body's revolution [on the wheel of rebirth] he shall be able to be born in the same place as *dhāraṇī(pratilabdha)bodhisattvas*; he shall be wise and of keen faculties; for a hundred thousand myriads of ages never dumb; his breath never fetid; his tongue never diseased; his mouth also never diseased; his teeth not dirty or black, not yellow or wide-spaced, not missing or falling out, not uneven or crooked; his lips not hanging down, also not tightly pursed, not rough or chapped, not scarred or scabbed, not defective or damaged, not askew, neither thick nor large, not black, in short having nothing hateful about them; his nose neither thin nor crooked and out of joint; his face not of dark complexion, nor long and narrow, nor concave and irregular—in short he shall have no disagreeable features, his lips, tongue, and teeth being all majestic and goodly; his nose long, prominent, and straight; the shape of his face full and round; his brows high and long; his forehead broad, flat, and even; his male member perfect. In birth after birth through generations he shall see the Buddha and hear the Dharma, believing and accepting the teachings. O Ajita, look you, now, how great is the merit of him who encourages but one man to go and listen to the Dharma! How much the greater is that of one who single-mindedly listens to the preachings, reads and recites, and in the great multitude explains them to others, practicing as he preaches!"

At that time, the World-Honored One, wishing to restate this meaning, proclaimed gāthās, saying:

If a man in the Dharma-assembly
  Can hear this scriptural canon
And, even for a single gāthā,
  Rejoice appropriately and preach it to others,
And if in this way it is taught by turns
  Till it reaches the fiftieth,
The happiness obtained by the last person
  I will now set forth with discrimination:
If there is a great donor
  Who makes presents to incalculable multitudes,
Full eighty years
  According with their wishes;
If he sees their aged and decrepit appearance,
  Their hair white and their faces wrinkled,
Their teeth wide-spaced, their bodily forms withered;
  If he thinks, "Their death is not far off.
I must now teach them,
  Enabling them to gain the fruit of the Path!";
If straightway he then preaches to them by resort to expedient devices
  The real dharma of nirvāṇa,
Saying, "The world is in no wise firm or secure,
  But it is like water-bubbles, like a will-o'-the-wisp!
You all must
  Speedily produce thoughts of revulsion!";
If men, hearing this dharma,
  All gain arhattva,
Perfecting the six supernatural penetrations,

The three clarities, and the eight deliverances;
If the last, the fiftieth [of those told of the Dharma Blossom],
Hearing a single gāthā, rejoices appropriately:
This man's happiness shall exceed the former
So that no likeness is possible.
If one hears it thus indirectly,
One's happiness even so shall be incalculable.
How much the more shall his be who in the Dharma-assembly
First hears and rejoices appropriately!
If there be one who encourages a single person,
Guiding him to listen to the Dharma Blossom,
Saying, "This scripture is profound and subtle,
Hard to encounter in a thousand myriads of kalpas!";
If he straightway, accepting the advice, goes and listens,
Hearing it for but a moment:
This man's reward of happiness
I will now state in specific detail.
Generation after generation he shall have no mouth ailments.
His teeth shall not be wide-spaced, yellow, or black.
His lips shall not be thick, pursed, or thin.
In short, he shall have no disagreeable features.
His tongue shall not be dry, black, or short.
His nose shall be prominent, long, and also straight.
His forehead shall be broad, also flat and even.
His face and eyes shall be perfectly regular and dignified.
Others shall be delighted to see him.
His breath shall not be fetid or foul.
The scent of the *utpala* [blue lotus] flower
Shall ever issue forth from his mouth.
If intentionally he goes to a saṃgha-cell,
Wishing to listen to the Scripture of the Dharma Blossom,
And if, hearing it even for a moment, he rejoices,
I now will tell of his happiness.
Afterward, being born among gods and men,
He shall get fine elephant- and horse-drawn carriages
And palanquins fashioned of precious gems,

And also ascend to the divine palaces.
If in a place where Dharma is expounded
He encourages others to sit and listen to the scriptures,
Then, by virtue of this merit, he shall gain
The thrones of Śakra, Brahmā, and the wheel-turners.
How much truer shall this be of one who single-mindedly listens to
And explains its purport,
Practicing it as he preaches it!
For his happiness shall be boundless.[4]

Chapter Nineteen: The Merits of the Dharma-Preacher

At that time, the Buddha declared to the bodhisattva-mahāsattva Ever Persevering (Satatasamitābhiyukta), "If any good man or good woman shall accept and keep this Scripture of the Dharma Blossom, whether reading it, reciting it, interpreting it, or copying it, that person shall attain eight hundred virtues of the eye, one thousand two hundred virtues of the ear, eight hundred virtues of the nose, one thousand two hundred virtues of the tongue, eight hundred virtues of the body, and one thousand two hundred virtues of the mind, by means of which virtues he shall adorn his six faculties, causing them all to be pure.[1] That good man or good woman, with the pure eye of flesh engendered by father and mother, shall see all mountains and forests, rivers and seas, both inner and outer,* that are in the thousand-millionfold world, down to the Avīci hell and up to the Pinnacle of Existence. He shall also see all living beings in their midst. Moreover, he shall thoroughly see and thoroughly know the causes and conditions, the fruits and retributions, of the beings' deeds and places of birth."[2]

At that time the World-Honored One, wishing to restate this meaning, proclaimed gāthās, saying:

If, in the midst of the great multitude, anyone,
  With a heart free of fear,
Shall preach this Scripture of the Dharma Blossom,
  Listen now to his merits!
This man shall attain eight hundred

* Probably in the sense "hidden and exposed."

Virtues distinguishing his eye,
With which adorned
His eye shall be very pure.
With the eye engendered by father and mother
He shall thoroughly see the thousand-millionfold world,
Its inner and outer mounts Meru,
Sumeru, and Iron-Rim,
As well as all other mountains, forests,
Great seas, rivers, streams, and rivulets,
Down as far as the Avīci prison
And up to the gods of the Pinnacle of Existence.
The living beings in their midst,
Every one of them, shall he see.
Though he may not yet have acquired a divine eye,
Such shall be the power of his fleshly eye.[3]

"Further, O Ever Persevering, if a good man or good woman shall accept and keep this scripture, whether reading it, reciting it, interpreting it, or copying it, he shall attain a thousand two hundred virtues of the ear, and by means of this pure ear he shall hear in the thousand-millionfold world, down to the Avīci hell and up to the Pinnacle of Existence, all manner of speech and sounds, both inner and outer: the voices of elephants, the voices of horses, the voices of cattle, the sounds of chariots, the sound of sobs, the sound of sighs, the sound of conch shells, the sound of drums, the sound of bells, the sound of gongs, the sound of laughter, the sound of speech, men's voices, women's voices, boys' voices, girls' voices, the sound of Dharma, the sound of nondharma, the sound of pain, the sound of pleasure, the voices of ordinary fellows, the voices of saints, the sound of happiness, the sound of unhappiness, the voices of gods, the voices of dragons, the voices of yakṣas, the voices of gandharvas, the voices of asuras, the voices of kinnaras, the voices of mahoragas, the sound of fire, the sound of water, the sound of wind, the voices of hell-dwellers, the voices of beasts, the voices of hungry ghosts, the voices of bhikṣus, the voices of bhikṣuṇīs, the voices of voice-hearers, the voices of pratyekabuddhas, the voices of Buddhas—in short, whatever sounds there may be, inner or outer, in the thousand-millionfold world. Though he may not yet have acquired a divine ear, with the pure ordinary ear engendered by father and mother he shall hear and know everything. In this way he shall discriminate among sundry sounds and yet not damage his aural faculty."

At that time the World-Honored One, wishing to restate this meaning, proclaimed gāthās, saying:

The ear engendered by father and mother
  Is pure and without defilement.
With this common ear he hears
  The sounds of the thousandfold world:
The sounds made by elephants, horses, and cattle;
  The sounds of bells, gongs, conchs, and drums;
The sounds of lutes and pipes;
  The sound of the voices of flutes.
To the sound of pure and lovely song,
  Though he hears it, he is not attached,
While the voices of numberless kinds of men
  He hears and can thoroughly understand.[4]
He also hears the voices of the gods,
  The sounds of their refined songs;
And he hears the voices of men and women,
  The voices of boys and girls.
Within mountains, streams, and deep ravines,
  The voice of the kalaviṅka,
And of the sundry other birds,
  All these voices does he hear.[5]
Of the multitudinous woes and pains of hell
  The various tormented screams;
Of hungry ghosts pressed by hunger and thirst
  The voices, as they seek food and drink;
The asuras,
  Dwelling by the edge of the great sea,
When they talk to one another
  What great sounds they utter:

Sounds like these [are heard by] the preacher of Dharma,
  Who dwells here securely;
This multitude of sounds does he hear from afar,
  Yet they do not damage his aural faculty.
Within the world-spheres in all ten quarters
  The birds and beasts cry out, calling to one another,
And the man preaching Dharma
  Hears all of them here.
Those above the Brahmā gods,
  Bright Sound and Universally Pure,
Up through the gods of the Pinnacle of Existence,
  The sound of the speech of these
Is the Dharma-master, dwelling here,
  Able to hear in its entirety.[6]
The multitude of all bhikṣus,
  As well as bhikṣuṇīs,
Whether reading and reciting the scriptural canon
  Or preaching it to others,
The Dharma-master, dwelling here,
  Is thoroughly able to hear.
Further, there are bodhisattvas
  Reading and reciting the scriptural Dharma
Or preaching it to others,
  Compiling commentaries that explicate its meaning.
The sounds of voices like these
  He is thoroughly able to hear.
The Buddhas, the most venerable among the great saints,
  Who teach and convert living beings,
Who in the midst of the great assemblies
  Expound the subtle Dharma,
He who holds this Dharma Blossom
  Is able to hear, every one of them.
Of the thousand-millionfold world,
  The inner and outer sounds,
From as far down as the Avīci prison
  To as high as the gods of the Pinnacle of Existence,

The sounds of all these voices does he hear,
Yet they do not damage his aural faculty.[7]
Since his ear is acute and perceptive,
He can know all with discrimination.
Whosoever holds this Dharma Blossom,
Though he has not yet acquired a divine ear,
By the mere use of the ear with which he was born
Already has virtues of this kind.[8]

"Again, O Ever Persevering, if a good man or good woman accepts and keeps this scripture, whether reading it, reciting it, explaining it, or copying it, he shall achieve eight hundred virtues of the nose, and shall, by the use of his pure nasal faculty, smell all manner of scents, superior and inferior, inner and outer, in the thousand-millionfold world, the scent of the *sumanā*-flower, the scent of the *jāti*-flower, the scent of the *mallikā*-flower,* the scent of the campaka-flower, the scent of the red lotus blossom, the scent of the green lotus blossom, the scent of the white lotus blossom, the scents of blossoming trees, the scents of fruit-bearing trees, the scent of candana, the scent of the scent that sinks in water, the scent of tamālapatra, the scent of *tagara* [East Indiān rosebay], and the scents of a thousand myriads of varieties of blended perfumes, whether powdered, or in lumps, or in the form of paint. One who holds this scripture, while dwelling in this very place, shall be able to distinguish them perfectly. He shall also know with discrimination the scents of living beings, to wit, the scent of elephants, the scent of horses, the scents of cattle and sheep, the scent of men, the scent of women, the scent of boys, the scent of girls, and the scents of grasses, trees, thickets, and forests. Be they near or far, whatever scents there are, he shall be able to smell them all, distinguishing among them without error. One who holds this scripture, though he may dwell here, shall yet smell the divine scents above the heavens, to wit, the scent of the pārijātaka and *kovidāra* [bauhinia] trees; as well as the scent of the māndārava-flower; the scent of the mahāmāndārava-flower; the scent

* These are three kinds of jasmine.

of the mañjūṣaka-flower; the scent of the mahāmañjūṣaka-flower; as well as the scents of candana, the scent that sinks in water, various powdered perfumes, and the perfumes of sundry flowers. Of such divine perfumes as these, or of perfumes produced from blending them, there is none that he shall not smell and know. He shall also smell the scents of the gods' bodies, to wit, the scent of Śakro Devānām Indraḥ when he sports atop his palace of victory and enjoys the pleasures of the five desires, or his scent when atop his fine Dharma-hall he preaches Dharma to the Trāyastriṃśa gods, or his scent when he amuses himself in his gardens, as well as the scents of the bodies of all the other gods and goddesses: all these he shall smell from afar. In this way, proceeding by degrees to the Brahmā-gods and up to the Pinnacle of Existence, he shall smell the scents of all the gods' bodies, and shall at the same time smell the incense burnt by the gods, as well as the scents of voice-hearers, the scents of pratyekabuddhas, the scents of bodhisattvas, and the scents of Buddha-bodies: these also shall he smell from afar, thus knowing where they all are. Though he may smell these scents, yet his nasal faculty shall not suffer or be misled. If he wishes to preach of them to others with discrimination, his mind shall not wander."

At that time the World-Honored One, wishing to restate this meaning, proclaimed gāthās, saying:

Since this man's nose is pure,
  Within this world-sphere,
Be they fragrant or fetid,
  All manner of things it smells and knows:
Sumanā and jāti,
  Tamāla and candana,
The scent that sinks in water and the perfume of the catalpa tree,
  In short, the perfumes of various blossoms and fruits.[9]
And he knows the scents of living beings,
  The scents of men and women.
Though dwelling afar off, the preacher of Dharma
  By smelling their scents knows where they are.
The wheel-turning kings of great might,

The lesser wheel-turners and their sons,
Their assembled ministers and those in their inner apartments—
Smelling their scents, he knows where they are.
The precious gems attached to the body
And the precious deposits within the earth,
As well as the precious daughters of the wheel-turning kings—*
Smelling their scents he knows where they are.[10]
The accouterments that adorn men's bodies,
Their clothing, their necklaces,
The sundry ointments with which they paint themselves—
Having smelt these, he then knows their bodies.
Of the gods, whether walking or sitting,
Their games and magical feats (*ṛddhibalaṃ ca sarvam* /),
He who holds this Dharma Blossom,
Having smelt their scents, can thoroughly know.
The blossoms and fruits of trees
And clarified butter—by their fragrant scent,
He who holds this scripture, dwelling here,
In every case knows where they are.[11]
In the deep ravines of the mountains
The spread of blossoms on the candana trees,
As well as the living beings who dwell in their midst,
By smelling the scents he can know thoroughly.
On Mount Iron-Rim, in the great ocean,
And within the earth are living beings,
And by the smell of their scents, the keeper of this scripture
Knows in every case where they are.
The asuras' sons' and daughters'
As well as their retinues'
Times of fight and of play,
By smelling their scents, he can know entirely.[12]
Open fields and ravines,
Lions, elephants, tigers, and wolves,

* This renders *chuan lun wang pao nü*, but I cannot help thinking that the *pao* and the *nü* have been transposed. This is supported by context and by the Skt. (see note 10).

Wild oxen and water oxen—
  Smelling their scents, he knows where they are.
If there are pregnant women,
  And it is not yet known whether theirs will be boy or girl,
Or defective or monstrous,
  By smelling their scents he can know in each case.
By virtue of his power of smell
  He shall know of their first conceiving,
Whether or not they shall come to fruition
  And whether in comfort they shall bear a happy child (*puṇya-mayaṃ kumāram* / /)
By virtue of his power of smell
  He shall know what men and women think,
Their thoughts of passionate desire, folly, and anger;
  He shall also know those who cultivate the good.[13]
The many deposits in the earth
  Of gold, silver, and precious gems,
The contents of copper vessels,
  By smelling their scents, he can know completely.
The various and sundry necklaces,
  Whose value none can know—
By smelling their scent, he knows their value,
  Their place of origin, and where they now are.[14]
The flowers above the heavens,
  Mandārava and mañjūṣaka
And flowers on the pārijāta tree,
  By smelling their scents, he can know thoroughly.
The palaces above the heavens,
  Whether superior, middle, or inferior,
Adorned as they are with a host of precious flowers,
  By smelling their scents, he can know completely.
The divine parks and groves, the palaces of victory,
  The temples, the halls of fine Dharma,
And the pleasures that are within,
  Smelling their scents, he can know completely.
The gods, either when listening to Dharma

Or when experiencing the pleasures of the five desires,
As they come, go, walk, sit, or lie,
Smelling their scents, he can know completely.[15]
The garments worn by the goddesses,
The lovely floral perfumes with which they adorn themselves,
The times at which they circle about in play,
By smelling their scents, he can know completely.[16]
Proceeding thus upward by degrees
Until he reaches the Brahmā-gods,
Those who enter dhyāna and those who leave dhyāna,
By smelling their scents, he can know completely.
From the gods Bright Sound and the Universally Pure
Up through the Pinnacle of Existence,
Those just born and those retired to oblivion,
By smelling their scents, he can know completely.[17]
The multitudes of bhikṣus
Ever striving vigorously toward Dharma,
Whether sitting or walking,
Whether reading or reciting the scriptural Dharma,
Or whether, at the foot of trees in a forest,
With single-minded vigor sitting in dhyāna,
He who holds this scripture, by smelling their scents,
Knows in every case where they are.[18]
The bodhisattvas of firm intent,
Seated in dhyāna, whether reading the scriptures
Or preaching Dharma to others,
By smelling their scent, he can know completely.[19]
Wherever he may be, the World-Honored One,
Humbly revered by all,
Preaching the Dharma out of compassion for the multitude,
By smelling his scent, [the preacher] can know completely.
The living beings who, in the Buddha's presence,
Hearing the scripture, all rejoice
And practice in accord with the Dharma,
By smelling their scents, he can know completely.
Though he has not yet attained the bodhisattva's

Dharma without outflows, or the nose engendered thereby,
Yet this person who holds this scripture
First attains this nasal mark.[20]

"Further, O Ever Persevering, if a good man or good woman accepts and keeps this scripture, whether reading it, reciting it, interpreting it, or copying it, he shall attain a thousand two hundred virtues of the tongue. All things, whether good or ugly, whether delicious or foul-tasting, or even bitter and astringent, shall all change for his lingual faculty into things of superior flavor like the sweet dew of the gods, none failing to be delicious. If in the midst of a great multitude he has anything to expound, then, producing a profound and subtle sound, with his lingual faculty he shall be able to penetrate their hearts, causing them all to rejoice and be cheerful. Also, the sons and daughters of the gods, as well as Śakra and Brahmā and other gods, hearing of the order in the words and remarks that he has to expound with this profound and subtle voice, shall all come to listen. And the dragons and dragons' daughters, the yakṣas and yakṣas' daughters, the asuras and asuras' daughters, the garuḍas and garuḍas' daughters, the kinnaras and kinnaras' daughters, the mahoragas and mahoragas' daughters, in order to listen to the Dharma shall all come and approach him with familiarity, revere him humbly, and make offerings to him. And the bhikṣus, bhikṣuṇīs, upāsakas, and upāsikās, the lords and princes of realms, the assembled ministers and their retinues, the lesser wheel-turning kings and the greater wheel-turning kings, their thousands of sons all endowed with the seven jewels, and the inner and outer retinues of these latter, atop their palaces,* shall all come to listen to the Dharma. Since this bodhisattva shall skillfully preach Dharma, the Brahmans, householders, and commoners within the realm shall follow him for the full length of their bodily lives, rendering service and offerings. Also, the voice-hearers, pratyekabuddhas, bodhisattvas, and Buddhas shall ever desire to see him. Wherever this person may be, the Buddhas shall all preach the Dharma facing that place, and he shall be able to accept and hold

* Extant Skt. has nothing corresponding, but K.'s original must have had *vimāna*, a word for "palace" that also means "flying chariot."

completely all the Buddhadharmas. He shall also be able to give forth the profound, subtle sound of Dharma."[21]

At that time the World-Honored One, wishing to restate this meaning, proclaimed gāthās, saying:

This man's lingual faculty shall be pure,
 Never experiencing ugly flavors,
But whatever he eats
 Shall all turn to sweet dew.[22]
With his profound, pure, and fine voice,
 In the great multitude he shall preach Dharma,
And by resort to causes, conditions, and parables[23]
 Shall draw to himself the hearts of the beings.
His hearers, all rejoicing,
 Shall prepare superior offerings.
The gods, dragons, yakṣas,
 And asuras,
All with humbly reverent thought,
 Shall come together to listen to Dharma.[24]
This preacher of Dharma,
 If he wishes with his subtle sound
To permeate the thousandfold world,
 Shall be able to do so directly, exactly as he wishes.[25]
The greater and lesser wheel-turning kings,
 As well as their thousands of sons and their retinues,
With palms joined and with hearts humbly reverent,
 Shall ever come to listen receptively to the Dharma.
The gods, dragons, yakṣas,
 Rākṣasas [kind of demon] and piśācas
Shall also, with rejoicing heart,
 Ever desire to come and make offerings.[26]
Brahmā, the king of the gods, and King Māra,
 The Self-Master and the Great Self-Master,
And a multitude of gods like these
 Shall all come into his presence.[27]
The Buddhas and their disciples,

Hearing the sound of him preaching Dharma,
Shall, ever mindful, protect him,
And at times shall display their own bodies to him.[28]

"Again, O Ever Persevering, if a good man or good woman accepts and keeps this scripture, whether reading it, reciting it, interpreting it, or copying it, he shall acquire eight hundred virtues of the body, for he shall acquire a body as pure as unblemished vaiḍūrya, one which the beings will delight to see. Because his body shall be pure, the living beings in the thousand-millionfold world, whether at the time of birth or at the time of death, whether superior or inferior, fair or ugly, born in a good place or in a bad place, shall all be visible therein. And Mount Iron-Rim, Mount Great Iron-Rim, Mount Meru, Mount Mahāmeru, and the other kings among mountains, as well as the living beings in their midst, shall all be visible therein. From the Avīci hell up to the Pinnacle of Existence, whatever there is, and whatever living beings are there, all shall be visible therein. If voice-hearers, pratyekabuddhas, bodhisattvas, or Buddhas preach Dharma, they shall all reveal their physical images within that body."[29]

At that time, the World-Honored One, wishing to restate this meaning, proclaimed gāthās, saying:

If anyone holds the Dharma Blossom,
His body shall be very pure,
Like that unblemished vaiḍūrya
The sight of which gives joy to all living beings.
Also, as in a pure, bright mirror
One sees all physical images,
The bodhisattva, in his pure body,
Sees whatever is in the world.
Only he alone in and of himself has clear perception,
For these are things that others do not see.[30]
Within the thousandfold world,
All germinating things,
Gods, men, asuras,
Hell-dwellers, ghosts, beasts,

And physical forms such as these
　Can all be seen in his body.[31]
Iron-Rim and Meru,
　Also Mahāmeru, these mountains,
The great oceans and rivers
　Can all be seen in his body.[32]
Buddhas and voice-hearers,
　Sons of Buddhas and bodhisattvas,
Whether alone or in a multitude,
　Preaching Dharma, can all be seen.
Though he has not yet acquired the outflow-free
　Subtle body of Dharmahood,
His common body being thus pure,
　Everything appears within it.

"Again, O Ever Persevering, if a good man or good woman after the extinction of the Thus Come One accepts and holds this scripture, whether reading it, reciting it, interpreting it, or copying it, he shall attain a thousand two hundred virtues of the mind. With this pure mental faculty, by hearing so much as a single gāthā or a single phrase, he shall penetrate incalculable, limitless meanings; and after having understood these meanings, he shall be able to expound a single phrase or a single gāthā for as much as a month, or four months, or even for a year, and the dharmas that he preaches shall be in accord with the import of that meaning, standing in absolutely no contradiction to the marks of reality. If he preaches secular classics, pronouncements on the governance of the world, occupations that sustain life, and things of this sort, he shall in every case do so in accord with the Fine Dharma. In the thousand-millionfold world, among the living beings of the six destinies, the actions they perform in thought, the motions they make in thought, and the frivolous assertions to which they resort in thought are all known to him. Though he shall not yet have attained knowledge without outflows, yet his mental faculty shall be as pure as this. Whatever intentions, or calculations, or speech this man has shall all match the Buddhadharma, none of it being out of keeping with true Reality, and all shall have been preached in the scriptures of previous Buddhas."

At that time, the World-Honored One, wishing to restate this meaning, proclaimed gāthās, saying:

This man's mind shall be pure,
 Clear, sharp, and undefiled.
With this fine mental faculty,
 He shall know superior, middle, and inferior dharmas.
By hearing so much as a single gāthā,
 He shall penetrate incalculable meanings,
In due sequence and in keeping with Dharma preaching them
 A month, four months, as long as a year.
Within and without this world-sphere,
 All living beings—
Whether gods, dragons, or men,
 Yakṣaṣ, ghosts, spirits, and the like—
Within the six destinies
 And the thoughts they think, in their sundry varieties,
As a reward for holding this scripture
 He knows all at once.[33]
The countless Buddhas in the ten quarters,
 Marked with a hundred happy adorning marks,
Preaching Dharma to the beings,
 He hears completely, and can accept and keep their message.[34]
He thinks on incalculable meanings,
 And his preaching of Dharma is also incalculable,
For from beginning to end he neither forgets nor confuses,
 And this because he holds to the Dharma Blossom.
He is thoroughly aware of the marks of the dharmas,
 And recognizes their order as it really is.
He has penetrated names and words
 And, as he knows them, so he expounds them.[35]
What this man has to preach
 Is all in accord with the Dharma of previous Buddhas.
Because he sets forth this Dharma,
 Within the multitude he is without fear.
He who holds to the Scripture of the Dharma Blossom

Has a mental faculty as pure as this.
Though he has not yet contrived to be free of outflows,
Yet he has such marks as these from before.
This man, holding this scripture
And dwelling securely on rare ground,
Is by all living beings
Enjoyed, loved, and revered.
For he can, by resort to a thousand myriads of varieties
Of skillful words,
Expound with discrimination,
Because he holds to this Scripture of the Dharma Blossom.[36]

Scripture of the Lotus Blossom of the Fine Dharma.
End of Roll the Sixth.

Roll 7

Chapter Twenty: The Bodhisattva Never Disparaging

At that time, the Buddha declared to the bodhisattva-mahāsattva Gainer of Great Strength (Mahāsthāmaprāpta), "You should now know this: if a bhikṣu, bhikṣunī, upāsaka, or upāsikā holds to this Scripture of the Dharma Blossom, and if anyone with a foul mouth abuses or maligns him or her, then that latter person shall receive retribution for a great sin, such as was formerly described; while the merit gained by the former shall be as just mentioned, for his eyes, ears, nose, tongue, body, and mind shall be pure.[1]

"O Gainer of Great Strength! Long ago, beyond incalculable, unlimited asaṃkhyeyakalpas, not subject to reckoning or discussion, there was a Buddha named King of Imposing Sound (Bhīṣmagarjitasvararāja), a Thus Come One, worthy of offerings, of right and universal knowledge, his clarity and conduct perfect, well gone, understanding the world, an unexcelled Worthy, a Regulator of men of stature, a Teacher of gods and men, a Buddha, a World-Honored One, whose kalpa was named Free of Deterioration (Vinirbhāga), whose realm was named Great Coming into Being (Mahāsaṃbhavā). That Buddha, King of Imposing Sound, in that world preached the Dharma to gods, men and asuras: to those who sought the rank of voice-hearers preaching a dharma corresponding to the Four Truths, with which to save them from birth, old age, sickness, and death and to enable them to achieve perfect nirvāṇa; to those who sought the rank of pratyekabuddha preaching a dharma corresponding to the twelve causes and conditions; to the bodhisattvas, in keeping with anuttarasamyaksaṃbodhi, preaching a dharma corresponding to the six pāramitās, with which to achieve perfect Buddha-knowledge. O Gainer of Great Strength! This Buddha, King of

Imposing Sound, had a life-span of kalpas equal in number to the sands of forty myriads of millions of nayutas of Ganges rivers. His True Dharma abided in the world for kalpas equal in number to the atoms in one Jambudvīpa. His Counterfeit Dharma abided in the world for kalpas equal in number to the atoms in four worlds under heaven. After that Buddha had benefited the beings, then and only then did he pass into extinction. After his True Dharma and Counterfeit Dharma had perished utterly, in that land there emerged yet another Buddha, also named King of Imposing Sound, a Thus Come One, worthy of offerings, of right and universal knowledge, his clarity and conduct perfect, well gone, understanding the world, an unexcelled Worthy, a Regulator of men of stature, a Teacher of gods and men, a Buddha, a World-Honored One. In a sequence such as this there were two myriads of millions of Buddhas, all of the same name. When the first Thus Come One named King of Imposing Sound had passed into extinction, and after his True Dharma had perished, in the midst of his Counterfeit Dharma bhikṣus of overweening pride had great power. At that time there was a bodhisattva-bhikṣu named Never Disparaging (Sadāparibhūta). O Gainer of Great Strength! For what reason was he named Never Disparaging? Whomever this bhikṣu saw, be it bhikṣu, bhikṣuṇi, upāsaka, or upāsikā, he would do obeisance to them all and utter praise, saying: 'I profoundly revere you all! I dare not hold you in contempt. What is the reason? You are all treading the bodhisattva-path, and shall succeed in becoming Buddhas!' So this bhikṣu did not simply read and recite the scriptural canon, but rather did obeisance, too, to the point that, when he saw the fourfold multitude from afar, he would make a special point of going to them, doing obeisance, and uttering praise, saying, 'I dare not hold you all in contempt, since you are all to become Buddhas!' Within the fourfold multitude were some who gave way to anger, whose thoughts were impure, who reviled him with a foul mouth, saying, 'This know-nothing bhikṣu! Whence does he come? He himself says, "I do not hold you in contempt," yet he presumes to prophesy to us that we will succeed in becoming Buddhas! We have no need of such idle prophecies!' In this way, throughout the passage of many years, he was constantly subjected to abuse; yet he did not give way to anger, but constantly said, 'You shall become Buddhas!' When he spoke these words, some in the multitude would beat him with sticks and staves, with tiles and stones. He would run away and abide at a distance, yet he would still proclaim in a loud voice, 'I dare not hold you all in contempt. You shall all become Buddhas!' Since he constantly said those words, the overweening bhikṣus, bhikṣuṇīs, upāsakas, and upāsikās called him Never Disparaging.[2]

"This bhikṣu, when faced with the end of his life, in open space heard distinctly twenty thousand myriads of millions of gāthās of the Scripture of the Dharma Blossom previously preached by the Buddha King of Imposing Sound, which he was able fully to accept and hold, and straightway he attained the above-mentioned purity of ocular faculty and purity of aural, nasal, lingual, bodily, and mental faculties. Having attained this purity of the six faculties, he increased his life-span yet further by two hundred myriads of millions of nayutas of years, broadly preaching to others this Scripture of the Dharma Blossom. At that time, the overweening fourfold multitude of bhikṣus, bhikṣuṇīs, upāsakas, and upāsikās, who had made light of this man and held him cheaply, who had dubbed him with the name Never Disparaging, saw that he had acquired the power of great supernatural penetration, the eloquent power of joy in preaching, and the power of great wholesome quiescence;[3] and hearing what he preached, all bowed down in belief and followed him. This bodhisattva also converted a multitude of a thousand myriads of millions, causing them to dwell in anuttarasamyaksaṃbodhi.

"After his life had ended, he was able to encounter two thousand millions of Buddhas, all named Sun-and-Moon-Glow. Within their Dharma he preached this Scripture of the Dharma Blossom, and by these means again encountered two thousand millions of Buddhas, identically named King of Illumination who is Master of the Clouds. Within these Buddhas' Dharma he received and held, read and recited, and for the fourfold multitude preached this scriptural canon, for which reason he attained this purity of his ordinary eye, as well as the purity of aural, nasal, lingual, bodily, and mental faculties, preaching Dharma within the fourfold multitude with a heart free of fear.[4]

"O Gainer of Great Strength! This bodhisattva-mahāsattva Never Disparaging, having made offerings to such great numbers of Buddhas, having humbly revered them, honored them, held them in solemn esteem, and praised them, thus planting wholesome roots, thereafter once again encountered a thousand myriads of millions of Buddhas, and within their Buddhadharma as well preached this scriptural canon, achieving merit and being on the point of becoming a Buddha. O Gainer of Great Strength! In your thinking, how is it? At that time, can the bodhisattva Never Disparaging possibly have been anyone else? For he was indeed myself! If I had not received and kept, read and recited, this scripture, nor preached it to others, in a previous age, I should not have been able quickly to attain anuttarasamyaksaṃbodhi. It is because in the presence of former Buddhas I did accept and hold, read and recite this scripture and preach it to others that I quickly attained anuttarasamyaksaṃbodhi. O Gainer of Great Strength! The fourfold multitude of that time, the bhikṣus, bhikṣunīs, upāsakas, and upāsikās, because they held me lightly and cheaply with their hateful thoughts, for two hundred millions of kalpas never met a Buddha, nor heard the Dharma, nor saw the saṃgha. For a thousand kalpas in the Avīci hell they suffered great pain and agony. When they had finished paying this penalty, once again they encountered the bodhisattva Never Disparaging, who converted them by teaching them anuttarasamyaksaṃbodhi. O Gainer of Great Strength! In your thinking, how is it? Can the fourfold multitude of that time, who constantly held this bodhisattva lightly, possibly have been anyone else? Nay, they are in the midst of this very assembly, to wit, the five hundred bodhisattvas headed by Bhadrapāla, the five hundred nuns headed by Lion Moon [Siṃhacandrā, "glowing like a lioness"], and the five hundred upāsakas[5] headed by Thoughtful of the Buddha [Sugatacetanā, "she who is conscious of the Well Gone One"], all persons who shall not backslide from anuttarasamyaksaṃbodhi. O Gainer of Great Strength! Let it be known that this Scripture of the Dharma Blossom greatly benefits the bodhisattva-mahāsattvas, being able to cause them to reach anuttarasamyaksaṃbodhi. For this reason, after the extinction of the Thus Come One, the bodhisattva-mahāsattvas are ever to accept and keep, read and recite, interpret and copy this scripture."

At that time the World-Honored One, wishing to restate this meaning, proclaimed gāthās, saying:

In the past there was a Buddha
  Whose name was King of Imposing Sound,
His superhuman wisdom incalculable,
  A Leader of all,
To whom gods and men, dragons and spirits,
  Together made offerings.
After this Buddha's extinction,
  When the Dharma was about to be exhausted,
There was a bodhisattva
  Named Never Disparaging.
At the time, the fourfold multitudes
  Were reckoning in terms of dharma.
The bodhisattva Never Disparaging
  Went before them
And spoke to them, saying,
  "I do not hold you in contempt!
You are all treading the Path,
  And shall all become Buddhas!"
The men, having heard,
  Held him lightly and maligned him, abused and reviled him,
But the bodhisattva Never Disparaging
  Was able to bear this with equanimity.
When his penalty had been paid,
  And he faced the end of his life,
He was able to hear this scripture,
  And his six faculties were purified.
Thanks to his power of supernatural penetration,
  He increased his life-span,
And again to others
  Broadly preached this scripture.
The multitude attached to the dharmas,
  All receiving the bodhisattva's
Doctrine and conversion, were perfected,
  And were caused to dwell in the Buddha Path.
When the life of Never Disparaging ended,

He encountered numberless Buddhas.
Because he had preached this scripture,
He attained incalculable happiness,
Gradually acquiring merit,
Then quickly achieving the Buddha Path.
At that time Never Disparaging
Was indeed myself!
The fourfold multitude of the time,
Those who clung to the dharmas,
Who heard Never Disparaging say,
"You shall become Buddhas!"
By virtue of that
Encountered numberless Buddhas.
The bodhisattvas of this assembly,
The multitude of five hundred,
And the fourfold assembly,
The gentlemen and ladies of pure faith,
Now in my presence
Abide, listening to Dharma.
In former ages, I
Encouraged these men
To listen receptively to this scripture,
The first of the dharmas.
Explaining and demonstrating, I taught men,
Causing them to dwell in nirvāṇa.
Age upon age they accepted and held
Scriptural canons like these,
For millions and millions of myriads of kalpas,
Whose number cannot even be discussed.
Then at last they were enabled to hear
This Scripture of the Dharma Blossom.
In millions upon millions of myriads of kalpas,
Whose number cannot even be discussed,
The Buddhas, the World-Honored Ones,
[Only] occasionally preach this scripture.
For this reason the practitioner

After the Buddha's extinction
When he hears a scripture like this one,
Is not to give way to doubts or second thoughts,
But is single-mindedly
And broadly to preach this scripture,
For age upon age encountering Buddhas
And quickly achieving the Buddha Path.[6]

Chapter Twenty-One: The Supernatural Powers of the Thus Come One

At that time the bodhisattva-mahāsattvas who had welled up out of the earth, equal in number to the atoms in the thousandfold world, all in the Buddha's presence single-mindedly joined palms, looked up at the August Countenance, and addressed the Buddha, saying, "O World-Honored One! After the Buddha's extinction, in those lands wherein are the emanations of the World-Honored One, in those places where he has passed into extinction, we will broadly preach this scripture. What is the reason? We also wish to gain this truly pure Great Dharma ourselves, to receive and keep it, to read and recite it, to preach it, to copy it, and to make offerings to it."

At that time, in the presence of Mañjuśrī and the others, of the whole multitude of incalculable hundreds of thousands of myriads of millions of bodhisattva-mahāsattvas who had long resided in the Sahā world-sphere, as well as of bhikṣus, bhikṣuṇīs, upāsakas, upāsikās, gods, dragons, yakṣas, gandharvas, asuras, garuḍas, kinnaras, mahoragas, humans, and nonhumans, the World-Honored One displayed great supernatural power, putting forth his long, broad tongue, which reached upward as far as the Brahmā-world, while his pores emitted rays in incalculable, numberless colors, all universally illuminating the world-spheres in all ten quarters. The Buddhas on the lion thrones at the foot of the multitudinous jeweled trees also in the same way put out their long, broad tongues and emitted incalculable rays of light.[1]

When Śākyamunibuddha and the Buddhas at the foot of the jeweled trees had displayed their supernatural power, after the passage of fully a hundred thousand years they drew back their tongues and at once both coughed and snapped their fingers. These two sounds reached throughout the world-spheres of the Buddhas in all ten quarters, and in all of them the earth trembled in six different ways. The living beings in those world-spheres, gods, dragons, yakṣas, gandharvas, asuras, garuḍas, kinnaras, mahoragas, humans, and nonhumans, thanks to the Buddhas' supernatural power, saw the Buddhas seated on lion thrones at the foot of a multitude of incalculable, limitless hundreds of thousands of myriads of millions of jeweled trees in the Sahā world-sphere, and saw Śākyamunibuddha together with Many Jewels the Thus Come One seated on a lion throne within a jeweled stūpa. They also saw incalculable, limitless hundreds of thousands of myriads of millions of bodhisattva-mahāsattvas and fourfold multitudes surrounding Śākyamunibuddha in humble reverence. When they had seen this, they were all overjoyed, having gained something they had never had before. Straightway in open space the gods with a loud voice declared, "Incalculable, limitless hundreds of thousands of myriads of millions of asaṃkhyeyas of world-spheres beyond this place is a realm called Sahā. Within it is a Buddha named Śākyamuni. To sundry bodhisattva-mahāsattvas he is now preaching a scripture of the Great Vehicle named the Lotus Blossom of the Fine Dharma, a Dharma to be taught to bodhisattvas, a Dharma which the Buddhas keep protectively in mind. You must all rejoice profoundly in your hearts. You must also worship and make offerings to Śākyamunibuddha."[2]

When those beings had heard the voice in open space, they faced the Sahā world-sphere, and with palms joined they said: "*Namaḥ Śākyamunibuddhāya. Namaḥ Śākyamunibuddhāya.*" Taking sundry floral scents, necklaces, banners, parasols, and other accouterments of bodily adornment, precious gems, and fine objects, all together they scattered them from afar on the Sahā world-sphere. The things they scattered came from all ten quarters, like clouds gathering, and, turning into jeweled canopies, completely covered the Buddhas in this region. At that time, through the world-spheres in all ten quarters passage was unobstructed, as if they had been one Buddha-land.[3]

At that time the Buddha declared to Superior Conduct and the great multitude of other bodhisattvas: "The supernatural powers of the Buddhas are as incalculable, as limitless, as far beyond reckoning and discussion as this. [Yet] if by means of these supernatural powers I were to preach the merits of this scripture for incalculable, limitless hundreds of thousands of myriads of millions of asaṃkhyeyakalpas, with the purpose of entrusting it to others, I could still not exhaust those merits. Briefly stated, all the dharmas possessed by the Thus Come One, all the Thus Come One's supernatural powers of self-mastery, the treasure house of all the Thus Come One's secrets, all the Thus Come One's profound affairs are entirely proclaimed, demonstrated, revealed, and preached in this scripture. For this reason, after the extinction of the Thus Come One, you all must single-mindedly receive and keep, read and recite, interpret and copy, and, as you preach, so practice it. In any land, if there is anyone who accepts and keeps, reads and recites, interprets and copies, and, as he preaches, so practices it, whether in a place where scriptural rolls are lodged, or in a garden, or in a grove, or at the foot of a tree, or in a saṃgha-cell, or in the home of a white-clad layman, or in a palace, or on mountains, or in valleys, or in open fields, there, in every case, is to be erected a stūpa, to which offerings are to be made. What is the reason? Be it known that that place is a Platform of the Path (*bodhimaṇḍo veditavyaḥ*); that the Buddhas there have achieved anuttarasamyaksaṃbodhi; that the Buddhas there have turned the Dharma-wheel; that the Buddhas there have achieved parinirvāṇa."

At that time, the World-Honored One, wishing to restate this meaning, proclaimed gāthās, saying:

The Buddhas, the Saviors of the world,
  Dwelling in their great supernatural penetrations,
In order to gladden living beings,
  Display incalculable supernatural powers.
A tongue-mark (*jihvendriya*) reaching to the Brahmā-world,
  A body that gives forth countless rays of light:
For those who seek the Buddha Path
  These are the rare things they display.
The Buddhas' voices as they cough
  And the sound of the snapping of their fingers
Are heard throughout the realms of the ten quarters,
  Whose lands all tremble in six ways.
Since after the Buddhas' passage into extinction
  [Those who listen to the Buddhas] can hold this scripture,

The Buddhas all joyfully
  Display incalculable supernatural powers.
In order to hand down this scripture,
  They praise those who accept and keep it,
Throughout incalculable kalpas
  Still unable to exhaust the praise.[4]
Those men's merits
  Shall be limitless and inexhaustible;
They shall be like open space in all ten quarters,
  Having no possible limit or end.
Those who can hold to this scripture
  On that account shall have already seen me.
They also shall have seen the Buddha Many Jewels
  And those who are emanations of my body.
They also shall have seen me this day
  Teaching and converting the bodhisattvas.
Those who can hold to this scripture
  Shall cause me and the emanations of my body,
As well as the Buddha Many Jewels, now passed into extinction,
  All without exception to rejoice.
The Buddhas of the present in all ten quarters,
  As well as those of past and future,
They shall both see and shower with offerings,
  Enabling them, too, to gain joy.
What the Buddhas seated on the Platform of the Path (*bodhimaṇḍa*),
  What secret, vital dharmas they attain,
He who can hold to this scripture
  Shall in no long time also attain.
He who can hold to this scripture,
  Shall, with respect to the meanings of the dharmas (*dharme 'pi cārthe ca*),
To names and words (*nirukti*),
  And to joy in preaching (*pratibhānu*), be inexhaustible,
As the wind in the midst of space

Is unobstructed by anything.
After the extinction of the Thus Come One
He shall know the scriptures preached by the Buddha,
The causes and conditions, and the order of sequence,
And preach them in accord with their meaning and with Reality.[5]
As the bright light of the sun and the moon
Can clear away all darkness and obscurity,
So this man, going through the world,
Can extinguish the darkness of the beings.
I teach incalculable bodhisattvas
To dwell absolutely in the One Vehicle.
For this reason one who has wisdom,
Hearing of the advantage of these merits,
After my passage into extinction
Should receive and keep this scripture.
This man, with respect to the Buddha Path,
Shall assuredly have no doubts.[6]

Chapter Twenty-Two: Entrustment[1]

At that time Śākyamunibuddha rose from his seat and, displaying great supernatural powers, with his right hand stroked incalculable bodhisattva-mahāsattvas on the crown of the head, then said: "For incalculable hundreds of thousands of myriads of millions of asaṃkhyeyakalpas, I practiced and cultivated this Dharma of anuttarasamyaksaṃbodhi, so hard to obtain. Now I entrust it to all of you. You must all single-mindedly propagate this Dharma, broadly causing others to benefit from it." In this way, thrice stroking the bodhisattva-mahāsattvas on the crown of the head, he said: "For incalculable hundreds of thousands of myriads of millions of asaṃkhyeyakalpas I practiced and cultivated this Dharma of anuttarasamyaksaṃbodhi, so hard to obtain. Now I entrust it to all of you. You must all accept and keep, read and recite, and broadly proclaim this Dharma, enabling all beings universally to know and hear it. What is the reason? The Thus Come One has great good will and compassion. He is in no way niggardly, nor is there anything he fears. He is able to give to the beings the wisdom of the Buddha, the wisdom of the Thus Come One, the wisdom that is so of itself. The Thus Come One is the Great Benefactor of all living beings. You all must also imitate the manner of the Thus Come One, never giving way to niggardliness. In an age yet to come, if there is a good man or good woman who believes in the wisdom of the Thus Come One, you must preach to him or her this Scripture of the Dharma Blossom, enabling him or her to hear and know it, in order to enable that person to attain Buddha-knowledge. If there are living beings who neither believe nor accept, then you are to show and to teach them, to afford them advantage and joy, by resort to the other profound dharmas of the Thus Come One. If you can do this, then you shall have repaid the kindnesses of the Buddhas."[2]

At that time the bodhisattva-mahāsattvas, having heard the Buddha make these remarks, all experienced a great joy that permeated their bodies and, all the more humble and reverent, bending their bodies and bowing their heads, with palms joined they faced the Buddha and spoke together, saying, "As the Buddha commands, so will we worshipfully do. Very well, O World-Honored One, we beg you to have no concern!" In this way, three times did they speak together, saying, "As the Buddha commands, so will we worshipfully do. Very well, O World-Honored One, we beg you to have no concern!"[3]

At that time Śākyamunibuddha caused the Buddhas who were emanations of his body and who had come from the ten quarters each to return to his original land, saying to them: "O Buddhas! Let each of you follow what course is most comfortable for him. The stūpa of the Buddha Many Jewels may again be as it was."

When he had spoken these words, in the ten quarters incalculable Buddhas who were emanations of his body, seated on lion thrones at the foot of jeweled trees, and the Buddha Many Jewels, as well as a great multitude consisting of Superior Conduct and limitless asaṃkhyeyas of bodhisattvas, the fourfold multitude of voice-hearers consisting of Śāriputra and others, and the gods, men, and asuras in all the worlds, having heard what the Buddha had preached, were all overjoyed.[4]

Chapter Twenty-Three: The Former Affairs of the Bodhisattva Medicine King

At that time, the bodhisattva Beflowered by the King of Constellations* (Nakṣatrarājasaṃkusumitābhijña) addressed the Buddha, saying: "O World-Honored One! How does the bodhisattva Medicine King travel in the Sahā world? O World-Honored One! This bodhisattva Medicine King has to his credit several hundreds of thousands of myriads of millions of nayutas of difficult deeds, of painful deeds. Very well, O World-Honored One, I beg you to explain a bit. For the gods, dragons, yakṣas, gandharvas, asuras, garuḍas, mahoragas, humans, and non-humans, as well as the bodhisattvas come from other lands and this multitude of voice-hearers, hearing, shall all rejoice."

At that time the Buddha declared to the bodhisattva Beflowered by the King of Constellations: "In time past, beyond kalpas as numerous as the sands of innumerable Ganges rivers, there was a Buddha named Pure and Bright Excellence of Sun and Moon (Candrasūryavimalaprabhāśrī), a Thus Come One, worthy of offerings, of right and universal knowledge, his clarity and conduct perfect, well gone, understanding the world, an unexcelled Worthy, a Regulator of men of stature, a Teacher of gods and men, a Buddha, a World-Honored One. That Buddha had eighty millions of great bodhisattva-mahāsattvas and a great multitude of voice-hearers equal in number to the sands of seventy-two Ganges rivers. The Buddha's life-span was forty-two thousand kalpas, and the life-span of his bodhisattvas was also the same. That realm had no women, hell-dwellers, hungry ghosts, beasts, or asuras,

* *Hsiu wang hua.* The Skt. form of the name means "one whose superknowledges have been beflowered by the kings of the constellations," which I take to signify one whose superhuman faculties have been blessed by lucky stars. The Ch. probably is a laconic way of saying the same thing.

or any troubles whatsoever. Its land was as flat as the palm of one's hand, made of vaiḍūrya, adorned with jeweled trees, hung with jeweled canopies, and draped with jeweled floral banners. Jeweled pots and censers ringed its borders, and its terraces were fashioned of the seven jewels. Trees alternated with terraces, the trees being removed from the terraces the distance of an arrow-shot. All those jeweled trees had bodhisattvas and voice-hearers sitting under them. The jeweled terraces each had atop them a hundred million gods making divine music and singing the praises of the Buddha as an offering. At that time that Buddha preached the Scripture of the Dharma Blossom to the bodhisattva Seen with Joy by All Living Beings (Sarvasattvapriyadarśana) and to the many bodhisattvas and multitude of voice-hearers. This bodhisattva Seen with Joy by All Living Beings, desiring to cultivate painful practices, within the dharma of the Buddha Pure and Bright Excellence of Sun and Moon went about persevering with vigor and single-mindedly seeking Buddhahood for full twelve thousand years. He then obtained the samādhi that displays all manner of physical bodies.[1] After he had obtained this samādhi, he was overjoyed at heart. Straightway he had this thought, saying to himself, 'My ability to obtain the samādhi that displays all manner of physical bodies is entirely due to my having contrived to hear the Scripture of the Dharma Blossom. I will now make offerings to the Buddha Pure and Bright Excellence of Sun and Moon and to the Scripture of the Dharma Blossom." Straightway then he entered into this samādhi, and in open space there rained down māndārava and mahāmāndārava flowers, while a finely powdered, hard, black candana, filling all of space, descended like a cloud. There also rained down the scent of the candana of the near seashore,[2] six *shu** of this scent having the value of the Sahā world-sphere, with which he made an offering to the Buddha.

"After he had made this offering, he arose from samādhi and thought to himself, 'Though by resort to supernatural power I have made an offering to the Buddha, it is not as if I had made an offering of my own body.' Straightway then he applied [to his body] various scents, candana, *kunduruka*, *turuṣka* [two kinds of frankincense], *pṛkkā*

* I.e., one-fourth of a tael; the Skt. has one *karṣa*, about 176 grains Troy.

[trigonella], the scent that sinks in water, and the scent of pine-tar;[3] and he also drank the fragrant oils of campaka-flowers. When a thousand two hundred years had been fulfilled, he painted his body with fragrant oil and, in the presence of the Buddha Pure and Bright Excellence of Sun and Moon, wrapped his body in a garment adorned with divine jewels, anointed himself with fragrant oils, with the force of supernatural penetration took a vow,[4] and then burnt his own body. The glow gave light all around to world-spheres equal in number to the sands of eighty millions of Ganges rivers. Within them the Buddhas all at once praised him, saying, 'Excellent! Excellent! Good man, this is true perseverance in vigor! This is called a true Dharma-offering to the Thus Come One. If with floral scent, necklaces, burnt incense, powdered scent, paint-scent, divine cloth, banners, parasols, the scent of the candana of the near seashore, and a variety of such things one were to make offerings, still they could not equal this former [act of yours]. Even if one were to give realm and walled cities, wife and children, they would still be no match for it. Good man, this is called the prime gift. Among the various gifts, it is the most honorable, the supreme. For it constitutes an offering of Dharma to the Thus Come Ones.' When they had made this speech, each kept silence.

"His body burnt in the fire a thousand two hundred years. When this had passed, his body was then consumed.[5] Because the bodhisattva Seen with Joy by All Living Beings had made such a Dharma-offering as this, after his life had ended he was born again in the realm of the Buddha Pure and Bright Excellence of Sun and Moon, where, in the household of King Pure Virtue (Vimaladatta), he was born suddenly, by transformation, sitting crosslegged. Straightway to his father he proclaimed a gāthā, saying:

O Great King! Now be it known that
  I, going about in that place,
Straightway attained the All-
  Body-Displaying Samādhi,
Whereby, striving and greatly persevering in vigor,
  I cast off the body to which I had been so attached.

"When he had proclaimed this gāthā, he addressed his father, saying, 'The Buddha Pure and Bright Excellence of Sun and Moon is still present. Having formerly made offerings to that Buddha, I have already contrived to understand the dhāraṇī of the speech of all living beings. I have also heard of this Scripture of the Dharma Blossom eight hundred thousands of myriads of millions of nayutas of *kaṅkara*, *vivara*, *akṣobhya*,* and the like, of gāthās. O Great King! I will now go back and make offerings to that Buddha!'[6] When he had spoken, he straightway sat on a platform made of the seven jewels, and rose up into open space to a height of seven tala-trees. He went into the Buddha's presence, made obeisance to his feet with head bowed, joined his ten fingernails, and with a gāthā praised the Buddha:

O most wondrous and fine of countenance,
  Whose bright glow illuminates all ten quarters,
Formerly I have made offerings to you,
  And now once again I come to behold you in person.

"At that time the bodhisattva Seen with Joy by All Living Beings, having proclaimed this gāthā, addressed the Buddha, saying, 'World-Honored One, World-Honored One, you are still in the world!' At that time the Buddha Pure and Bright Excellence of Sun and Moon declared to the bodhisattva Seen with Joy by All Living Beings, 'Good man, my time of nirvāṇa has come, my time of total extinction has arrived. You may lay out my couch and seat, for this night will I achieve parinirvāṇa.'

"Again, he commanded the bodhisattva Seen with Joy by All Living Beings: 'Good man, I entrust the Buddha's Dharma to you. Also, bodhisattvas and their great disciples, as well as the dharma of anuttarasamyaksaṃbodhi, also the seven-jeweled world-spheres of the thousand-millionfold world, its jeweled trees and jeweled terraces, and the gods who wait upon it I entrust entirely to you. After my passage into extinction, whatever śarīra there may be I entrust to you also. You

* *Kaṅkara, vivara, akṣobhya*: each is an unspecified high number.

are to spread them about and broadly arrange for offerings to them. You are to erect several thousand stūpas.' In this way the Buddha Pure and Bright Excellence of Sun and Moon, having commanded the bodhisattva Seen with Joy by All Living Beings, in the last watch of the night entered nirvāṇa.

"At that time, the bodhisattva Seen with Joy by All Living Beings, seeing that the Buddha had passed into extinction, was sore moved with grief and longing for the Buddha. Straightway, using the candana of the near seashore for firewood and as an offering to the Buddha's body, he then burnt the latter. When the fire had gone out, he collected the śarīra and, making eighty-four thousand jeweled pots, with it erected eighty-four thousand stūpas the height of three world-spheres, displaying chattras as ornaments, draped with banners and parasols, and hung with a multitude of jeweled bells. At that time the bodhisattva Seen with Joy by All Living Beings again had a thought, saying to himself, "Though I have made this offering, at heart I am still not satisfied. I will now make still further offerings to the śarīra.' He then said to the bodhisattvas, their disciples, the gods, dragons, yakṣas, and the others, to all the great multitude, 'You are all to attend single-mindedly. For I will now make an offering to the śarīra of the Buddha Pure and Bright Excellence of Sun and Moon.' Having spoken these words, straightway, before the eighty-four thousand stūpas, he burnt his forearm, adorned as it was with a hundred happy qualities, making this his offering for seventy-two thousand years, thus causing a numberless multitude seeking the rank of voice-hearers, incalculable asaṃkhyeyas of human beings, to open up their thought to anuttara-samyaksaṃbodhi, enabling them also to dwell in the samādhi that displays all manner of physical bodies.

"At that time the bodhisattvas, gods, men, asuras, and others, seeing that he was without an arm, grieved and mourned, then said: 'This bodhisattva Seen with Joy by All Living Beings is our master, the one who has taught and converted us. Yet, now he has burnt his forearm, his body is lacking something.' At that time, the bodhisattva Seen with Joy by All Living Beings in the midst of the great multitude took this oath, saying, 'I have thrown away both arms. May I now without fail gain the Buddha's gold-colored body! If this oath is reality and not vanity, then may both arms be restored as before!' When he had taken this oath, they were restored of themselves, an achievement due to the purity of this bodhisattva's merit and wisdom.[7] At that time, the thousand-millionfold world trembled in six ways, the gods rained down jeweled flowers, and all men and gods gained something they had never had before."

The Buddha demanded of the bodhisattva Beflowered by the King of Constellations, "In your thinking, how is it? Can the bodhisattva Seen with Joy by All Living Beings possibly have been anyone else? He was none other than the present bodhisattva Medicine King! Gifts of his own body, such as this one, number in the incalculable hundreds of thousands of myriads of millions of nayutas. O Beflowered by the King of Constellations! If there is one who, opening up his thought, wishes to attain anuttarasamyaksaṃbodhi, if he can burn a finger or even a toe as an offering to a Buddhastūpa, he shall exceed one who uses realm or walled city, wife or children, or even all the lands, mountains, forests, rivers, ponds, and sundry precious objects in the whole thousand-millionfold world as offerings. If again there is a man who offers a thousand-millionfold world full of the seven jewels to Buddhas, great bodhisattvas, pratyekabuddhas, and arhants, the merit gained by him shall not match that of one who holds of this Scripture of the Dharma Blossom so much as a single four-foot gāthā, for the latter's merit shall be the greatest.[8]

"O Beflowered by the King of Constellations! Just as, for example, among all streams, rivers, and bodies of water the sea is first, this Scripture of the Dharma Blossom, also in the same way, is the deepest and greatest among the scriptures preached by the Thus Come One. Also, just as among Earth Mountain, Black Mountain, the lesser Mount Iron-Rim, the greater Mount Iron-Rim, the Mount of Ten Jewels, and the whole multitude of mountains Mount Sumeru is the first, this Scripture of the Dharma Blossom, also in the same way, is supreme among the scriptures.[9] Further, just as among a multitude of stars the moon, child of the gods, is first, this Scripture of the Dharma Blossom, also in the same way, is the brightest among a thousand myriads of millions of kinds of scriptural dharmas. Further, just as the sun, child of the gods, can clear away all darkness, this scripture, also in the same way, can demolish the obscurities of all kinds of unwholesomeness. Further, just as among lesser kings the wheel-turning sage-king is first, this scripture also, in the same way, is the most honorable among a multitude of scriptures. Just as the divine Śakra is king among the thirty-three gods, this scripture, also in the same way, is king among scriptures. Further, just as the great god king Brahmā is father of all living beings, this scripture also, in the same way, is father of all saints and sages, of all learners and of those who having nothing more to learn, and of all who have launched bodhisattva-thought. Further, just as among all ordinary fellows the srota'āpanna, sakṛdāgāmin, anāgāmin, arhant, and pratyekabuddha are first, this scripture also, in the same way, is first and foremost among all scriptural dharmas, whether preached by the Thus Come One, or preached by bodhisattvas, or preached by voice-hearers.[10] If anyone can accept and hold this scriptural canon, he, too, in the same way, shall be first among all living beings. Among all voice-hearers and pratyekabuddhas the bodhisattva is first, and this scripture too, in the same way, is first and foremost among all scriptural dharmas. Just as the Buddha is the king of the dharmas, this scripture is also, in the same way, the king of the scriptures.[11] O Beflowered by the King of Constellations! This scripture can save all living beings. This scripture can enable all living beings to separate themselves from pain and torment. This scripture can greatly benefit all living beings, fulfilling their desires. Like a clear, cool pond, it can slake the thirst of all. As a chilled person finds fire, as a naked person finds clothing, as a merchant finds a chief, as a child finds its mother, as a passenger finds a ship, as a sick person finds a physician, as darkness finds a torch, as a poor person finds a jewel, as the people find a king, as a commerical traveler finds the sea, as a candle dispels darkness, this scripture of the Dharma Blossom also, in the same way, can enable the beings to separate themselves from all woes, from all sickness and pain, and can loose all the bonds of birth and death. If a man contrives to hear this Scripture of the Dharma Blossom, and if he writes it down himself, or causes another to write it, then no limit can be found to the merit he shall obtain, even if its quantity be measured with Buddha-wisdom. If, having written down this scriptural roll, he makes offerings with floral scent, necklaces, burnt incense, powdered incense, perfumed paint, banners and parasols, garments, and sundry torches, such as sesame torches, oil torches, torches of sundry fragrant oils, torches of campaka oil, torches of sumanā oil, torches of *pāṭala* [trumpet-flower] oil, torches of *vārṣika* and torches of *navamālikā* oil [two varieties of Arabian jasmine], the merit he gains shall also be incalculable. O Beflowered by the King of Constellations! If a man hears this Chapter of the Former Affairs of the Bodhisattva Medicine King, he also shall gain incalculable, limitless merit. If a woman, hearing this Chapter of the Former Affairs of the Bodhisattva Medicine King, can accept and keep it, she shall put an end to her female body, and shall never again receive one. If after the extinction of the Thus Come One, within the last five hundred years, there is then a woman who, hearing this scriptural canon, practices it as preached, at the end of this life she shall straightway go to the world-sphere Comfortable (Sukhāvatī), to the dwelling place of the Buddha Amitāyus, where he is surrounded by a multitude of great bodhisattvas, there to be reborn on a jeweled throne among lotus blossoms, never again to be tormented by greed, never again to be tormented by anger or folly, never again to be tormented by pride, envy, or other defilements.[12] But he shall gain the bodhisattva's supernatural penetrations, his acceptance of the principle of unborn dharmas. When he has attained this acceptance, the faculty of his eye shall be pure. With this pure ocular faculty he shall see Buddhas, Thus Come Ones, equal in number to the sands of seven hundred myriad two thousand millions of nayutas of Ganges rivers. At that time the Buddhas shall together praise him from afar, saying, 'Excellent! Excellent! Good man, you have been able, within the dharma of Śākyamuni-buddha, to receive and hold, to read and recite, and to think on this scripture, as well as to preach it to others. The merit you have obtained is incalculable and limitless, such as fire cannot burn nor water carry off. Your merits are such that a thousand Buddhas, speaking of them together, could not exhaust them. You have now already proved able to smash Māra's assorted rabble, to destroy the army of birth and death. The remaining enemies you have completely annihilated. Good man, a hundred thousand Buddhas with their power of supernatural penetrations shall together protect you.[13] Among the gods and men in all the worlds there is none like you, save only the Thus Come One.

Among voice-hearers and pratyekabuddhas, yes, and bodhisattvas too, for wisdom and dhyāna-concentration there is none to equal you.' O Beflowered by the King of Constellations! Such was the force of merit and wisdom achieved by this bodhisattva!

"If there is a man who, hearing this Chapter of the Former Affairs of the Bodhisattva Medicine King, can rejoice appropriately and praise it as good, this man in the present age shall ever exhale from his mouth the fragrance of pure lotus, from his pores the scent of ox-head candana; and the merits he obtains shall be as just stated. For this reason, O Beflowered by the King of Constellations, I entrust this Chapter of the Former Affairs of the Bodhisattva Medicine King to you. After my passage into extinction, within the last five hundred years, broadly proclaim and propagate it in Jambudvīpa, never allowing it to be cut off, nor evil Māra's people, or gods, dragons, yakṣas, kumbhāṇḍas, and the like to get the better of it. O Beflowered by the King of Constellations! With the power of supernatural penetration, you are to protect this scripture. What is the reason? This scripture, for the people of Jambudvīpa, is a good physic for their sicknesses. If a man has an illness and can hear this scripture, the illness shall immediately vanish. He shall neither grow old old nor die. O Beflowered by the King of Constellations! If you see that there is anyone who accepts and holds this scripture, then you must heap powdered incense in a green lotus blossom and scatter it on top of him as an offering, then, having scattered it, say to yourself, 'This man in no long time shall without fail take grass, sit on the Platform of the Way [after spreading the grass over its surface], and smash the armies of Māra. He shall blow the conch of the Dharma, beat the drum of the Dharma, and ferry all beings over the sea of birth, old age, sickness, and death.' For this reason, when one seeking the Buddha Path sees that there is a person who accepts and keeps this scriptural canon, he is to produce in this way a thought of humble reverence."[14]

When this Chapter of the Former Affairs of the Bodhisattva Medicine King was preached, eighty-four thousand bodhisattvas attained the dhāraṇī enabling them to understand the speech of all living beings,[15] and the Thus Come One Many Jewels within the jeweled stūpa praised the bodhisattva Beflowered by the King of Constellations, saying, "Excellent! Excellent, O Beflowered by the King of Constellations! It is because you have achieved merits beyond reckoning and discussion that you are able to question Śākyamunibuddha about such matters as these and to benefit the incalculable totality of living beings."[16]

Chapter Twenty-Four: The Bodhisattva Fine Sound

At that time Śākyamunibuddha emitted a glow from the knot of flesh that was one mark of the Great Man, as well as a ray of light from the mark of the white tuft between his brows, universally illuminating Buddha world-spheres in the eastern quarter as numerous as the sands of a hundred and eight myriads of millions of nayutas of Ganges rivers. Beyond these there was a world-sphere named Adorned with Pure Light (Vairocanaraśmipratimaṇḍitā). In that realm was a Buddha named Knowledge [Conferred] by the King of Constellations [named] Pure Flower (Kamaladalavimalanakṣatrarājasaṃkusumitābhijña), a Thus Come One, worthy of offerings, of right and universal knowledge, his clarity and conduct perfect, well gone, understanding the world, an unexcelled Worthy, a Regulator of men of stature, a Teacher of gods and men, a Buddha, a World-Honored One,[1] surrounded in humble reverence by an incalculable, limitless multitude of bodhisattvas, to whom he preached the Dharma. The glow of Śākyamunibuddha's white tuft universally illuminated that realm. At that time, within the realm Adorned with All Pure Light was a bodhisattva named Fine Sound (Gadgadasvara), who had long since planted the roots of a multitude of excellences, made offerings to and approached with familiarity incalculable hundreds of thousands of myriads of millions of Buddhas, achieving profound wisdom and attaining the samādhi of the fine standard (*dhvajāgrakeyūrasamādhilabdhaḥ*), the samādhi of the Dharma Blossom (*saddharmapuṇḍarīka*°), the samādhi of pure excellence (*vimaladatta*°), the samādhi of the sport of the king of constellations (*nakṣatrarājavikrīḍita*°), the samādhi of no objects (*anilambha*°), the Samādhi of the seal of knowledge (*jñānamudrā*°), the samādhi that Enables one to understand the speech of all living beings (*sarvarutakauśalya*°), the samādhi that collects all merits (*sarvapuṇyasamuccaya*°), the pure samādhi (*prasādavatī*°), the samādhi of the play of magical powers (*ṛddhivikrīḍita*°), the samādhi of the lamp of knowledge (*jñānolkā*°), the samādhi of the king of adornments (*vyūharāja*°), the samādhi of pure glow (*vimalaprabhāsa*°), the samādhi of the pure womb (*vimalagarbha*°), the unshared samādhi (*apkṛtsna*°), and the samādhi that turns to the sun (*sūryāvarta*°)—attaining, in sum, great samādhis of this sort equal in number to the sands of a hundred thousand myriads of millions of Ganges rivers.[2] As soon as Śākyamunibuddha had illuminated his body, straightway [Fine Sound] addressed the Buddha Knowledge [Conferred] by the King of Constellations [named] Pure Flower, saying, "O World-Honored One! I will go to the Sahā world-sphere, there to worship, to approach with familiarity, and to make offerings to Śākyamunibuddha and to see the bodhisattva Mañjuśrī, the Dharma-prince, the bodhisattva Medicine King, the bodhisattva Brave Donor (Pradānaśūra), the bodhisattva Beflowered by the King of Constellations, the bodhisattva Superior Conduct, the bodhisattva King of Adornments (Vyūharāja), and the bodhisattva Above Medicine (Bhaiṣajyarājasa mudgata)."[3]

At that time the Buddha Knowledge [Conferred] by the King of Constellations [named] Pure Flower declared to the bodhisattva Fine Sound, "Do not hold that realm lightly, nor conceive notions of its inferiority. Good man, that Sahā world is of uneven height. Its earth, stones, and mountains are full of filth.[4] Its Buddha's body is mean and small. The multitude of its bodhisattvas is also small-shaped. Yet your body is of forty-two thousand yojanas, while my body is of six hundred and eighty myriads of yojanas. Your body is most superbly erect, especially wonderful with the glow of a hundred thousands of myriads of happy qualities. Do you therefore go, but do not hold that realm in light esteem, nor toward its Buddha, its bodhisattvas, and its lands conceive notions of [their] inferiority."

The bodhisattva Fine Sound addressed his Buddha, saying, "O World-Honored One! That I go now to the Sahā world-sphere is due entirely to the Thus Come One's power, to the Thus Come One's play of magical powers, to the adornments of the Thus Come One's wisdom and merit." Thereupon the bodhisattva Fine Sound, not rising from his seat nor moving his body, entered into samādhi, by the force of which on Gṛdhrakūṭa mountain, not far from the Dharma-seat, he magically created eighty-four thousand jewel-clustered lotus blossoms, their stems of Jāmbūnada gold, their leaves of white silver, their bristles of diamond, their sepals of *kiṃśuka* [red-blossomed tree, the Eastern kino].[5]

At that time Mañjuśrī, the Dharma-prince, seeing these lotus blossoms, addressed the Buddha, saying, "O World-Honored One! What is the cause of this wondrous display, whereby there are several thousands of myriads of lotus blossoms, their stems of Jāmbūnada gold, their leaves of white silver, their bristles of diamond, their sepals of kiṃśuka?

At that time Śākyamunibuddha declared to Mañjuśrī, "Fine Sound the bodhisattva-mahāsattva wishes to come, together with his surrounding retinue of eighty-four thousand bodhisattvas, from the realm of the Buddha Knowledge [Conferred] by the King of Constellations [named] Pure Flower to this Sahā world-sphere, here to make offerings, to approach me with familiarity, and to worship. He also wishes to make offerings and listen to the Scripture of the Dharma Blossom."

Mañjuśrī addressed the Buddha, saying, "O World-Honored One! What wholesome roots has this bodhisattva planted, what merit has he cultivated, that he can have this great power of supernatural penetration? Whatever samādhi he may have performed, we beg that the name of that samādhi be told us, for we, too, wish to practice it zealously. For it is only by practicing this samādhi that we shall be able to see this bodhisattva's physical marks, his majestic posture, his comings and goings. We beg the World-Honored One, by resort to his powers of supernatural penetration, to enable us to see that bodhisattva when he shall have arrived."[6]

At that time, Śākyamunibuddha declared to Mañjuśrī: "This Thus Come One Many Jewels, long extinct, for your sakes will display marks."

At the time the Buddha Many Jewels declared to that bodhisattva [Fine Sound], "Good man, come! Mañjuśrī, the Dharma-prince, wishes to see your body." Then the bodhisattva Fine Sound disappeared from that realm and came hither together with eighty-four thousand bodhisattvas. The realms through which they passed trembled in six different ways, and all alike rained down lotus blossoms of the seven jewels. A hundred thousand instruments of divine music, unbeaten, sounded of themselves. This bodhisattva's eyes were like broad, great leaves of the green lotus. Even if one could have combined a hundred thousand myriads of moons, the classic beauty of his facial features would have exceeded theirs. His body was the color of pure gold, adorned with incalculable hundreds of thousands of merits. His majesty was imposing and glorious, his glow lustrous, his marks as perfect as those of the firm body of Nārāyaṇa. When he entered the seven-jeweled terrace, he rose straight up into space to a distance of seven tala-trees from earth. A multitude of bodhisattvas, surrounding him in humble reverence, came to this Sahā world-sphere, to Gṛdhrakūṭa mountain. When they arrived, he descended from his seven-jeweled terrace and, taking a necklace worth a hundred thousands, brought it before Śākyamunibuddha, where with head bowed he did obeisance to his feet and, presenting the necklace, addressed the Buddha, saying, "O World-Honored One! The Buddha Knowledge [Conferred] by the King of Constellations [named] Pure Flower inquires after the World-Honored One, whether he is in good health and free of annoyances; whether his risings and stayings are easy and pleasant; whether he conducts himself comfortably or not; whether the four elements are in harmony in him or not; whether he finds the affairs of the world bearable or not; whether the beings are easy to ferry to salvation or not; whether they do not have much lust, anger, folly, envy, and greed; whether they are not unfilial toward father and mother, disrespectful toward śramaṇas, of crooked views and unwholesome thoughts, not restraining the five feelings.* O World-Honored One! Can the beings subdue the Māra-foes or not? Has the Thus Come One Many Jewels, long passed into extinction, come to hear the Dharma in his seven-jeweled stūpa or not? He also asks concerning the Thus Come One Many Jewels whether he is serene and free of annoyances, whether he dwells long in forbearance or not. O World-Honored One! We now wish

* The desires of the senses.

to see the body of the Buddha Many Jewels. We beg the World-Honored One to show it to us, to let us see it!"[7]

At that time Śākyamunibuddha said to the Buddha Many Jewels, "This bodhisattva Fine Sound wishes to see you." Then the Buddha Many Jewels declared to Fine Sound, "How excellent! How excellent that in order to make offerings to Śākyamunibuddha, in order to listen to the Scripture of the Dharma Blossom, and in order to see Mañjuśrī and the others, you are able to come to this place!"

At that time the bodhisattva Floral Excellence (Padmaśrī) addressed the Buddha, saying, "O World-Honored One! What wholesome roots did this bodhisattva Fine Sound plant, what merits did he cultivate, that he has these supernatural powers?"

The Buddha declared to the bodhisattva Floral Excellence, "In the past there was a Buddha named King of the Sound of Thunder in the Clouds (Meghadundubhisvararājas) tathāgato 'rhan samyaksaṃbuddhaḥ, whose realm was named Manifesting All Worlds (Sarvarūpasaṃdarśanā), whose kalpa was named Joy to Behold (Priyadarśana). For twelve thousand years the bodhisattva Fine Sound made offerings of ten myriads of varieties of music to the Buddha King of the Sound of Thunder in the Clouds. He also presented him with eighty-four thousand *pātras* [alms bowls] made of the seven jewels. As a reward for this, he has now been reborn in the realm of the Buddha Knowledge [Conferred] by the King of Constellations [named] Pure Flower and has these supernatural powers. O Floral Excellence! In your thinking, how is it? As for the bodhisattva Fine Sound, who at that time, in the place of the Buddha King of the Sound of Thunder in the Clouds, made an offering of music and presented jeweled vessels—can he possibly have been anyone else? The present bodhisattva-mahāsattva Fine Sound is that very person. O Floral Excellence! This bodhisattva Fine Sound has already, in time past, made offerings to and approached with familiarity incalculable Buddhas. He has long planted the roots of excellence. He has also encountered hundreds of thousands of myriads of millions of nayutas of Buddhas, equal in number to the sands of the river Ganges. O Floral Excellence! All you see is the bodhisattva Fine Sound whose body is here. Yet this bodhisattva displays a variety of bodies, here and there preaching this scriptural canon to the beings. Now he displays the body of King

Brahmā; now he displays the body of the god Śakra; now he displays the body of the Self-Mastering God; now he displays the body of the Great Self-Mastering God; now he displays the body of the great general of the gods; now he displays the body of the god king Vaiśravaṇa; now he displays the body of a wheel-turning sage-king; now he displays the bodies of lesser kings; now he displays the body of an elder; now he displays the body of a householder; now he displays the body of a civil official; now he displays the body of a Brahman; now he displays the body of bhikṣu, bhikṣuṇī, upāsaka, or upāsikā; now he displays the body of the wife of an elder or householder; now he displays the body of the lady of a civil official; now he displays the body of a Brahman lady; now he displays the body of a boy; now he displays the body of a girl; now he displays the body of god, dragon, yakṣa, gandharva, asura, garuḍa, kinnara, mahoraga, human, or nonhuman: and thus he preaches this scripture.[8] Whoever is in hell, or in the rank of hungry ghost or beast, or indeed in any other troublesome place, he can rescue them all. Even in the inner quarters of a king's palace, changing into a female body, he preaches this scripture. O Floral Excellence! This bodhisattva Fine Sound is one who can save the living beings of the Sahā world-sphere. This bodhisattva Fine Sound, displaying sundry magical transformations of his body, in this Sahā land preaches this scriptural canon to the beings. Of his supernatural penetrations, magical transformations, and wisdom he loses nothing. This bodhisattva, by resort to several kinds of wisdom, illuminates the Sahā world-sphere, causing all living beings each to gain an object of knowledge, and doing the same thing in all ten quarters in world-spheres as numerous as the sands of the Ganges river. If a person is one who can be rescued by a voice-hearer's form, he preaches Dharma to him in the form of a voice-hearer. If a person is one who can be rescued by a pratyekabuddha's form, he preaches Dharma to him in the form of a pratyekabuddha. If a person is one who can be rescued by a bodhisattva's form, he preaches Dharma to him in the form of a bodhisattva. If a person is one who can be rescued by a Buddha's form, he preaches Dharma to him in the form of a Buddha. Thus in a variety of ways, depending on the one to be rescued, he displays the appropriate form. This includes one who can be rescued by passage into extinction, for whom he then displays passage into extinction. Floral

Excellence! As to the bodhisattva-mahāsattva Fine Sound's achievement of the powers of great supernatural penetration and wisdom, such is the manner of it."[9]

At that time the bodhisattva Floral Excellence addressed the Buddha, saying, "O World-Honored One! This bodhisattva Fine Sound has deeply planted wholesome roots. O World-Honored One! In which samādhi does this bodhisattva dwell, that in this way, wherever he may be, he can make magical demonstrations and rescue living beings?"

The Buddha declared to the bodhisattva Floral Excellence, "Good man, the samādhi is called 'manifestation of the body of all forms' (*sarvarūpasaṃdarśano nāma samādhiḥ*). The bodhisattva Fine Sound, dwelling within this samādhi, can in this way benefit incalculable living beings."

When this Chapter of the Bodhisattva Fine Sound was preached, those who had come with the bodhisattva Fine Sound, eighty-four thousand persons, all attained the samādhi of the manifestation of the body of all forms, and in this Sahā world-sphere incalculable bodhisattvas also attained this samādhi and dhāraṇī.

At that time, the bodhisattva-mahāsattva Fine Sound, having made offerings to Śākyamunibuddha and to the stūpa of the Buddha Many Jewels, returned to his original land. The realms he passed through trembled in six different ways, then rained down jeweled lotus blossoms, and a hundred thousand myriads of millions of varieties of music sounded. After arriving in his original country, accompanied and surrounded by eighty-four thousand bodhisattvas, he went before the Buddha knowledge [Conferred] by the King of Constellations [named] Pure Flower, where he addressed the Buddha, saying, "O World-Honored One! I arrived in the Sahā world-sphere, where I benefited the beings, saw Śākyamunibuddha, also saw the stūpa of the Buddha Many Jewels, worshiped and made offerings; where I also saw the bodhisattva Mañjuśrī the Dharma-prince, and the bodhisattva Medicine King, the bodhisattva He Who Attains the Power of Vigorous Perseverance through Effort (Vīryabalavegaprāpta), the bodhisattva Brave Donor (Pradānaśūra), and the like, and enabled these eighty-four thousand bodhisattvas to attain the samādhi of the manifestation of the body of all forms."

When this Chapter of the Comings and Goings of the Bodhisattva Fine Sound was preached, forty-two thousand sons of gods attained acceptance of [the doctrine of] the unborn dharmas, while the bodhisattva Floral Excellence attained the samādhi of the Dharma Blossom.

Scripture of the Lotus Blossom of the Fine Dharma.
End of Roll the Seventh.

Roll 8

Chapter Twenty-Five: The Gateway to Everywhere of the Bodhisattva He Who Observes the Sounds of the World

At that time the bodhisattva Inexhaustible Mind (Akṣayamati) straightway rose from his seat and, baring his right shoulder and facing the Buddha with palms joined, said: "O World-Honored One! For what reason is the bodhisattva He Who Observes the Sounds of the World (Avalokiteśvara)* called Observer of the Sounds of the World?" The Buddha declared to the bodhisattva Inexhaustible Mind, "Good man, if incalculable hundreds of thousands of myriads of millions of living beings, suffering pain and torment, hear of this bodhisattva He Who Observes the Sounds of the World and single-mindedly call upon his name, the bodhisattva He Who Observes the Sounds of the World shall straightway heed their voices, and all shall gain deliverance.

"If there is one who keeps the name of this bodhisattva He Who Observes the Sounds of the World, even if he should fall into a great fire, the fire would be unable to burn him, thanks to the imposing supernatural power of this bodhisattva.

"If he should be carried off by a great river and call upon this bodhisattva's name, then straightway he would find a shallow place.[1]

"If a hundred thousand myriads of millions of living beings enter the great sea in quest of gold, silver, vaiḍūrya, giant clamshell, agate, coral, amber, pearl, and other such gems, even if a black wind blows their ship away, carrying it off and plunging it into the realm of the rākṣasa-ghosts, if there is among them but one man who calls upon the name of the bodhisattva He Who Observes the Sounds of the World,

* *Kuan Shih Yin.* Kumarajiva's original undoubtedly had *Avalokitasvara.*

those men shall be delivered from the troubles [caused by] the rākṣasas. It is for this reason that he is called Observer of the Sounds of the World.

"If, again, a man who is about to be murdered calls upon the name of the bodhisattva He Who Observes the Sounds of the World, then the knives and staves borne by the other fellow shall be broken in pieces, and the man shall gain deliverance.[2]

"If there should be a thousand-millionfold world of lands filled with yakṣas and rākṣasas who wish to come and do harm to others, if they should but hear the name of the bodhisattva He Who Observes the Sounds of the World, these malignant ghosts would not be able even to look upon those others with an evil eye, how much the less to inflict harm on them!

"Even if there is a man, whether guilty or guiltless, whose body is fettered with stocks, pillory, or chains, if he calls upon the name of the bodhisattva He Who Observes the Sounds of the World, they shall all be severed and broken, and he shall straightway gain deliverance.[3]

"If in a thousand-millionfold world of lands full of malicious bandits there is a merchant chief whose men are carrying precious gems over a road by a steep drop, if there is among them one man who makes this proclamation: 'Good men, do not let terror take possession of you! You all must single-mindedly call upon the name of the bodhisattva He Who Observes the Sounds of the World. For that bodhisattva can confer fearlessness upon living beings. If you all call upon his name, then from these malicious bandits you shall contrive to be delivered'; and if the multitude of merchants, hearing this, speak these words in unison, saying, 'Namo bodhisattvāya He Who Observes the Sounds of the World!'; then, by the mere calling upon his name, they shall forthwith gain deliverance.

"Inexhaustible Mind, the imposing, supernatural power of the bodhisattva He Who Observes the Sounds of the World is as sublime as this![4]

"If there are beings of much lust who are constantly mindful of and humbly respectful to the bodhisattva He Who Observes the Sounds of the World, they shall straightway contrive to be separated from their lust. If those with much anger are constantly mindful of and humbly respectful to the bodhisattva He Who Observes the Sounds of the World, they shall straightway contrive to be separated from their anger.[5] If those of much folly are constantly mindful of and humbly respectful to the bodhisattva He Who Observes the Sounds of the World, they shall straightway contrive to be separated from their folly. Inexhaustible Mind! Such imposing supernatural power has the bodhisattva He Who Observes the Sounds of the World, so many are the benefits he confers! For this reason the beings should ever bear him in mind.

"If there is a woman, and if she is desirous and hopeful of having a son, making worshipful offerings to the bodhisattva He Who Observes the Sounds of the World, she shall straightway bear a son of happiness, excellence, and wisdom. If she be desirous and hopeful of having a daughter, she shall straightway bear a daughter, upright and endowed with proper marks, one who has previously planted wholesome roots, who is loved and honored by a multitude of men. O Inexhaustible Mind, such is the power of the bodhisattva He Who Observes the Sounds of the World![6]

"If there are beings who in humble reverence worship the bodhisattva He Who Observes the Sounds of the World, their happiness shall not be vainly cast aside,[7]

"For this reason the beings must all receive and keep the name of the bodhisattva He Who Observes the Sounds of the World. Inexhaustible Mind! If there is anyone who receives and keeps the names of bodhisattvas as numerous as the sands of sixty-two million Ganges rivers, also exhausting his whole physical being in offering food and drink, clothing, bedding, and medicine, in your thinking how shall it be? Shall the merit of this good man or good woman be much or not?"

Inexhaustible Mind said, "Very much, O World-Honored One!"

The Buddha said, "If again there is a man who receives and keeps the name of the bodhisattva He Who Observes the Sounds of the World, making worshipful offerings to it but once, the happiness of these two shall be equal and undifferentiated, not to be exhausted in a hundred thousand myriads of millions of kalpas. Inexhaustible Mind! One who accepts and keeps the name of the bodhisattva He Who Observes the Sounds of the World shall gain the benefit of merits as incalculable and as limitless as these!"

The bodhisattva Inexhaustible Mind addressed the Buddha, saying, "O World-Honored One! How does the bodhisattva He Who Observes the Sounds of the World travel in this Sahā world-sphere? How does he preach Dharma to living beings? As to his power of resorting to expedient devices, what is the manner of it?"

The Buddha declared to the bodhisattva Inexhaustible Mind, "Good man, if there are beings in the land who can be conveyed to deliverance by the body of a Buddha, then to them the bodhisattva He Who Observes the Sounds of the World preaches Dharma by displaying the body of a Buddha. To those who can be conveyed to deliverance by the body of a pratyekabuddha he preaches Dharma by displaying the body of a pratyekabuddha. To those who can be conveyed to deliverance by the body of a voice-hearer he preaches Dharma by displaying the body of a voice-hearer. To those who can be conveyed to deliverance by the body of a Brahmā-king he preaches Dharma by displaying the body of a Brahmā-king. To those who can be conveyed to deliverance by the body of the god Śakra he preaches Dharma by displaying the body of the god Śakra. To those who can be conveyed to deliverance by the body of the Self-Mastering God he preaches Dharma by displaying the body of the Self-Mastering God. To those who can be conveyed to deliverance by the body of the Great Self-Mastering God he preaches Dharma by displaying the body of the Great Self-Mastering God. To those who can be conveyed to deliverance by the body of the general of the gods he preaches Dharma by displaying the body of the general of the gods. To those who can be conveyed to deliverance by the body of Vaiśravaṇa he preaches Dharma by displaying the body of Vaiśravaṇa. To those who can be conveyed to deliverance by the body of a lesser king he preaches Dharma by displaying the body of a lesser king. To those who can be conveyed to deliverance by the body of an elder he preaches Dharma by displaying the body of an elder. To those who can be conveyed to deliverance by the body of a householder he preaches Dharma by displaying the body of a householder. To those who can be conveyed to deliverance by the body of an official he preaches Dharma by displaying the body of an official. To those who can be conveyed to deliverance by the body of a Brahman he displays the body of a Brahman. To those who can be conveyed to deliverance by the body of bhikṣu, bhikṣuṇī, upāsaka, or upāsikā he preaches Dharma by displaying the body of bhikṣu, bhikṣuṇī, upāsaka, or upāsikā. To those who can be conveyed to deliverance by the body of the wife of elder, householder, official, or Brahman he preaches Dharma by displaying the body of a woman. To those who can be conveyed to deliverance by the body of boy or girl he preaches Dharma by displaying the body of boy or girl. To those who can be conveyed to deliverance by the body of god, dragon, yakṣa, gandharva, asura, garuḍa, kinnara, mahoraga, human, or nonhuman he preaches Dharma by displaying the appropriate body. To those who can be conveyed to deliverance by the body of the spirit who grasps the thunderbolt (Vajrapāṇi) he preaches Dharma by displaying the body of the spirit who grasps the thunderbolt. Inexhaustible Mind! The bodhisattva He Who Observes the Sounds of the World, having achieved such merit as this and by resort to a variety of shapes, travels in the world, conveying the beings to salvation. For this reason you must all single-mindedly make offerings to the bodhisattva He Who Observes the Sounds of the World. This bodhisattva-mahāsattva He Who Observes the Sounds of the World in the midst of terror, emergency, and trouble can confer the gift of fearlessness. For this reason this whole Sahā world-sphere calls him the One Who Confers the Gift of Fearlessness."[8]

The bodhisattva Inexhaustible Mind addressed the Buddha, saying, "O World-Honored One! I will now present an offering to the bodhisattva He Who Observes the Sounds of the World." Straightway he undid his necklace of many precious gems, whose value was a hundred thousand taels of gold, and gave it to him, saying these words: "Sir, accept this Dharma-gift, this necklace of precious jewels!" But at the time the bodhisattva He Who Observes the Sounds of the World would not accept it. Inexhaustible Mind again addressed the bodhisattva He Who Observes the Sounds of the World, saying, "Out of pity for us, accept this necklace!" At that time, the Buddha declared to the bodhisattva He Who Observes the Sounds of the World that he should, out of pity for that bodhisattva Inexhaustible Mind and his fourfold assembly, as well as for the gods, dragons, yakṣas, gandharvas, asuras, garuḍas, kinnaras, mahoragas, humans and nonhumans, accept that necklace. Immediately thereupon the bodhisattva He Who Observes the Sounds of the World, out of pity for the fourfold assembly and for the gods, dragons, humans, and nonhumans, accepted the necklace, dividing it into two parts, one of which he presented to Śākyamuni-buddha, the other of which he presented to the stūpa of the Buddha Many Jewels.

"O Inexhaustible Mind! In possession of such supernatural powers of self-mastery as these does the bodhisattva He Who Observes the Sounds of the World travel in the Sahā world-sphere!"[9]

At that time, the bodhisattva Inexhaustible Mind questioned by resort to a gāthā, saying:

O World-Honored One, fully endowed with subtle signs!
Now again I ask about that
Son of the Buddha for what reason
He is named the One Who Observes the Sounds of the World.

[The Buddha replied:]

Listen you to the conduct of the Sound-Observer,[10]
The one who responds well to all places in all directions!
His broad vows as deep as the ocean,
Throughout kalpas beyond reckoning or discussion
He has served many thousands of millions of Buddhas,
Uttering great and pure vows.
I will tell it to you in brief.[11]
The hearing of his name, the sight of his body,
And the recollection of him in thought do not pass away in vain,
For he can extinguish the woes of existence.
Even if someone whose thoughts are malicious
Should push one into a great pit of fire,
By virtue of constant mindfulness of Sound-Observer
The pit of fire would turn into a pool.[12]
Or, one might be afloat in a great sea,
In which are dragons, fish, and sundry ghosts.
By virtue of constant mindfulness of Sound-Observer
The waves could not drown one.[13]
Or, being on the peak of Sumeru,
One might by another be pushed off.

By virtue of constant mindfulness of Sound-Observer,
  Like the sun itself one would dwell in space.
Or, one might by an evil man be chased
  Down from a diamond mountain.
By virtue of constant mindfulness of Sound-Observer
  He could not harm a single hair [on one's head].[14]
Or, one might be surrounded by enemies,
  Each carrying a knife and intending to inflict harm.
By virtue of one's constant mindfulness of Sound-Observer
  All would straightway produce thoughts of good will.
Or, one might encounter royally ordained woes,
  Facing execution and the imminent end of one's life.[15]
By virtue of one's constant mindfulness of Sound-Observer
  The knives would thereupon break in pieces.
Or, one might be confined in a pillory,
  One's hands and one's feet in stocks.
By virtue of constant mindfulness of Sound-Observer
  One would freely gain release.[16]
When either by spells, or by curses, or by various poisonous herbs,
  [Someone] wishes to harm his body, the victim,
By virtue of his constant mindfulness of Sound-Observer,
  Shall send them all back to plague their authors.[17]
Or, one might encounter evil rākṣasas,
  Poisonous dragons, ghosts, and the like.
By virtue of one's constant mindfulness of Sound-Observer,
  They would not dare to do one harm.[18]
Or, one may be surrounded by malicious beasts,
  Sharp of tooth and with claws to be dreaded.
By virtue of one's constant mindfulness of Sound-Observer,
  They shall quickly run off to immeasurable distance.
There may be poisonous snakes and noxious insects,
  Their breath deadly, smoking and flaming with fire.
By virtue of one's constant mindfulness of Sound-Observer,
  At the sound of one's voice they will go away of themselves.[19]
The clouds, rolling the thunder drums and dispatching the
    lightning,

Send down the hail and pour forth the great rains.
By virtue of one's constant mindfulness of Sound-Observer,
At that very moment one can dry up and dissipate them.
The beings suffer embarrassment and discomfort;
Incalculable woes press in upon them.
The Sound-Observer, by virtue of his unblemished knowledge,
Can rescue the world from its woes.
He is fully endowed with the power of supernatural penetration
And broadly cultivates wisdom and expedient devices;
In the lands of all ten quarters
There is no kṣetra where he does not display his body.
The various evil destinies,
Those of hell, ghosts, and beasts,
As well as the pains of birth, old age, sickness, and death,
All little by little are extinguished.[20]
O you of the true gaze, of the pure gaze,
Of the gaze of broad and great wisdom,
Of the compassionate gaze and the gaze of good will!
We constantly desire, constantly look up to,
The spotlessly pure ray of light,
The sun of wisdom that banishes all darkness,
That can subdue the winds and flames of misfortune
And everywhere give bright light to the world.
The thunder of the monastic prohibitions, whose essence is good will,
And the great and subtle cloud, which is the sense of compassion,
Pour forth the Dharma-rain of sweet dew,
Extinguishing and removing the flames of agony.
When disputes go through civil offices,
When they terrify military camps,
By virtue of constant mindfulness of Sound-Observer
The multitude of enemies shall all withdraw and scatter.
The delicate-voiced One Who Observes the Sounds of the World
And the Brahmā-voiced sound of the tide

Are superior to the sounds of the world.
　Therefore one must ever be mindful of them.
From moment to moment conceive no doubts,
　For the pure saint Who Observes the Sounds of the World
In the discomforts of pain, agony, and death
　Can be a point of reliance.
Fully endowed with all the merits,
　His benevolent eye beholding the beings,
He is happiness accumulated, a sea incalculable.
　For this reason one must bow one's head to him.[21]

At that time the bodhisattva Earth-Holder (Dharaṇiṃdhara) straightway rose from his seat and, coming forward, addressed the Buddha, saying, "O World-Honored One! If there is a living being who shall hear this Chapter of the Bodhisattva He Who Observes the Sounds of the World, the deeds of self-mastery, the manifestation of the gateway to everywhere, the powers of supernatural penetration, be it known that that person's merit shall not be slight."

When the Buddha preached this Chapter of the Gateway to Everywhere, within the multitude were eighty-four thousand living beings all of whom opened up their thoughts to unequaled anuttara-samyaksaṃbodhi.

Chapter Twenty-Six: Dhāraṇī[1]

At that time, the bodhisattva Medicine King straightway rose from his seat and, baring his right shoulder, faced the Buddha with palms joined and addressed the Buddha, saying, "O World-Honored One! If among good men and good women there is anyone who can receive and keep this Scripture of the Dharma Blossom; or read, recite, and derive benefit from it; or copy it into a scroll, how much happiness shall he obtain?"

The Buddha declared to Medicine King, "If there is a good man or good woman who makes offerings to Buddhas equal in number to the sands of eight hundred myriads of millions of nayutas of Ganges rivers, in your thinking how is it? Shall the happiness gained thereby be much or not?"

"Very much, O World-Honored One!"

The Buddha said, "If a good man or good woman can accept and keep so much as a single four-foot gāthā of this scripture, read and recite it, understand its meaning, and practice as it preaches, his happiness shall be very great."[2]

At that time the bodhisattva Medicine King addressed the Buddha, saying, "O World-Honored One! I will now give to the preachers of Dharma a dhāraṇī-charm for their protection." He then pronounced a dhāraṇī, saying:*

anye manye mane mamane citte carite same samitā viśānte mukte muktame[3]
same aviṣame samasame[4] *kṣaye akṣaye akṣiṇe śānte sami*[5]
dhāraṇi ālokabhāṣe pratyavekṣaṇi niviṣṭe[6] *abhyantaraniviṣṭe atyantapāriśuddhi*
utkule mutkule[7] *araḍe paraḍe sukānkṣi asamasame buddhavikliṣṭe*[8]

* Translation of the dhāraṇīs has not been attempted because the meanings are frequently obscure, and the results would be pure guesswork. Most of the words are Indic, some pure Sanskrit and some just mumbo-jumbo, and most are or have been made to look like feminine singular vocatives.

dharmaparīkṣite saṃghanirghoṣaṇi[9] *bhayābhayaviśodhi*[10] *mantra mantrākṣayata*[11] *uruta*[12] *urutakauśalya akṣara*[13] *avaru*[14] *amanyanatāya*

"O World-Honored One! This dhāraṇī, this supernatural charm, has been pronounced by Buddhas equal in number to the sands of sixty-two millions of Ganges rivers. If anyone offends this teacher of Dharma, thereby he shall have offended these Buddhas."

At that time Śākyamunibuddha praised the bodhisattva Medicine King, saying, "Good, good! O Medicine King, it is out of pity for this teacher of Dharma and to protect him that you have pronounced this dhāraṇī; thus you are the source of much benefit to living beings."

At that time the bodhisattva Brave Donor addressed the Buddha, saying, "O World-Honored One! I, too, in order to protect those who read and recite, accept and keep the Scripture of the Dharma Blossom, will pronounce a dhāraṇī. If this teacher of Dharma has this dhāraṇī, no being, whether yakṣa, or rākṣasa, or *pūtana*, or *kṛtya* [both are kinds of demons], or kumbhāṇḍa, or hungry ghost, seeking his weaknesses, shall contrive to get the better of him."

Straightway in the Buddha's presence he then pronounced a charm, saying:

jvale mahājvale ukke mukke aḍe aḍāvati nṛtye nṛtyāvati iṭṭini viṭṭini ciṭṭini nṛtyani nṛtyāvati[15]

"O World-Honored One! This dhāraṇī, this supernatural charm, is one preached by as many Buddhas as there are sands on the Ganges river, and has also duly delighted them. If anyone offends these teachers of Dharma, thereby he shall have offended these Buddhas."

At that time the god king Vaiśravaṇa, protector of the world, addressed the Buddha, saying, "O World-Honored One! I, too, out of pity for the living beings, and in order to protect these teachers of Dharma, will pronounce this dhāraṇī." He straightway then pronounced a charm, saying:

aṭṭe[16] *naṭṭe vanaṭṭe*[17] *anaḍe*[18] *nāḍi kunaḍi*

"O World-Honored One! By means of this supernatural charm will I protect the teachers of Dharma. I will also personally protect the holders of this scripture for as far as a hundred yojanas off, so that they shall suffer neither decline nor care."

At that time the god king Realm-Holder[19] was in this assembly. With a multitude of a thousand myriads of millions of nayutas of gandharvas circumambulating him in humble reverence, he came forward to the Buddha's presence and addressed the Buddha with palms joined, saying, "O World-Honored One! I, too, with the divine charm of a dhāraṇī will protect those who keep the Scripture of the Lotus Blossom." He straightway pronounced a charm, saying:

agaṇe gaṇe gauri gandhāri caṇḍāli mātaṅgi[20] *saṅkule vrūsuli*[21] *atte*[22]

"O World-Honored One! This dhāraṇī, this supernatural charm, is one pronounced by forty-two millions of Buddhas. If anyone offends these teachers of Dharma, thereby he shall have offended these Buddhas."

At that time, there were daughters of rākṣasas, the first named Lambā, the second named Vilambā, the third named Crooked Teeth [Kūṭadantī, prop. "pointed teeth"], the fourth named Flowery Teeth (Puṣpadantī), the fifth named Black Teeth [Makuṭadantī, prop. "crested teeth"], the sixth named Much Hair (Keśinī), the seventh named Insatiable [Acalā, prop. "immoveable"], the eighth named Necklace Bearer [Mālādhārī, prop. "garland bearer"], the ninth named Kuntī, the tenth named Robber of the Vital Vapors of All Living Beings (Sarvasattvojohārī). These ten daughters of rākṣasas, with the mother of the ghosts' children, as well as their own children and retinue, together approached the Buddha's presence, where with one voice they addressed the Buddha, saying, "O World-Honored One! We, too, wish to protect those who read and recite, accept and keep the Scripture of the Dharma Blossom, and to keep them from decline and care; so that if any seek the weaknesses of the teachers of Dharma, they shall not be allowed to get the better of them."

Straightway in the Buddha's presence they pronounced a charm, saying:

itime itime itime atime itime nime nime nime nime nime ruhe ruhe ruhe ruhe tahe tahe tahe tuhe thuhe[23]

"Let anyone rather climb upon our heads than hurt these teachers of Dharma, be the attacker yakṣa, or rākṣasa, or hungry ghost, or pūtana,[24] or kṛtya, or *vetāla*, or *ghaṇṭa*,[25] or *omāraka*,[26] or *apasmāraka*, or *yakṣakṛtya*[27] [various types of demons], or human kṛtya (*manuṣyakṛtya*), or fever, whether of one day, or of two days, or of three days, or of four days, or of as many as seven days, or perpetual fever,[28] or anyone in the form of a man, or of a woman, or of a boy, or of a girl, even in a dream: let none of these harm them!"

Then in the Buddha's presence they proclaimed gāthās, saying:

If anyone, not obedient to our protective charms,
  Torments or disturbs a preacher of Dharma,
Then may his head split into seven parts
  Like a branch of the *arjaka* tree [East Indian basil].
Like [punishment] for the sin of having killed father or mother,
  Also like the calamity visited on one for having pressed oil,*
Or for cheating others in weights and measures,
  Or for Devadatta's sin of disuniting the saṃgha,
He who offends these teachers of the Dharma
  Shall inherit calamities such as these.[29]

When the daughters of the rākṣasas had spoken these gāthās, they addressed the Buddha, saying, "O World-Honored One! We, too, with our own persons will protect those who accept and keep, read and recite, and put into practice this scripture, thus enabling them to gain tranquillity and to separate themselves from decline and care, to dry up the multitude of noxious medicines."

The Buddha declared to the daughters of the rākṣasas, "Good! Good! All of you, for being able to do no more than protect those who receive and keep the name of the Dharma Blossom, shall have happiness incalculable. How much the more so for protecting those who receive

* According to Kato, this is the crime of taking life: there is a danger, in pressing sesame seeds to produce oil, that one will kill the tiny insects that make their home among the sesame seeds. See Bunno Kato, trans., *Myōhō Renge Kyō: The Sutra of the Lotus Flower of the Wonderful Law*, revised by W. E. Soothill and Wilhelm Schiffer (Tokyo, Risshō Kōsei-kai, 1971), p. 421.

and keep it in its entirety and make offerings to the scriptural roll, offerings of floral perfume and garlands, of powdered scent, perfumed paint, burnt incense, banners and parasols, and skillfully played music; who burn all manner of candles, candles of sesame, candles of oil, candles of fragrant oils, candles of the oil of the sumanā-flower, candles of the oil of the campaka-flower, candles of the oil of the vārṣika-flower, candles of the oil of the utpala-flower; who make offerings of this sort in a hundred thousand varieties! Kuntī! You and your retinue must protect such Dharma-teachers as these!"

When this Dhāraṇī Chapter was preached, sixty-eight thousand persons attained acceptance of [the doctrine of] the unborn dharmas.

Chapter Twenty-Seven: The Former Affairs of the King Fine Adornment

At that time, the Buddha declared to the great assemblies, "In an ancient age long past, beyond incalculable, endless asaṃkhyeyakalpas past reckoning or discussion, there was a Buddha named Wisdom Adorned with Flowers [i.e., blessed with luck] by the King of Constellations [named] Thunder-Sound of Clouds (Jaladharagarjitaghoṣasusvara-nakṣatrarājasaṃkusumitābhijñas) tathāgato 'rhan samyaksaṃbuddhaḥ. His realm was named Lustrous Adornment (Vairocanaraśmipratimaṇḍitā), and his kalpa was named Joy to Behold (Priyadarśana). Within that Buddha's dharma was a king named Fine Adornment (Śubhavyūha). That king's lady was named Pure Virtue [Vimaladattā, "gift of the Spotless One"]. She had two sons, one named Pure Womb [Vimalagarbha, "Pure Womb" or "Pure Embryo"], the second named Pure Eye (Vimalanetra). These two sons had great supernatural power, merit, and wisdom, and were long practiced in the Path trodden by bodhisattvas, that is, in dānaparamitā, śīlapāramitā, kṣāntipāramitā, vīryapāramitā, dhyānapāramitā, prajñāpāramitā, the pāramitā of expedient devices; good will, compassion, joy, and indifference; in short, in everything up to and including the dharmas in thirty-seven parts that conduce to the Path.[1] In all of these they had clear understanding, they had arrived at all. They had also attained the bodhisattva's pure samādhi; the samādhi of sun, stars, and constellations (*nakṣatrarājāditya*); the samādhi of pure ray (*vimalanirbhāsa*); the samādhi of pure color; the samādhi of pure sparkle (*vimalabhāsa*); the samādhi of eternal adornment [*alaṃkāraśubha*, "lovely in adornment"]; and the samādhi of the womb of great, imposing excellence [*mahātejogarbha*, "the womb/embryo of great glow"]: at all of these samādhis as well had they arrived. At that time the Buddha, wishing to draw to him the king Fine Adornment, and being compassionately mindful of the beings, preached this Scripture of the Dharma Blossom. At the time the two sons, Pure Womb and Pure Eye, went before their mother and, joining their palms, ten fingers to ten fingers, deferentially spoke: 'We beg leave, Mother, to go before the Buddha Wisdom Adorned with Flowers by the King of Constellations [named] Thunder-Sound of Clouds, where we too, will attend him, approach him with familiarity, make offerings to him, and worship him. What is the reason? In the midst of a multitude of all gods and men this Buddha preaches the Scripture of the Dharma Blossom, and we must listen to it receptively.' The mother declared to her sons, 'Your father believes in and accepts external ways, being profoundly attached to the dharma of the Brahmans. You must report to your father, and only then go off together.'[2] Pure Womb and Pure Eye addressed their mother with palms joined, ten fingers to ten fingers: 'We are Dharma-princes, yet we have been born into a household of crooked views such as this!' The mother declared to her sons, 'Taking thought for your father with concern, you must show him some magical feats, for, if he is enabled to see them, without fail his thoughts shall be purified, and he may permit us to go before that Buddha.'

"Thereupon the two sons, taking thought for their father, danced in empty space at a height equal to that of seven tala-trees and displayed a variety of magical feats in empty space: walking, remaining still, sitting, lying down, emitting water from the upper part of their bodies, emitting fire from the lower part of their bodies, emitting water from the lower part of their bodies, emitting fire from the upper part of their bodies, or else displaying a body large enough to fill empty space, then displaying a small one, or a small one and then displaying a large one, vanishing in empty space and then suddenly appearing on the ground, sinking into the earth as if it were water, treading on the water as if it were earth. Displaying such a variety of magical feats as these, they caused the king their father to believe and understand with a pure heart.[3] At that time the father, seeing his sons' magical powers to be of this kind, was at heart overjoyed, having gained something he had never had before, and, facing his sons with palms joined, asked, 'Who is your teacher? Whose pupils are you?' The two sons spoke deferentially: 'O great king! That Buddha Wisdom Adorned with Flowers by the King of Constellations [named] Thunder-Sound of Clouds, who, seated on a Dharma-throne at the foot of a bodhi-tree made of the seven jewels, in the midst of a multitude of gods and men of all the worlds, broadly preaches the Scripture of the Dharma Blossom—he is our Master, and we are his disciples.' The father told his sons, "Now I also wish to see your Teacher. Let us go together."

"Thereupon the two sons descended from empty space and arrived before their mother, where, with palms joined, they deferentially addressed her: 'The king our father now already believes and understands, and is capable of opening up his thought to anuttarasamyaksaṃbodhi. For our father's sake we have already done the Buddha's business. We beg permission, Mother, to leave the household and cultivate the Path before that Buddha!'

"At that time the two sons, wishing to restate this meaning, in gāthās addressed their mother:

> We beg you, Mother, to let us
>   Leave the household and become śramaṇas,
> For Buddhas are very hard to encounter,
>   And we would learn as a Buddha's followers.
> [Rare] as the udumbara-flower,
>   Nay, harder yet to encounter is a Buddha.
> Shaking off one's troubles is also difficult.
>   We beg permission to leave the household.[4]

"The mother straightway declared, 'I permit you to leave the household. What is the reason? That a Buddha is hard to encounter.'[5]

"Thereupon the two sons addressed their father and mother, saying, 'Excellent! Father and Mother, we entreat you.* It is time to go before the Buddha Wisdom Adorned with Flowers by the King of Constellations named Thunder-Sound of Clouds, to approach him with familiarity and to make offerings to him. What is the reason? A Buddha is as hard to encounter as an udumbara-flower, as hard as it would be

* Having attained their parents' general consent to join the Buddha, they now ask for permission to leave immediately.

for a one-eyed tortoise to encounter a hole in a floating piece of wood.[6] Yet, our former merits having been profound and of great proportions, we have been born into the Buddhadharma. For this reason, Father and Mother, you must grant us permission, thus enabling us to leave the household. What is the reason? The Buddhas are hard to meet, and the time is also hard to encounter.'

"At that time, in the rear palace of the king Fine Adornment, eighty-four thousand persons all became capable of receiving and holding this Scripture of the Dharma Blossom. The bodhisattva Pure Eye was already long accomplished in the samādhi of the Dharma Blossom.[7] The bodhisattva Pure Womb for incalculable hundred thousands of myriads of millions of kalpas had been accomplished in the samādhi that separates one from evil destinies, for he wished to enable all living beings to separate themselves from their own evil destinies. The royal lady attained the samādhi of the Buddhas' assemblies, and was able to know the treasure house of the Buddhas' secrets.[8] In this way the two sons, by resort to the power of expedient devices, skillfully converted their father, causing his heart to believe and understand and to love the Buddhadharma. Thereupon the king Fine Adornment, together with his assembled ministers and his retinue, the lady Pure Virtue, and the harem women and retinue of the rear palace, as well as his two sons together with their own forty-two thousand men, at the same time went to the Buddha's place. When they reached it, with head bowed they did obeisance to his feet, circumambulated him three times, and then stood off to one side.

"At that time, that Buddha preached Dharma to the king, demonstrated to him, taught him, benefited him, and afforded him advantage. The king was overjoyed. Then the king Fine Adornment and his lady undid their pearl necklaces, whose value was a hundred thousands, and scattered them over the Buddha. In the midst of empty space they magically created a jeweled terrace with four pillars. Within the terrace was a great jeweled couch, over which were spread a hundred thousand myriads of divine cloaks, and on top of them was a Buddha, seated with legs crossed and emitting a great ray of light. At that time the king Fine Adornment thought: 'A Buddha's body is rare, erect and awesome, most distinguished, having perfected matter of supreme subtlety.' At that time the Buddha Wisdom Adorned with Flowers by the King of Constellations [named] Thunder-Sound of Clouds declared to the fourfold multitude, 'Do you see this king Fine Adornment, standing before me with palms joined, or do you not? This king, within my dharma, shall become a bhikṣu. With subtle striving he shall cultivate and practice the dharmas that conduce to the Buddha Path, and shall contrive to become a Buddha whose name shall be King of the Śāla Trees, whose realm shall be called Great Light, and whose kalpa shall be called [Age of the] Great Exalted King. That Buddha, King of the Śāla Trees, shall have an incalculable multitude of bodhisattvas and an incalculable number of voice-hearers. His realm shall be flat and even. Such shall be his merits.' Straightway that king conferred the realm upon his younger brother, and with his lady, his two sons, and his varied retinue, left the household within the Buddhadharma and cultivated the Path. When the king had left the household, for eighty-four thousand years, constantly striving and vigorously persevering, he put into practice the Scripture of the Blossom of the Fine Dharma. When this time had passed, he attained the samādhi of the adornment of all pure merit, and straightway ascended into empty space to a height equal to that of seven tala-trees.[9]

"Then he addressed the Buddha, saying, 'O World-Honored One! These two sons of mine have already done the business of the Buddha, by resort to supernatural penetrations and magical feats turning my crooked thoughts and enabling me to dwell secure in the midst of the Buddhadharma and to see the World-Honored One. These two sons are my good friends. It is because they wished to raise up my wholesome roots of former ages, to confer benefit upon me, that they came to be born in my house.'

"At that time the Buddha Wisdom Adorned with Flowers by the King of Constellations [named] Thunder-Sound of Clouds addressed the king Fine Adornment, saying, 'It is so! It is so! It is as you have said! If a good man or good woman, in order to plant wholesome roots, in age after age gains a good friend, that good friend can do the Buddha's business, demonstrating, teaching, profiting, delighting, and causing entry into anuttarasamyaksaṃbodhi. O great king! Let it be known that a good friend is a great cause and condition. This means that he converts and guides, making possible the vision of a Buddha and the opening up of the thought to anuttarasamyaksaṃbodhi. O great king! Do you see these two boys, or do you not? These two boys have already made offerings to Buddhas equal in number to the sands of sixty-five hundred thousand myriads of millions of nayutas of Ganges rivers, approaching them with familiarity, doing them humble reverence, before the Buddhas receiving and keeping the Scripture of the Dharma Blossom, taking compassionate thought for the beings with their crooked views and enabling them to dwell in right view.'

"The king Fine Adornment straightway descended from the midst of empty space and addressed the Buddha, saying, 'O World-Honored One! The Thus Come One is most rare! By reason of his merit and wisdom, a knot of flesh on the crown of his head shines with a bright glow. His eyes are long and broad, deep blue in color. The mark of the tuft between his brows is as white as a crystal moon. His teeth are white, even, and close, ever glistening. His lips are red in color and as lovely as the fruit of the *bimba* [a bright red gourd].'

"At that time the king Fine Adornment, having praised incalculable hundred thousands of myriads of millions of the Buddha's merits such as these, in the presence of the Thus Come One, single-mindedly and with palms joined, again addressed the Buddha, saying, 'O World-Honored One! This is something that has never been before! The Dharma of the Thus Come One is perfect, its fine and subtle merits beyond reckoning or discussion. He teaches what is to be done. He is tranquil, cheerful, and good. From this day forward, I will no longer follow the course of my own thought. I will not give way to the evil thoughts of crooked views, pride, or anger.' When he had spoken these words, he did obeisance to the Buddha and left."

The Buddha demanded of the great multitude, "To your minds, how is it? Can the king Fine Adornment possibly have been anyone else? The present bodhisattva Floral Excellence is that very person. The lady Pure Virtue is the very bodhisattva Marks of Adornment who now shines in the Buddha's presence. It is because he pitied the king Fine Adornment and his assorted retinue that he was born among them. The two sons are the present bodhisattvas Medicine King and Above Medicine. When these bodhisattvas, Medicine King and Above Medicine, shall have achieved such great merits as these, then in the presence of incalculable hundreds of thousands of myriads of millions of Buddhas they shall plant a multitude of wholesome roots and achieve wholesome merit past reckoning or discussion. If any man knows the names of these two bodhisattvas, then the gods and men of all the worlds must do obeisance to him also."

When the Buddha pronounced this Chapter of the Former Affairs of the King Fine Adornment, eighty-four thousand persons put off their grime, separated themselves from their defilements, and attained purity of the Dharma-eye with respect to the dharmas.[10]

Chapter Twenty-Eight: The Encouragements of the Bodhisattva Universally Worthy

At that time the bodhisattva Universally Worthy (Samantabhadra , who was renowned for awe-inspiring excellence because of his powers of supernatural penetration, together with great bodhisattvas i numbers incalculable, limitless, not subject to measure or count, came from the eastern quarter. The realms through which he passed all trembled throughout, rained down jeweled lotuses, and resounded with incalculable hundreds of thousands of myriads of millions of kinds of skillfully played music. He was also accompanied and surrounded by a great multitude of countless gods, dragons, yakṣas, gandharvas, asuras, garuḍas, kinnaras, mahoragas, humans, and nonhumans, who circumabulated him, each displaying powers of awe-inspiring excellence and supernatural penetration. Reaching the Sahā world-sphere, arriving at the very midst of Mount Gṛdhrakūṭa, with head bowed he did obeisance to Śākyamunibuddha and, circumambulating him clockwise seven times, addressed the Buddha, saying, "O World-Honored One! In the realm of the Buddha King Surpassing the Awe-Inspiring Excellence of Gems, I heard from afar that in this Sahā world-sphere the Scripture of the Dharma Blossom is preached, and with a multitude of incalculable, limitless hundreds of thousands of myriads of millions of bodhisattvas I have come to listen receptively. I beg the World-Honored One to preach it to us! After the extinction of the Thus Come One, how may a good man or good woman attain this Scripture of the Dharma Blossom?"

The Buddha declared to the bodhisattva Universally Worthy, "If a good man or good woman perfects four dharmas, after the extinction of the Thus Come One he shall attain this Scripture of the Dharma Blossom. First, he must be the object of the protectively mindful thoughts of the Buddhas. Second, he must plant the roots of a multitude of excellences. Third, he must enter into a collection of right concentrations. Fourth, he must launch the thought of rescuing all living beings. If a good man or good woman in this way perfects the four dharmas, after the extinction of the Thus Come One he shall without fail attain this scripture."[1]

At that time the bodhisattva Universally Worthy addressed the Buddha, saying, "O World-Honored One! In the last five hundred years, in the midst of a muddied, evil age, if there is anyone who receives and keeps this scriptural Canon, I will guard and protect him, keep him from decline and care, enable him to gain tranquillity, and prevent those who seek to get the better of him from doing so, Be it Māra, or a son of Māra, or a daughter of Māra, or a subject of Māra, or one possessed by Māra, or yakṣa, or rākṣasa, or kumbhāṇḍa, or piśāca, or kṛtya, or pūtana, or vetāla, or any other tormentor of men, none shall get the better of him. If that person, whether walking or standing, reads and recites this scripture, at that time I, mounted on a white elephant-king with six tusks, together with a great multitude of bodhisattvas will go to that place and, personally revealing my body, make offerings to him, guard and protect him, and comfort his thoughts. Also, if, as an offering to the Scripture of the Dharma Blossom, that person, seated, thinks on this scripture, at that time also I will appear before that person, mounted on a white elephant-king. If that person suffers the loss from memory of a single phrase or a single gāthā of the Scripture of the Dharma Blossom, I will teach him, reading and reciting it together with him, thereby enabling him to regain the advantage thereof. At that time anyone who receives and keeps, reads and recites the Scripture of the Dharma Blossom, having contrived to see my body, shall be overjoyed, and shall persevere all the more vigorously for having seen me. He shall straightway attain samādhis and dhāraṇīs, the latter named the Turning Dhāraṇī (*Dhāraṇyāvartā*), the dhāraṇī that can be turned to a hundred thousand myriads of millions [of uses] (*koṭīśatasahasrāvartā*), and the dhāraṇī of skill in the [use of] Dharma-sounds (*sarvarutakauśalyāvartā*): such dhāraṇīs as these shall he attain.[2]

"O World-Honored One! If in the latter age, in the last five hundred years, in the midst of a muddied and evil age, a bhikṣu, or bhikṣuṇī, or upāsaka, or upāsikā who seeks, accepts and keeps, reads and recites, and copies, wishes to cultivate and practice this Scripture of the Dharma Blossom, then for three weeks he must single-mindedly persevere with vigor. When he has fulfilled three weeks, I, mounted on my white elephant with six tusks, will together with incalculable bodhisattvas personally circumambulate him, appearing before that person in a body beheld with joy by all living beings, preaching Dharma to him, demonstrating to him, teaching him, benefiting and delighting him. I will also give him this dhāraṇī-charm. Once he has that dhāraṇī, no nonhuman shall be able to destroy him, nor shall he be led astray or confused by women. I will also personally ever protect that person. I beg the World-Honored One to permit me to pronounce this dhāraṇī-charm." Straightway in the Buddha's presence he pronounced a charm, saying:

> *adaṇḍe daṇḍapati daṇḍapate daṇḍakuśale daṇḍasudhāri sudhāri sudhārapati buddhapaśyane sarvadhāraṇyāvartani svāvartani saṃghaparīkṣaṇi saṃghanirghātani asaṃkhye saṃghāvaghāṭi tiryādhasaṃghātulya araḍe paraḍe sarvasaṃgha samādhigarandhi sarvadharmasuparīkṣite sarvasattvarutakauśalyānugate siṃhavikrīḍite*[3]

"O World-Honored One! If a bodhisattva is able to hear this dhāraṇī, let it be known that this ability is the work of the supernatural penetrations of Universally Worthy.

"If the Scripture of the Dharma Blossom is abroad in Jambudvīpa, and if there is anyone who receives and keeps it, one must have this thought: 'This is all the awesome, supernatural doing of Universally Worthy.' If there is anyone who receives and keeps it, reads and recites it, properly recalls it, interprets the import of its meaning, and practices as it preaches, let it be known that this person is doing the work of Universally Worthy, that in the presence of incalculable, limitless Buddhas he has deeply planted wholesome roots, that he has had his head caressed by the hands of the Thus Come Ones. If he but copies it, that person at the end of his life shall be born in the Trāyastriṃśa Heaven. At that time, eighty-four thousand goddesses, making music with a multitude of instruments, shall come to receive him. That man shall straightway don a crown of the seven jewels, and among the women of the harem shall enjoy himself and be gay. How much the more shall this be true of one who receives and keeps it, reads and recites it, and interprets the import of its meaning! To that man at life's end shall be extended the hands of a thousand Buddhas, causing him not to fear, nor to fall into evil destinies. He shall straightway ascend to the top of the Tuṣita Heaven, to the place of the bodhisattva Maitreya. The bodhisattva Maitreya has thirty-two marks, is surrounded by a great multitude of bodhisattvas, and has a retinue of a hundred thousand myriads of millions of goddesses, born within his retinue. Such are the merits and advantages that he shall have! Therefore a wise person must single-mindedly write it himself, or cause others to write it, receive and keep it, read and recite it, recall it properly, and practice as it preaches. O World-Honored One! By resort to my powers of supernatural penetration, I will now guard and protect this scripture. After the extinction of the Thus Come One, within Jambudvīpa I will broadly propagate it and cause it never to perish."

At that time Śākyamunibuddha uttered praise, saying, "Excellent! Excellent! O Universally Worthy, you are able to protect this scripture, to afford comfort and advantage to many beings. Having already achieved merit beyond reckoning and discussion, with deep and great good will and compassion from the distant past until now launching the thought of anuttarasamyaksaṃbodhi, you are able to take this vow of supernatural penetration, to guard and protect this scripture. I, by resort to my power of supernatural penetration, will guard and protect whoever can accept and keep the name of the bodhisattva Universally Worthy. O Universally Worthy! If there is anyone who can receive and keep, read and recite, recall properly, cultivate and practice, and copy this Scripture of the Dharma Blossom, be it known that that person has seen Śākyamunibuddha, that he might have heard this scriptural canon from the Buddha's mouth. Be it known that that person has made offerings to Śākyamunibuddha. Be it known that that person has been praised by the Buddha with the word 'Excellent!' Be it known that that person has had his head stroked by Śākyamunibuddha. Be it known that that person has been covered with Śākyamunibuddha's cloak. Such a person as this shall never again crave worldly pleasures, shall never again be fond of the classical books or the manuscripts of the external paths, shall also take no pleasure in approaching with familiarity persons [associated with these things] or other wicked ones, be they butchers, or those who raise pigs, sheep, fowl, and dogs, or hunters, or those who advertise and sell female flesh. That man's thought and mind shall be straightforward and honest. He shall have right recall. He shall have the power of merit. That man shall not be tormented by the three poisons, nor shall he be tormented by envy, pride, conceit, or haughtiness. That man's desires shall be slight, and he shall know satisfaction. He shall be able to cultivate the conduct of Universally Worthy. O Universally Worthy! After the extinction of the Thus Come One, in the last five hundred years, if then there is a person who sees one that receives and keeps the Scripture of the Dharma Blossom, he is to think: 'Ere long this person shall arrive at the Platform of the Path. He shall smash Māra's hosts. He shall attain anuttarasamyaksaṃbodhi. He shall turn the Wheel of the Dharma. He shall beat the drum of the Dharma. He shall blow the conch of the Dharma. He shall precipitate the rain of the Dharma. He shall sit, amid a great multitude of gods and men, on a lion throne of the Dharma.' O Universally Worthy! If anyone in the latter age accepts and keeps, reads and recites this scriptural canon, that person shall never again want for clothing, bedding, food and drink, or for the things that support life. His wishes shall not be in vain. He shall also in the present age gain his happy recompense. If there is a man who utters words of disparagement: 'You are nothing but a madman! In vain are you performing these practices! You shall never get anything for them!'; the retribution for sins such as this shall be that from age to age he shall have no eyes. If there is anyone who makes offerings and gives praise, in this very age he shall get his present reward. If, again, one sees a person receiving and holding this scripture, then utters its faults and its evils, be they fact or not fact, that person in the present age shall get white leprosy. If anyone makes light of it or laughs at it, from age to age his teeth shall be far apart and decayed, he shall have ugly lips and a flat nose, his arms and legs shall be crooked, his eyes shall be pointed and the pupils out of symmetry, his body shall stink, he shall have sores running pus and blood, his belly shall be watery and his breath short: in brief, he shall have all manner of evil and grave ailments. For this reason, O Universally Worthy, if you should see one who accepts and keeps this scriptural canon, you must arise and greet him from a distance, you must behave as if you were paying homage to a Buddha."

When this Chapter of the Encouragements of Universally Worthy was preached, incalculable, limitless bodhisattvas, equal in number to the sands of the river Ganges, attained the dhāraṇī that can be turned to a hundred thousand myriads of millions of uses, and bodhisattvas equal in number to the fine grains in the thousand-millionfold world perfected the path of Universally Worthy. When the Buddha had preached this scripture, Universally Worthy and the other bodhisattvas, Śāriputra and the other voice-hearers, and the gods, dragons, humans, and nonhumans—in short the whole great assembly—were all overjoyed and, accepting and keeping the Buddha's Word, they did obeisance and departed.

Scripture of the Lotus Blossom of the Fine Dharma.
Roll the Eighth. The End.[4]

Glossary

abhijñā Higher or supernatural knowledge; intuition. There are five or six, depending on the tradition. In the *Lotus* there are five: (1) *divyacakṣus*, divine eye; (2) *divyaśrotra*, divine ear; (3) *paracittajñāna*, knowledge of the thoughts of others; (4) *pūrvanivāsānusmṛti*, recollection of former incarnations; (5) *ṛddhivimokṣakriyā*, which seems to mean "deeds [leading to] magical power and release." For this last, Eugène Burnouf, in *Le Lotus de la Bonne Loi* (new ed., Paris, Maisonneuve, 1925, p. 11*n*), gives instead *ṛddhisākṣātkriyā*, "direct experience of magical power." For *abhijñā*, Kumārajīva gives *shen t'ung*, "supernatural penetration."

adbhuta Astonishing; amazed, wonder-struck. Kumārajīva must have understood this as *abhūta*, "unprecedented, never having been before," for he consistently renders it with *wei ts'eng yu*.

adhimukti Strong inclination, attachment; earnest, zealous application. Kumārajīva's consistent equivalent is *hsin chieh*, "belief and understanding." On the other hand, *chieh* and *mukti* both mean "release," and I am certain that in this Ch. equivalent there is something at work that I do not understand.

agaru, *aguru* Aloeswood, agalloch (*aquilaria agallocha*), a shrub with an aromatic wood, or incense made from it. The Chinese name, as given in the *Pen ts'ao kang mu*, is *ch'en shui hsiang*, lit. the "scent that sinks in water," a name apparently based on the process by which the incense is made, a process of concentration that makes it quite heavy.

ajita The "unbeaten one," *Invictus*, an eponym of Maitreya.

ājīvaka A member of a non-Buddhist ascetic fellowship or order. In the form *ājīvika*, this is sometimes identified with *nirgrantha*, presumed to signify a Jain.

akaniṣṭha (In pl.) "they of whom none is the youngest," name of the highest class of gods in the Rūpadhātu, the "Sphere of Form," a world (or, depending on the point of view, a state of trance) in which there are still visible shapes, but shapes for which the denizens feel no desire.

akṣobhya An unspecified high number.

amanuṣyakṛtya A *kṛtya* (q.v.) having inhuman form.

anāgāmin A "nonreturner," one who has reached a stage of religious development that frees him from rebirth in the Kāmadhātu, the "Sphere of Desire," i.e., the world of ordinary mortals.

anuttarasamyaksaṃbodhi Supreme perfect enlightenment, that of a Buddha.

apasmāraka A sort of demon or supernatural evil being. Since the same word also means "epilepsy," is it possible that this is a sort of epilepsy-demon?

āraṇyaka Forest-dwelling hermit.

arhant (Usually found, in European-language works, in the weak form *arhat.*) While the etymology is obscure, the meaning is not. It refers to a person who has intuited the Truth, and who consequently will not be reincarnated. The Mahāyāna before the *Lotus* denigrated him, saying that, while he was indeed enlightened, still he was inferior to a Buddha. The *Lotus* says, in effect, that the *arhant* does not exist. In the present translation, the word, when translated, is consistently rendered "worthy one."

arhattva The quality or state of being an *arhant*, for which see the previous entry.

arjaka The East Indian basil (*Ocimum gratissimum*).

asaṃkhyeya Incalculable; an incalculable number.

asura A demon of the first order, in perpetual hostility with the gods, more or less equivalent to the Greek Titans.

atimukta, *atimuktaka*. "Whiter than pearl," the name of a shrub, bursage (*Gaertneria racemosa*).

aupamya Parable.

avīci Lit. "lower, facing downward," but by Kumārajīva's time the etymology had been forgotten. In the *Lotus*, implied to be the lowest and most terrible of all the hells.

avivartika (also *avaivartika* or, as a state of being, *avaivartya*). "Not to be turned back." Up to a certain stage in their development, all religious practitioners are subject to backsliding. The bodhisattva, when he has reached the seventh (in some traditions, the eighth) of ten stages, cannot backslide.

bhavāgra The pinnacle of existence. Another name for *naivasaṃjñānāsaṃjñāyatana*, the "realm where there is neither perception nor nonperception," the very top of the Ārūpyadhātu, the "Sphere of No-Form," the highest stage in the world, above and beyond which begins the unworldly, i.e., the path to enlightenment.

bheruṇḍaka Some sort of beast of prey that makes a terrible sound and eats human flesh.

bhikṣu "Mendicant [monk]," this being, together with *śramaṇa*, "ascetic," the most common Buddhist Sanskrit designation for a Buddhist monk.

bhikṣuṇī "Mendicant nun," feminine form of *bhikṣu*.

bhikṣusaṃgha The company of Buddhist monks; synonymous with *saṃgha*.

bimba A plant (*Momordica monadelpha*) bearing a bright red gourd. The balsam apple and balsam pear belong to the same genus.

bodhi Enlightened intuition, the attainment that, *par excellence*, characterizes a Buddha. Also used as an abbreviation of *bodhivṛkṣa*, the tree under which a Buddha has his experience of *bodhi*.

bodhimaṇḍa Platform, terrace, seat of enlightenment, name given to the spot under the bodhi tree on which the Buddha sat when he became enlightened. Rendered consistently by Kumārajīva with *tao ch'ang*, "Platform of the Path."

bodhisattva A word of uncertain etymology, whose meaning, however, is clear. It refers to a being well on the way to Buddhahood, a being who devotes a good bit of his career to bringing others besides himself nearer the Goal. Traditionally, the bodhisattva's career is subdivided into many stages, of which, however, the *Lotus* tells us almost nothing. An epithet for *bodhisattva* is *mahāsattva*, "great being," and the two words frequently occur together as a pair.

buddha Lit. "awakened," the highest stage of enlightenment in the Mahāyāna tradition. Though in the same tradition the number of Buddhas is infinite, the title, when used without qualification, refers to Gautama.

buddhaśarīra The Buddha's relics; synonymous with *śarīra*.

campaka Champac (*Michelia campaka*), name of a tree bearing a yellow, sweet-smelling flower.

caṇḍāla The lowest of the outcastes, being born of a Śūdra father and a Brahman mother.

candana Sandal (*Sirium myrtifolium*), whether the tree, the wood, or the unctuous preparation of the wood, held in high esteem as a perfume. The English word is borrowed from the Skt., but the etymology of the latter is itself unknown.

chattra Lit. "covering," i.e., a parasol. (Occasionally *chatra*.)

dhāraṇī Magical formula.

dhāraṇīpratilabdha Having obtained, i.e., being in possession of, a *dhāraṇī*.

dharma Of the many possible meanings of this word in Buddhist Sanskrit, two seem to stand out in the *Lotus*: (1) A constituent of existence, even a "thing;" (2) A truth, a true idea, or even the Buddha's Truth in its totality; a doctrine. In the sense of the Buddha's Truth or Doctrine, the word is always capitalized in the present translation.

dhuta, *dhūta* Lit. "shaken [off]," referring now to ascetic practices, from which worldly defilements have been shaken off, now to ascetic practitioners, who have achieved the said "shaking off." At times, the word can be so weak in meaning as to signify little more than "morality."

dhyāna Meditation or contemplation; mystic trance. The Ch. frequently renders this with *ting*, "concentration," which, strictly speaking, renders not this but *samādhi*, q.v.

gandharva While this is a very ancient word, in Buddhist Sanskrit it acquired the meaning of a sort of musician-demigod. Incidentally, the word itself is akin to "centaur."

garuḍa A mythical bird.

gāthā While in theory these are supposed to be preachings made entirely in verse, neither accompanying nor accompanied by prose, in fact, in the *Lotus*, they seem to be synonymous with the next entry.

geya Verses repeating in substance the content of a prose preaching immediately preceding.

ghaṇṭa One name of Śiva.

guhyaka Name of a class of demigods who, like the *yakṣas*, are attendants on Kubera, the god of wealth, and guardians of his treasures.

gūthoḍigalla Cesspool. In the *Lotus*, this word appears in two other guises, *gūthoḍilla* and *gūtholilla*.

itivṛttaka Story of past events.

jāmbūnada Adjective derived from *Jambūnadī*, the river Jambū (or Jambu), the latter alleged to be formed of the juice of the *jambu* fruit and to flow down from Mount Sumeru into our continent, which thus bears the name *Jambudvīpa*, "jambu island." In Kumārajīva's version, *jāmbūnada* bears the deceptive appearance of *yen-fou-t'an* (ancient pronunciation approximately *yem-bu-dan*), while the Skt., as we have it, does not have the word at all.

jātaka Story of a previous incarnation of a Buddha.

jāti Large-flowered variety of common jasmine (*Jasminum officinale grandiflorum*).

kalaviṅka The Indian cuckoo; occasionally a sparrow.

kalpa Cosmic age.

kiṃśuka The dhak or Bengal kino (*Butea frondosa*), a tree bearing beautiful blossoms.

kinnara Lit. "what sort of man?" A mythical being reckoned as a horse with a man's head or a man with a horse's head, sometimes associated with the heavenly musicians (*gandharva*, a word related to "centaur").

kleśa Impurity, depravity. They are usually of three kinds: (1) *rāga*, lust; (2) *dveṣa*, hatred (consistently rendered by the Chinese with "anger"); (3) *moha*, delusion (rendered by the Chinese with *ch'ih* or *yü ch'ih*, "folly" in the present translation). *Kleśa* appears in Chinese as *fan nao*, which here appears usually as "agony," something very close to the word's original meaning. The kleśas, in our terms, are attachment to the unwholesome, hatred of the wholesome and the inability to distinguish between the two.

koṭi, koṭī Ten millions.

kovidāra The Buddhist bauhinia (*Bauhinia variegata*), a small tree with variegated flowers.

kṛtya A kind of demon.

kṣaṇa A moment.

kṣatriya A member of the governing or military caste.

kṣetra Lit. "field," specifically the area over which a Buddha holds sway.

kumbhāṇḍa, kumbhāṇḍaka A kind of evil spirit, pictured with testicles the size of water-pitchers, which is what the name literally means.

kunduruka, kundurūka Frankincense.

lokāyata A materialist.

mahāmāndārava A large *māndārava*, q.v.

mahāsattva A "great being," i.e., a *bodhisattva* (q.v.); almost always used in conjunction with the latter.

mahoraga A great serpent.

mallikā One variety of the Arabian jasmine (*Jasminum sambac*).

mandārava, māndārava The blossom of the coral tree, but here used, in all likelihood, to refer to some mythical flower.

maṇi Jewel.

mañjūṣaka A species of celestial flower.

manuṣyakṛtya A *kṛtya* (q.v.) in human form.

māra Lit. "killing." The Destroyer, the Evil One, who tempts men to indulge their passions and is thus the great enemy of the Buddha and his teaching. In later Buddhist folklore, there is an incalculable number of Māras.

nāga A serpent-demon. The Ch. almost consistently render this with *lung*, "dragon."

nama, namaḥ, namas, namo. Homage.

nārāyaṇa An eponym of Viṣṇu.

naṭa A dancer, player, mimic, actor.

navamālikā A variety of the Arabian jasmine (*Jasminum sambac*).

nayuta A large number, supposedly 100,000,000,000, but clearly used to indicate a meteoric quantity.

nidāna Cause, underlying and determining factor; cause of action, motive, motivation; beginning, introduction (which states the factors underlying the narration that is to follow).

nirgrantha A non-Buddhist monk, commonly assumed to refer to a Jain.

nirvāṇa The end of reincarnation, the goal of all Buddhists.

omāraka Name of a demoniac being.

ostāraka Name of a demoniac being.

pāpīyaṃs Lit. "the More Evil One," eponym of Māra (q.v.).

pāramitā Perfection. The bodhisattva is traditionally regarded as possessing six of them, viz., (1) *dāna*, the capacity to give without stint, even if it means giving up his own life; (2) *śīla*, perfect moral conduct, i.e., absolutely no violation of the monastic code; (3) *kṣānti*, absolute forbearance; (4) *vīrya*, vigorous exertion or perseverance, which means sparing oneself no effort or hardship; (5) *dhyāna*, contemplation that will succumb to no disturbances; (6) *prajñā*, wisdom.

pārijāta, pārijātaka The Indian coral tree (*Erythrina indica*).

parinirvāṇa "Perfect extinction," that of a Buddha as opposed to that of an *arhant*, q.v.

pāṭala The trumpet-flower (*Oroxylum indicum*).

piśāca Demon, goblin, sprite.

piśācikā Female *piśāca*.

pratyekabuddha A being that attains to enlightened intuition thanks entirely to his own efforts, but who then benefits no one but himself with this intuition. Usually translated *yüan chüeh*, which here is always rendered with "condition-perceiver."

preta A ghost. In one tradition, the *pretas* are depicted as beings with stomachs the size of a mountain and throats the size of a needle, so that they can never possibly be sated. The Ch. accordingly renders *preta* with *o kuei*, "hungry ghost."

pṛkkā An herb, the horned trigonella (*Trigonella corniculata*).

pūtana A particular class of demons or spirits.

rākṣasa An evil or malignant demon.

ṛṣi Originally, a person who alone, or with others, invokes the deities in song or in speech of sacred character; later, a seer or sage.

śakra Lit. "the Able One," eponym of Indra. (One may also take the view that *indra* is an eponym of Śakra, for in the Lotus the Skt. title is always *śakro devānām indraḥ*, "the Able One, Lord of the Gods.") In later Buddhism there is a potential infinity of Śakras, as there is of Māras, etc.

sakṛdāgāmin A person who will have but one rebirth more in the Kāmadhātu, the world or ordinary mortals.

śakya Name of the clan to which Gautama belonged.

śākya A member of the Śakya clan, specifically Gautama the Buddha.

śāla The sal tree (*Shorea robusta*), under which a Buddha has his experience of enlightenment.

samādhi Concentration, preparatory to meditation.

saṃgha Any collective body, specifically the collective brotherhood of Buddhist monks.

samyaksaṃbuddha "Properly and fully enlightened," a Buddha.

śarīra Lit. "body," specifically the relics of a Buddha when he has attained *nirvāṇa*.

skandha Lit. "mass." Buddhism divides existence into *dharmas* (q.v.), which it classifies, for practical purposes, in five groups, viz., (1) *rūpa*, visible matter (lit. "form"), (2) *vedanā*, sensation, (3) *saṃjñā*, notion or perception, (4) *saṃskāra*, constituent impulses, (5) *vijñāna*, cognition. None of these Eng. equivalents is very satisfactory. The fifth is frequently rendered with "consciousness."

sphāṭika Crystal.

śramaṇa "Ascetic," specifically a Buddhist monk.

śrāmaṇera A Buddhist novice.

śrāvaka "Auditor," a person already on the way to Buddhist salvation, a salvation to be gained for himself alone by hearing the preachings of a Buddha. Thanks to a false etymology, the Ch. consistently renders this with *sheng wen*, "voice-hearer."

srota'āpanna The occupant of the first stage of the *śrāvaka*, q.v.

stabdha Name of some demoniac being.

stūpa A reliquary for *śarīra*, q.v.

sumanā One variety of the great-flowered common jasmine.

sūtra A recorded sermon of the Buddha; a book containing the same.

sūtradharma The doctrinal content of a *sūtra*; the *sūtra* itself.

tagara The shrub of the East Indian rosebay (*Tabernaemontana coronaria*); a fragrant powder or perfume obtained from it.

tala The palmyra tree, the fan-palm (*Borassus flabelliformis*).

tāla See preceding entry; also used as a measure of height.

tamālapatra, tamālapattra The leaf of the *Garcinia xanthochymus*, a resin-bearing tree related to the gamboge.

tathāgata "He who is thus gone" or "thus come," i.e., the one who has trodden the very same Path as all the other Buddhas to Supreme Enlightenment. Frequent epithet of a Buddha.

trāyastriṃśa Traditionally, this referred to thirty-three gods presided over by Indra. The Buddhists imagined the Kāmadhātu to have six god-worlds, of which this one is the second from the bottom. It lies atop Mount Sumeru and is presided over, in the Buddhist tradition as well, by Indra.

turuṣka Frankincense.

udumbara The cluster-fig tree (*Ficus glomerata*).

upadeśa Discussion, in the form of questions and answers, between the Buddha and his disciples on matters of doctrine.

upāsaka A lay brother, one who binds himself to abstain from five forms of sinful action, viz., (1) taking the life of anything animate, (2) taking anything not freely given by the possessor, (3) speaking untruth, (4) drinking anything alcoholic, and (5) sexual misconduct; and who is worshipful toward the Buddha and his community, providing them always with the necessary food and drink, clothing, shelter, and medicines.

upāsikā The female equivalent of the preceding.

uṣṇīṣa A lump of flesh on the crown of the head of every Buddha.

utpala The blossom of the blue lotus.

vaiḍūrya A cat's-eye gem. The word "beryl" is cognate with this.

vaiśāradya Self-confidence, almost always a quality of a Buddha or bodhisattva.

vaiśravaṇa Name of the protective deity of the northern quarter.

vārṣika The Arabian jasmine.

vetāla A kind of demon, ghost, spirit, goblin, vampire.

vimokṣa Release, salvation, deliverance. There are three, consisting of the intuitive awareness that everything is (1) *śūnya*, "empty," i.e., devoid of own-being; (2) *animitta*, "signless," i.e., devoid of characteristics; (3) *apraṇihita*, "wishless," i.e., not a thing on which to premise any hopes or conclusions.

vivara A high number.

vyākaraṇa An explicit statement, specifically of a Buddha to a bodhisattva, telling him that one day he too will be a Buddha. This includes some indication of the time at which it will happen, his name as a Buddha, the name of his *kṣetra* (q.v.) and of his *kalpa* (q.v.) and the length of the duration of his True Dharma and of his Counterfeit Dharma, i.e., of how long his activity as a Buddha will make itself felt and how long it will merely occasion religious forms devoid of content.

yakṣa A living supernatural being, spiritual apparition, ghost, spirit; name of a class of semidivine beings attendant on Kubera. Though generally regarded as beings of a benevolent and inoffensive disposition, they are occasionally classed with *piśācas* (q.v.) and other malignant spirits, and are sometimes said to cause demoniacal possession.

yakṣakṛtya A *kṛtya* (q.v.) in the form of a *yakṣa* (q.v.).

yojana A unit of distance, supposed to measure several miles.

Notes on the Sanskrit Text

Notes for Chapter One

1. *Candrasūryapradīpas tathāgato 'rhan samyaksaṃbuddho vidyācaraṇasaṃpannaḥ sugato lokavid anuttaraḥ puruṣadamyasārathiḥ śāstā devānāṃ ca manuṣyāṇāṃ ca buddho bhagavān.* The separate epithets are explained in the glossary. Unless otherwise noted, the Skt. quotations are from H. Kern and Bunyiu Nanjio, eds., *Saddharma-puṇḍarīka*, Bibliotheca Buddhica, vol. 10 (St. Petersburg: Académie Impériale des Sciences, 1912), and the translations are made from the same text.

Notes to Chapter Two

1. These two paragraphs of Kumārajīva's version are so different from the Skt. that it behooves us, for comparison, to quote the latter in full:

"And then the Blessed One (*bhagavān*), mindful and conscious, arose from that samādhi. Having arisen, he addressed the long-lived Śāriputra: 'Hard to see, hard to understand is the Buddha-knowledge directly and intuitively perceived by the Thus Gone Ones, the Worthy Ones, the Properly and fully Enlightened Ones, hard to discern for all auditors and individually enlightened ones. For what reason is that? The Thus Gone Ones, the Worthy Ones, the Properly and Fully Enlightened Ones have sat at the feet of many hundreds of thousands of koṭīs of nayutas of Buddhas, Śāriputra; they have fulfilled their obligation with respect to unexcelled proper and complete enlightenment under many hundreds of koṭīs of nayutas of Buddhas, having followed them far, having done deeds of valor, endowed with wonderful and miraculous dharmas, endowed with dharmas hard to discern, accepting dharmas hard to discern.

" 'Hard to discern, Śāriputra, is the intentional speech (*saṃdhābhāṣya*) of the Thus Gone Ones, the Worthy Ones, the Properly and Fully Enlightened Ones. For what reason is that? The self-dependent dharmas they do illustrate by means of divers skills in [the employment of] means—knowledge and insight, demonstration of causes and conditions, enunciation of reasons, and predications—in order, through these several skills in [the employment of] means, to release the beings bogged down in the sundry objects of their respective attachments. They, the preachers of the divers dharmas, are endowed with the wondrous dharmas of the self-confidence born of the power of unattached and impalpable knowledge and insight, born of the power of their unique faculties, of the components of enlightenment, of the release born of meditation, of the attainment to concentration. They have arrived at great wonders and miracles, Śāriputra, the Thus Gone Ones, the Worthy Ones, the Properly and Fully Enlightened Ones. Enough, Śāriputra! Let this statement, at least, stand: the Thus Gone Ones, the Worthy Ones, the Properly and Fully Enlightened Ones, have arrived at the supremely wonderful, Śāriputra. Therefore let it be the Thus Gone One, Śāriputra, who shall teach the Dharma of the Thus Gone One, what dharmas the Thus Gone One knows. All the dharmas, every one of them, Śāriputra, does the Thus Gone One himself teach. All the dharmas, every one of them, Śāriputra, does the Thus Gone One himself know. Which the dharmas are, how the dharmas are, what the dharmas are like, of what appearance the dharmas are, and of what essence the dharmas are: which and how and like what and of what appearance and of what essence the dharmas are, indeed it is the Thus Gone One who is the manifest eyewitness of these dharmas.' "

My guess is that *bhagavant*, by this time, was a pure honorific, for which Kumārajīva substituted another honorific, standing for *lokasaṃmata* (?).

Saṃdhābhāṣya perhaps requires some explanation. Its meaning is this: if, for example, it is understood to both of us, but to us alone, that, whenever I say "black" to you, I mean "white," then "black" is *saṃdhābhāṣya.* When the Buddha had spoken to the earlier schools in terms of *dharma*, they took him at his word, not realizing the intention (*saṃdhā*) of his speech (*bhāṣya*). Such was the standard Mahāyāna position. Here in the *Lotus*, the Buddha seems to be implying that, on the highest level, the Absolute Truth is not in contradiction with the orthodox view of the dharmas or, for that matter, with the data of everyday experience.

2. *Ananyathāvādi jino maharṣī cireṇa pī bhāṣati uttamārthaṃ.*

3. *Amantrayāmī imi sarvaśrāvakān pratyekabodhāya ca ye 'bhiprasthitāḥ.*

4. "Since, O Śāriputra, at the breakup and deterioration of a cosmic age, the many living beings are such, greedy and of scant wholesome roots, then the Thus Gone Ones, the Worthy Ones, the Properly and Fully Enlightened Ones, by resort to skill in means demonstrate that very course of the Buddha, one though it be, as if it were three separate courses."

5. "And then again, O Śāriputra, whatever mendicant monk or mendicant nun experiences the state of a Worthy One without laying a foundation for unexcelled, right, perfect enlightened intuition, saying, 'I am cut off from the course of the Buddhas!' or saying, 'This is the final and complete extinction of this body of mine,' know, Śāriputra, that that person is one of overweening pride. For what reason is that? There is no place, Śāriputra, no room for the possibility that a mendicant monk, a Worthy One [with] his outflows exhausted, having heard this Dharma in the very presence of the Thus Gone One, shall not believe it, unless it happens that the Thus Gone One shall already be completely at peace (*nirvṛta*). For what reason is that? At that time or on that occasion, when

the Thus Gone One is completely at peace, Śāriputra, there shall not be any auditors or bearers and teachers of such scriptures as this one."

6. "Wherever the Self-Originated One stands firm of himself, and whatever has been intuitively perceived by him, of whatever sort and howsoever, / what also are his strengths, his contemplations, his deliverances, and his faculties, in those very things does he confirm the beings as well. //"

7. "The sin of greed would be mine if, having touched upon spotless enlightened intuition, in the inferior course I should establish a single living being: that would be wicked of me."

8. "No greed is to be seen in me anywhere, no envy, nor indeed any lust of mine. / All my dharmas are cut off from sin: therefore am I the Awakened One, by the common acknowledgment of the world. //"

9. "For since I am variously adorned with marks, illuminating this whole world, / placed at their head by many hundreds of living beings, so do I teach this Seal of the own-being of the dharmas. //"

10. "And whosoever honor the relics of the extinguished Victorious Ones / [with] many thousands of reliquaries made of jewels, or of gold and silver, or of crystal; //78// whosoever also make reliquaries of emerald, or of quartz crystal and pearl, whoever they may be, // or [whoever make reliquaries] of the finest cat's-eye gem, or, again, of sapphire, they all have become recipients of enlightened intuition. //79// And whosoever make reliquaries on the crags, or [reliquaries] of sandalwood or aloeswood, whoever they may be, / and whosoever make reliquaries of deodar wood, or of parquetry, whoever they may be; //80// and whoso fashion lovely reliquaries of the Victorious Ones, whether of sand or of earth, / or whoso make even lines of dust, displaying them in forests or caves, //81// making mounds of gravel, for that matter, to represent the reliquaries of the Victorious Ones, whoever they may be, / even children in play here and there, all have become recipients of enlightened intuition. //82// And whosoever fashioned any images whatsoever, made of jewels and representing the forms of the thirty-two marks, / they also became, all of them, recipients of enlightened intuition. //83// Whosoever of the seven jewels, or of copper (*tāmrika*) or of bronze (*kāmṣika*), / made images of the Victorious Ones, they all, whoever they may be, became recipients of enlightened intuition. //84// Whosoever of lead, or of iron (*loha*), or of clay, made images of the Well Gone Ones, / [or] beautiful ones fashioned of plaster, they all became recipients of enlightened intuition. //85 // And whoso on particolored walls make images, full-limbed and marked with hundreds of meritorious marks, / whether these persons draw them themselves or cause another to draw them, all have become recipients of enlightened intuition. //86// And whatever pupils, albeit whiling away their time in play, / with fingernail or with stick of wood fashioned images on the walls, be they men or boys, //87// they, too, all became compassionate and rescued millions of living beings; / impelling many bodhisattvas, they all became recipients

of enlightened intuition. //88// And whoever in relics or in reliquaries of the Thus Gone Ones, or on earthen images of them, / or on inscribed walls or in sand, have given reliquary flowers and perfumes, //89// or whoever have played sounding instruments, whether *bherī*-drums, or conch shells, or pleasant-sounding *paṭaha*-drums, / or who have played *dundubhi*-drums to honor those at the supreme pinnacle of enlightened intuition, //90// or whoever played lutes, or *tāla*-cymbals, or *paṇava*-cymbals, or *mṛdaṅga*-drums, or *vaṃsa*-flutes, or *tuṇava*-flutes, all pleasing to the senses, / they all, whether in the first flush of youth or in youthful maturity, have become recipients of enlightened intuition. //91// And whoever sounded *jhallarīs* [kind of drum or cymbal], or *jalamaṇḍukas*, or *carpaṭakamaṇḍukas*, / in the performance, for the honor of the Well Gone Ones, of song well sung, sweet, and pleasing to the senses, //92// all of them, too, became Buddhas, having done honor to many varieties of relics, / or having sounded over the relics of the Well Gone Ones an instrument however trifling. //93// With so much as a single flower having done honor to images of the Well Gone Ones on an inscribed wall, / or having honored them, albeit with thoughts distracted, they shall in due course see millions of Buddhas. //94// Or whosoever have joined palms at a reliquary, or offered one handful of groats [?] (*paripūrṇa ekā talasaktikā*), / or inclined their heads [assuming *unnāmitaṃ* to signify *onnāmitaṃ*, i.e., *avanāmitam*] for a moment, or bowed down the body but once, //95// or whoever recited 'Homage be to Buddha!' but once by those reliquaries, / even be they distracted in thought and albeit one time only, they have all attained this supreme enlightened intuition. //96// From those Well Gone Ones, be they at that time extinct or still present, / whatever beings have heard but mention of the Dharma, they all became recipients of enlightened intuition. //97//"

It is more likely that *jalamaṇḍuka* refers to the sound made by the splashing of water, while *carpaṭamaṇḍuka* refers to that made by the clapping of hands. As for *talasaktikā*, a variant reading is *talaśaktikā*, which means one hand raised in salutation.

11. "For permanent is this dharma-eye, and the nature of the dharmas ever radiant. Having seen [this eye,] the Buddhas, the Supreme among the Two-Legged Beings, shall set forth my One Vehicle. //"

12. "The stability of the dharmas, and the ever-enduring certainty of the dharmas, this thing unshakable in the world, / this enlightened intuition, shall the Buddhas on a platform of earth demonstrate with their skill in means [?]. //" (*dharmasthitiṃ dharmaniyāmatāṃ ca nityasthitāṃ loki imām akampyām / buddhāś ca bodhiṃ pṛthivīya maṇḍe prakāśayiṣyanti upāyakauśalam //*)

13. "They reveal their skill in means, they make a display of various courses, / and the One Course do the Buddhas illuminate, that supremely quiet Stage. //"

14. ". . . // Difficult of belief will it be this day for those of slight understanding who entertain notions of signs, / affected as they are by overweening

pride and having no knowledge. But these bodhisattvas, on the other hand, *will* listen. //131// Accordingly, with confidence and joy setting aside all clinging, / I speak in the midst of the sons of the Well Gone Ones and endow those very ones with enlightened intuition. //132// When you have seen such Buddha-sons as these, your doubts, too, shall be taken away, / and the twelve hundreds that are [here] shall be without outflows in the world, all of them. //133// As the dharmahood of those former Saviors and of the Victorious Ones to come, / by me also has it [my dharmahood] been freed of discrimination, and just so have I showed it to you. //134//"

Notes to Chapter Three

1. "Then the long-lived Śāriputra, at that time satisfied, enraptured, his mind transported with joy, delighted, and affected with pleasure and gladness (*prītisaumanasyajāta*), bowed with palms joined in the direction of the Blessed One and, facing the Blessed One himself, said to him: 'Affected by wonder and astonishment am I, O Blessed One, affected by excess of joy, having heard words such as this in the presence of the Blessed One. For what reason is that? Never having heard, O Blessed One, such a Dharma as this in the presence of the Blessed One, but having seen other bodhisattvas and having heard the Buddha-names that those bodhisattvas shall have in time to come, I was exceedingly grieved, in exceeding pain, thinking, "I have fallen away from the field of this knowledge of the Thus Gone One, from knowledge and insight!" Now, O Blessed One, whenever I go to mountains, hills, and valleys, or to forests and thickets, or to pleasure groves, to rivers, or to the foot of trees, remote places all, there to spend the day, then, too, O Blessed One, do I behave in the manner just indicated. [I kick myself for having missed the Message.] Though the entry into the Dharma-realm is the same, we have been conveyed by the Blessed One on a deficient vehicle. Then, O Blessed One, the following occurs to me: It is we who are to blame for this, not the Blessed One. For what reason is that? If we had given the Blessed One due attention when he pronounced the most excellent Dharma-doctrine, namely, when he had recourse to unexcelled and proper enlightened intuition, then, O Blessed One, we should have been conveyed to those dharmas. But, O Blessed One, as soon as the Dharma doctrine of the Thus Gone One had been spoken, no bodhisattvas being near at hand, it was heard by us, and, having heard it, we immediately took it up, bore it, realized it, considered it, and took it to heart, ignorant of the intentional speech of the Blessed One and consumed by haste; for this reason, O Blessed One, I have been spending my days and nights for the most part in self-reproach. But today, O Blessed One, I have attained extinction (*nirvāṇaprāptaḥ*)! I am perfectly at peace (*parinirvṛtaḥ*)! Today, O Blessed One, my arhattva has been reached! Today, O Blessed One, I am the eldest son of the Blessed One, his own, born of his mouth,

born of the Dharma, made of the Dharma, heir to the Dharma, sprung from the Dharma! Free of anguish am I this day, O Blessed One, having heard such a wonderful Dharma as this, a sound never before heard in the presence of the Blessed One."

2. "I have no further questions, for I am matured in the Supreme Course."

3. "Completely letting go the products of arbitrary views, and touching upon empty dharmas, / I then perceive, 'I am at peace!', and that this former was not to be called 'extinction.' // In other words, it is only when I have achieved freedom from all views whatever, when I realize that the much-touted dharmas are themselves devoid of reality, that is, when I am a Buddha, that I understand that this alone is *nirvāṇa*, and that *arhattva* is illusory.

4. "But when he becomes a Buddha, a Supreme Being, placed at their head by men, maruts [storm gods], yakṣas, and rākṣasas, / then and there he gains peace, bearing all thirty-two marks without exception. //"

5. "But when—by resort to causes, and reasons, and parables—demonstrated/and well established is that choice enlightened intuition of the Buddhas, then I am free of doubt, having heard the Dharma. //"

6. "And those bodhisattvas shall be beings whose deeds have no beginning, whose wholesome roots shall have been long planted, who shall have practiced asceticism under the tutelage of many hundreds of thousands of Buddhas, who shall have been praised by the Thus Gone Ones; [beings] intent on Buddha-knowledge, born of service to the great forms of superknowledge, skilled in the practices of all the dharmas, gentle, and mindful. For the most part, Śāriputra, such are the bodhisattvas of whom that Buddha-field shall be full."

7. "And that man goes out of that house."

8. "And to those children would belong many playthings, varied, pleasing, desirable, lovely, dear, appealing to the senses, and they would be hard to obtain."

9. "Then, Śāriputra, this man gives to his sons, to every child, ox-drawn carriages having the speed of the wind; made of the seven jewels; having benches; hung with nets having small bells; high and prominent; adorned with wonderful and marvelous jewels; beautified with jeweled cords; decorated with flower garlands; strewn with cotton and wool; spread over with woven calico; [furnished with] red cushions on both sides; yoked to white, gleaming, swift oxen; attended by many men; and hung with banners: ox-drawn carriages possessing the might and speed of the wind, of one color and one type."

10. "This having been said, the Blessed One said to the long-lived Śāriputra: 'Good, good, Śāriputra! It is just as you say. Just so, Śāriputra, is the Thus Gone One, the Worthy One, the Properly and Fully Enlightened One, released from all fears, freed altogether, by all means and in all ways from the covering film and from all the bonds of all calamities, weariness, troubles, woes, ill dis-

positions (*daurmanasya*), darkness, gloom, and obscurity. The Thus Gone One is the Father of the world, endowed with such unique Buddhadharmas as knowledge, strength, and self-confidence; most strong with the strength of magic; having attained the supreme perfection of great devices and knowledge; greatly compassionate; of untiring mind; seeking the good of others, and sympathizing with them. He emerges in the triple sphere, which is like a shelter or abode with an old roof aflame with the great mass of woes and ill dispositions, for the purpose of releasing from lust, hatred, and delusion and establishing in unexcelled, right, and perfect enlightened intuition the beings, [who are] confined within the film and bonds of birth, old age, sickness, death, pain, grief, woe, ill disposition, weariness, ignorance, darkness, gloom, and obscurity. Having emerged, he serenely sees the beings burning, cooking, roasting, and baking in birth, old age, sickness, death, pain, grief, woe, ill disposition, and weariness; for it is because of acquisition and by reason of desire that they experience many kinds of woe. It is because of greed and acquisition in this life that, after passage into the next, they experience the many kinds of woes of hell, beasts, and the world of Yama; that directly they experience poverty as gods or men, union with the unwanted, and woes such as separation from the wanted. And, remaining in that very mass of woes, they play, enjoy themselves, and amuse themselves, and are not afraid, nor alarmed, nor do they feel terror, nor are they aware, nor do they think, nor are they anxious, nor do they seek an escape. On the contrary, in that some triple sphere, similar though it is to a burning house, they amuse themselves, and run about hither and yon. And, smitten though they are by this great mass of woe, they have no notion of a perception of woe.' "

11. "And in this way, O gentle beings, do I instill a keen desire for the carriages, noble, praised by the noble, and endowed with very pleasant features: 'Without stint, good sirs, shall you play with these, enjoy them, make use of them, experience great pleasure by virtue of your faculties, strengths, contemplations, deliverances, attainments of concentration, and be endowed with great joy and good disposition.' "

12. "He tells them of the house's faults: 'This woe, O gentle children of good family, is a terrible one. / For there are sundry beings and this fire, a great series of woe. //65// Yakṣas of strong poison and of most frightening thought, kumbhāṇḍas, and many ghosts of the departed dwell herein, / as well as *bheruṇdakas*, packs of dogs and jackals, and vultures, all hunting prey //66// So many are they that dwell herein, even without the fire a most frightening thing! / Such is this woe in and of itself, and now from all sides burns this fire!' //67//"

13. "I apply my skill in means and tell them of three courses, / for, knowing the many faults in the three spheres, I pronounce a device for their escape. //89// And, whatever sons, relying on me, have great mastery over the six kinds of superknowledge and the threefold skills, / also whatever individually enlightened ones there may be, also what bodhisattvas may be here who do not

backslide, //90// to all those sons equally at that moment, by resort to this choice parable, O wise one, / do I pronounce this Buddha-course: 'Seize it! You shall all be Victorious Ones.' //91//"

14. "Strengths, contemplations, as well as deliverances and many hundreds of koṭis of concentrations: / such is this choicest chariot in which the sons of the Buddha ever take pleasure. //93// Playing with it, they while away nights and days, half-months and seasons, months/and years; they while away an intermediate kalpa or thousands of koṭis of kalpas. //94// This is the chariot made of jewels wherein, to the site of enlightened intuition, go/the many bodhisattvas at play and those auditors who listen to the Well Gone One. //95//"

15. "And whatever bodhisattvas are here, all of them hear of my Buddha-eye; / this is the skill in means of the Victorious One, whereby he guides many bodhisattvas. //"

16. "Whence, O son of Śāri, are they delivered? From grasping at the unreal are they delivered. / Yet for all that they are not wholly delivered, and the Leader here declares them to be not at peace. //103// For what reason do I not speak of their deliverance, of this unattainable, supreme peak of enlightened intuition?/ [Because] this is my wish: I am the Dharma King, born into this world for the purpose of leading them to happiness." //104//

17. "For the weal of the world with its gods, teach it in the primary and intermediate quarters!"

18. "You are not to tell this to stubborn men, nor to proud ones, nor to those attached to the notion of 'I.' / For fools, ever drunk with their desires and ignorant, would reject the spoken Dharma. //111// For rejecting my skill in means, which is my Buddha-eye standing ever secure in the world, / for knitting their brows and rejecting my course, hear forthwith what shall be their retribution! //112//"

19. "He to whom they render a service will wish to give them nothing,/ and whatever is given vanishes immediately: such is the fruit of their sin. //"

20. The Skt. has nothing to correspond to this quatrain.

21. "And whatever medicinal herb they may take, well formed and given by skillful men, / by it, too, their disease is aggravated, and that illness never comes to an end. //"

22. "By others are thefts perpetrated on them, and tumult, riot, and discord. / Also, their things are taken from them by others, and evildoers pounce upon them besides. //"

23. "Also, attaining to human existence, he arrives at blindness, deafness, and stupidity. / He becomes a poor servant. Such [being the case] at that time, [these attributes] are ever [his] ornaments. //132// Diseases become his apparel, as do the millions of millions of millions of wounds on his body, / also the mange, the itch, the *pāman* [kind of skin disease], leprosy, white leprosy, and raw stench. //133// And the view of a substantial body becomes his wealth, and the power of

anger arises within him. / Also, lust forms within him fiercely, and he ever disports himself in the wombs of beasts. //134//"

24. "A full kalpa, Śāriputra, could I tell of the thousands of koṭis of shapes/ of those who have set out for the supreme peak of enlightened intuition. At the head of them you might preach this scripture. //"

Notes to Chapter Four

1. "O Blessed One, we made no efforts toward unexcelled, proper, enlightened intuition, we were powerless to achieve it, we were without energy sufficient to undertake it, telling ourselves that we were old; advanced in age; senior, honored elders in the community of mendicant monks; well stricken in years; and [moreover, that we had already] attained to extinction. Even when the Blessed One taught the Dharma—when the Blessed One was long seated, and when we were present at that Dharma teaching—even then, O Blessed One, since we were long seated, long in the presence of the Blessed One, our primary and secondary members ached, our primary and secondary joints were in pain; and thus, O Blessed One, when the Blessed One was teaching the Dharma, we [failed] totally to become aware of emptiness, signlessness, and wishlessness. There was produced in us no desire for these Buddhadharmas, manifestations of Buddha-fields, sport of bodhisattvas, or sport of Thus Gone Ones. For what reason was that? Because, O Blessed One, we [felt we] had escaped from this triple sphere and [because we] had notions of extinction; also because we are advanced in age. Therefore, O Blessed One, even when other bodhisattvas were taught and instructed by us in unexcelled proper enlightened intuition, there was not produced in us, O Blessed One, a single thought of desire. O Blessed One, having heard here, in the presence of the Blessed One, that there is a prophecy of unexcelled, proper, enlightened intuition even for auditors, we have found a wonder, a marvel, we have obtained a great gain. O Blessed One, this day, having heard all at once this speech of the Thus Gone One, never heard by us before, we have gained a great jewel as well. O Blessed One, we have gained an immeasurable jewel. O Blessed One, we have gained such a great jewel as this, one not striven after by us, nor sought for, nor thought of, nor desired. We understand perfectly, O Blessed One, we understand perfectly, O Well Gone One! For it is as if, O Blessed One, a certain man left his father's presence. Leaving, he went to a different community. He there dwelt as an exile for many years, twenty, or thirty, or forty, or fifty. Then, O Blessed One, [the father] became a great man, while [the son] was poor. And he, in quest of a livelihood and for the sake of food and clothing going in all directions and intermediate directions, went to yet another community. And his father went to a different settlement yet. He became a man of much grain, money, gold, treasure, and storehouses. He became the owner of much gold and silver, gems and pearls, cat's-eye and conch shells, crystal [*śilā*] and corals, gold and silver.

He became the master of many bondmen and bondwomen, servants and menials. He became the owner of many elephants, horses, carriages, cattle, and sheep. He was a rich man even for a large community. [?] (*mahājanapadeṣu ca dhanikaḥ syāt* /) He became a man rich in actions and undertakings, in agriculture and commerce."

2. "And then that householder left his house, put off his necklaces, put off his fine garments, covered himself with clean, yet coarse and dark garments, took a basket in his right hand, and covered his limbs with dust; then he approached the place where that poor man was, addressing him from a distance. Approaching, he said, 'Sirs, take the baskets and gather dirt! Do not stand about.' By this device he could talk to his son. He said to him, 'Sir workman, do your work only here. You are not to go elsewhere any more. I will give you a special wage. Whatever your payment is to be, you may ask for it unconcerned, be it a basin, or a water-pot, or a lamp-pot, or a staff, or salt, or food, or clothing. Sir, I have a tattered garment. If that is to be your payment, ask for it, and I will give it to you. Whichever useful thing of this kind your pay is to be, I will give it to you. Be at ease, sir! You are to think of me as a father. For what reason is this? I am old, and you are young. You have done much work for me, sweeping out this privy. Nor have you ever been while working here, nor are you now, guilty of wickedness, crookedness, falsehood, pride, or hypocrisy. Never in any way have I noticed the least misdeed on your part, though these faults are indeed evident in the other men who work here. As my own son would be to me, so are you to be from this day forward.' And then, O Blessed One, that householder gave that poor man the name of 'son.' And that poor man, when in that householder's presence, thought of him as a father. In that way, O Blessed One, that householder, delighted with the love of a son, had his son cleaning latrines for twenty years. Then, after the passage of twenty years, that poor man was at ease in that householder's home, both in coming and in going; but he continued to make his home in the same straw hut."

3. "In just this way, O Blessed One, we are like the Thus Gone One's sons. And the Thus Gone One says to us, 'You are my sons,' just as did that householder. And we, O Blessed One, were sore pressed by the three kinds of woe. By which three? Namely, by the woe of suffering itself, by the woe intrinsic to anything conditioned, and by the woe implicit in vicissitude. And in the round of transmigration we were inclined toward the inferior. Therefore the Blessed One made us think on many lowly dharmas similar to latrines. And we were attached to them, were busy with them, were contending about them. And we were seeking nirvāṇa also, O Blessed One, as if desiring a day's wages. And we were satisfied, O Blessed One, once that nirvāṇa had been attained. And we thought we had gained much in the presence of the Thus Gone One, being attached to, being busy with, and contending about these dharmas. And the Thus Gone One understood our inclination toward the inferior; hence the

Blessed One was tolerant of us, did not chastise us, nor did he tell us, 'The treasure house of knowledge that is the Thus Gone One's shall be yours, too.' On the contrary, the Blessed One by his skill in means established us as heirs to this treasure house of knowledge of the Thus Gone One. And we were without desire, O Blessed One. From this very fact we now know how great a kindness was being done us, as if we were getting nirvāṇa in payment for a single day's work. Here we were, O Blessed One, taking the knowledge and insight of the Thus Gone One and conferring this noble teaching on the bodhisattvas, those great beings! We were revealing, showing, demonstrating the gnosis of the Thus Gone One. And yet, O Blessed One, we were without desire and quite even-tempered! For what reason is that? Through his skill in means the Thus Gone One understood our inclinations perfectly. We, for our own part, however, did not know, had not understood what had, in fact, already been told us by the Blessed One, namely, that we are real sons of the Blessed One, that he was designating us heirs to the gnosis of the Thus Gone One. Why is this? Because, true sons of the Thus Gone One though we were, even so we were inclined toward the inferior. The Blessed One would utter bodhisattva sounds to us when he observed that the strength of our religious inclinations had matured. We have thus been assigned two roles by the Blessed One. In the first instance we were declared to be of inferior inclinations vis-à-vis the bodhisattvas, while the noble, superior enlightened intuition of the Buddha was assigned to them. In the second instance, which is now, the Blessed One, aware of the full force of our religious inclinations, has made this declaration to us. For this reason, O Blessed One, we now say this: 'Suddenly, quite suddenly, though not expecting it, we have received the jewel of omniscience, unhoped for, unsought, unwished for, unthought of, and unsolicited, like the sons of the Thus Come One that we are.'"

4. "The man reached him and stood by him. Some were counting grain and gold, / while some were writing documents and conducting business. //"

5. "Coming down, taking a basket, and putting on dirty clothes, / he came into the presence of that man, scolding him: 'You men are not doing your work! //25// Yet I give you a double wage, double foot ointment and more; I give you salted food, I give you even vegetables and cloth!' //26// In this way he scolded him at this time, but yet again, as he was wise, he soothed him: 'You do your work here well. Clearly, you are my son, of that there is no doubt!' //27//"

6. "And, knowing that this son of his was now of a noble disposition, inviting his friends and acquaintances, he [said] 'I give all my affairs in charge!' //31// And gathering townsmen and city-dwellers, as well as many merchants, he spoke thus in the midst of the assembly: 'This is my long-lost son!'"

7. Throughout this poetic section, the Chinese is so much at variance with the Sanskrit that it is virtually impossible to ascertain the meaning of an obscure passage in the one by resort to the other.

8. This involves a play on the word *śrāvaka*. The word-game is doubly obscured, however, in that (1) it is an attempt to manipulate Sanskrit in Chinese and (2) the Chinese is here being reproduced in English. *Śrāvaka* is a *vṛddhi*-derivative of the root *śru-* ("to hear," a word cognate with the Sanskrit), to which the suffix *-ka* has been appended. What the present verse is attempting is an etymology of *śrāvaka* through *śrāvayati*, the causative of the same verb. In other words, the verse is trying to make *śrāvaka* mean two things at the same time, viz., "one who hears" and "one who enables others to hear."

9. "They are characterized by great spirit, by immeasurable capacity, and by great supernatural power, and dwell firmly in the might of forbearance; / the Buddhas, the Great Kings, the Victorious Ones without outflows, bear such powers as these. //59// In constant conformity, he speaks the Dharma to those who follow appearances, / He the Lord of the Dharma, the Lord in all the world, the Great Lord, the Chief Guide of the world. //60// The proper course of conduct he demonstrates in many ways to the beings, wisely understanding their respective states, / and, seeing their several inclinations, by invoking thousands of causes he speaks the Dharma to them. //61// The Thus Gone One, wisely understanding the conduct of all living beings and of men, / in many ways speaks the Dharma, demonstrating this supreme enlightened intuition. //62//"

Notes to Chapter Five

1. "One who has attained to mastery over the meanings of all dharmas, one who has attained to the abodes of all dharmas, one who has attained to the supreme perfection of knowledge of the skill of ascertaining all dharmas, a demonstrator of all-knowing knowledge, one who makes his appearance in all-knowing knowledge, one who deposits all-knowing knowledge [in his memory?], O Kāśyapa, is the Thus Gone One, the Worthy One, the Properly and Fully Enlightened One."

2. "Just as, O Kāśyapa, the great cloud, covering the whole thousand-millionfold world, releases the same water, and delights all the grasses, shrubs, herbs, and great trees with the water, and just as those grasses, shrubs, herbs, and great trees drink in the water, each in accord with its strength, its abode, and its station, and attain their divers natural sizes, just so, Kāśyapa, is that whole Dharma which the Thus Gone One, the Worthy One, the Properly and Fully Enlightened One, preaches of one flavor, namely, the flavor of deliverance, the flavor of disenchantment, the flavor of suppression, leading to the knowledge of the All-Knowing One. At that, Kāśyapa, those beings who hear the Thus Gone One preaching the Dharma, who keep it, who apply themselves to it, do not of themselves know themselves, nor do they feel themselves, nor are they aware of themselves. For what reason is that? It is the Thus Gone One, O

Kāśyapa, who knows those beings: who they are, and how they are, and of what kind they are; and whom they think of, and how they think, and by what means they think; and what degree [of power in meditational vision] they realize, and how they realize it, and by what means they realize it; and what degree [of power at conversion] they attain, and how they attain it, and by what means they attain it. It is the Thus Gone One, O Kāśyapa, who bears eyewitness, direct eyewitness, to those things. And, as I am the viewer of those beings, standing on their respective grounds, of the grasses, shrubs, herbs, and great trees, whether lowly, exalted, or intermediate, I, O Kāśyapa, seeing a Dharma of one flavor—to wit, the flavor of deliverance, the flavor of disenchantment, leading to extinction, eternally disenchanted, on one ground, gone into space [reading *ākāśagatam* for °*gatim*]—and keeping to the preferences of the beings, do not immediately proclaim to them the knowledge of the All-Knowing One. Struck by wonder, struck by marvel, are you all, O Kāśyapa, in that you are unable to understand the intentional speech of the Thus Gone One. For what reason is that? Because the intentional speech of the Thus Gone Ones, the Worthy Ones, the Properly and Fully Enlightened Ones, Kāśyapa, is difficult to understand."

3. "And having emerged, the Leader of the World speaks, and demonstrates the real course of conduct to living beings."

4. "They who go about in wise understanding of the Dharma without outflows and who have attained extinction, / and who realize the six sorts of superknowledge and the three kinds of wisdom, are called the minor herbs. //29// And they who go about on mountains and in the valleys and who desire individual enlightened intuition, who are intermediate in pure understanding of this sort, are called intermediate herbs. //30//"

Notes to Chapter Six

1. *Tasyāṃ ca velāyāṃ pṛthak pṛthaṅ manaḥsaṃgītyā imā gāthā abhāṣanta* "and at that time, separately yet in a chorus of minds, spoke these verses."

2. I am not certain of this, and the Skt. is so different as to be of no help: *avaśyam avasāraṃ jñātva asmākaṃ pi narottama / amṛteneva siñcitvā vyākuruṣva vibhojana* //"Knowing without fail that we, too, are a proper receptacle for it, O Supreme among Men, / sprinkle us with nectar and confer a prophecy upon us, O Distributor of Nourishment. //" (?)

3. "Many shall be the bodhisattvas, turners of the irreversible wheel, / of sharp faculties, who under the tutelage of that Victorious One shall purify that Buddha-field. //21// Many shall be his auditors—there shall be no number of them, nor shall there ever be a measure of them; / and they shall possess the six sorts of superknowledge, the three skills, great magical power, and be firmly

set in the eight deliverances. //22// And inconceivable shall be the magical power of him who clarifies this supreme enlightened intuition. / Gods and men like to Ganges' sands shall ever face him with palms joined. //23//"

4. "And he shall make reliquaries to those Thus Gone Ones who are completely at peace, a thousand yojanas in height, fifty yojanas in circumference, fashioned of the seven jewels, to wit, gold, silver, beryl, crystal, carnelian [?] (*lohitamukti*), emerald, and the seventh one, namely, coral. And he shall make offerings to those reliquaries, offerings of flowers, perfumes, scents, garlands, pastes, powders, garments, parasols, flags, standards, and banners."

5. *Jāmbunadābhāsu sa cāpi nāmnā saṃtārako devamanuṣyakoṭinām*, "the savior of millions of gods and men."

Notes to Chapter Seven

1. "And then, O mendicant monks, those sixteen princes, youths that they were, having praised to his face with these beautiful verses the Blessed Mahābhijñājñānābhibhū [Master of the Gnosis (called) Great Superknowledge] the Thus Gone One, the Worthy One, the Properly and Fully Enlightened One, entreated that Blessed One to turn the Dharma-wheel: 'May the Blessed One teach the Dharma! May the Well Gone One teach the Dharma for the weal of many men, for the happiness of many men, out of compassion for the world, for the sake of the great body of men, for the weal, for the happiness of gods and humans!'"

2. "What full twenty-five thousands of millions of worlds exist elsewhere, / whence we have come hither to greet the Victorious One, altogether forsaking the choicest of palaces, //22// by former deeds done in those very worlds are these flying chariots variously adorned. Accepting them out of favor to us, may He Who Knows the World enjoy them as he sees fit! //23//"

3. "And then, O mendicant monks, the great Brahmās, having praised the blessed Mahābhijñājñānābhibhū, the Thus Gone One, the Worthy One, the Properly and Fully Enlightened One, to his very face with this beautiful verse, said to that Blessed One: 'Let the Blessed One turn the Dharma-wheel! Let the Well Gone One turn the Dharma-wheel in the world! Let the Blessed One reveal his Blessed Peace! Let the Blessed One convey the beings to salvation! Let the Blessed One show a kindly disposition to this world! Let the Blessed One, the Lord of the Dharma, reveal the Dharma to the world with its Māras and its Brahmās, to the population with its multitude of ascetics and Brahmans, of gods, men, and titans! That shall be for the benefit of many men, for the weal of many men, out of compassion for the world, for the benefit of the body of men, for the weal of both gods and men!'

"Then indeed, O mendicant monks, those fifty hundreds of thousands of nayutas of Brahmās with one voice and in concert addressed that Blessed One with these beautiful verses:

Reveal the Dharma, O Blessed One! Reveal it, O Supreme among Two-Legged Beings! /
And reveal the power of good will! Save the woe-beset beings! //24//

Hard to obtain is the Light of the World as if it were the *udumbara* flower. /
You have arisen, O Great Hero! We seek the Thus Gone One. //25//

"And then, O mendicant monks, that Blessed One assented in silence to the great Brahmās.

"Moreover, at that very time, O mendicant monks, in the southeast quarter, what Brahmā palaces there were in fifty hundreds of thousands of millions of nayutas of worlds, they all sparkled, glowed, shone gloriously and splendidly. And then, O mendicant monks, this occurred to those Brahmās: 'Now these Brahmā palaces are, indeed, sparkling, glowing, shining gloriously and splendidly. Now of what can this be a sign?' And then, O mendicant monks, in those fifty hundreds of thousands of millions of nayutas of worlds, what great Brahmās there were, they all went to one another's homes and talked. Then indeed, O mendicant monks, a great Brahmā named Adhimātrakāruṇika addressed that great Brahmā multitude with these verses."

4. "And then, O mendicant monks, those great Brahmās, having praised that Blessed Mahābhijñājñānābhibhū the Thus Gone One, the Worthy One, the Properly and Fully Enlightened One, to his face with these beautiful verses, said to that Blessed One: 'May the Blessed One turn the Dharma-wheel! May the Well Gone One turn the Dharma-wheel in the world! May the Blessed One teach us his Peace! May the Blessed One ferry the beings to salvation! May the Blessed One favor this world! May the Blessed One teach the Dharma to this world with its Māras and its Brahmās, to the creatures with their ascetics and their Brahmās, with their gods and men! That shall be for the weal of many men, for the happiness of many men, out of compassion for the world, for the sake of the great body of men, for the weal, for the happiness of gods and humans.' Then indeed, O mendicant monks, those fifty koṭīs of nayutas of hundreds of thousands of Brahmās with a single voice addressed that Blessed One in these two verses."

5. "And then, O mendicant monks, that Blessed One assented to those great Brahmās as well in silence. Again, indeed, at that time, O mendicant monks, what Brahmā-palaces there were in those fifty koṭīs of nayutas of hundreds of thousands of world-spheres in the eastern quarter, they gleamed, glowed, and shone most gloriously and splendidly. Then indeed, O mendicant monks, this occurred to those great Brahmās: 'These Brahmā-palaces, indeed, gleam, glow, and shine most gloriously and splendidly. What appropriate prior cause can there be?' And then, O mendicant monks, what great Brahmās there were in those fifty koṭīs of nayutas of hundreds of thousands of world-spheres, all of

them, going to one another's homes, addressed one another. And then, O mendicant monks, a great Brahmā named Sudharma addressed that great multitude of Brahmās in a pair of verses.' "

6. "It is through a teaching and with a foundation [of bodhisattvahood] that you have attained unexcelled Buddha-knowledge."

7. "At that time indeed, O mendicant monks, seeing that those young princes had wandered forth and turned into novices, as great as was the retinue of that wheel-turning king, one-half of it wandered forth, eighty koṭīs of nayutas of hundreds of thousands of living beings."

8. Sarvalokadhātūpadravodvegapratyuttīrṇa, "saved from the calamities and agitations of all the worlds."

9. Going back to a presumable *megheśvara*, where our Skt. has *meghasvaradīpa*, "Lamp of Cloud Sounds," or "He Whose Lamp is Full of the Sounds of Clouds"; and *megheśvararāja*, where our Skt. has *meghasvararāja*, "King of Cloud Sounds." In both cases, "cloud sounds" presumably refers to auspicious thunder, while a "thunder-lamp" would presumably be lighting.

10. "Who, O mendicant monks, are the beings who by me as a bodhisattva under the tutelage of that Blessed One—beings numbering in the hundreds of thousands of nayutas of koṭīs, like to immeasurable, innumerable sands of Ganges rivers—were made to hear the Dharma of omniscience? You, O mendicant monks, were those beings at that time and on that occasion."

11. "And in the upper air drums resounded to do honor to that Victorious One, / well afflicted [*sic*] also by the Victorious One, who by enlightened intuition of long standing had attained to the unexcelled stage." The conundrum is *suduḥkhitā*, "well afflicted," probably a copyist's error, perhaps for *sukhitā*, "blessed." The Chinese version clearly bears this second ardhaśloka no resemblance whatsoever.

12. " 'It is in this place alone in the wide world of the ten directions that you have made your appearance, O Great Leader!' say the Brahmā gods, shaking their chariots in order to produce appropriate signs in the living beings. //66// In the eastern quarter fifty thousand koṭīs of fields trembled, / and there, too, the Brahmā chariots that were chief were exceedingly brilliant. //67// " But of verse 66 I am far from certain. The Chinese, free as it is, appears after all to be saying the same thing as the Sanskrit.

13. "The One of Vision speaks of the woe whose latter end is death, putting nescience at its beginning: / 'All these faults issue from birth. Understand this thing known as human death.' //"

14. "There was yet another, a second moment for that Victorious One preaching many dharmas, / when purified beings, as numerous as Ganges' sands, became auditors in a moment. //"

15. "And that Victorious One spoke this *sūtra* and, entering this cell, contemplated/full eighty-four kalpas in a composed sitting posture, the Leader

of the World. //" This is based on the assumption that *vilakṣayīta* is a misprint for *vilakṣayati*, for the former I cannot construe.

16. "Each of them, designating his seat apart from the others, spoke that *sūtra* to them. / Under the tutelage of that Well Gone One, they established this authority of mine, just as it is now. //"

17. "They then caused to hear persons as innumerable as the sands of sixty thousand Ganges rivers, / for each son of that Well Gone One guided beings not few in number. //"

18. "When that Victorious One was at peace, they, by practicing, saw koṭīs of Buddhas; / then, together with the latter, who had been caused to hear, they did honor to the Supreme Ones among the Two-Legged Beings, //87// and, performing broad and distinguished practice, they were awakened to enlightened intuition in the ten directions, / and those sixteen sons of that Victorious One are themselves Victorious Ones, [standing] two by two at all [compass] points. //88//"

19. "Then he, being both wise and skilled, thinks up a device to lead them on, saying to himself, / 'How sad if, deprived of their jewels, these foolish children should all fall away by turning themselves back!' //"

20. "In this very way, O mendicant monks, I am the Guide, or the Leader, of thousands of koṭīs of living beings. / In the same way I see living beings sore tormented, unable to break through the shell of the defilements. //103// Thereupon I think of this matter: 'These persons are at peace, they are satisfied. This is the suppression of all woe. At the arhant stage you did what had to be done.' //104//"

Notes to Chapter Eight

1. " 'What can we then do, O Blessed One? It is the Thus Gone One who knows where we are based, as well as our former religious practices.' Bowing to the Blessed One's feet, he stood to one side, doing obeisance to the Blessed One and gazing at him with unblinking eyes."

2. "O mendicant monks, apart from the Thus Gone One, there is none other able to outdo Pūrṇa, the son of Maitrāyaṇī, in respect of either sense or expression."

3. "For what reason is that? O mendicant monks, with my superhuman memory I recall that in time past, ninety-nine Buddha-koṭis ago, [the Dharma] was comprehended by that very person under the tutelage of those blessed Buddhas. Just as [he is] here, in my presence, so everywhere was he the chief of the Dharma-narrators, everywhere the one who trod the course leading to Emptiness, everywhere the possessor of analytical faculties, and everywhere the one who trod the path to the bodhisattva's superknowledge. He was also a most certain demonstrator of Dharma, an undoubting demonstrator of Dharma, a

pure demonstrator of Dharma, and under the tutelage of those blessed Buddhas he cultivated chaste conduct."

4. "And everywhere he stood by the living beings with the performance of Buddha-deeds. And everywhere he purified his own Buddha-field. And everywhere he was committed to the maturation of the living beings."

5. "What assemblage of Buddhas there shall also be at that time, O mendicant monks, in this kalpa Goodly numbering a thousand less four, under their tutelage, as well, this very Pūrṇa, the son of Maitrāyaṇī, shall be the chief of the Dharma-narrators, as well as one who comprehends the True Dharma. In this way, in time to come, he shall support the True Dharma of immeasurable, innumerable blessed Buddhas; shall work the weal of immeasurable, innumerable living beings; and shall mature immeasurable, innumerable living beings in unexcelled, right, perfect, enlightened intuition."

6. "Hear, O mendicant monks, this message of mine, how practice was cultivated by my son / and how this bodhi-practice was performed by one learned in skill-in-means. //"

7. "And they act as if unknowing, as much as to say, 'Truly we are auditors, men of negligible practice!' Disgusted with all birth and death, they purify each his own field. //5// They make a show of lust on their own part, of hatred, and of delusion, / and seeing others bogged down in their own views, they go along with their views as well. //6// Acting in this way, my many auditors deliver the beings by resort to skillful devices. / [For, if not], ignorant men would proceed to go mad; [otherwise, the bodhisattva] would explain his whole conduct [to them]. //7//"

8. ". . . and comprehend their True Dharma, seeking this Buddha-knowledge."

9. "Having trodden the course with respect to the great sorts of super-knowledge, he was also a possessor of the analytical faculties, / and, knowing the purview of the faculties of the beings, he constantly taught a pure Dharma. // And, setting forth the most excellent True Dharma, he matured thousands of koṭis of beings, / purifying his own most excellent field here in the supreme, unexcelled course. //"

10. ". . . and the kalpa shall be Jewel-Glow, and the world shall be Right Pure. //"

11. "And all beings in that Buddha-field shall be pure and chaste, / all born spontaneously, of golden hue, and of physical form marked with the thirty-two marks. //"

12. "There, Kāśyapa, Kauṇḍinya the mendicant monk, the great auditor, shall, after sixty-two koṭis of nayutas of hundreds of thousands of Buddhas, be a Thus Come One . . . named Samantaprabha. . . . There, Kāśyapa, shall be five hundred Thus Come Ones of that same name. Thereafter five hundred great auditors shall all directly experience unexcelled . . . intuition,

namely, five hundred self-controlled ones, headed by Gayākāśyapa . . . and Svāgata."

13. "This auditor of mine, of the Kauṇḍinya clan, shall be a Thus Gone One, a Leader of the World. /
In time to come, in a limitless kalpa, he shall guide thousands of *koṭis* of living beings. //21//

He shall be a Victorious One, Samantaprabha by name, and his field shall be purified, /
For he shall have seen, in time yet to come, many limitless Buddhas in a limitless kalpa. //22//

Prabhāsvara, endowed with Buddha-might, much bruited about in the ten directions, /
And honored by thousands of koṭis of living beings, shall teach supreme, excellent, enlightened intuition. //23//

Thereupon bodhisattvas, intent in appearance and mounting the choicest of airborne chariots, /
Traveling there, shall think thereon, ever of pure moral conduct and excellent deportment. //24//

Hearing the Dharma of the Supreme among Two-Legged Beings, to other fields also shall they ever /
Go, those worshipers of a thousand Buddhas, and do them, too, extended honor. //25//

And in a moment they shall come back then to the field of this Guide, /
For such shall be the power of the conduct of the Supreme of Men, Prabhāsa by name. //26//

Full sixty thousand kalpas shall be the life-span of that Well Gone One, /
Then twice as long shall last the Dharma of that Tāyin [Savior] when he is perfectly at peace. //27//

And the Counterfeit Image [of the Dharma] shall last for a time thrice that, /
Then men and gods shall be woebegone after the decline of the True Dharma of that Tāyin. //28//

Of those Victorious Ones, identically named Samantaprabha, Supreme among Men, /
Of those Leaders, these shall be the five hundreds in order of sequence. //29//

And such shall be the array of them all, and their supernatural power, also their Buddha-fields, /

And such also shall be their number and their True Dharma, and the duration of their True Dharma shall be the same. //30//

And such shall be the name of them all at that time in the world with its gods, /
As I have previously said, to wit, Samantaprabhāsa Supreme among Men. //31//

In sequence, in this way, shall each, in his benevolent mercy, prophesy to the next, /
And this shall happen today, in immediate succession to me [?] (*anantarāyaṃ*), just as I, too, teach the whole world. //32//

So bear them in mind today [?], Kāśyapa, these five hundred, /
And whatever other self-controlled auditors there may be of mine, and tell of them to other auditors as well. //33//"

14. "It is as if there were a certain man who had entered his friend's mansion, / while his friend, a rich and propertied man, gave him much food, //36// then, having delighted him with food, gave him a highly priced jewel / and, tying it to the inside of his garment and giving him a *granthi* [a knotted string attached to the interior of a garment as a device for keeping money], was satisfied.' //37//"

15. "Just the same, O Blessed One, are we, ignorant as we are of the former vow. / For this was given us by the Thus Gone One himself in previous existences throughout the long night of time. //"

Notes to Chapter Nine

1. "Then indeed the long-lived Ānanda at that time thought: 'Truly, may we also receive such a prophecy as this!' Then thinking, reflecting, and praying in this way, rising from his seat and bowing down to the feet of the Blessed One, and the long-lived Rāhula also thinking, reflecting, and praying in this way, and bowing down to the feet of the Blessed One, [they] spoke as follows: [If the English of this does not parse as a sentence, it is because the Sanskrit, too, is not grammatically coherent.] 'May our turn also come in the same way, O Blessed One! May our turn also come in the same way, O Well Gone One! For the Blessed One is our Father, our Progenitor, our Refuge, our Salvation. For we, O Blessed One, in this world with its gods, men, and asuras, have been variously depicted in such words as these: "These are the sons of the Blessed One, as well as the attendants of the Blessed One, and they carry the storehouse of the Dharma of the Blessed One." Now, O Blessed One, let that [prophecy] be right quickly matched [by you], in that the Blessed One shall prophesy to us concerning unexcelled, right, perfect, enlightened intuition."

2. "... reflecting on this very thought, to wit, 'Buddha-knowledge is *this*! Now may we too receive a prophecy concerning unexcelled, right, perfect enlightened intuition!' "

3. *Sāgaravaradharabuddhivikrīḍitābhijño nāma*. If I am not mistaken, the name means "the one whose superknowledge makes child's play of the intelligence necessary to carry the choicest of oceans," i.e., the Buddha for whom the intelligence necessary to carry the greatest of oceans about with one would be a mere trifle.

4. "And perfect shall your Buddha-field be, made of beryl. And Unbent Banner shall be the name of that world. And Resounding with Delightful Sound shall that kalpa be."

5. "... shall in time yet to come be a Victorious One, having honored six hundred million Well Gone Ones."

6. "He shall be renowned by name as the Bearer of the Wisdom of the Ocean, the One Who Has Attained Superknowledge, there / in the very beautiful Perfectly Pure Field of the Unbent Banner of Victory. //"

7. "Then indeed, within that assembly, to eight thousand bodhisattvas newly set out on the Path the following occurred: 'Not even on bodhisattvas have we ever before heard such an august prophecy conferred, not to mention auditors! What cause can there be for this, what condition?' Then indeed the Blessed One, recognizing in his own mind what was going on in the minds of those bodhisattvas, addressed those bodhisattvas as follows: 'Identically, O sons of good family, in the same moment, at the same instant, was our thought, mine and that of Ānanda, raised up to unexcelled, right, perfect, enlightened intuition in the presence of Dharmagaganābhyudgatarāja [the King Ascended to the Dharma Sky] the Thus Gone One, the Worthy One, the Properly and Fully Enlightened One. There this man, O sons of good family, was bent on the status of one who has heard much, while I was bent on vigorous undertaking. Therefore I was the quicker to experience unexcelled, right, perfect, enlightened intuition. This fellow, on the other hand, this goodly Ānanda, became the very bearer of the treasure of the True Dharma of the Blessed Buddhas. That is to say, whatever vow is taken for the perfection of bodhisattvas, that belongs, O sons of good family, to this very son of good family as well.' "

8. *āścaryabhūtā jina aprameyā ye smārayanti mama dharmadeśanām / parinirvṛtānāṃ hi jināna tāyināṃ samanusmarāmī yatha adya śvo vā //6//* If this is to be taken at face value, the first ardhaśloka can only mean, "Wondrous, O Victorious One, are the innumerable ones who mention my teaching of Dharma!" If *jina* is for *jinā*, it means, "Wondrous are the Victorious Ones who ..." If *ye* is somehow for *yāṃ*, it means one of three things: (1) "Wondrous, O Victorious One, are the innumerable ones who mention my teaching of Dharma!" (2) "Wondrous, O Victorious One, and immeasurable is my teaching of Dharma that they mention!" (3) "Wondrous, O Victorious One, is my teaching of Dharma that

the innumerable ones mention!" The second ardhaśloka means, "For I remember that of the now thoroughly extinguished victorious Tāyins as if it were today or tomorrow [sic]." Kumārajīva's version departs from the first *ardhaśloka* rather radically, though it represents the second well enough.

9. "This unknown conduct of Rāhula, his former vows, I know."

10. *guṇāna koṭīnayutāprameyāḥ pramāṇu yeṣāṃ na kadā cid asti / ye rāhulasyeha mamaurasasya tathā hi eṣo sthitu bodhikāraṇāt* //11// If I understand this right, it means, "Incalculable are the koṭis of nayutas of good qualities, whose measure in no wise exists, / belonging to this Rāhula here, my own true son. For it is thus he stands, by reason of [or "for the sake of"?] enlightened intuition."

11. "Doing reverence before the Buddhas with limitless parables and doctrinal expositions, / they shall achieve my supreme enlightened intuition, occupying their last bodies. //"

12. "Rich in magical powers shall they be here in all the worlds, on all sides, and in the ten directions, / setting forth the Dharma; and, even when they are extinguished, their True Dharma shall abide as evenly as ever. //"

13. "We are delighted, O Light of the World, having heard this prophecy! / We are as happy, O Thus Gone One, as if we had been sprinkled with nectar! //17// We have neither doubts nor second thoughts: we shall be Supreme among Men. / Today we have attained happiness, now that we have heard this prophecy. //18//"

Notes to Chapter Ten

1. "Moreover, whosoever, O Bhaiṣajyarāja, whatever being he may be, of hateful thought, or of evil thought, or of violent thought, gives an unfavorable account of the Thus Gone One in his presence, or utters so much as a single unpleasant sound, true or untrue, of such Dharma-preachers as these, bearers of this scripture (*sūtrānta*), whether householders or gone forth from the household, I say that this evil deed of his shall be more grave. ["More grave" than what? The implication seems to be that he who maligns these preachers is guilty of a more serious offense than he who maligns the Buddha. In this respect, Kumārajīva's original must have been better than the Sanskrit as we now have it.] For what reason? That son of good family or daughter of good family, O Bhaiṣajyarāja, is to be designated as one set about with the adornments of the Thus Gone One. He carries the Thus Gone One about on his shoulder, O Bhaiṣajyarāja, who, having written down this Circuit of the Dharma (*dharmaparyāya*) and reduced it to book form, carries it about on his shoulder. Wherever he may go, in those places he is to be greeted by the beings with palms joined, treated as one truly honorable, held in solemn esteem, respected, showered with offerings, praised, and set about with both heavenly and earthly flowers, perfume, scent, ointment, powder, garments, parasols, ensigns, banners, music, delicacies, sweetmeats, food, drink, chariots, and strings of divine jewels that

have attained the pinnacle of perfection. That Dharma-preacher is to be treated as one truly honorable, held in solemn esteem, respected, and showered with offerings, and strings of divine jewels are to be presented to that Dharma-preacher. For what reason? Only once, truly, need he proclaim this Dharma-circuit in order for immeasurable, incalculable living beings, on hearing it, to perfect themselves [The text as I have it reads *parinişpadyeyuḥ*, which poses two difficulties: (1) It is not a classically attested form. (2) It makes little sense, being active. I interpret it to mean *parinişpadyeran*, which is free of both draw-backs.] most quickly in unexcelled, right, perfect, enlightened intuition."

2. "Rejecting his fine associations, that firm one is come hither, / who out of sympathy for the beings bears this scripture."//

3. "And whoever, standing here in the presence of the Victorious One, may utter insults for a full kalpa, / with malicious intent and knitting his brows, that man shall produce a great heritage of sin. //"

4. These eight verses correspond to Skt, *ślokas* 14 and 15, which say the same thing, albeit in very different words. The four verses that follow have no analogue in the Sanskrit text as we now have it.

5. "I declare this to you, Bhaişajyarāja, I inform you. For many, Bhaişajyarāja, are the Dharma-circuits I have spoken, speak, and shall speak. And of all those Dharma-circuits, Bhaişajyarāja, this Dharma-circuit runs counter to all the worlds and is incredible to all the worlds. For this, Bhaişajyarāja, is the internal secret of the Thus Gone One himself, guarded by the might of the Thus Gone One, never before an object of detailed presentation, never before an object of predication or of declaration. By many men, Bhaişajyarāja, shall this Dharma-circuit be rejected while yet the Thus Gone One remains. What need to speak of what will happen after he is extinct?"

6. "In whatever quarter of earth, morever, O Bhaişajyarāja, this Dharma-circuit should happen to be spoken, or taught, or written, or studied, or sung, in that quarter of earth, O Bhaişajyarāja, a reliquary of the Thus Gone One should be made, great, fashioned with jewels, high and prominent. Nor need relics of the Thus Gone One necessarily be lodged in it. For what reason is that? The body of the Thus Gone One in a solid mass is deposited there, in whatever quarter of earth this Dharma-circuit happens to be spoken, or taught, or read, or sung, or written, or, if already written, left in the form of a book. And that reliquary is to be treated as something truly honorable, held in solemn esteem, respected, showered with offerings, and worshiped with all manner of flowers, perfumes, scents, garlands, ointments, powders, garments, parasols, banners, flags, and standards. Offering is to be made thereto in the form of all manner of vocal and instrumental music, dance, instruments, *tālāvacara* [kind of musical instrument], choruses, and symphony. Furthermore, whatever beings, Bhaişajyarāja, accept that reliquary of the Thus Gone One for worship, offering, or view, all of them, Bhaişajyarāja, are to be declared close to unexcelled, right,

perfect, enlightened intuition. For what reason is that? Many householders and many gone forth from the household, Bhaiṣajyarāja, perform bodhisattva-conduct but do not even accept this Dharma-circuit for viewing, or for hearing, or for writing, or for the making of offerings. Nor, Bhaiṣajyarāja, are they skilled in bodhisattva-conduct, so long as they do not hear this Dharma-circuit. But whoever hear this Dharma-circuit and, having heard it, feel an inclination for it, enter into it, understand it, or carry it about, all of them shall at that time stand close to unexcelled, right, perfect, enlightened intuition, and be near it."

7. "O Medicine-King! Into other countries I will send magically conjured men to be multitudes gathered to listen to Dharma. I will also send magically conjured bhikṣus, bhikṣuṇīs, upāsakas, and upāsikās, who shall listen to the preaching of Dharma." The Skt. reads as follows: *anyalokadhātusthitaś cāhaṃ Bhaiṣajyarāja tasya kulaputrasya nirmitaiḥ parṣadaḥ samāvartayiṣyāmi / nirmitāṃś ca bhikṣubhikṣuṇyupāsakopāsikāḥ saṃpreṣayiṣyāmi dharmaśravaṇāya /* The word on which the interpretation hinges is *nirmita*. The word is composed of the prefix *nis-* and of the perfect passive participle of the verb *mā-*. The latter, however, has two meanings, the primary one being to "measure," a secondary one being to "make" (both Eng. words being almost certainly cognate to it). In the former case, it is the participle *mita* with *nis-* as a negative prefix, hence "unmeasured," the sense in which Kumārajīva took it. In the latter case, it is the participle of the verb *nirmimāti*, "to turn out, create, produce, fashion." Now there is a class of gods whose collective name is *nirmāṇarati*, "they who take pleasure in creation," i.e., who can turn themselves into any shape at will, and who take pleasure in doing so for their own amusement. *Nirmita* is, among other things, an alternate name for the Nirmāṇarati gods. In the Skt. text, the Buddha is predicting to Bhaiṣajyarāja that he will send Nirmāṇarati gods in the form of auditors to hear his disciples' sermons. This is partly to make the disciples' efforts worthwhile, but gods need salvation as much as men do—more, from one point of view. So much for the second sentence. The first sentence means that the Buddha will provide those disciples with entourages by making use of Nirmāṇarati gods, which is why *nirmitaiḥ* is in the instrumental. Kumārajīva, on the other hand, must have had not *nirmitaiḥ* but *nirmitāḥ*, making the word an adjective in the accusative plural modifying *parṣadaḥ*. For the Ch., at face value, means "magically conjured audiences."

8. These last eight verses correspond to ślokas 32 and 33, but in reverse order. The second ardhaśloka of 33 reads *eko vihāre vanakandareṣu svādhyāya kurvantu mamā hi paśyet*. For *vihāre* Kern-Nanjio has *vihārī*, while for *mama* Wogihara-Tsuchida has *mamaṃ* (U. Wogihara and C. Tsuchida, eds., *Saddharmapuṇḍarīka-sūtra* . . . [rpt; Tokyo: Sankobo Buddhist Book Store, 1958]. Of the last two, neither can be construed at face value, and again Kumārajīva's text, on which the fourth verse above is based, appears to have had a better reading, presumably *māṃ* or *mā*.

Notes to Chapter Eleven

1. The difference between the Sanskrit and Kumārajīva's Chinese is one of detail. The Skt. says that the stūpa was as wide as it was high. The seven jewels in Skt. are *suvarṇa* (gold), *rūpya* (silver), *vaiḍūrya* (beryl), *musāragalva* (a kind of coral), *aśmagarbha* (emerald), *lohitamukti*, and *karketana* (a kind of quartz). As noted earlier, I cannot positively identify either Skt. *lohitamukti* or Ch. *mei kuei*; but I suspect they are the same or nearly the same.

2. *etad asya praṇidhānaṃ yadā khalv anyeṣu buddhakṣetreṣu buddhā bhagavanta imaṃ Saddharmapuṇḍarīkaṃ dharmaparyāyaṃ bhāṣeyuḥ tadāyaṃ mamātmabhāvavigrahastūpo 'sya Saddharmapuṇḍarīkasya dharmaparyāyasya śravaṇāya gacchet tathāgatānām antikam / yadā punas te buddhā bhagavanto mamātmabhāvavigraham udghāṭya darśayitukāmā bhaveyuś catasṛṇāṃ parṣadām atha tais tathāgatair daśasu dikṣv anyonyeṣu buddhakṣetreṣu ya ātmabhāvanirmitās tathāgatavigrahā anyānyanāmadheyāḥ teṣu teṣu buddhakṣetreṣu sattvānāṃ dharmaṃ deśayanti tān sarvān saṃnipātya tair ātmabhāvanirmitais tathāgatavigrahaiḥ sārdhaṃ paścād ayaṃ mamātmabhāvavigrahastūpaḥ samudghāṭya upadarśayitavyaś catasṛṇāṃ parṣadām /*

"This was his vow: 'Whenever indeed in the other Buddha-fields the Blessed Buddhas happen to speak this Dharma-circuit, the White Lotus of the True Dharma, then may this my reliquary, to which my body has been assigned, go into the presence of the Thus Gone Ones to hear this Dharma-circuit, the White Lotus of the True Dharma. Moreover, whenever, the Blessed Buddhas wish to uncover this body of Mine and show it to the four assemblies, then may this body of mine be uncovered by those several Thus Gone Ones and shown to the four assemblies, together with those physical forms of the Thus Gone Ones, fashioned from their very being, after [the Buddhas] have assembled whichever physical forms of the Thus Gone Ones, fashioned from their very being, teach Dharma to the beings in the several Buddha-fields under a variety of names.' "

3. "And then at that time the Blessed One emitted a ray from the tuft of hair between his brows, by which ray, as it reached everywhere, whatsoever Blessed Buddhas traveled in *koṭīs* of nayutas of hundreds of thousands of world-spheres equal in number to the sands of fifty Ganges rivers, they all became visible. And those Buddha-fields were visible as made of quartz crystal, variously resplendent with jeweled trees, well adorned with cords of cotton and fine silk, filled with many hundreds of thousands of bodhisattvas, hung with canopies, covered with gold nets decked out with the seven jewels. In every one of them were seen Blessed Buddhas teaching the Dharma to the beings in sweet, lovely voices. And full of hundreds of thousands of bodhisattvas did those Buddha-fields appear. So in the southeastern quarter, so in the southern, so in the south-western, so in the western, so in the northwestern, so in the northern, so in the northeastern, so in the nether region, so in the upper region, so in every one of all the ten directions were seen many koṭīs of nayutas of hundreds of thousands of

Buddha-fields like to the sands of the river Ganges; and what Blessed Buddhas stand in the many koṭīs of nayutas of hundreds of thousands of Buddha-fields like to the sands of the river Ganges, they were all visible."

4. "And then those Thus Gone Ones, those Worthy Ones, those Properly and Fully Enlightened Ones, addressed their several multitudes of bodhisattvas: 'It will be incumbent on us now, O sons of good family, to go to the Sahā world-sphere, into the presence of the Blessed Śākyamuni, the Thus Gone One, the Worthy One, the Properly and Fully Enlightened One, to do homage to the reliquary of Prabhūtaratna [Many Jewels] the Thus Gone One, the Worthy One, the Properly and Fully Enlightened One.' And then those Blessed Buddhas, each accompanied by his attendants, his seconds and his thirds, came to this Sahā world-sphere. For the following, at that time, was the manner of all this world-sphere: adorned it was with jeweled trees; fashioned out of beryl; covered with a gold net decked with the seven jewels; permeated by the perfumed scent of great jewels; strewn with *māndārava* and great-*māndārava* flowers; decorated by nets fitted out with tinkling bells; bound by gold cords in the pattern of a chess-board; free of villages, cities, towns, empires, kingdoms, and metropolises; free of Kāla mountains; free of Mucilinda and Great Mucilinda mountains; free of Cakravāla and Great Cakravāla mountains; free of Sumeru mountains; free of all other mountains; free of great oceans; free of streams and rivers: thus was it on all sides: free of the bodies of gods, men, and asuras; free of hells, of beasts, and of Yama worlds. For in this way, at that time, whatever beings had arrived at the six destinies in this Sahā world-sphere had all been pushed off into other world-spheres, the exception being those who were assembled in this congregation. And then those Blessed Buddhas, accompanied by their attendants, their seconds, and their thirds, arrived in this Sahā world-sphere. And, having severally arrived, those Thus Gone Ones, reclining on lion thrones, disported themselves. And each jeweled tree was five hundred yojanas in height, decked in due order with branches and leaves, adorned with blossoms and fruits. And at the foot of every jeweled tree was a lion throne, five hundred yojanas in height and adorned with great jewels. There each and every Thus Gone One was seated with legs crossed. In this way, in the whole thousand-millionfold world, at the foot of all jeweled trees, there were Thus Gone Ones seated with legs crossed."

5. "Then indeed at that time the sphere of this thousand-millionfold world was filled with Thus Gone Ones. Nor is this to say that those fashioned from the Body of the Thus Gone One Śākyamuni arrived even from one quarter. [*na tāvad bhagavataḥ Śākyamunes tathāgatasyātmabhāvanirmitā ekasmād api digbhāgāt sarva āgatā abhūvan* / I am by no means certain of the meaning of this. Two possibilities come to mind: (1) From no direction, no not one, did any Buddhas arrive who had been fashioned by Śākyamuni. This is as much as to say that they were all self-created. (2) Not by any means did they all come from any particular quarter,

but from all sides at once. No more am I certain that I have correctly rendered Kumārajīva's version ("and still there was no limit to the emanations of Śākyamunibuddha in even one quarter"), but I cannot think what else it might mean. Perhaps, as a third possibility, both the Skt. and Kumārajīva's Ch. come to this: "You may imagine that it was beyond Śākyamuni's power to create all those Buddhas, and that it was only those issuing from one of the eight quarters that were fashioned by him. If that is what you think, you are mistaken." There is need to compare this with Dharmarakṣa's version and with the Tibetan.] Śākyamuni the Thus Gone One, the Worthy One, the Properly and Fully Enlightened One, made accommodation for those bodies of the Thus Gone Ones which had severally arrived. In all eight quarters at once he fashioned twenty koṭīs of nayutas of hundreds of thousands of Buddha-fields, all made of beryl; covered with gold nets fitted out with the seven jewels; decorated by nets with tinkling bells; strewn with *māndārava* and great-*māndārava* flowers; covered over with divine tapestries; hung about with cords made of divine flowers; scented with perfume of divine scent; all those twenty koṭīs of nayutas of hundreds of thousands of Buddha-fields, moreover, free of villages, cities, towns, empires, kingdoms, and metropolises, free of Kāla mountains; free of Mucilinda and Great Mucilinda mountains; free of Cakravāla and Great Cakravāla mountains; free of Sumeru mountains; free of all other great mountains; free of great oceans; free of streams and rivers; free of the bodies of gods, men, and asuras; free of hells, beasts, and Yama worlds. And all of those Buddha-fields did he fashion as one single Buddha-field, as one single quarter of earth, level, delightful, and variously decorated with trees made of the seven jewels. And those jeweled trees were five hundred yojanas in length and breadth, all decked in due order with branches, leaves, blossoms, and fruits. And at the foot of every jeweled tree was a lion throne, five hundred yojanas in height and breadth, made of divine jewels, variegated, and sightly. At the foot of those jeweled trees the Thus Gone Ones, severally arrived, sat with legs crossed on their lion thrones. Moreover, in that way, Śākyamuni the Thus Gone One cleared twenty koṭis of nayutas of hundreds of thousands of world-spheres to provide accommodation for those Thus Gone Ones who had arrived." This passage is here repeated, to the point where the Buddhas seat themselves on their lion thrones.

6. The Skt. adds: "And both those Thus Gone Ones, seated on a lion throne in the midst of that great jeweled reliquary, were seen situated in midair."

7. "Such was the vow taken by this Leader in a former existence / that, though extinct, he seeks out this whole world in all ten directions. //"

8. "Such is this zeal of mine, thinking how this eye of Dharma shall shine, / that these Buddhas stand innumerable, like a row of lotuses at the foot of trees. //"

9. "The appealing scent of the Leaders of the world blows in all ten directions, / thanks to which, as the wind blows, all these living beings constantly thrive. //"

10. ". . . let him hear his lion's roar who makes strenuous efforts. //"
11. "I, the second, and these many koṭis of Leaders who have come hither /
Will hear the commitment from the son of the Victorious One who is able to explain this Dharma. //12//

And I will ever be showered with offerings—as shall the victorious self-existent Prabhūtaratna—by him /
Whoever comes through the primary and secondary quarters to hear a Dharma such as this one. //13//

And what Leaders of the world are come hither, by whom this variegated earth is beautified, /
To them, too, not a few offerings, broad in scope, shall have been made by the preacher of this scripture. //14//

And I will be seen on this throne, as shall the Blessed One who stands in the midst of this reliquary /
And these many other Leaders of the world who have come to the many hundreds of fields. //15//

Think on it, O sons of good family! Out of compassion for all living beings /
The Leaders are able to undertake this most difficult task. //16//"

12. *yas tu īdṛśakaṃ sūtraṃ nirvṛtasmiṃs tadā mayi / paścātkāle likhec cāpi idaṃ bhavati duṣkaram* //23// "But if by anyone such a scripture as this, when I am extinct, / in that latter time, should be written, even that would be difficult. //" The *ca* contained in *cāpi* leads one to suspect that there may also have been another version, in which *likhec ca* was accompanied by *likhāpayec ca*, or something similar. If so, this is another case in which Kumārajīva's version is closer to the presumed original than the Skt. as we now have it.

13. "Whoever might place the whole earth-sphere on the tip of his nail / and, flinging it, go away [as if nothing had happened] or mount to the Brahmā world, //24// he would be doing no difficult thing, nor anything of a piece with heroic effort, / having achieved that hardest of all worldly feats. //25// More difficult yet, when I am extinct, / at that latter time, would it be if anyone should speak this scripture for a single moment. //26//"

14. "Let one bear eighty-four thousand dharma-aggregates and teach them/to koṭis of living beings, together with their commentaries as officially pronounced! //29// For that would not be difficult for monks at that time. / Let one, for that matter, guide the auditors and establish them in five sorts of super-knowledges. //30// But let one do something that *is* difficult: Let one bear this scripture / and believe in it, or feel an inclination toward it, or pronounce it again and again. //31//" This is a not-so-veiled disparagement of Hīnayāna

scholasticism: Let the preachers spell out the five *abhijñās*, or let them dwell with all the traditional verbose commentary on all eighty-four dharmas. (The Theravāda school, for example, lists the dharmas at eighty-four.) If it comes to that, let them multiply their precious dharma-catalogue by a thousand. What's so so hard about that? The *real* challenge to a preacher's ability is the exposition of the essence of the Buddha's message, which is contained in the Mahāyāna, of which the *Lotus* is the purest expression. The Skt. conveys this idea unmistakably, but Kumārajīva's version obscures it somewhat.

15. . . . *śūraḥ śauṭīryavāṃś cāpi kṣiprābhijñaś ca bodhaye //38// dhurāvāhaś ca so bhoti* . . . "a hero and a manly fellow, also one quick in superknowledge to the end of enlightened intuition. // A bearer of the burden also is he . . ." This interpretation is based on the assumption that the *dhurāvāha* of Vaidya's text is identical in meaning with classical *dhurāvaha* (see P. L. Vaidya, ed., *Saddharma-puṇḍarīkasūtraṃ* Buddhist Sanskrit Texts, no. 6 [Darbhanga: Mithilā Institute of Post-Graduate Studies and Research in Sanskrit Learning, 1960]). Wogihara-Tsuchida have *dhṛtāvāhaś ca*, which presumably means the same thing. Kumārajīva has *t'ou-t'o*, a phonetic transcription of Skt. *dhūta*, which as a Buddhist term means "morality." The likelihood is that Kumārajīva's original read *dhūtāvāhaś ca*, which a copyist wrongly reproduced as *dhṛtāvāhaś ca*, and which an even later copyist, one too clever for his own good, converted into the almost classical *dhurāvāhaś ca*. If this assumption is correct, the opening words of *śloka* 39 mean, "A bearer of morality also is he," i.e., a consistent adherent of the moral code of the Buddhist monk.

16. "And worthy of worship shall that most learned of all beings be, / who in the final time speaks this scripture for but one moment. //"

Notes to Chapter Twelve

1. Again, the difference between the Skt. and Kumārajīva's version is one of detail, the only detail worthy of note being that the king, once he had gone into the *ṛṣi*'s service, in addition to the tasks just mentioned acted as his door-keeper and sat at the foot of his bed, holding his feet the night long.

2. "I recall past kalpas, when I was a Dharma-king obedient to Dharma, / and when my kingship was exercised for the sake of Dharma, most excellent Dharma, and not of lust. //42// This proclamation was made by me to the four quarters: 'Whosoever shall preach Dharma, into his service will I go!' / There was at that time a wise seer; a preacher of the scripture by the name of True Dharma. //43// He said to me, 'If you have a craving for Dharma, come into my service, then I will preach Dharma.' / Then I, delighted at hearing that speech, performed work and the charges of a slave. //44// Nor did weariness of body and mind touch me, once gone into service for Dharma's sake, / but my [deeds] had a [firm] foundation, to wit, the interest of all beings, not of lust; for I was not

looking to myself. //45// That king had taken vigorous effort upon himself, doing no other deeds in the ten directions, / untiring for fully a thousand kalpas, having received the scripture named Dharma. //46//"

3. "Now what do you suppose, O mendicant monks? Was the king at that time and on that occasion anyone else? Such a view is not to be taken! For what reason is that? I was the king at that time and on that occasion. Is it possible, for that matter, O mendicant monks, that the seer at that time and on that occasion was someone else? Neither is such a view to be taken! For this very mendicant monk Devadatta was the seer at that time and on that occasion."

4. "And in whatsoever Buddha-field he shall be reborn, there on a self-originated lotus made of the seven jewels he shall be reborn in the presence of the Thus Gone One."

5. "And then at that time Mañjuśrī, seated on a thousand-petaled lotus of about the dimensions of a carriage wheel, and surrounded by and at the head of many bodhisattvas, came up out of the midst of the sea, from the palace of the nāga-king Sāgara, and went the path of the birds through the upper air into the presence of the Blessed One on Mount Gṛdhrakūṭa [Vulture Peak]. Then the youthful Mañjuśrī, descending from his lotus and bowing with his head to the feet of the Blessed Śākyamuni and Prabhūtaratna the Thus Gone One, went to that place where the bodhisattva Prajñākūṭa was. Having approached, and having exchanged all manner of pleasant and delightful talk together with and in the presence of the bodhisattva Prajñākūṭa, he sat down to one side."

6. "O great worthy One, whose name is Sun, what countless ones have been guided by you today, / these are the beings. But whose power is this? Tell us this, O you god among men, now that you have been asked! // Or what Dharma have you taught, what scripture, what indicator of the path to enlightened intuition, / hearing which their thoughts have been reborn to enlightened intuition, and they have been assured of omniscience by their acquisition of firm ground? //"

7. "There is, O son of good family, the daughter of the nāga king Sāgara, eight years of age; of great wisdom and sharp faculties; endowed with deeds of body, speech, and mind, with knowledge at their head; having mastered the magical charms for grasping the meanings of the syllables spoken by all the Thus Gone Ones; having mastered in a single moment the concentration that combines in one place all the dharmas and all the beings; not turning back from the thought of enlightened intuition; having a foundation of vows well spread out; following all living beings as if they were her own dear ones and able to produce good qualities in them."

8. "Meritorious, meritorious and profound, throughout all directions gleams / the subtle body, with the thirty-two marks well adorned, //49// bound also to the secondary marks and bowed down to by all beings, / to be approached by all beings as if it were a marketplace. //50// Mine is perfect enlightened

intuition, as if it were at will, and my witness thereof is the Thus Gone One. / I will teach the broad Dharma that liberates from woe. //51//" The first *ardhaśloka* of 51 is far from a certainty. It may also mean: "*How* my *saṃbodhi* is a matter of the will, *of that* the Thus Gone One is an eyewitness." One would like to think that the next to last couplet of Kumārajīva says the same thing, but the second character, *wen* (to hear), will not allow that.

9. "And then at that time the long-lived Śāriputra said to the daughter of the nāga king Sāgara: 'No sooner, O daughter of good family, has your thought been raised up to enlightened intuition than you become one who has the immeasurable wisdom that knows no backsliding. But the status of a properly and fully enlightened one is hard to obtain. O daughter of good family, there is a woman, and she does not let her efforts lapse, but for many hundreds of kalpas, many thousands of kalpas, does deeds of merit and fulfills the six perfections, yet even today has not attained Buddhahood. What is the cause? Five stations a woman even today does not attain. Which five? The first is the station of Brahmā, the second the station of Śakra, the third the station of a great king, the fourth the station of a wheel-turner, the fifth the station of a nonbacksliding bodhisattva.'

"Now at that time the daughter of the nāga king Sāgara had a jewel. in value equal to the whole millionfold world. Now that jewel was given by the daughter of the nāga king Sāgara to the Blessed One. And it was accepted by the Blessed One out of sympathy. Then the daughter of the nāga king Sāgara said to the bodhisattva Prajñākūṭa and the elder Śāriputra, 'Was this jewel, given by me to the Blessed One, received by him quickly?' The elder said, 'It was both quickly given by you and quickly received by the Blessed One.' The daughter of the nāga king Sāgara said, 'If, O venerable Śāriputra, I were a great magician, I should achieve right, perfect, enlightened intuition more quickly yet. Nor would there be any recipient for this jewel.'

"Then at that time the daughter of the nāga king Sāgara showed herself, in the presence of all the world and before the eyes of the elder Śāriputra, with her female faculties suppressed and male faculties displayed, herself become a bodhisattva. At that time the bodhisattva proceeded to the southern quarter. Now in the southern quarter was a world-sphere named Vimalā [Spotless]. There he showed himself seated enlightened at the foot of a bodhi-tree made of the seven jewels, the bearer of the thirty-two primary marks and appropriately fitted out with all the secondary marks, teaching Dharma while illuminating all ten directions with a glow. And what living beings were in the Sahā world-sphere all saw that Thus Gone One, being bowed down to by all gods, nāgas, yakṣas, gandharvas, asuras, garuḍas, kinnaras, humans and nonhumans, and teaching Dharma. And what beings heard the teaching of Dharma by that Thus Gone One all became nonbacksliders with respect to unexcelled, right, perfect, enlightened intuition. And that Vimalā world-sphere and this Sahā world-sphere trembled in six ways. And for three thousand living beings out of the circle of the assembly of the Blessed Śākyamuni there was the gain of acceptance of [the doctrine of] the unborn dharmas. And for three thousand living beings there was the gain of a prophecy with respect to unexcelled, right, perfect, enlightened intuition. Then Prajñākūṭa the bodhisattva-mahāsattva and the elder Śāriputra were silent."

This twelfth chapter in Kumārajīva's version corresponds to the end of chapter 11 in the Sanskrit. From here to the end, there is a gap of at least one chapter between the Sanskrit and the Chinese.

Notes to Chapter Thirteen

1. ". . . surrounded by twenty hundreds of thousands of bodhisattvas, uttered this speech to the face of the Blessed One. . . ."

2. "And then, together with six thousand mendicant nuns, learning nuns and those who had nothing more to learn, Mahāprajāpatī Gautamī, maternal aunt of the Blessed One, rose from her seat, joined palms in the direction of where the Blessed One was and, looking up at him, remained standing. Then indeed the Blessed One addressed Mahāprajāpatī Gautamī: 'Why, O Gautamī, do you stand there so downhearted, looking at the Blessed One? [You think] "I was not announced [as a future Buddha], nor granted a prophecy with regard to unexcelled, right, perfect, enlightened intuition." Yet, O Gautamī, you have been included in the prophecy conferred on the whole assembly. For, O Gautamī, hereafter, in the presence of thirty-eight koṭīs of nayutas of hundreds of thousands of Buddhas, you shall give the recognition due the truly honorable, indicating solemn esteem and respect, making offerings and showing homage and awe, having done which you shall become a bodhisattva-mahāsattva preaching the Dharma. These six thousand mendicant nuns also, the learners and those who have nothing more to learn, together with you yourself, in the presence of those Thus Gone Ones, those Worthy Ones, those Properly and Fully Enlightened Ones, shall become Dharma-preachers. Thereafter, in time far beyond that, having fulfilled bodhisattva-conduct, you shall become Dharma-preachers. Thereafter, in time far beyond that, having fulfilled bodhisattva-conduct, you shall become in the world a Thus Gone One, a Worthy One, a Properly and Fully Enlightened One named Sarvasattvapriyadarśana [Pleasant for All Beings to Behold], one perfectly endowed with knowledge and [proper] conduct, a Well Gone One, an unexcelled Knower of the world, a Guide of men who have to be tamed, a Teacher of gods and men, an Awakened One, a Blessed One. And, O Gautamī, that Sarvasattvapriyadarśana the Well Gone One, the Worthy One, the Properly and Fully Enlightened One, shall in successive prophecies prophesy to those six thousand bodhisattvas with regard to their future unexcelled, right, perfect, enlightened intuition.' "

3. ". . . named Raśmiśatasahasraparipūrṇadhvaja [He Whose Flag is Full of Hundreds of Thousands of Stripes] . . . in the Bhadra world. And immeasurable shall the life-span of . . . be."

4. In the Skt., the two thoughts of the bodhisattvas are (1) *asmākaṃ bhagavān adhyeṣati asya dharmaparyāyasya saṃprakāśanatāyai* / "The Blessed One desires us to preach this circuit of the Dharma" and (2) *kathaṃ vayaṃ kulaputrāḥ kariṣyāmo yad bhagavān adhyeṣati asya dharmaparyāyasyānāgate 'dhvani saṃprakāśanatāyai*, "How shall we act, O sons of good family, to preach this circuit of the Dharma as the Blessed One desires us to do in time to come?" While neither of these lends itself to smooth translation into English, the second English version is free in the extreme. The Chinese translators may have been confronted with a similar difficulty, but the likelihood is that their original was different from ours.

5. "And of *us* they will say, 'Bent on gain and honor, / these heretical mendicants teach their own verse, // having themselves written their scriptures, motivated by gain and honor.'/[Thus] in the midst of the assembly do our ruinous detractors speak. //" In other words, in my interpretation of Kumārajīva's version, I understand the speech of the pseudo-āraṇyakas to consist of the last seven verses. In the Skt., on the other hand, if I have understood it correctly, their speech begins with *lābhasatkāraniśritāḥ* ("bent on gain and honor") and consists, for the remainder, of the second ardhaśloka of 8 and the first of 9.

6. *ye cāsmān kutsayiṣyanti tasmin kālasmi durmatī / ime buddhā bhaviṣyanti kṣamiṣyāmatha sarvaśaḥ* //12// While the Skt. and the Ch. may conceivably mean the same thing, the former may also be understood as follows: "And whoever, ill disposed, shall despise us at that time,/they shall all be Buddhas, and we will by all means endure it. //" If this latter interpretation is correct, it means that the latter-day detractors will be Buddhas in disguise, whose purpose is to test the fortitude of these practitioners.

7. "In the great harsh fear, so frightening by reason of cosmic agitation, / many shall be our monkish detractors in the shape of yakṣas. // Yet, out of our veneration for the Lord of the World, we will endure these most difficult things, / having girt ourselves with the girdle of forbearance to preach this scripture. //"

8. "Mindful of the instructions of the Leader of the World in the final time, / we will speak this scripture with confidence in the midst of the assembly. //"

9. "Your bidding will we do, Lord of the World, O Great Ascetic. / Be therefore of slight care, having attained tranquillity and being at peace. //"

Notes to Chapter Fourteen

1. "Then indeed the youthful Mañjuśrī said to the Blessed One: 'A thing hard to do, O Blessed One, very hard to do, has been undertaken by these

bodhisattva-mahāsattvas out of veneration for the Blessed One. How, O Blessed One, by these bodhisattva-mahāsattvas is this Dharma-circuit at the last time and on the last occasion to be clarified?' When this had been said, the Blessed One said to the youthful Mañjuśrī: 'By a bodhisattva-mahāsattva rooted in four dharmas, Mañjuśrī, is this Dharma-circuit at the last time and on the last occasion to be clarified. In which four? Now, O Mañjuśrī, by a bodhisattva-mahāsattva rooted in [the proper] conduct and [in the proper] field of action (*ācāragocarapratiṣṭhitena*) is this Dharma-circuit at the last time and on the last occasion to be clarified. And how, O Mañjuśrī, does a bodhisattva-mahāsattva become rooted in [the proper] conduct and [in the proper] field of action? When, O Mañjuśrī, a bodhisattva-mahāsattva is tranquil and subdued, having attained a subdued stage, in mind not alarmed or terrified, nor indignant; and when, O Mañjuśrī, a bodhisattva-mahāsattva courses in no dharma, but views the own-mark of the dharmas exactly as it is; and when, moreover, with regard to these dharmas he neither discriminates nor reflects, that is called, O Mañjuśrī, the conduct of the bodhisattva-mahāsattva. And what, O Mañjuśrī, is the field of action of the bodhisattva-mahāsattva? When, O Mañjuśrī, the bodhisattva-mahāsattva does not frequent a king, nor princes, nor the king's ministers, nor the king's men, does not frequent them, nor cultivate them, nor sit next to them, nor approach them; when he does not frequent, or cultivate, or sit next to adherents, or practitioners, or itinerants of other schools, or Ājīvakas, or Nirgranthas, or those devoted to [worldly] verses and treatises; when he does not frequent, nor cultivate, nor sit next to, those who bear the mystical verses of the Lokāyatas or, for that matter, the Lokāyatas themselves, nor strike up an acquaintance with them; when he does not approach outcastes, cheats, dealers in pork, poulterers, deer-hunters, butchers, dancers, cudgel players, wrestlers, or those of any other station having to do with sport or play, nor strike up an acquaintance with them; when he preaches Dharma only from time to time, to persons he has not himself sought out, and then without committing himself to them; when he does not frequent, or cultivate, or sit next to mendicant monks and nuns and lay adherents, male and female, who belong to the course of the auditors, nor strike up an acquaintance with them, nor share the same space with them, whether in walking or in dwelling; and when he preaches Dharma only from time to time, to persons he has not himself sought out, and then without committing himself to them—this, Mañjuśrī, is the field of action of the bodhisattva-mahāsattva.

" 'Then again, Mañjuśrī, the bodhisattva-mahāsattva does not pointedly teach Dharma to women again and again out of motives of civility, nor is he keenly eager to see women. Nor does he approach families, nor does he feel a particular need to talk to daughter, wife, or young woman, nor does he entertain them. Nor does he teach Dharma to a eunuch, nor does he strike up an acquaintance with him, nor entertain him. Nor does he go alone in quest of alms into the inner quarters, unless cultivating recollection of the Thus Gone One. If, on the other hand, he does teach Dharma to women, he does it not even out of attachment to the Dharma, how much less to the women! He does not show even his row of teeth, how much the less coarse facial expressions! Nor does he [?] (*sātīyati*, *sādīyati*) a novice, male or female, or monk or nun, or young man or young woman, nor does he strike up an acquaintance with them, nor does he hold conversation with them. For he attaches great weight to retirement to privacy, and cultivates it exceedingly. This is called, O Mañjuśrī, the first field of action of the bodhisattva-mahāsattva.

"Again, O Mañjuśrī, the bodhisattva-mahāsattva views all dharmas as empty, as it were firmly rooted, standing [on the] uninverted, standing just as they are, untrembling, unshakable, not to be turned aside, not characterized by turns, standing ever just as they are, of the nature of open space, inaccessible to verbalization or formulation, unborn, neither become nor not become, unconditioned, without continuity, products of the pronouncement of what is not real, the manifest products of false perception, having made their appearance thanks to perversity of notion. [This is a veiled attack on the older notion of the dharmas, viz., that they are emerging and disappearing at every moment. They are in fact motionless, says the *Lotus*, and it is only thanks to perverse notions that they *appear*—for it is no more than that—to emerge.] For it is thus, O Mañjuśrī, that the bodhisattva-mahāsattva conducts himself, repeatedly viewing all dharmas. By conducting himself in that way, the bodhisattva-mahāsattva has his stand in the [proper] field of action. This, O Mañjuśrī, is the second field of action of the bodhisattva-mahāsattva.' "

2. "And whoever are king's men, with them let him strike up no acacquaintance nor, by any means, with outcastes, cheats, drunkards, and worshipers at sacrificial altars. //"

3. "Let him avoid the mendicant nun whose constant activity is laughter and chatter, and let him avoid the lay sisters who stand out in prominent view. // What lay sisters seek Peace in this very life, / let him avoid their acquaintance. *This* is called [proper] conduct. //"

4. "What beings are female or eunuchs, with them let him strike up no acquaintance. / Let him also avoid young wives and young girls within the households. //8// Let him not encourage them to inquire smilingly after his well-being [?], / but let him avoid acquaintance with them, as with dealers in pork and with herders of sheep. //9// And whoever harm sundry living beings for profit / and sell their flesh in the slaughterhouse, let him avoid acquaintance with them. //10// And whoever keep women, let him avoid acquaintance with them, / as with dancers, cudgel-players, wrestlers, and whosoever else may be of that sort. //11// Nor let him cultivate courtesans or whoever else may live off pleasure *vāramukhyā na seveta ye cānye boghavṛttinaḥ (boghavṛttayaḥ) / pratisaṃmodanaṃ (pratisaṃmodatāṃ) tebhiḥ sarvaśaḥ parivarjayet* //12// [Vaidya's edition reads

bhogavṛttinaḥ, while the Gilgit (Kashmir) MS reads *bhogavṛttayaḥ*, both masculine forms, an obvious reference to pimps. Kumārajīva's *hsüan mai nü se* (which I have rendered "those who advertise and sell female flesh") may correspond to this, or to the *strīpoṣakāś ca* in 10 ("whoever keeps women"), or to both. On the other hand, K. may have been dealing with a different original.], but let him by all means avoid exchanging salutations with them. //12//"

5. "This is the first [mode of] conduct, the first field of action set forth by me, / in which the wise conduct themselves, bearing a scripture like this one. //"

6. "Because of the unbornness of all dharms, though seeking them, he does not see them. //"

7. "What their field of action is, hear that now from him who explains it clearly: // Nonexistent have these dharmas been declared, unemerged, unborn all, / standing throughout all time empty and intentionless: this is called the field of action of the wise. //"

8. The Skt. adds *manyanavarjitāṃś ca*, "and beyond thought."

9. While the general tone of the passage is clear enough, vv. 99–102 ("Then that *bodhisattva* . . . with the doctrine") caused a bit of trouble. I am not certain that I have them right or, even if I have, that I have related them properly to the context. At any rate, the last twenty-three verses are far enough from the Sanskrit to warrant giving the latter as well: "For whosoever, keeping my positions [*īryāpatha*, postures and attitudes], shall become a mendicant monk after I am at peace / shall explain this scripture in the world, and he shall have no attachment. // Or, from time to time, entering his abode in thought, also in agitation, / and viewing this whole Dharma fundamentally, he shall rise up and teach it with thought unattached. // Kings shall thereupon attend to his protection, and also whatever princes shall hear the Dharma. / Others, moreover, householders and Brahmans, shall all remain standing about him as retinue. //"

10. "Again, O Mañjuśrī, the bodhisattva-mahāsattva who wishes to clarify this Dharma-circuit at the last time and on the last occasion, when the breakdown of the True Dharma is in process after the final peace of the Thus Gone One, shall enjoy a happy situation [?] (*sukhasthito bhavati*). He, enjoying a happy situation, shall preach the Dharma, whether it has become a part of him or is written in a book. Nor, when teaching others, is he to be excessively abusive by nature; nor to speak slightingly of other mendicant monks who preach Dharma; nor to speak of their negative qualities; nor to bring out their negative qualities; nor, mentioning them by name, to speak of the negative qualities of other mendicant monks of the course of the voice-hearers; nor to bring out their negative qualities; nor to entertain hostile notions in their presence. For what reason is that? Because he has taken his stand in a happy situation [*sukhasthānasthitatvāt*, "he is standing on a *sukha*-stand"]. To all who come to hear the Dharma he teaches it with favor and without resentment. Nor does he, when asked a

question, answer it, unless challenged, by recourse to the course of the voice-hearers [*avivadamāno na ca praśnaṃ pṛṣṭaḥ śrāvakayānena visarjayati* / What this seems to mean is that the bodhisattva, when questioned about Buddhist doctrine, answers in terms of pure Mahāyāna, not even mentioning the Hīnayāna doctrine except to refute it. For *avivadamāna*, possibly "unless engaged in disputation" would be better than "unless challenged."], but he answers it in such a way that the questioner shall become intuitively aware of Buddha-knowledge."

11. "He enjoys a happy situation; he is ever resplendent and, seated happily, pronounces the Dharma, / having made his seat high and well-arranged in a quarter of earth both clean and pleasant, //23// and wearing a clean garment, one well-tinted in auspicious hues, / and also donning a black one of great dimensions for ordinary wear [?], //24// sitting on a seat with feet and a pedestal, well strewn with variegated ornaments, / having mounted with feet washed, and with head and face glistening. //25// And, seated on that throne, to those who have come together with thought concentrated / let him tell many varied tales . . ."

12. "When he has heard such a Dharma as this, that wise one is then to keep it; / in happy concentration disposed to the practice of it, he is well guarded by millions of living beings. //"

13. "Ever demonstrating the power of good will, ever pitying all beings, / let one explain such a Dharma as this, a scripture of distinction narrated by the Well Gone Ones. //"

14. "Whoever might be householders and those gone forth, and also bodhisattvas at that last time, he would demonstrate the power of good will to all of them: 'May they not cast it away, once having heard the Dharma!//"

15. "Nor shall his be pain, nor obstruction, nor yet weariness that ill affects the color, / nor shall his skin be dark, nor yet shall his dwelling be in an inferior city. //"

16. These four verses have no analogue in the Skt., while the Skt., as we have it, has no analogue in the Ch.: *so bandhubhūto bhavatīha prāṇinām ālokajāto vicarantu medinīm / timiraṃ haranto bahuprāṇakoṭinām yo sūtra dhāre imu nirvṛte mayi* //58// "He becomes a kinsman here to animate beings, the one of natural radiance, travelling over the earth, / taking the darkness away from millions of living beings, who bears this scripture after I am at peace. //59//"

17. ". . . Such shall that dream be. // And many, yea endless, shall his sweet-voiced praisers be, / who in the final time shall explain this Scripture of the Supreme Dharma, so well taught by me. //"

Notes to Chapter Fifteen

1. This presumably means all thousand-millions of lands. All the Skt. says is *atheyaṃ Sahā lokadhātuḥ sphuṭitā visphuṭitā abhūt* / "then this Sahā world-sphere split asunder and burst open."

2. The Skt. is much more prolix, but in essence says the same thing. Specifically, there were bodhisattvas equal in number to a hundred thousand koṭis of nayutas multiplied by the number of sands in sixty Ganges rivers, each one of them at the head of a like number of bodhisattvas. The number progressively increases as the particular bodhisattva's retinue dwindles to the same meteoric figure multiplied by the sands of fifty Ganges rivers, then forty, then thirty, twenty, ten, five, four, three, two, one, one-half, one-quarter, one-sixth, one-eighth, one-tenth, one-twentieth, one-fortieth, one-fiftieth, one-hundredth, one-thousandth, one-hundred-thousandth, one-ten-millionth, one-ten-thousand-millionth, one-million-millionth, finally one-million-million-nayutath of a Ganges river. The number of bodhisattvas in leadership continues to increase as their respective retinues dwindle to a million million nayutas of individuals, then to ten million, then to a hundred thousand, etc., down to one. The most numerous of all are those bodhisattvas who come with no retinue at all.

3. The Skt. says that the bodhisattvas honored those two and also the innumerable emanations of Śākyamuni, of whom mention was made above.

4. "Are you conducting yourself happily, O lustrous Leader of the World? / Are you free of obstacles? Do the things that touch your body cause it no illness? // Of most goodly appearance are your beings, easy to lead, well purified. / May they not cause you any weariness, O World-Honored One, as you speak! //"

5. "Whoever also have attended to their devotions on the ground of the auditor or on the ground of the individually enlightened, wherever that may have been, them also have I ferried over here into knowledge of Buddha and Dharma and enabled to hear the Prime Meaning."

6. The Skt. adds: *kutaḥ khalv ime bodhisattvā mahāsattvā āgatā iti*, "Whence come then these bodhisattva-mahāsattvas?"

7. "And all of them are firm, mindful, great seers, / their form lovely to behold. Whence is their provenance? //"

8. The Skt. phrases this very differently. However, since the idea is the same, and since the principal discrepancies have to do with meteoric numbers and similar flourishes, the points of difference shall not be dwelt on here.

9. "Of all the magnanimous, vigorous Tāyins, / of the manly bodhisattvas, whence is the provenance? //24// By whom was the Dharma taught to them? By whom were they established in enlightened intuition? / Whose teaching do they desire? Of whose teaching are they the bearers? //25// For, splitting the whole earth, with its four directions, from every quarter, /they well up, they of great wisdom, of great magical power, all resplendent, //26// This world-sphere has been torn to pieces from all sides, O Silent One, / by these fearless bodhisattvas welling up here. //27// For we have not seen these before at any time. / Tell us the name of that world-sphere, O Leader! //28// For we have wandered over the ten quarters again and again, / but we have not seen these bodhisattvas

at any time. //29// Not one of your sons have we seen, / yet today we have suddenly seen these. Tell us what they have done, O Silent One! //30// Thousands, hundreds, yea nayutas of bodhisattvas, / all seized with astonishment, look at the Supreme among Two-Legged Beings //31// Explain, O Great Hero, O Immeasurable, Attributeless One, whence come these fearless hero-bodhisattvas! //32//"

10. "And then the Blessed One addressed the bodhisattva Maitreya: 'Good, good, O Ajita [Unconquered One]! This is an important matter, O Ajita, that you ask me.' And then the Blessed One addressed the whole multitude of bodhisattvas: 'For that very reason, O sons of good family, let every one of you be intent, well-girt, of firm strength, both you and this whole multitude of bodhisattvas. The Thus Gone One's knowledge and insight, O sons of good family, the Thus Gone One, the Worthy One, the Properly and Fully Enlightened One, shall directly explain, the manliness of the Thus Gone One, the deeds of the Thus Gone One, the sport of the Thus Gone One, the exploits of the Thus Gone One, the bold advance of the Thus Gone One.'"

11. "Be all of you enduring, mindful, concentrated, and remain so, / for an unprecedented Dharma is to be heard today, a wonder of the Thus Gone Ones. //"

12. "What bodhisattvas these may be, incalculable, unthinkable, of whose number there is no means of measurement, / through their magical power, their wisdom, and what they have heard, practiced in gnosis throughout many koṭis of kalpas, // all these have been ripened by me to enlightened intuition, and all of them dwell in my very own field, / all these bodhisattvas being my very own sons, ripened by none other than me. // All of them, bent on the ascetic forest life, avoid the soil of contact, / in their practice of nonattachment learning by example my own supreme conduct, these sons of mine. //"

13. The Skt. describes the bodhisattvas in this way: "In the very same way the Blessed One has for no long time been fully awakened to unexcelled, right, perfect, enlightened intuition; yet these bodhisattva-mahāsattvas are so numerous as to be immeasurable, having cultivated chaste conduct for many koṭīs of nayutas of hundreds of thousands of kalpas, having won certainty of Buddha-knowledge throughout the long night of time, being skilled at attaining and at leaving hundreds of thousands of the gateways of samādhi, having emerged from actions attendant on the great superknowledges, having attended to these same actions, wise with respect to the ground of Buddhahood, skilled at singing the praises of the dharmas of the Thus Gone One, marveled at by the world, having attained to the strength of great manliness."

14. "But these noble confident ones are many, who, having practiced with their great assemblies for koṭīs of kalpas, / stand rooted in the might of magical power, unshakable, well learned, having gone the course in the strength

of wisdom. // Unsullied as a lotus by water, they who, having cleft the great earth, are here come / stand all with palms joined, solemn and mindful, these sons of the Overlord of the World. //"

15. "In the very same way, the Blessed One is young and in the prime of life, while these many bodhisattvas of discerning wisdom, / mindful of wisdom and confident, have been well trained for thousands of koṭis of kalpas. // Holding firmly to wisdom, resplendent, of favorable appearance and fair to behold, all of them, / confident of their definitions of Dharma, thoroughly praised by the Leaders of the World, // unattached in conduct, dwell in pure open space, never leaning on anything. / They generate vigor, these sons of the Well Gone One, seeking this Buddha-soil. //"

Notes to Chapter Sixteen

1. By this count, the plea was made four times, whereas in the Skt. it was made only three.

2. "I take many bodhisattvas and set them up in Buddha-knowledge."

3. "Thereupon I preside over myself and over all living beings, / and deluded men, their understanding set on its head, though standing right there, do not see me. //"

4. ". . . their desires released."

5. ". . . and scatter them over me and the auditors and over whichever other wise ones have set forth for enlightened intuition. //"

6. The Skt. adds: "Nor do I ever tell them of this so unexcelled doing of mine. /"

7. "How now shall I lead them toward enlightened intuition? How shall they become recipients of the Buddhadharmas? //"

Notes to Chapter Seventeen

1. The above twenty-four verses occupy the same position as ślokas 4 to 6 in the Skt., but, as will be noted, the correspondence is rather thin: "And others, who have set out for the unexcelled Buddha-knowledge of the *paramāṇukṣetra*, / shall in some cases in eight rebirths become Victorious Ones of endless vision. //4// Some, on the other hand, after the passage of four, some of three, others of one, / shall receive enlightened intuition as viewers of the Supreme Meaning, having heard this Dharma of the Leader. //5// And some, having stood for a single rebirth [i.e., having heard of the *āyuṣpramāṇa* in this incarnation], shall become omniscient in the next existence, / having heard of the life-span of the Leader. Such shall be the fruit without outflows gained by them. //6//" The meaning of *paramāṇukṣetra* is not clear to me. On the surface, it means "atom-field." If it means world-spheres as numerous as the atoms in a single

world-sphere as known to us, it should be plural (°*kṣetrāṇām*), not singular. Kumārajīva is, in this case, of no help.

2. "Such a deed as this has been done by the Great Seer, preaching this enlightened intuition of the Buddhas / which is so endless it has no yardstick, as immeasurable as open space. //"

3. "Broad this day is this gain in all ten quarters, [broad] also the Voice of the Leaders, which has issued forth. / Delighted are the thousands of koṭīs of living beings, fitted for enlightened intuition by their wholesome [deeds]. //"

4. Throughout the whole poetic passage just given in the text, the wording of the Skt. is greatly at variance with that of Kumārajīva, but there is virtually no difference in substance. It should be pointed out that "happiness" renders *fu*, which in turn, when there is a word-for-word correspondence, stands for *puṇya*, "merit."

5. *Suvarṇasūtrāṣṭāpadavinaddhāṃ ratnavṛkṣair vicitritām* / "its highways in eight directions being bound by gold cords, [the world-sphere itself being] variously adorned with jeweled trees."

6. *aṣṭatalā bhikṣusahasrāvāsāḥ*, of which the former is more likely to mean "octagonal," while the latter refers to accommodations for only *one* thousand monks. Kumārajīva may have had *aṣṭatalā bhiksulakṣāvāsāḥ*, in which he interpreted the former word to mean what the English translation says.

7. The Skt. is just different enough to warrant a separate translation:

"His is a boundless mass of merit, which I have described again and again, /
Who shall bear this scripture when the Leader of Men is at peace. //37//

And he shall have made offerings to me, and constructed reliquaries, /
Made of jewels, variegated, sightly, and made beautiful; //38//

As high as the Brahmā-world, equipped with rows of parasols, /
Of broad circumference, glorious, fitted out with victorious standards. //39//

And there shall be clear bells, adorned with bands of fine cloth, ringing /
As they tremble in the wind: so shall the bells sparkle in the reliquaries of the Victorious Ones. //40//

And to them offerings broad in scope, with flowers and incense and paints, /
And with musical instruments, and with garments, and with repeated drumbeats shall have been made. //41//
And sweet musical instruments shall be sounded in those reliquaries, /
And candles of scented wax presented from all sides. //42//

Whoever may keep this scripture and teach it at the time of destruction, /
Such shall be the various limitless offerings he shall make to me: //43//

Many millions of lofty monasteries made of sandalwood, /
Thirty-two palaces eight tālas in height, //44//

Furnished with beds and chairs, stocked with delicacies, /
Done with pieces of colored woolen cloth; also designated dwellings [i.e., donated by the pious] by the thousands; //45//

Promenades and walks [are also] given, decorated with flower plots, /
Many also uncovered [?], variegated with many designs. //46//

To the religious community varied offerings shall have been made in my presence by him /
Who shall bear this Scripture when the Leader is at peace. //47//

Ever greater than [the merit] of him who is the soul of faith shall be his /
Merit, who shall speak this scripture or write it down, //48//

Or who, whatever man he may be, shall cause this discourse, which the Buddha has done well to pronounce, to be written in a book /
And shall make to the book offerings of scent, garlands, and paint, //49//

Or who shall give a lamp, ever filled with scented sesame oil. /
And with red and white lotuses, *atimuktas*, and scattered heaps of champac flowers, //50//

Whoever shall make such offerings to the books /
Shall generate merit that would have no measure. //51//

Just as of open space no measure can be taken, /
So in the ten quarters shall his mass of merit ever be. //52//

What need then to mention him who shall be forbearing, sedate, collected, /
Of disciplined moral conduct, contemplative, given to retirement, //53//

Neither irascible nor slanderous, standing at the reliquary in dignity, /
Ever bowed down before the mendicant monks, neither arrogant nor indifferent, //54//

Wise also and firm, who, when asked a question, does not get angry, /

But agreeably teaches, being of merciful intent toward living beings? //55//

Whosoever shall be thus, whoever he may be, and bear this scripture, /
Of his mass of merit no measure can be taken. //56//

If any man should see such a preacher of Dharma /
Bearing this scripture, let him do him honor! //57//

Let him strew him with divine flowers and cover him with divine garments. /
Having bowed down his head to his feet, let him conceive the notion, 'This is a Thus Gone One!' //58//

And, having beheld him, let him think at that time, 'This man shall go to the foot of the Tree! /
He shall experience the supreme, blessed, enlightened intuition for the benefit of the world with its gods.' //59//

And, wherever such a wise one shall walk, or stand, or sit, /
Let the hero prepare a couch for him somewhere, and let them speak even a single verse from one scripture. //60//

And, wherever he may have built a reliquary of the Supreme among Men, variegated and most sightly, /
And where, pointing to the Buddha, the Blessed One, the Leader, he may also make varied offerings to him, //61//

By me that quarter of the earth shall have been enjoyed, by me myself trodden, /
And I myself will have entered there, where that son of the Enlightened One shall be standing. //62//"

Notes to Chapter Eighteen

1. *puṇyakāmo hitakāmaḥ*, i.e., desirous of merit for himself and the weal of others.

2. The Skt. says in essence the same thing but, as often, at greater length and in more detail.

3. *divyānāṃ ca vimānānām lābhī bhaviṣyati* /, meaning that the man shall be the recipient of divine *vimānas*, a word which means both "chariot" and "palace." Given the context, the former certainly seems to be the meaning intended. Somewhere the translators slipped, for, while the Skt. says *lābhī* (recipient), the Ch. rendered it with *ch'eng* (mount, ride), then undid it by rendering *vimāna* with *kung* (palace). A *vimāna* is traditionally regarded as a palace or chariot that flies.

4. "And whoso, the fiftieth in succession, may hear one verse of this scripture, /
Rejoicing with favorable intent, hear what shall be his merit! //2//

For that man shall ever be a giver of gifts to koṭīs of nayutas of beings; /
Those whom formerly I have depicted in allegories, all these shall he delight for eighty years. //3//

Seeing their impending old age, their wrinkles, their broken teeth, and their hoary heads, he /
Shall think, 'O joy! For all beings are inclined to me, whence I will now address them with Dharma.' //4//

He preaches Dharma to them, and afterward clarifies nirvāṇa's ground: /
'All forms of existence are like to foam and to will-o'-the wisp. Have done with existence, and quickly!' //5//

All those beings, having heard the Dharma in that very donor's presence, /
Shall become Worthy Ones (*arhantabhūtā bhavi*) all at once, their outflows exhausted, bearers of a final body. //6//

More than that shall be his merit, who in sequence shall hear a single verse /
Or rejoice at the merit of one who has. For the former mass of merit shall not be slight. [?] //7//

[This seems to mean the following: Greater by far than the merit of the preacher of Buddhist doctrine in general is that of the person who indirectly, albeit at the end of a queue of fifty persons, hears but one verse of the *Lotus*. So great, in fact, shall his merit be that a person who but hears of him and rejoices at his good fortune shall accumulate more merit thereby than a Dharma-preacher.]

So great shall his merit be, so limitless, as to have no measure, /
For having heard but one verse indirectly. What, then, is to be said of him who hears it in the very Presence itself, //8//

Or who says to but one living being in exhortation, 'Come! Hear the Dharma! /
Most hard to obtain is this scripture in several koṭīs of nayutas of kalpas'; //9//

Whereupon that person, having been exhorted by him, hears this scripture for but a moment! /

Hear the fruit of his dharma as well: He shall never have mouth disease. //10//

His tongue also shall never be afflicted. His teeth shall never fall out, /
Or be black, or yellow, or uneven, nor shall he ever have disgusting lips. //11//

Crooked, or dry, or, indeed, elongated shall his face never be, nor flat, /
But well-shaped shall be his nose, and his forehead, and his teeth, and his lips, and the design of his face. //12//

Fair to behold shall he ever be among men, nor shall anything fetid or crooked ever be his. /
As is ever [wafted] the fragrance of the blue lotus, so, too, shall his fragrance be wafted. //13//

A man of firm will, wandering forth from his house, may go to a monastery to hear this scripture, /
And, having gone, may hear it for but a moment. Hear the fruit to be gained by this man of favorable intent! //14//

Most dignified shall his body be, and that man of firm will shall go about in horse-drawn carriages. /
Mounting also lofty elephant-drawn carriages, variously adorned with gems, shall he promenade. //15//

He shall acquire a variously adorned palanquin, drawn by several men, /
For so lovely shall be the fruit he shall gain from having gone to hear the Dharma. //16//

Having seated himself there in the assembly, by virtue of the pure deeds done by him, /
He shall receive Śakra-thrones, Brahmā-thrones, and royal thrones. //17//"

Notes to Chapter Nineteen

1. "Virtues" renders *kung te*, the usual equivalent of *puṇya*. Here, however, the Skt. has *guṇa*, "quality."

2. "And whatever beings shall be born there, the retribution of all their deeds shall he see. //"

3. "Whosoever may speak this scripture and in the assemblies, confident /
And unattached, explain it, hear his qualities from me! //1//

Eight hundreds of [excellent] qualities shall be his eye's by all means, /
Whereby his eye shall be pure and unattached. //2//

With that eye of flesh produced by father and mother, he /
Shall see this world-sphere, with its mountains, its forests, and its groves. //3//

All Merus, Sumerus, and Cakravālas shall he see, /
Also whatever other mountains and thickets [taking *khaṇḍāh* to mean *ṣaṇḍāḥ*] there may be, and oceans also shall he see. //4//

As far as Avīci below and as Bhavāgra above, /
All shall this man of firm will see in this way with his eye of flesh. //5//

Neither shall he even have a divine eye, nor shall one be born to him, /
But such as this shall be the sphere of his fleshy eye. //6//"

4. "His aural faculty becomes pure, not turbid, natural though it be, / for with it he hears the sundry sounds in this world-sphere, all of them without exception, does this fellow. //7// Of elephants and horses he hears the sounds, of chariots and oxen, of goats and rams, / of lovely-sounding kettle-drums and tabours, of *vīṇā*-lutes and pipes, as well as *vallakī*-lutes. //8// The lovely, sweet song does he hear, yet is not attached to it, firm fellow that he is; / he hears the voices of millions of men, whatever they say and wherever they say it. //9//"

5. The Skt. specifies *kalaviṅkā kokila barhiṇaś ca*, i.e., the sparrow, the black cuckoo, and the peacock.

6. *ye brahmaloke nivasanti devā akaniṣṭha ābhasvara ye ca devāḥ / ye cānyam anyasya karonti ghoṣān śṛṇoti tat sarvam aśeṣato 'sau* //15// "What gods dwell in the Brahmā-world, what gods also are Akaniṣṭhas ["of whom none is the youngest"] and Ābhāsvaraṣ ["shining, bright"], / and what gods make sounds to one another, all that does this fellow hear without exception. //" "Those above the Brahmā gods," *chu fan t'ien shang*, corresponds exactly to *ye brahmaloke nivasanti devā*, while "those of Bright Sound" (*kuang yin*), albeit mistranslated, matches *ābhāsvara*. *Akaniṣṭha*, on the other hand, has no counterpart in Kumārajīva's version, while his "Universally Pure" (*pien ching*, his rendition of *śubhakṛtsna*) and "Pinnacle of Existence" (*yu ting*, the standard equivalent of *bhavāgra*) are absent from the Skt. as we now have it.

7. The Skt. has *na cāpi kṣetraṃ uparudhyate 'sya*, "nor is his field even obstructed," which on the face of it does not make much sense. In view of Kumārajīva's "aural faculty" (*erh ken*), I suspect his original read *śrotraṃ* rather than *kṣetraṃ*.

8. "Of sharp faculties, he knows each place, for such is his natural aural faculty. //20// Nor does he even make an effort for the divine, since this ear of

his exists by nature. / For, whosoever holds this scripture with confidence, such are his qualities. //21//"

9. "The scent of the great-flowered jasmine and the Arabian jasmine, of garcinia and sandalwood, / the scent of rosebay and aloeswood, as well as of sundry blossoms and fruits. //23//"

10. *strīratnabhūtāni bhavanti yāpi gandhena so jānati bodhisattvaḥ* //26// "Which also have become ornaments of women, them does that bodhisattva know by their scent." Hence "the gems of the daughters of wheel-turning kings."

11. "In this very way, the scents of fragrant sesame and the assorted scents of blossoms and fruits, / these scents he knows and smells, standing still in this very place. //29//"

12. "The gods does he know and the asuras, and the asuras' daughters does he also discern, / and the games and pleasures of the asuras does he know, for such is his power of smell. //32//"

13. "He discerns well the intentions of men, and in the same way smells the scent of their intentions. / He likewise smells the scent of hypocrites and of those whose thought is at peace. //"

14. "The *hāra* and *ardhahāra* necklaces, the priceless jewels and pearls, and the sundry [other] jewels / by their odor he knows, every one of them, and the one called Priceless, which is like a ray of light. //" The *hāra*, according to some traditions, had 108 or 64 strands; the *ardhahāra*, 64 or 40. Of the meaning of *anarghanāmaṃ dyutisaṃsthitaṃ ca* I am not certain.

15. "Likewise he intuitively perceives the park land by the Vaijayanta [the palace of Indra], with its divine throne on which the good Dharma is preached, / and he discerns the choicest of the palaces and what sons of gods amuse themselves therein. // Standing here, he smells their scent, and by the scent he knows the sons of the gods, / who does what deed where, where he stands, or lies, or goes.//"

16. The Skt. speaks of flowers, garments, garlands, and jewels.

17. Here again Bright Sound stands for *ābhāsvara*, but Universally Pure (*pien ching*), presumably rendering *śubhakṛtsna*, has no analogue in our Skt. text. Also, this quatrain mentions the Pinnacle of Existence, i.e., *bhavāgra*, but śloka 45, which corresponds to it, does not, while śloka 44 does, but the corresponding Ch. does not.

18. The Skt. specifies mendicant monks who take pleasure both in their own study and in the teaching imparted by others, *uddeśasvādhyāyaratāś ca bhikṣavo*.

19. The same specification is made here in the same language.

20. "Moreover, whatever living beings hear his Dharma and, having heard it, are glad at heart, / the bodhisattva, standing here, knows that whole assembly of the Victorious One. // Such is his nasal power; nor does he even

have a divine sense of smell, / but this is for him a precursor of the divine sense of smell, free of outflows. //"

21. The principal difference between the Skt. and Ch. on this point is one of detail, the Skt. being, for one thing, much wordier. The Skt. does, however, list among the preacher's devotees one group not found in the Ch., viz., *piśācas* (a sort of carnivorous demon, yellow in color) and their daughters.

22. *nikṣiptamātrāś ca bhavanti divyā rasena divyena samanvitāś ca* //52// "And whatever he places on his tongue, as soon as placed, shall become divine, fully endowed with divine flavor. //" "Sweet dew" renders *kan lu*, which, in turn, usually renders *amṛta* or *rasāyana*, "nectar" or "ambrosia," as the case may be. There can be little doubt that the *rasena* of our text has a double meaning, the one just mentioned as well as its original meaning of "flavor." Thus Kumārajīva's *kan lu* is perfectly in order.

23. *dṛṣṭāntakoṭīnayutair anekaih*, "with several koṭis of nayutas of parables."

24. "The gods also, and the nāgas, asuras, and guhyakas, shall desire to see him constantly / and shall hear the Dharma respectfully, for such in every case shall be his qualities. //" A *guhyaka* is a class of demigod who, like the yakṣas, is in attendance on Kubera, the god of wealth.

25. "By his mere wish he shall inform this whole world-sphere with his voice, / and the sound of it shall be smooth and sweet, deep and lovely, most delightful. //"

26. The Skt. specifies yakṣa, nāga, gandharva, piśāca, and *piśācikā* (female piśāca).

27. The Skt. specifies Brahmā, Maheśvara, Īśvara, Śakra, and other sons and daughters of the gods, but makes no mention of Māra. It also says that Brahmā shall do the preacher's bidding.

28. "Shall display their own bodies to him" renders *wei hsien shen*, which corresponds to *karonti rakṣāṃ mukhadarśanāya*, whose meaning, however, is not perfectly clear. If it is to be interpreted as pure Sanskrit, it may mean that the Buddhas protect the preacher in order that his face may be seen by all. If it is to be taken as hybrid, it may mean that they protect him by showing him their faces. This is obviously the sense in which Kumārajīva took it.

29. The only significant difference here is that, whereas the Ch. says that all these things "shall appear" in that body, the Skt. says that the preacher, without changing his bodily form, "shall see" (*drakṣyati*) them all. But see note 32.

30. The Skt. adds *pariśuddhi kāyasmi ima evarūpā* //62// "Such is this purity within his body."

31. Again the Skt. mentions guhyakas in addition to the above.

32. "The palaces of the gods, up as far as the Pinnacle of Existence and Mount Cakravāla, / as well as the Snow-Capped [Himalaya], Sumeru, and Great Meru, are completely visible in his body. //"

33. Once again the Skt. includes guhyakas and Kumārajīva omits them.

34. "What Dharma also the Buddha, marked with a hundred merits, explains in all the world, / the pure sound of that too does he hear, and what he says is grasped. //" Kumārajīva clearly took this to mean that the preacher hears the Buddha and has a clear understanding of his message. The Skt. may very well mean that, but it may also mean that the Buddha's message, as transmitted by the preacher, is understood to men in general because of the preacher's clear exposition.

35. "He has a discerning knowledge of conjunction and disjunction, as well as of the sundry marks in all dharmas. / He also knows meanings and expressions and, as he knows them, so does he speak of them. //"

36. "Nor does he even acquire nonattachment, but this is previous knowledge belonging to him. // For, standing on teacher's ground, he shall tell all beings of Dharma, / and shall be skilled in millions of expressions, holding to this scripture of the Well Gone One. //"

Notes to Chapter Twenty

1. "Then indeed the Blessed One addressed the bodhisattva-mahāsattva Mahāsthāmaprāpta [attained to Great Strength]: 'In that way, O Mahāsthāmaprāpta, the following is to be known: if any reject in any way a Dharma-circuit of this kind, or abuse, malign, or address with false and rough speech such scripture-bearers as these mendicant monks, mendicant nuns, lay brethren, and lay sisters, such persons shall have an undesirable retribution that words cannot describe. But whoever shall bear, speak, teach, study, or explain in detail to others a scripture such as this one, theirs shall be a desirable retribution, such as previously described by me. For they shall acquire such purity as this of eye, ear, nose, tongue, body, and mind.' "

2. There are only two significant differences. The Skt. does not mention the pratyekabuddha at all, but has the "twelve causes and conditions" (i.e., the pratītyasamutpāda) preached to the śrāvakas also. Second, the Skt. has Sadāparibhūta urging the religious practitioners to stay on course, in addition to prophesying that one day they shall be Buddhas. Apart from this, there appears to be a double meaning to the word *paribhūta*. While in Sanskrit it is strictly passive, it seems likely from the context that in some of the Prakrits it may have been active. Thus *sadāparibhūta* may very well mean "conquering, overcoming, despising" and "overcome, conquered, despised" at one and the same time. Kumārajīva takes it in the active sense, but complicates the issue by interpreting it not as *sadā* + *paribhūta* but as *sadā* + *aparibhūta*, in the sense of "never overcoming," etc.

3. "Seeing his exalted magical power, his strength of logical argument and eloquence, and his strength of wisdom."

4. "Then again, O Mahāsthāmaprāpta, that bodhisattva-mahāsattva, after perishing there, encountered twenty hundred koṭīs of Thus Gone Ones, Worthy Ones, Properly and Fully Enlightened Ones, all having the name Candrasvararāja [King of Moonglow], and to all of them he explained this Dharma-circuit. In the same way, by virtue of former wholesome roots, once again in due course he met similarly twenty koṭīs of nayutas of hundreds of thousands of Thus Gone Ones, Worthy Ones, Properly and Fully Enlightened Ones, having in common the name Dundubhisvararāja [King of Drum Sound], and all of them he provided with this very same Dharma-circuit of the White Lotus of the True Dharma, and explained it to their fourfold assemblies. [Then] thanks to this very same previous wholesome root, he met once again in the same way twenty hundreds of thousands of koṭīs of Thus Gone Ones, Worthy Ones, Properly and Fully Enlightened Ones, having the common name Meghasvararāja [King of Thunder], and all of them he provided with this very same Dharma-circuit of the White Lotus of the True Dharma, and explained it to their fourfold assemblies. And on all these occasions he was endowed with ocular purity of this sort, endowed with aural purity, nasal purity, lingual purity, bodily purity, and mental purity of this sort."

5. The Skt. has "upāsikās," which must surely be correct.

6. All supreme Dharmas have been pronounced by me, and all of those persons have been ripened by me. / Moreover, when I am at peace, these firm ones shall all bear this supreme scripture. // For millions of cosmic ages incalculable multitudes have not heard such a Dharma as this at any time; / there are hundreds of millions of Buddhas, yet they do not explain this scripture. // Therefore, whoever has heard such a Dharma as this, bruited about of itself, from him who exists of himself, / and has acquired it, let him explain this scripture again and again when I here am at peace. //"

Notes to Chapter Twenty-One

1. "And then the many koṭīs of nayutas of hundreds of thousands of bodhisattvas with Mañjuśrī at their head, who had to do with this Sahā world-sphere, as well as the monks, nuns, lay brethren, lay sisters, gods, nāgas, yakṣas, gandharvas, asuras, garuḍas, kinnaras, mahoragas, humans, nonhumans, and the many bodhisattva-mahāsattvas like to the sands of the river Ganges, said to the Blessed One: 'We, too, O Blessed One, will explain this Dharma-circuit by the invisible spiritual being (*adṛṣṭenātmabhāvena*) of the Thus Gone One when he is at peace. O Blessed One! Standing in open space, we will cause our voices to be heard. We will cause to be planted those wholesome roots of the beings who have not yet planted wholesome roots.'

"And then the Blessed One at that time addressed the principal one of those bodhisattva-mahāsattvas of long standing, of the heads of groups, of the heads of great groups, of the teachers of great groups, [one] whose name was Viśiṣṭacāritra [Distinguished Conduct], a bodhisattva-mahāsattva, head of a great group, teacher of a great group: 'Good, good, Viśiṣṭacāritra! That is precisely what you are to do for the sake of this Dharma-circuit. You have been ripened by the Thus Gone One!'

"And then the Blessed Śākyamuni the Thus Gone One and the Blessed Prabhūtaratna [Many Jewels] the Thus Gone One, the Worthy One, the Properly and Fully Enlightened One, within the reliquary seated on the lion throne, both produced smiles, and from within their mouths bent out their tongues. And with their tongues they reached as far as the Brahmā world. And from those tongues issued forth many koṭīs of nayutas of hundreds of thousands of rays. And from every one of those rays issued forth many koṭīs of nayutas of hundreds of thousands of bodhisattvas, golden in color, their bodies endowed with the thirty-two marks of the Great Man, each seated on a lion throne in the womb of a lotus. And those bodhisattvas scattered into hundreds of thousands of world-spheres in all the primary and secondary directions and, standing in open space in all primary and secondary directions, taught Dharma. Just as the Blessed Śākyamuni, the Thus Gone One, the Worthy One, the Properly and Fully Enlightened One, with his tongue performed feats of magic, as did also Prabhūtaratna the Thus Gone One, the Properly and Fully Enlightened One, so did also all those Thus Gone Ones, Worthy Ones, Properly and Fully Enlightened Ones who had arrived from koṭīs of nayutas of hundreds of thousands of other world-spheres, seated each on a lion throne at the foot of a tree, perform feats of magic with their tongues"

2. In the Skt., the bodhisattvas are instructed to pay their respects to Prabhūtaratna as well as to Śākyamuni.

3. "Then indeed all those beings, having heard such a sound as this issue out of open space, standing just where they were uttered the words, 'Homage to the Blessed Śākyamuni, the Thus Gone One, the Worthy One, the Properly and Fully Enlightened One (*namo bhagavate Śākyamunaye tathāgatāyārhate samyak-saṃbuddhāyeti vācaṃ bhāṣante sma*),' 'with palms joined. And, where this Sahā world-sphere was, thither they threw sundry flowers, perfumes, scents, garlands, ointments, pastes, garments, parasols, banners, flags, and standards, as well as sundry attached ornaments, hāra and ardhahāra necklaces, jewels and gems, as offerings to the Blessed Śākyamuni and to Prabhūtaratna the Thus Gone One, as well as to this Dharma-circuit of the White Lotus of the True Dharma. And those flowers, perfumes, scents, garlands, ointments, pastes, garments, parasols, banners, flags, and standards, as well as the hāra- and ardhahāra-necklaces, the jewels and gems, arrived in this Sahā world-sphere as thrown. And by means of these heaps of flowers, perfumes, scents, garlands, ointments, pastes, garments, parasols, banners, flags, and standards, as well as the hāra- and ardhahāra-necklaces, jewels and gems, whatsoever Thus Gone Ones were seated in this Sahā

world-sphere, together with the other koṭīs of nayutas of hundreds of thousands of world-spheres joined with it, over all of them in the open sky from all sides was spread a great floral canopy."

4. "Those Buddhas who cough or who make a sound by snapping their fingers / are informing [giving a message to] all this world and this world-sphere in all ten quarters. // These and other miraculous qualities do they show who have compassion for the world, / thinking, "Now how shall they joyfully bear this scripture at that time, when the Well Gone One is at peace? // For many thousands of millions of cosmic ages will I speak the praises of the sons of the Well Gone Ones, / who shall bear the supreme scripture when the Leader of the world is at peace. //"

5. "Of the scriptures preached with intentional language ever does he know what has been said by the Leaders in intentional language, / and even when the Leader is at peace he knows the real meaning of the scriptures. //"

6. "Of their [eventual attainment of] enlightened intuition there can be no doubt. //"

Notes to Chapter Twenty-Two

1. This corresponds to the final chapter, number twenty-seven, of the Skt.

2. There are some differences between the two texts, the most significant being that in the Skt. the Buddha does not stroke the bodhisattvas' heads but puts his right hand in theirs.

3. To this, in the Skt., the bodhisattvas add a promise to do the bidding of *all* Buddhas.

4. "Then indeed the Blessed Śākyamuni, the Thus Gone One, the Properly and Fully Enlightened One, released all those Thus Gone Ones, those Worthy Ones, those Properly and Fully Enlightened Ones who had come from other world-spheres. And he saluted those Thus Gone Ones, wishing them well: 'Farewell, O Thus Gone Ones, O Worthy Ones, O Properly and Fully Enlightened Ones!' And he left the jeweled reliquary of the Blessed Prabhūtaratna the Thus Gone One, the Worthy One, the Properly and Fully Enlightened One, in its original place. That Thus Gone One too, that Worthy One, that Properly and Fully Enlightened One, he saluted, wishing him well.

"So said the Blessed One, pleased in mind. And those incalculable, innumerable Thus Gone Ones, Worthy Ones, Properly and Fully Enlightened Ones who had come from other world-spheres, seated on lion thrones at the foot of trees, as well as Prabhūtaratna the Thus Gone One, the Worthy One, the Properly and Fully Enlightened One, and his whole multitude of bodhisattvas; the incalculable, innumerable bodhisattva-mahāsattvas with Viśiṣṭacāritra at their head, who had issued forth from an opening in the earth; the great auditors, the fourfold assembly; and the world, with its gods, men, asuras, and gandharvas, were delighted by the speech of the Blessed One.

"Thus, in the august Dharma-circuit of the White Lotus of the True Dharma, is the twenty-seventh chapter, entitled Entrustment, complete.

> "What dharmas have their origin in causes, their causes, you see, the Thus Gone One has told,
> As well as that which is the suppression of [causes], has the Great silent One (*muni*), who tells of things exactly as they are. //"

Notes to Chapter Twenty-Three

1. *sarvarūpasaṃdarśanaṃ nāma samādhiṃ pratilabhate sma* /

2. *uragasāracandanavarṣam abhipravṛṣṭam* /, "a rain of sandalwood of essence of snake [?] was rained down."

3. 'The scent that sinks in water' renders *ch'en shui*, which in turn renders *agaru*. Besides this, the Skt. list consists only of *kunduruka* and *turuṣka*. Kumārajīva is obviously in a different tradition on this point.

4. *svakam adhiṣṭhānam akarot* /, "he provided himself with a spiritual basis."

5. While the Skt. may have this meaning, it may equally well mean that for the first twelve hundred years the flame did not abate, and that the fire went out only after a second period of twelve hundred years.

6. The Skt. has Sarvasattvapriyadarśana addressing this petition to both parents.

7. The Chinese speaks of two arms, the Sanskrit throughout of only one: *svaṃ mama bāhuṃ tathāgatapūjakarmaṇe parityajya . . . / . . . ayaṃ mama bāhur yathāpaurāṇo bhavatu . . . / . . . / . . . sa bāhur yathāpaurāṇaḥ saṃsthito 'bhūt . . .* /

8. The only significant difference between the two versions is that the Skt. is considerably more verbose.

9. The Skt. is somewhat different. To "Earth Mountain" (*t'u shan*) nothing corresponds. The counterpart of "Black Mountain" (*hei shan*) is Kālaparvata. To the two Mountain Rims correspond Cakravāla and Mahācakravāla, respectively, while the "Mount of Ten Jewels" (*shih pao shan*) has no analogue.

10. The Skt. does not specify by whom the other scriptures may have been preached.

11. "Just as, O Nakṣatrarājasaṃkusumitābhijña [Adorned with the Superknowledge of the King of Constellations], the Thus Gone One is the diadem-crowned king of all auditors, individually enlightened ones, and bodhisattvas, in just that way, O Nakṣatrarājasaṃkusumitābhijña, is this Dharma-circuit of the White Lotus of the True Dharma the Thus Gone One for those set out on the bodhisattva-course."

12. "Nor shall his lust constitute an obstacle, nor his hatred, or pride, or greed, or anger, or malice."

13. "You have warded off Māra the adversary, O son of good family, passed over a host of fears, blunted your enemies' edge. You are supported by a hundred thousand Buddhas."

14. This paragraph has no analogue in the Skt. text as we now have it.

15. *Sarvarutakauśalyānugatāyā dhāraṇyāḥ pratilambho 'bhūt.* |

16. "It is good, good, O Nakṣatrarājasaṃkusumitābhijña, that you have been declared by the Thus Gone One to be a bearer of incalculable qualities, and that you, in turn, question the Thus Gone One, who himself is endowed with the dharmas of incalculable qualities."

Notes to Chapter Twenty-Four

1. "There a Thus Gone One, a Worthy One, a Properly and Fully Enlightened One, named K., stands, is borne, and sets things in motion that have a very broad life-span."

2. Some of the Ch. equivalents are exact, some only approximate. "Unshared," however, seems not to correspond at all to *apkṛtsna*, which appears to mean "totally aquatic, made entirely of water." Also, between *jñānamudrāsamādhipratilabdhaḥ* and *sarvarutakauśalya°* is *candrapradīpasamādhipratilabdhaḥ*, "have acquired the Concentration of the Light of the Moon," for which the Ch. has no counterpart.

3. In view of the Ch., this must surely be an error for *Bhaiṣajyasamudgata*.

4. *mṛnmayī kālaparvatākīrṇā gūthoḍillaparipūrṇā* | "made of earth, covered with black mountains, and full of cesspools."

5. "And then at that time Gadgadasvara the bodhisattva-mahāsattva, not moving from that Buddha-field nor rising from that seat, entered into such a samādhi that, as soon as Gadgadasvara bodhisattva had entered into it, in this very Sahā world-sphere, on Vulture Peak Mountain, before the Dharma-seat of the Thus Gone One, eight-four koṭīs of nayutas of hundreds of thousands of lotuses appeared, gold-stalked, silver-leaved, the color of lotus and kino."

6. "Let us, O Blessed One, see that bodhisattva-mahāsattva, see what that bodhisattva's color is like, what his form is like, what his marks are like, what his appearance is like, what his manner of behavior is. Very well, O Blessed One! Let the Thus Gone One make such a sign that that bodhisattva-mahāsattva, impelled by that sign, shall come serenely [?] (*samāna*) to this Sahā world-sphere."

7. "And then the Blessed Śākyamuni, the Thus Gone One, the Worthy One, the Properly and Fully Enlightened One, said to the Blessed Prabhūtaratna the Thus Gone One, the Worthy One, the Properly and Fully Enlightened One, who was at peace: 'Let the Blessed One make such a sign that Gadgadasvara the bodhisattva-mahāsattva shall come to this Sahā world-sphere.' And then the Blessed Prabhūtaratna the Thus Gone One, the Worthy One, the Properly

and Fully Enlightened One, who was at peace, at that time produced such a sign to impel Gadgadasvara the bodhisattva-mahāsattva, [as much as to say]: 'Come, O son of good family, to this Sahā world-sphere! For this Prince Mañjuśrī rejoices at the thought of seeing you.' And then Gadgadasvara the bodhisattva-mahāsattva, bowing to the feet of the Blessed Kamaladalavimalanakṣatra-rājasaṃkusumitābhijña [He Whose Superknowledges Are Adorned by the King of Constellations of Lotus Petals] the Thus Gone One, the Worthy One, the Properly and Fully Enlightned One, and circumambulating him thrice clockwise, together with and surrounded and placed at their head by those eighty-four koṭīs of nayutas of hundreds of thousands of bodhisattvas, disappeared from that Vairocanaraśmipratimaṇḍita world-sphere and came to this Sahā world-sphere aglow with trembling fields, raining lotuses, koṭīs of nayutas of hundreds of thousands of sounding instruments. The eyes in his face like blue lotuses, his body gold-colored, he was a being adorned with a hundred thousand merits and with glory, blazing with splendor, his limbs variegated with marks, his body as solid as that of Nārāyaṇa. Mounting an upper room [probably meant as a kind of *vimāna*, flying palace] made of the seven jewels, at a height of about seven tālas in open space, surrounded and placed at their head by a troop of bodhisattvas, he arrived. Where the Sahā world-sphere was, where also the Vulture Peak Mountain, thither he approached. Approaching, and alighting from that upper room, he went up to where the Blessed One was, holding a pearl necklace worth a hundred thousands. Approaching, bowing with his head to the feet of the Blessed One, and circumambulating him clockwise seven times, he presented that pearl necklace as an offering to the Blessed One. Presenting it, he said to the Blessed One: 'The Blessed Kamaladalavimalanakṣatrarājasaṃkusumitābhijña the Thus Gone One, the Worthy One, the Properly and Fully Enlightened One, inquires after the Blessed One's freedom from hindrances, freedom from disease, carefree condition, passage of time, strength, and pleasant diversions. And that Blessed One has spoken thus: "Are things tolerable for you, O Blessed One? Are they manageable? Do the elements work against you? Are your people of decent appearance, easy to guide, well tended medically [?]? Are they clean in body, not excessively motivated by lust, nor excessively motivated by hatred, nor excessively motivated by delusion, nor, O Blessed One, beings excessively jealous, nor greedy, nor unmindful of their mothers, nor unmindful of their fathers, nor indifferent to ascetic monks, nor indifferent to Brahmans, nor given to false views, nor untamed in thought, nor immodest [lit., "failing to conceal their organs"]? Have these beings, O Blessed One, beaten down Māra the foe? O Blessed One, has Prabhūtaratna the Thus Gone One, the Worthy One, the Properly and Fully Enlightened One, now at peace, come to this Sahā world-sphere within his reliquary made of the seven jewels to hear the Dharma?" And that Blessed One also inquires after that Blessed Thus Gone One, that Worthy One, that Properly and Fully Enlightened One:

"Are things, O Blessed One, tolerable for Prabhūtaratna the Thus Gone One, the Worthy One, the Properly and Fully Enlightened One? Are they manageable? O Blessed One, shall Prabhūtaratna the Thus Gone One, the Worthy One, the Properly and Fully Enlightened One, remain long?" May we too, O Blessed One, see the shape of the relics of Prabhūtaratna the Thus Gone One, the Worthy One, the Properly and Fully Enlightened One! Very well, O Blessed One, let the Thus Gone One show the form of the relics of that Blessed Prabhūtaratna the Thus Gone One, the Worthy One, the Properly and Fully Enlightened One!' "

8. The Skt. gives them in the following order: Brahmā, Rudra (i.e., Śiva), Śakra (i.e., Indra), Īśvara, Senāpati (i.e., Kārttikeya, son of Śiva and Pārvatī), Vaiśravaṇa, *cakravartin* (wheel-turing king), *koṭṭarāja* (king of a walled city), *śreṣṭhin* (rich merchant), *gṛhapati* (householder), *naigama* (townsman), Brahman, bhikṣu, bhikṣuṇī, upāsaka, upāsikā, *śreṣṭhibhāryā* (wife of a rich merchant), *gṛhapatibhāryā* (wife of a householder), *naigamabhāryā* (townswoman), *dāraka* (boy), and *dārikā* (girl). Thus the Chinese list lacks Rudra, while the Indian lacks Maheśvara (the "Great Self-Mastering God") and *brāhmiṇī* ("Brahman lady"). "Self-Mastering God" renders Īśvara, and the "great general of the gods" translates Senāpati. "Lesser kings" is a less exact equivalent of *koṭṭarāja*. "Elder" (*chang che*) is the usual equivalent of *śreṣṭhin*. "Civil official" (*tsai kuan*) is a somewhat surprising rendition of *naigama*.

9. Apart from what has been noted above, the only differences between the two versions are, again, differences of detail.

Notes to Chapter Twenty-Five

1. "If again, O son of good family, beings carried off by rivers should call upon Avalokiteśvara the bodhisattva-mahāsattva, all those rivers would provide those beings with a ford."

2. "If, O son of good family, anyone at all exposed to a murderous attack should call on Avalokiteśvara the bodhisattva-mahāsattva, the knives of those murderers would be cut to pieces."

3. "Such, O son of good family, is the power of Avalokiteśvara the bodhisattva-mahāsattva."

4. "If, O son of good family, this thousand-millionfold world were to be full of crafty and malicious bandits, armed with knives; if therein a caravan chief should be going, charged with a great caravan rich in jewels, whose value could not be reckoned; if his companions should behold those crafty and malicious bandits, armed with knives, and, seeing them, should be all the more frightened, thinking themselves helpless; if the caravan chief should address the caravan, saying, 'Fear not, sons of good family, fear not! But call with one voice on the granter of asylum, Avalokiteśvara the bodhisattva-mahāsattva, for then you shall with all speed be delivered from this danger of bandits, from the danger

of enemies!'; if then that caravan with a single voice should call upon Avalokiteśvara, 'Homage, homage to that granter of asylum, to Avalokiteśvara the bodhisattva-mahāsattva! (*namo namas tasmai abhayaṃdadāyāvalokiteśvarāya bodhisattvāya mahāsattvāyeti |*)' then directly upon appeal to his name that caravan would be delivered from all fears. Such, O son of good family, is the power of Avalokiteśvara the *bodhisattva-mahāsattva.*"

5. "What beings are motivated by hatred, they, having declared their homage to Avalokiteśvara the bodhisattva-mahāsattva, are then free of hatred."

6. The Skt. characterizes the son as "well-formed, pleasant, a sight to behold, endowed with the marks of a son, dear to many men, appealing, one who has planted wholesome roots," the daughter in the same terms with two differences, viz., (a) she is endowed with the marks of a daughter, not of a son, and (b) she is endowed with the "florescence of supremely lovely beauty."

7. *teṣām amoghaphalaṃ bhavati |* "the fruit thereof is not empty."

8. The list of beings in the Skt. is as follows: buddha, bodhisattva, pratyekabuddha, śrāvaka, Brahmā, Śakra, gandharva, yakṣa, Īśvara, Maheśvara, cakravartirāja, piśāca, Vaiśravaṇa, Senāpati, a Brahman, and Vajrapāṇi, the "spirit who grasps the thunderbolt." This last may mean a Brahman or may be, like Śakra, another name for Indra. On the other hand, it may refer to a certain type of bodhisattva. Then again it may be something quite different from all of them. "The One Who Confers the Gift of Fearlessness" (*shih wu wei che*) corresponds to Abhayaṃdada, for which a better English equivalent would be "The One Who Grants Asylum."

9. In the Skt., however, the Buddha does not intervene. When Avalokiteśvara first refuses Aksayamati's gift, the latter says to him, "Accept it out of pity for us," and Avalokiteśvara does so.

10. In the Skt. it is supposedly the Buddha speaking. On the face of it, this is very puzzling. It seems to me, however, that this must be a survival from the primitive *Lotus*, which was presumably a work entirely in verse. If so, then the first śloka was Akṣayamati's question introduced by narrative, while the second śloka begins the Buddha's answer, likewise introduced by narrative. Later editors of the text, however, who knew the *Lotus* only as a work of combined verse and prose, misunderstood the passage and garbled it. As we have it, then, "Akṣayamati of the particolored banner questioned this matter, namely, the reason (*kāraṇāt*): | 'For what cause is the son of the Victorious One called Avalokiteśvara?' || Then by the discerning Teacher was Akṣayamati, the sea of vows, | he of the particolored banner, addressed: 'Hear of the conduct of Avalokiteśvara!' " || The only conundrum is then *kāraṇāt*, which one might emend to read *kāraṇam.*

11. "For many incalculable koṭis of kalpa-centuries, by many thousands of koṭis of Buddhas | how the basis of his religious practice was purified—this hear from me as I teach it. ||"

12. "For one mindful of Avalokiteśvara the fire goes out as if sprinkled."

13. "One mindful of Avalokiteśvara never sinks in the king of waters."

14. The Skt. as we now have it means that not a single hair of a man's head would be harmed if a whole diamond mountain were to fall on top of him.

15. "If one should be standing on a ground of execution in the power of those who put murderers to death. . . ."

16. *saci dārumayair ayomayair haḍinigaḍair iha baddhabandhanaiḥ / smarato Avalokiteśvaraṃ kṣipram eva vipaṭanti bandhanā //11//* Assuming *baddhabandhanaiḥ* to be for *baddhabandhanaḥ*, "If he is bound in fetters made of wood and iron, / then for one mindful of Avalokiteśvara the bonds split with all speed. //"

17. The Skt. specifies *mantrā* (spells, incantations), *bala* (forces), *vidya* (skills), *oṣadhī* (herbs), *bhūta* (ghosts), and *vetāla* (goblins, vampires).

18. "If one is surrounded by vigor-robbing nāgas, yakṣas, gods, ghosts, and rākṣasas, / they are not able to harm a hair of the head of him who is mindful of Avalokiteśvara."

19. "If surrounded by beings whose very gaze is poisonous, malignant and destructive with glow and flame, / for one who is mindful of Avalokiteśvara with all speed they are deprived of their poison. //"

20. "Having arrived at the ultimate limit of magical powers, broad in knowledge and learned in means, / everywhere in the world with its ten directions, everywhere without exception, he is seen. // All those frightened victims of untimely destinies, in the grip of hell, wearing the form of beasts, or under the control of Yama, / who are hard pressed by birth, old age, and sickness—all these living beings in due course are put at peace. //" The remaining gāthās in this passage, are, in the Skt., the speech of Akṣayamati.

21. "O you of the auspicious eyes, of the benevolent eyes, of the eyes distinguished by wisdom and gnosis, / of the merciful eyes, of the pure eyes, O friendly one, O you of goodly countenance, of goodly eyes, //20// whose spotless glow is beyond the clean and the unclean, O you free of darkness, who have the glow of the Sun of gnosis, / from whose glow has been taken the flame of fire, burning you give light in the world! //21// O you who resound with good will and with the true qualities of pity, O you of the auspicious qualities, of the benevolent mind, the firmly solid one, / you extinguish the fire of the afflictions of animate beings and send down a Dharma-rain of nectar! //22// When quarrel, dispute, and discord come to the community of man, bringing great fears, / for one who is mindful of Avalokiteśvara the evil multitude of enemies is put to rest. //23// [Gone to] the sounds of all the clouds, the sound of drums, the sound of rainfall, the goodly sound of Brahmā, / gone to the ultimate limit of the whole range of sounds is this Avalokiteśvara, the one worthy of recollection. //24// Recollect, recollect, do not doubt the pure being Avalokiteśvara! / In death, in distraction, in misfortune he is salvation, refuge, escape. //25// Gone to the utmost limit of all qualities, with eyes of pity and good will for all beings, / the

good qualities personified, and ocean of great qualities, is the venerable Avalokiteśvara. //26// To him who, full of pity for the world, shall be a Buddha in time yet to come, / to him who destroys all pain, fear, and anguish do I bow down, to Avalokiteśvara. //27// Lokeśvara the Leader of kings, the repository of the Dharma of the mendicant monks, honored of the world, / having practiced for many hundreds of kalpas, has attained supreme, immaculate, intuitive wisdom. //28// O you who stand now to his right, now to his left, fanning the Leader Amitābha, / O you who are like to an illusion, to you in a state of concentration do the Victorious Ones in all the fields go, there to do you honor. //29// In the eastern quarter is the gladdening world-sphere, the immaculate Sukhāvatī, / where this Leader Amitābha stands plain to view, the Caravan Chief of living beings. //30// There is no birth of women there, nor any dharma of copulation whatsoever, / but those sons of the Victorious One are self-produced, seated spotless in the wombs of lotuses. //31//That Leader Amitābha, too, in the immaculate, appealing womb of a lotus, / seated on a lion throne, glows like a king at court. //32// He, too, is thus, the Leader of the world, who has not his like in this triple existence; / for the accumulated merit of his praise may I quickly become like you, O supreme among men! //33//

Notes to Chapter Twenty-Six

1. This corresponds to the twenty-first chapter in the Skt.

2. Apart from great prolixity, the Skt. says that the merit of the latter shall be greater than that of the former.

3. The Skt. reads *muktatame.*

4. Between *samasame* and *kṣaye*, the Skt. has *jaye.*

5. The Skt reads *samite.*

6. The Skt. reads *nidhiru.*

7. For these three, the Skt. has *abhyantarapāriśuddhimutkule.*

8. The Skt. reads *buddhavilokite.*

9. Following *saṃghanirghoṣaṇi*, the Skt. has *nirghoṇi*, almost certainly by mistake for *nirghoṣaṇi.*

10–11. For these two, the Skt. has forms ending in *-e*, thus indicating a feminine singular vocative, the usual thing in mantras (along with the fem. sing. acc.). These forms, unless they represent slovenly transcription, are masculine vocative.

12. Apart from the difference mentioned in note 10–11, the Skt. lacks the initial *u-*.

13. The Skt. reads *akṣaye.*

14. Since the Skt. has nothing to correspond to this, and given the imprecise nature of the Ch. transcription, there can be no certainty in this

restoration. The first syllable may be *a* or *ā*; the second may be *ba*, *bā*, *bha*, *bhā*, *va*, or *vā*; the third may be *ru*, *rū*, *ro*, *lu*, *lū*, or *lo*. Quite apart from this, the end of the mantra, after *akṣaye*, reads: *akṣayavanatāye vakkule baloḍra amanyanatāye svāhā* //

15. Between *ukke* and *mukke*, the Skt. has *tukke*. Also, as elsewhere, the Ch. omits the *svāhā* with which the Skt. ends.

16. Between *aṭṭe* and *naṭṭe*, the Skt. has *taṭṭe*.

17. This is how the Skt. reads. The Ch. transcription presumably goes back to something like *nunaṭṭe*, but I have not given it, because I am not certain of it.

18. The transcription represents something more like *anaḍu*, but again I am not certain.

19. This renders *ch'ih kuo t'ien*, which in turn renders *Dhṛtarāṣṭra*. The Skt., however, plainly speaks of *Virūḍhako mahārājo*.

20. Between *mātaṅgi* and *saṅkule*, the Skt. has *pukkasi*.

21. The Ch. transcription is closer to something like *vrūsuni*.

22. The Skt. has *sisi*. What the Ch. transcription represents is difficult to say, since the first syllable may represent *aṭ*, *at*, *ar*, or *al*, while the second may represent *ṭi*, *ṭī*, *ṭe*, *ti*, *tī*, or *te*.

23. The Skt. has *itime*, *nime*, *ruhe*, and *stuhe*, each five times. The Ch. must be corrupt.

24. Between *preta* and *pūtana*, the Skt. has *piśāca*.

25. Between *vetāla* and *omāraka* the Skt. has *kumbhāṇḍa* and *stabdha*, both missing from the Ch., which instead has *ch'ien-t'u*. The transcription being what it is, there can be no certainty about the reconstruction. *Ghaṇṭa* is another name for Śiva.

26.· Between *omāraka* and *apasmāraka*, the Skt. has *ostārika*.

27. Between *yakṣakṛtya* and *manuṣyakṛtya*, the Skt. has *amanuṣyakṛtya*.

28. The Skt. specifies a fever of one, two, three, or four days, a perpetual fever, and an uneven fever.

29. "May his head split seven ways like the blossom of the East Indian basil, / [the head of him] who, having heard this charm, shall transgress against a preacher of Dharma. // Whatever is the course of matricides, what the course of parricides, / may he tread that course, who shall transgress against a preacher of Dharma. // Whatever is the course of pressers of sesame oil, what the course of cheats in sesame oil, / may he tread that course, who shall transgress against a preacher of Dharma. // Whatever is the course of cheats in weights and measures, what the course of cheats in copper and brass, / may he tread that course, who shall transgress against a preacher of Dharma. //" The reference to those who press sesame oil I do not understand, and might be prepared to dismiss it as a copyist's error, but that the Chinese has the same thing. See footnote in text for possible interpretation.

Notes to Chapter Twenty-Seven

1. *upāyakauśalyapāramitāyāṃ maitryāṃ karuṇāyāṃ muditāyām upekṣāyāṃ yāvat saptatriṃśatsu bodhipakṣikeṣu dharmeṣu* /

2. "O sons of good family, this father of yours, this king Śubhavyūha, is attached to the Brahmans. Therefore you will get no permission to go see that Well Gone One."

3. The Skt. contains two miracles that the Ch. does not. (1) They shook the dust off themselves in mid-air (*tatraivāntarīkṣe rajo vyadhunītām*). (2) They would sink into the earth and reemerge in open space. This is worded *pṛthivyām unmajjitvā ākāśa unmajjataḥ* /, but the first two words must surely be an error for *pṛthivyāṃ nimajjitvā* or more probably for *pṛthivyām avamajjitvā*.

4. The Skt. ends with the observation that the right moment is very hard to catch (*durlabhā kṣaṇasaṃpadā*).

5. In the Skt., the mother's answer, too, is in verse: "I release you. Go today in peace, you two boys! / We, too, will wander forth, for a Thus Gone One is hard to encounter. //"

6. The Skt. reads *mahārṇavayugacchidrakūrmagrīvāpraveśavat* / This seems to mean that the chance of encountering a Buddha is as great a tortoise's chance of getting its head through a knothole, a tortoise that surfaces once in a *yuga* (cosmic age). The difficulty is that *yuga* is not a Buddhist term, and that the compound is itself hard to construe. The Chinese, on the other hand, seems not to be speaking of time at all, but to be saying that the above-mentioned encounter is as difficult as it would be for a one-eyed tortoise to slip its head through a knothole by pure chance.

7. "And the boy Vimalanetra was practiced in this Dharma-circuit."

8. "And the two boys' mother, the queen Vimaladattā, came to know the chorus of all Buddhas and the secret objects of all Buddhadharmas."

9. "And then, O sons of good family, that Blessed Jaladharagarjitaghoṣasusvaranakṣatrarājasaṃkusumitābhijña [He Whose Superknowledges are Adorned by the King of Constellations (named) the One of the Sweet Sound of the Roaring Voice (i.e., thunder) of the Water-Bearers (i.e., clouds)] the Thus Gone One, the Worthy One, the Properly and Fully Enlightened One, seeing that the king Śubhavyūha had approached with his retinue, demonstrated to him, established him, sharpened him, and delighted him with talk of Dharma. And then, O sons of good family, the king Śubhavyūha, having been well and firmly taught, established, sharpened, and delighted by that Blessed One with talk of the Dharma, at that time, pleased, elated, his mind transported, joyful, and affected by satisfaction and cheer, fixing the diadem on his younger brother and establishing him in the kingship, surrounded by his sons and by his own men, with faith in the pronouncements of the Blessed Jaladharagarjitaghoṣasusvaranakṣatrarājasamkusumitābhijña the Thus Gone One, the Worthy One, the Properly and Fully Enlightened One, wandered forth out of the household

into the houseless life, as did the queen Vimaladattā, surrounded by her whole band of women, and the two boys, together with their forty-two thousand living beings, all together and in a body. And, having wandered forth, the king Śubhavyūha, accompanied by his retinue, for forty-two thousand years practiced with dedication this Dharma-circuit of the White Lotus of the True Dharma, thinking on it, realizing it, and purifying it. Then indeed, O sons of good family, that king Śubhavyūha, after the passage of those forty-two thousand years, gained the concentration named Display of the Adornments of All Qualities (*sarvaguṇālaṃkāravyūhaṃ nāma samādhiṃ pratilabhate sma* /). Directly that concentration had been gained, he rose up into open space to a distance of about seven talas."

10. "When this had been said, Jaladharagarjitaghoṣasusvaranakṣatrarājasaṃkusumitābhijña the Thus Gone One, the Worthy One, the Properly and Fully Enlightened One, said to the king Śubhavyūha: 'It is just so, O great king, just exactly as you say! For, O great king, for sons of good family and daughters of good family who have planted wholesome roots, whatever the state of being, or destiny, or death, or birth, upon which they chance, good friends are not easy to get, good friends who for the Teacher's sake stand right by them, who with respect to unexcelled, right, perfect enlightened intuition (*anuttarāyāṃ samyaksaṃbodhau*) are teachers and guides to understanding and to maturation. A noble status is this, O great king, namely, the assumption of the role of the good friend who establishes one in the view of the Thus Gone One. Do you, O great king, see these two boys?' He said, 'I see them, O Blessed One! I see them, O Well Gone One!' The Blessed One said, 'These very two boys, O great king, in the presence of Thus Gone Ones, of Worthy Ones, of Properly and Fully Enlightened Ones equal in number to the sands of sixty-two Ganges rivers, shall make offerings. They shall also carry about the Dharma-circuit of the White Lotus of the True Dharma out of compassion for the beings and to generate in beings of false views the vigor necessary to achieve right views.'

"And then, O sons of good family, that king Śubhavyūha, descending from the sky and joining ten fingers to ten fingers, said to Jaladharagarjitaghoṣasusvaranakṣatrarājasaṃkusumitābhijña: 'Very well, O Blessed One! Let the Thus Gone One teach us: with what sort of knowledge is the Thus Gone One, the Worthy One, the Properly and Fully Enlightened One, endowed, that on his head there shines an *uṣṇīṣa*, that the Blessed One is pure-eyed, that between his brows there shines a tuft of hair with the pale yellow glow of the moon or of a conch shell, that his row of even and well-placed teeth glistens in the opening of his mouth, that the Blessed One has red lips, the Well Gone One lovely eyes?'

"And then, O sons of good family, the king Śubhavyūha, praising the Blessed Jaladharagarjitaghoṣasusvaranakṣatrarājasaṃkusumitābhijña the Thus

Gone One, the Worthy One, the Properly and Fully Enlightened One for these many qualities, praising that Blessed One also for koṭīs of nayutas of hundreds of thousands of other qualities, said to the Blessed Jaladharagarjitaghoṣasusvaranakṣatrarājasaṃkusumitābhijña the Thus Gone One, the Worthy One, the Properly and Fully Enlightened One: 'It is wonderful, O Blessed One, how great is the meaning of this teaching of the Thus Gone One, how incalculable are the qualities of the code of Dharma-conduct made known by the Thus Gone One, how well conceived is the teaching of the Thus Gone One! From this day forward, O Blessed One, we will no longer be under the control of our thought, no longer under the control of false views, no longer under the control of anger, no longer under the control of the rise of evil thought-formulations. Endowed with such unwholesome dharmas as these, O Blessed One, I have no desire to go into the presence of the Blessed One.' He, bowing his head to the feet of the Blessed Jaladharagarjitaghoṣasusvaranakṣatrarājasaṃkusumitābhijña, remained standing in open space.

"And then the king Śubhavyūha and the queen Vimaladattā threw to the Blessed One in the upper air a pearl necklace worth a hundred thousands. No sooner was the pearl necklace thrown on the head of the Blessed One than the pearl necklace became a palace with four corners and four pillars, evenly proportioned, well divided [into rooms], and sightly. In that palace appeared a carriage, strewn with several hundreds of thousands of ornaments. And in that carriage was visible an image of the Thus Gone One, sitting crosslegged. And then, this occurred to the king Śubhavyūha: 'Of great power is this Buddha-knowledge, and incalculable are the qualities with which the Thus Gone One is endowed, wherein is visible, namely, this image of the Thus Gone One in the midst of a palace, pleasant, sightly, endowed with the florescent beauty of extremely auspicious colors!'

"And then the Blessed Jaladharagarjitaghoṣasusvaranakṣatrarājasaṃkusumitābhijña the Thus Gone One addressed the fourfold assembly: 'Do you see, O mendicant monks, the king Śubhavyūha, standing in the sky and roaring a lion's roar?' They said, 'We see, O Blessed One.' The Blessed One said, 'This king Śubhavyūha shall indeed, O mendicant monks, having become a mendicant monk under my instruction, be in the world a Thus Gone One, a Worthy One, a Properly and Fully Enlightened One named Śālendrarāja, perfect in knowledge and conduct, a Well Gone One, an unexcelled knower of the world, a leader of those men who are to be tamed, a Teacher of gods and men, an Awakened One, a Blessed One, in the world-sphere Vistīrṇavatī. His cosmic age shall be Abhyudgatarāja by name. Again, O mendicant monks, the bodhisattva-community of Śālendrarāja, that Thus Gone One, that Worthy One, that Properly and Fully Enlightened One, shall be immeasurable, immeasurable his community of auditors. As even as the palm of one's hand, made of beryl, shall be that world-sphere Vistīrṇavatī. So inconceivable shall that Thus Gone

One be, that Worthy One, that Properly and Fully Enlightened One! It may be now, O sons of good family, that you have uncertainties, second thoughts, or doubts [e.g.]: "Was that king named Śubhavyūha at that time and on that occasion someone else?" You are not ever to take this view, O sons of good family! For what reason is that? This very bodhisattva-mahāsattva named Padmaśrī was at that time and on that occasion the king Śubhavyūha. It may be now, O sons of good family, that you have uncertainties, second thoughts, or doubts: "Was that queen named Vimaladattā at that time and on that occasion someone else?" You are not ever to take this view, O sons of good family! For what reason is that? This very bodhisattva-mahāsattva named Vairocanaraśmi-pratimaṇḍitadhvajarāja [King Whose Banner is Adorned by the Rays of the Effulgent (Sun)] was at that time and on that occasion the queen named Vimaladattā. Out of compassion for the king Śubhavyūha and for those beings he took the form of Śubhavyūha's lady. It may be now, O sons of good family, that you have uncertainties, second thoughts, or doubts: "Were those two boys at that time and on that occasion someone else?" You are not ever to take this view, O sons of good family! For what reason? These two, Bhaiṣajyarāja and Bhaiṣajyasamudgata, were at that time and on that occasion the two sons of the king Śubhavyūha. So inconceivable are the qualities with which the bodhisattva-mahāsattva Bhaiṣajyarāja and Bhaiṣajyasamudgata are endowed, both of these good men having planted wholesome roots under the tutelage of many koṭīs of nayutas of hundreds of thousands of Buddhas, both endowed with incalculable dharmas! And whoever shall carry about the names of these two good men, they shall all be fit objects of obeisance on the part of the world with its gods.'

"When this Chapter of the Former Practices was being preached, for eighty-four thousands of animate beings a Dharma-eye, spotless and free of taint, was purified."

Notes to Chapter Twenty-Eight

1. The beginning of this passage is similar enough in the two versions. The bodhisattva is Samantabhadra, and the Buddha from whose realm he has come is Ratnatejobhyudgatarāja, meaning "the king who has risen above the glow of gems." Beyond Samantabhadra's speech the Skt. is different enough to merit translation in its own right: "When this had been said, the Blessed One said to the bodhisattva-mahāsattva Samantabhadra: 'These bodhisattva-mahāsattvas, you see, O son of good family, are of an understanding that has been unlocked. Also, this is the Dharma-circuit of the White Lotus of the True Dharma, which is unbroken Thusness.' Those bodhisattvas said, 'It is so, O Blessed One! It is so, O Well-Gone One!' Then indeed, whatever bhikṣus, bhikṣuṇīs, upāsakas, and upāsikās there were in that assembly, in order to

establish them in the Dharma-circuit of the White Lotus of the True Dharma, the Blessed One now said the following also to the bodhisattva-mahāsattva Samantabhadra: 'This Dharma-circuit of the White Lotus of the True Dharma shall be within the grip of a woman endowed with four dharmas. Which four? Namely, she must be backed by the Blessed Buddhas, she must have planted wholesome roots, she must be set in her series of departures [?], and she must raise up her thought to unexcelled, right, perfect, enlightened intuition for the purpose of saving all beings. It is a woman endowed with these four dharmas who shall have this Dharma-circuit of the White Lotus of the True Dharma within her grip.' " The phrase followed by a question mark renders *nirayarāśi-vyavasthitaś ca bhaviṣyati*, whose meaning really escapes me. I have taken it to refer to a woman who adheres to a series of actions that will eventuate in escape from the world. The difficulty is that *niraya*, which has the literal meaning of "exit," in Buddhist contexts is usually another name for hell. In addition, the first word is a masculine adjective, which thus cannot refer to a woman. The Chinese analogue, *ju cheng ting chü*, means something quite different, and may represent an original such as *samyaksamādhiskandham avatariṣyati*.

2. In the Skt. the three names seem to mean (1) the charm that brings all other charms into one's power, (2) the one that brings all manner of things into one's power, and (3) the one that enables one to understand all sounds. There are other differences in detail between the two versions, but not of significant magnitude.

3. The Skt. is in places quite different: *adaṇḍe daṇḍapati daṇḍāvartani daṇḍakuśale daṇḍasudhāri sudhārapati buddhapaśyane sarvadhāraṇi āvartani saṃvartani saṃghaparīkṣite saṃghanirghātani dharmaparīkṣite sarvasattvarutakauśalyānugate siṃha-vikrīḍite anuvarte vartani vartāli svāhā* // Where my version departs from the Skt., my reconstructions are no more than tentative.

4. "Then indeed at that time the Blessed Śākyamuni, the Thus Gone One, the Worthy One, the Properly and Fully Enlightened One, gave his approval to the bodhisattva-mahāsattva Samantabhadra: 'Good, good, O Samantabhadra, that you have put yourself out so for the weal of many men, for the happiness of many men, out of compassion for the world, for the sake of a great body of men, for their weal and happiness! You are endowed with such incalculable dharmas by virtue of a disposition in which great compassion is included, by virtue of an excitation of thought in which incalculable things are included, in that you yourself furnish a basis for those preachers of Dharma. Whichever sons of good family shall carry about the name of Samantabhadra, be it known that by them Śākyamuni, the Thus Gone One, has been seen; and this Dharma-circuit of the White Lotus of the True Dharma heard in the presence of that Blessed Śākyamuni; and Śākyamuni, the Thus Gone One, honored by them with offerings; and the approval of Śākyamuni, the Thus Gone One, given to them as he taught the Dharma; and this Dharma-circuit

duly enjoyed; and his hand placed on their heads by Śākyamuni, the Thus Gone One; and the Blessed Śākyamuni covered by them with their cloaks. Those sons of good family or daughters of good family are also, O Samantabhadra, to be designated recipients of the teaching of the Thus Gone One. Nor shall there be any pleasure for them in the Lokāyata, nor shall beings devoted to fine verse be agreeable to them, nor dancers, nor wrestlers, nor actors, nor vintners, nor shepherds, nor poulterers, nor swineherds, nor keepers of women. Once they have heard such a scripture as this one, or written it down, or carried it about, or recited it, nothing else shall appeal to them. Those beings, moreover, are to be designated as endowed with the Dharma of own-being. And the attention they pay shall be their own. Those beings shall be supported by the might of their own merit, pleasant for other beings to behold. Whatsoever mendicant monks shall be bearers of that scripture in this way, lust shall not obstruct them, nor hatred, nor delusion, nor envy, nor greed, nor hypocrisy, nor pride, nor arrogance, nor conceit. Those preachers of Dharma, O Samantabhadra, shall be content with what they get. Whosoever, O Samantabhadra, may at the latter time, on the latter occasion, when the last five hundred years are in progress, see a mendicant monk bearing this Dharma-circuit of the White Lotus of the True Dharma, he should entertain the following thought: 'This son of good family shall go to the seat of enlightened intuition, this son of good family shall triumph over Māra's wheel of strife, he shall turn the Wheel of Dharma, he shall beat the drum of Dharma, he shall blow the conch of Dharma, he shall precipitate the rain of Dharma, he shall mount the lion's throne of Dharma.' Whosoever shall carry about this Dharma-circuit at the latter time, on the latter occasion, when the last five hundred years are in progress, those mendicant monks shall not be greedy, not eagerly longing for clothing, nor eagerly longing for alms-bowls. Straight also shall those preachers of Dharma be. Recipients of the three deliverances shall those preachers of Dharma be. In the present life shall their release take place [?]. Whoever shall delude such mendicant monks as these, bearers of this scripture, preachers of Dharma, those beings shall be blind from birth. And whoever shall bruit about evil reports of such scripture-bearing mendicant monks as these, in this very life their bodies shall be many-colored. And whoever shall laugh inwardly at, or speak derisively to [?], such scriptural copyists as these, they shall be of broken teeth, of teeth spaced far apart, of hideous lips, flat-nosed, of inverted hands and feet, of inverted eyes, of stinking bodies, their bodies covered with goiters, boils, scabs, leprosy, and the itch. Whoever shall bruit about unpleasant talk, whether true or untrue, about such scriptural copyists, such preachers of scripture, such bearers of scripture, or such teachers of scripture as this, their sinful deed is to be designated as more profound yet. Therefore, O Samantabhadra, one is to rise even from afar to greet the mendicant monks who bear this Dharma-circuit. Just as obeisance is to be done in the presence of the Thus

Gone One, so is obeisance to be done in that of those very mendicant monks who bear this scripture.'

"When this very Chapter of the Encouragements of Samantabhadra was being taught, there was acquisition of the Charm that Brings Hundreds of Thousands of Koṭīs of Things, acquisition on the part of bodhisattva-mahasattvas like to the sands of the river Ganges."

Index

This is principally an index of proper names and technical terms, predominantly Sanskrit. Titles and geographical names are generally not included, nor are constantly recurring words such as Buddha, etc.

Buddhist Studies and Translations

The Awakening of Faith, attributed to Aśvaghosha, tr. Yoshito S. Hakeda*	1967
The Platform Sutra of the Sixth Patriarch, tr. Philip B. Yampolsky*†	1967
Essays in Idleness: The Tsurezuregusa of Kenkō, tr. Donald Keene*†	1967
The Zen Master Hakuin: Selected Writings, tr. Philip B. Yampolsky*†	1971
Kūkai: Major Works, tr. Yoshito S. Hakeda*†	1972
The Lion's Roar of Queen Śrīmālā, tr. Alex and Hideko Wayman*	1974
Scripture of the Lotus Blossom of the Fine Dharma, tr. Leon Hurvitz*†	1976

* Translations from the Asian Classics

† Records of Civilization: Sources and Studies